D0555918

GANDHI IN INDIA

ndhi, Mahatma, 1869–19
ndhi in India, in his
n words /
87. WITHDRAWN
305222172607
01/27/11

GANDHI IN INDIA

IN HIS OWN WORDS

EDITED BY

MARTIN GREEN

PUBLISHED FOR TUFTS UNIVERSITY BY
UNIVERSITY PRESS OF NEW ENGLAND
HANOVER AND LONDON, 1987

UNIVERSITY PRESS OF NEW ENGLAND

BRANDEIS UNIVERSITY   DARTMOUTH COLLEGE

BROWN UNIVERSITY   UNIVERSITY OF NEW HAMPSHIRE

CLARK UNIVERSITY   UNIVERSITY OF RHODE ISLAND

UNIVERSITY OF CONNECTICUT   TUFTS UNIVERSITY

UNIVERSITY OF VERMONT

M. K. Gandhi's writings © 1987 by the Navajivan Trust.
Introduction, Members of the Gandhi Family Mentioned in the Text, chronologies, Glossary of Terms and Persons Mentioned, and Index © 1987 by Martin Green.

All rights reserved. Except for brief quotation in critical articles or reviews, this book, or parts thereof, must not be reproduced in any form without permission in writing from the publisher. For further information contact University Press of New England, Hanover, NH 03755. All writings of M. K. Gandhi are reproduced with the permission of the Navajivan Trust, which holds copyrights on all the writings of M. K. Gandhi.

Item 118, "My Sexual Practices," is reprinted from N. K. Bose, *My Days With Gandhi*, courtesy of Orient Longman Limited, Hyderabad, India. Item 119, "The Calcutta Fast," is reprinted from D. G. Tendulkar, *Mahatma*, courtesy of the late D. G. Tendulkar Charitable Trust, Bombay, India, and Publications Division, Ministry of Information and Broadcasting, Government of India, New Delhi, India.

Printed in the United States of America

LIBRARY OF CONGRESS CATALOGING-IN-PUBLICATION DATA

Gandhi, Mahatma, 1869–1948.
  Gandhi in India, in his own words.

  Includes index.
    1. Gandhi, Mahatma, 1869–1948. 2. Nationalists—
India—Biography. 3. Statesmen—India—Biography.
I. Green, Martin Burgess, 1927– . II. Tufts
University. III. Title.
DS481.G3A3 1987   954.03'5'0924 [B]   86–40385
ISBN 0–87451–390–1
ISBN 0–87451–418–5 (pbk.)

5   4   3   2   1

CONTENTS

NOTE

All of these pieces, with the exception of the last two, have been taken from *The Collected Works of Mahatma Gandhi*, published by Navajivan Press in India. The original volume and page numbers are included in parentheses. Only a few have been cut, and in those cases a footnote to that effect has been included. Their order has on occasion been changed slightly if something mentioned in one essay is more fully explained in a later one; and some titles and footnotes have been revised to provide more background for non-Indian readers. A glossary of Indian terms and the proper names that Gandhi refers to immediately precedes the Index.

INTRODUCTION: GANDHI AS AN AUTOBIOGRAPHICAL WRITER

Gandhi's works usually are read by students of history or political science, especially those interested in South Asia, or by students of peace making and social change. The works are, in my experience, much less often read by the general reader, and least of all by those trained in literature. *They* respond to his personality quite uneasily. I would like to present Gandhi as an autobiographical writer, and to unearth and disarm the hidden sources of the resistance to him.

Gandhi's native language was of course Gujarati, and it is to be presumed (his biographers do not make this entirely clear) that he wrote most of this material first in that language and then translated it into English, often with considerable help from other people. Had he been an ordinary man of letters, we might hesitate to judge him on the basis of translations. However, it seems clear that one could never have called Gandhi a Gujarati writer. There are many references to his imperfect command of literary Gujarati, and it may be that—on public themes, at least—he was as much at home with English as with any other language. In South Africa, after all, he moved in an English language environment for nearly twenty-five years, and later only a small minority of his collaborators, even the Indians, were Gujarati-speakers. These materials are, thus, quite unlike, say, a collection of poems written in French and then translated into English. These texts are what Gandhi presented to the world—his words for his ideas and his experience.

We don't usually think of Gandhi as any kind of writer, but he edited and in large part wrote a series of weekly newspapers and left behind him about ten million printed words, which means that he wrote an average of five hundred words a day for fifty years. Such a record would make any man a professional writer. To read him is, moreover, a richly rewarding experience, at least for naïve readers. The sophisticated may find they have prejudices to overcome before they can take him seriously. Why? Perhaps first because he seems intellectually inane.

Even the two *books* he wrote, his autobiography and *Satyagraha in South Africa*, are simple to the point of naïveté in vocabulary and syntax, in the structure of individual chapters, and in the lack of structure of the whole. They are equally naïve in mood and tone.

Sometimes, as Gandhi comments on his dealings with other people, one has the impression of an almost infantile simplemindedness; and when he expounds an idea, his language is so flatly rationalist and declarative that he offers nothing with which a sophisticated mind can sympathize. In fact, Gandhi was a subtle-minded man, and his writing yields subtle pleasures, but literary readers are often affronted by what seems like—what *is*, taking their point of view—crudity.

Thus part way through *Satyagraha in South Africa* he says, "My object in writing the present volume is that the nation might know how Satyagraha, for which I live, for which I wish to live, and for which I believe I am equally prepared to die, originated and how it was practised on a large scale." His text is to be heroically relevant and quite un-self-ironic. "The reader will note South African parallels for all our experiences in the present struggle to date. [That is, the struggle for freedom in India.] . . . I have neither the time nor the inclination to write a regular detailed history. My only object in writing this book is that it may be helpful in our present struggle."

Literary readers tend to disbelieve a writer who says things such as that, or they turn away from him. Serious writers, in their experience, are always ironic about heroism, always do more than *tell*, and have all the time in the world to write. They offer to extend their readers' very *awareness*, their consciousness itself, either by describing modes of being that lie beyond the moral-rational limits we ordinarily acknowledge or by making us aware of slumbering powers within our own minds. Perhaps Gandhi gets as close to that sort of writing as he ever does in the series of essays on "My Jail Experiences," some of which appear in this collection. These do extend the *field* of his readers' consciousness, but only in the simple sense that Gandhi wanted to familiarize them with life in jail in order to prepare them for similar experiences, thereby training them for political action and cultural regeneration.

He wanted his readers to be ready for hardships and for social ignominy, ready to identify themselves with "the insulted and injured." But if one compares his essays to Dostoevsky's *House of the Dead* (which also describes the author's prison experience) one sees how little Gandhi gives us of the rawer facts and rawer feelings of that experience. When, for instance, he lets the reader know that incidents of homosexual rape occurred where he was imprisoned, the fact is signaled (not described) to us by the phrase "unnatural vice." Gandhi treated literature as one of the provinces of polite culture, which should represent only a polite selection from the range of experience. Modern literature, from Dostoevsky on, has included more and more impolite material, extending its harmonic range by including the shrieks and groans of the reader's (and the writer's) consciousness and sense of taste, as they struggle against so much that challenges and offends. Reading Gandhi offers a respite from that struggle, but at first it also seems to be a relapse from adulthood.

Let us begin by considering what kind of a life story this is: We shall find it in some ways undeniably "autobiographical," while in other ways atypical of the form. Gandhi began writing an autobiography in 1925, giving the book the title *The Story of My Experiments with Truth*. That book covered his life as a child in India, as a student in England, as a struggling lawyer and then politician in South Africa, and as the religious reformer who arrived back in India in 1915 and, between then and 1920, rose rapidly to the position of supreme national leader. This was a much more systematic account of the main events in his life than the present volume can offer, but Gandhi was quite aware of its not being autobiography in the full sense. Introducing it, he said, "It is not my purpose to attempt a real autobiography. I simply want . . ." Although he was not explicit about the criteria he was declining to meet, it seems likely that he was thinking of the bare simplicity of his narrative and its narrow utilitarianism—the lack of description and fancy, of literary expansiveness and inventiveness, and of all we call "creativity." Its magic lay entirely in the deeds described and not in the language used in describing them.

Thereafter he continued to write autobiographically for his various weekly newspapers: He always offered his readers a personal encounter, but he did not narrate the events of his life in any complete way. Those short essays from his newspapers, some of them reminiscences or dialogues with critics, form the material of this volume, together with letters. It gives us a week-by-week account of Gandhi's thoughts and feelings during the second half of his life—indeed, the two-thirds of his career that followed 1920. The texts are taken directly from his *Collected Works*, of which eighty-five volumes, of as many as six hundred pages each, have been published.

This volume can offer itself as orthodox autobiography much less than *The Story of My Experiments with Truth* can. Rich though these pieces are in that kind of interest, they lack the structure and the purpose of a self-descriptive book. There are two sets of criteria for what constitutes autobiography; some apply to content, some to form. An autobiography must describe the important events of the writer's life, and it must be written retrospectively and reflectively.

Nearly everything included here fits one or the other of those criteria, but practically nothing fits both. On the one hand, the events of
his political life in India—for instance, his fateful dealings with
M. A. Jinnah and the Muslim League—certainly are reflected in his
writings; one might even say that they are enacted there, in his
letters to Jinnah, his statements to the press, his notes to Nehru on
how the negotiations were going; but they are not retrospectively
and reflectively described. On the other hand, there is plenty of reflective writing, but it is about general topics or about pre-1920
events. (Having written about them in his autobiography, he had entered them in the category "Memory.") So we have the raw materials
for a biography, and we have the skills of a reflective writer; but the
two do not come together.

I exaggerate. I should say, they come together only rarely, as in the
series on "Jail Experiences." The rest of this volume could be called
reflections on personal topics (such as "What I Believe") plus letters,
speeches, and interviews, in which Gandhi's sense of himself crys-
tallizes, plus others in which his intimate relationships with family,
disciples, and co-workers become visible. They were chosen with
this broader criterion in mind and not with an eye to reminding the
reader of the main events in Gandhi's life.

One consequence of this choice is that this volume cannot count
as, or take the place of, a biography of the man. Involuntarily, in presenting the personal truth of his life, it stresses the devotional, emotional, and sexual aspects, at the expense of the organizational, political, and economic. That is, of course, a distribution of emphasis
often to be found in autobiographies. The public events of his life are
sometimes only dimly visible in the background. I therefore have
prompted the reader's memory with a series of seven chronologies,
one for every four or five years between 1920 and 1948, to put the
writing in its historical context.

By describing the first few pieces in this collection, I can both exemplify what I have just been saying and prepare the reader for some
of the unusual aspects of Gandhi's writing. The first is a public letter
of 1920 addressed to a literary scholar in Gujarati, a man who had
criticized Gandhi for compromising his spirituality by engaging in
politics: answering him, Gandhi can both argue his case for a religious politics and describe his early life for the benefit of others (this
letter was written before his autobiography). Thus his actual policies
in 1920 are only implicit. The second essay declares Gandhi's self-
affiliation to the Maharashtran reformer, Gopal Krishna Gokhale, as

his political patron, model, and guru; it is at the same time a repudiation of Gokhale's more fiery and militant rival, Bal Gangadhar Tilak. The writing is again naïvely personal, but there are clear political implications as to which group Gandhi is going to ally himself with, for both Gokhale and Tilak left organized and devoted parties behind them. The third is an Aesopian dialogue, between Gandhi and two little girls, about his constant need for contributions to his various causes, contributions involving sacrifice. Taken together, the three pieces exemplify both the variety of Gandhi's autobiographical essays and their oblique relation to the political events of his life. Those events, the stuff of biography, are seen only from a distance.

However, in one nonformal sense, this book is almost uniquely autobiographical. Each piece was published soon after it was written, and we know exactly when and why it came into being. The writing is rooted in the author's life as practically no other such book is—not even his own autobiography, and much less the works of literary artists. If we look at, say, Proust's autobiographical novel, we see how such a writer creates around him, as a precondition for writing, a vacuum of silence and solitude in which his mind can expand, in which his memories, his fantasies, his aesthetic ambitions, can swell out to enormous bulk; and he can concentrate his will into a series of prestidigitations performed upon that material. To do all that, he must have the ordinary life around him held in check, banished, reduced to minimal and manageable proportions. Proust had the walls of his apartment lined with cork to keep noise out; Tolstoy closed a series of doors between him and his family when he went to write. The writing came out of another reality, one constituted by the writer. It did not come out of the reality of those days' events during which it was written. But Gandhi's writing does come out of the days' events. This is week-by-week reporting and reflecting, essentially unrevised, untransformed by the writer's ambitions for his book as a whole. There is a date for each item, a day of the month of the year, and the reader's mind is invited to follow the connections to the events of that month and that year.

By the same token, Gandi does not give us a rounded and perfected image of those times. He is involved and immersed, he is pressed on all sides, and his writing has to be a weapon of defense and a tool of purpose. Nor does he allow himself the language of mystification employed by some leaders, political and religious.

But if, comparatively speaking, Gandhi was a pedestrian and occasional writer, he was also a professional one, and a profoundly original mind. The reader who enters the world of his writing, especially the literary reader, will find himself in very unfamiliar territory, which will—if he resists the temptation to call it "simple" and "moralistic" and "old-fashioned"—absorb his attention and compel his imagination as much as that of the greatest man of letters. Of course, Gandhi exerts this power not only by his success in meeting the criteria of literary critics, but also by putting those criteria to the question, by making them tremble, as modern critics say. He was not a man of letters, even though he was a master craftsman in language; he did not belong to "letters"—rather, they belonged to him. He leads his readers to the point at which they begin to question the very activities of writing and reading.

Gandhi's most obvious character as a writer was simplicity. He wrote in a plain, neat, precise, factual, rational style, with very few rhetorical ornaments and no evocations of the mystical or transcendental; no music, no color, no translations of effects from one sensory realm into another; not to mention those magical meltings of mood and tone, those elegant tricks of perspective and reminiscence, which we find in masters of modern prose such as Nabokov. Gandhi used only one or two out of the orchestra of instruments available to the modern writer, though he was able to produce literary effects with them that give aesthetic pleasure as intense and pure as more elaborate writers. (After 1918, D. H. Lawrence tells us in *Aaron's Rod* that the unaccompanied flute is musically authentic, while the sound of a big orchestra and even a piano are ruined by their associations with the war. Gandhi's prose has that sort of authority.)

Seen in his Indian context, Gandhi *was* a modern stylist, in a simple sense. He had a strong influence on Indian writers of the next two generations, or so Indian critics say, and that influence is generally acknowledged to be in the direction of simplification. In the late nineteenth century Indian writers in English imitated the more elaborate among the various models available to them in England, taking an extra ration of jewels and flowers to themselves because they were Oriental. Two of those well known to Gandhi were Rabindranath Tagore, who won the first Nobel Prize for Literature awarded to a non-Westerner, in 1913, and Sarojini Naidu, the poet and later the Gandhian politician known as the Nightingale of Bombay.

We can use these writers as a contrastive background to Gandhi's literary character. (Because I cannot read them in their native languages, I have to treat them the same way I treat Gandhi, as writers in English. This is not quite fair to them, for they were poets, and he

was not; but in the good cause of praising Gandhi, they would perhaps have made the sacrifice and swallowed the insult.) Tagore was
certainly a remarkably gifted writer, but he was addicted to the transcendental—to the exalted manner and evasive statement—and the
reader does well not to ask too often exactly what he means. Mrs.
Naidu began by imitating William Morris and Arthur Symons in
verse, and went on to a style of political oratory whose character is
suggested by a couple of comments from her friends. Gokhale told
her, "Like all Hindus, you begin with a ripple and end in eternity!"
and Motilal Nehru was heard to ask, as all Congress applauded one
of her speeches, "Yes, but what did she *say?*"

Gandhi was the very opposite, as speaker and writer. At least the
mature Gandhi was. When he first went to London, in 1888 at the
age of nineteen, he was what he called a "reformer," which meant
that he intended to learn English ways and to take them home with
him, to change India to make it more like England. In London, for
instance, he began to read newspapers—three a day—and to spend
ten minutes before a mirror every morning, brushing his hair. (At
home he read no papers and saw a mirror only when a barber shaved
him.) He wore elegant English clothes, including a top hat, morning
coat, leather gloves, patent leather boots and spats, and carried a
silver-mounted cane.

In step with all that, as a speaker and writer he cultivated certain
elegancies of literary style. In 1893–94 he wrote a *Guide to London*
of over a hundred manuscript pages, which began by asking, "Who
should go to England? All who can afford it should go to England. [He
was soon to give Indians quite opposite advice, but it is the manner
as much as the idea that is so un-Gandhian.] . . . The movements
alike of students and laymen in London are shrouded in mystery. . . .
The writer of the following pages proposes to uncover the mystery."

And this manner did not change overnight when he took up political activity, for the good reason that his early political activity was
Victorian Liberal, in ethos and mythos. In 1893 he wrote to the
Natal Advertiser, complaining about a lead article that had called
the Indians in South Africa "wily wretched Asian traders" and said
they were "the real canker that is eating into the very vitals of the
community." The letter of protest shows Gandhi at his most literary,
his least Gandhian.

But they spend nothing, says the leading article under discussion. Don't
they? I suppose they live on air or sentiments. We know that Becky lived on
nothing a year in *Vanity Fair*. And here a whole class seems to have been

found doing the same. It is to be presumed they have to pay nothing for shop rents, taxes, butcher's bills, grocer's bills, clerks' salaries, etc., etc. One would indeed like to belong to such a blessed class of traders, especially in the present critical condition of the trade all the world over. . . . It seems on the whole, that their simplicity, their total abstinence from intoxicants, their peaceful and above all, their businesslike and frugal habits, which should serve as a recommendation, are really at the bottom of all this contempt and hatred of the poor Indian traders. And they are British subjects. . . . Is this Christian-like? . . . Is this civilization? I pause for a reply.

There again is the profusion of literary ornament: the rhetorical question, the playful irony, the rippling rhythms, and above all the confident and familiar allusion to *Vanity Fair*—referring to the main character by her Christian name alone. Gandhi here plays the game of English high culture, assuming that everyone is familiar with the "classics." Writing of this kind is, or was at the time, all too accessible to the Western literary reader.

The character of Gandhi's prose changed radically as his general character changed, as he ceased to be a reformer/westernizer/modernizer and became something like the opposite. He had always had, judging by his earliest memories, deep and strong traits of piety—familial, cultural, and moral, as well as religious piety. He had always been puritanical (though he could also be gentle and generous) in his judgments on modern luxury. And he was profoundly responsive to those ideals of the New Life which he met in London and South Africa, and which constituted a criticism of Victorian civilization. Those ideas were embodied for him above all in the life and teachings of Tolstoy, but also in such Englishmen as John Ruskin and Edward Carpenter (the prophet of the "simple life") and in the German *Lebensreformer* and Nature Cure practitioners, such as Adolf Just and Louis Kuhne.

All these men were, in their different ways, enemies of capitalism and its culture. Gandhi read their books, and put their ideas into practice, in South Africa. His experiences there, culminating in 1910 at Tolstoy Farm, confirmed his calling to repudiate capitalism and city civilization in favor of the village and the ashram, of experiments in the simple life. This vocation, working in the depths of Gandhi's emotional as well as rational life, expressed itself in his political activity, too, for he became the leader of the Indian population of South Africa in *satyagraha*, or nonviolent protest against the white rulers. Tolstoy became his great teacher, and Tolstoy had called on the nations of the East to save the human race from the disaster into which the West was leading it.

Thus Gandhi was driven back, or found his way back, to his origins in traditional Hindu culture. Though many of his new convictions came to him from modern and European sources, they allied themselves to other convictions of his that were old and conservative and Hindu. Altogether, they made a rich mixture—one of the most fascinating in all cultural history—but the main purpose of the whole, paradoxically, was simplicity. And this simplicity expressed itself in his literary techniques, too, thereby constituting a problem for the literary reader.

Perhaps the best way to make the point is to look at Gandhi's literary work globally and to see its likeness to Tolstoy's popular writing and publishing. Gandhi's letters and newspaper articles, his many narratives and anecdotes, direct addresses and expositions of an idea, sketch out as a whole a "literature for the people"—the people as distinct from the reading public. This phrasing seems appropriate partly because Tolstoy turned away from the reading public in the second half of his life—stopped writing fiction such as *Anna Karenina*—and began writing, translating, abridging, and even publishing a quite different kind of literature, for the people of Russia. Gandhi's forms, like those of Tolstoy, were short and simple, his style clear and unpretentious, the range of effect running from a modest gay inventiveness to a severity of logic and a mood of memento mori. One might call it a religio-pastoral literature, reminiscent of that of the Christian Middle Ages.

Some famous examples of his writing in this style are his letters from jail to the children of the ashram, written with a playfulness and tender gaiety that prompted his Western admirers to compare Gandhi to Saint Francis of Assisi. And writing of this kind was practiced by other Gandhians, too, for instance, in their narratives of the Gandhi campaigns. Mirabehn made the story of his midnight arrests (in 1930 and 1932) sound like the Gospel story of Jesus' arrest before the Crucifixion. Rajendra Prasad described the Champaran campaign; Mahadev Desai described the Bardoli campaign.[1] Rabindranath Tagore said about Desai's *Story of Bardoli*, "It has the spirit of the Epic Age in its narrative of the triumph of moral right over arbitrary power. . . ." In fact, of course, such writing is epic only by a paradoxical transvaluation of the term; it is epic transformed into pastoral. The same transvaluation is clear in Pyarelal's title for his pamphlet about the 1932 fast, "The Epic Fast." The story of a fast

1. Champaran was the scene of Gandhi's agitation against European indigo planters in 1917. Bardoli is a district in Gujarat, the scene of Gandhian antitax peasant agitation in 1928.

can only paradoxically be compared to, say, *The Iliad*. The real significance of such terms is to testify to our sense that time has been
turned back, and that we are escaping from the sordid empiricism
and complexity of the modern into an earlier, naïver, nobler age.

Perhaps the most gifted of the Gandhians in literature was Rajagopalachari, and he continued and extended this work after Gandhi's
death by his retelling of the great epics *Ramayana* and *Mahabharata*.
But there were many gifted writers among them—for instance, Vinoba Bhave, whose special field was the philosophical and religious
pensée, and J. C. Kumarappa, who wrote about village economy and
about history. Kumarappa's tone is sharp enough at times to be called
Orwellian, but he is also Gandhian in the pastoral picturesqueness
of his intellectual schemes.

Kumarappa was temperamentally fiery and intellectually proud.
Vinoba's criticism could be very biting and Rajagopalachari's cyni-
cism is sometimes all-engulfing. But they were all Gandhian writers,
and this Gandhian writing can be described as a soothing idyll by
modern standards. It transforms the ashram, the campaigns, the jail-
going, the battles with the police, and even the political dealings with
other leaders, British and Indian, into something simple, gentle,
colorful, idyllic. When Gandhi got a disappointing reply from the
viceroy, he told the world: "On bended knees I asked for bread, and
was given a stone instead." He usually presents his allies and himself
as "in love with" each other, able to deny each other nothing, making each other a gift of a favorite disciple; they plead with each
other, they yield, tears of joy spring to their eyes, they embrace, and
so on. It all rings very oddly in the modern ear, Indian as well as
Western. Nehru wrote to Dr. Ansari on October 10, 1931, about the
negotiations at the Round Table Conference:

There seems to me too much sugariness in its proceedings, at least so far as
our side is concerned. That of course is Gandhiji's way, and we must not
complain. But a little pepper would add to the taste.

As is usual with Gandhi, one can find an answer to this complaint
in another place. In 1925 a correspondent protested that Gandhi had
edited his letter (in publishing it) and said he himself always followed W. L. Garrison's motto, "I will be as harsh as truth, and as uncompromising as justice." Gandhi replied: "I do not mind harsh
truth, but I do object to spiced truth. Spicy language is as foreign to
truth as hot chilies to a healthy stomach. . . . truth suffers when it is
harshly put."

Gandhi did not use such terms as pastoral, epic, or idyll, but he did use the Hindu terms for "qualities"—terms that can be applied to anything from food through art to temperaments—*tamas, rajas,* and *sattva.* The first can be translated as dark, gloomy, inert, or chaotic; the second as fiery, passionate, energetic, or enthusiastic; while the last is marked by peace and reason and is what I have called "pastoral." Touring the United Provinces in 1924, Gandhi had a sheet of paper thrown into his car by a peasant, which he found to be covered with couplets and quatrains from his favorite poet, Tulsidas. Gandhi talked about this incident some time after, for he found it significant and moving.

Historians have testified that nowhere in the world are the peasants as civilised as in India. This sheet of paper is proof of it. . . . I firmly believe that in our country it is not tamas which rules supreme but sattva. . . . people who have such ideas [as that peasant] have a sattvic civilisation.

This sattvic civilization was what Gandhi intended to build up in India, and he thought he remembered it as having been fragmentarily realized in his home district in his boyhood. We get glimpses of that in his reminiscences of his childhood, and we can see correspondences to his adult ideas. Stories Gandhi says he dwelt on as a child include that of Harishchandra, the Hindu Job, and Prahlad, a boy so good he even defied his father for love of God. Both of these characters are unbelievable and, therefore, for many Westerners, uninteresting. We in the West have, I think, almost lost the power to respond to such tales—as to our own legend of the patient Griselda—for two reasons. The first is because our ideology has no use for such "negative" virtues, being built around instead such "positive" ones as appetite and its satisfaction, bold ambition, and achieved power. If we are to understand Gandhi we must reach across this enormous abyss, a difference which derives, in part, from the West's economy of abundance over the last three centuries. Stories like those of Harishchandra, Prahlad, and Griselda make more sense in an economy of frequent famines, where putting up with misery is an important virtue.

The second reason is that our imagination has become, in modern times, so "realistic." It demands the stimulus of empirical, and often sordid, fact. Even Tolstoy, and his great predecessor, Rousseau, differ from Gandhi in this way, for they find even their transcendent truths rooted in the grit of empiricism. Gandhi does not. The single author in Gandhi's life who corresponds most clearly to Rousseau in Tolstoy's is Tulsidas, author of one of the most famous versions of the *Ramayana;* and one of the legends about Tulsidas himself may help us to understand Gandhi and may be taken in contrastive parallel with the stories Rousseau tells about himself in the *Confessions.* Tulsidas was so passionately fond of his wife that he followed her when she went, without his permission, to visit her parents. She reproached him, saying, "My body is nothing but skin and bone; and if such love as you have for it had been devoted to the Lord Rama, you would have no reason to dread rebirth." (Gandhi reproaches Mirabehn for idolizing him, in much the same terms, in a letter included in this volume.) Hearing this, Tulsidas at once abandoned all his ties to his home and became an ascetic votary and pilgrim, and later composed this and other poems about Rama.

There are many differences between that legend and Rousseau's story, in his *Confessions,* of how he left *his* home or of how he stole some ribbon and let a fellow servant take the blame. But all those differences imply the larger truth that the Western story is imbued with reverence before sordid empirical experience, and with the ambition to exalt such experience to the level of revelation, to give it transcendental significance. The story of Tulsidas, on the other hand, is clearly unrealistic; it is a nonempirical legend in which the important thing is the moral lesson (which is not something suddenly revealed but something repeated for the thousandth time) that we must be ready to give up everything at a moment's notice. Rousseau's "lesson," we might say, is that we need give up nothing, because our self continues. Whatever we do, however ugly, if we but remember it, write it down, embalm it in *consciousness,* it will always be ours; and all other truths and duties take their places within that universe of thought. However good or bad we may be, we can remain interesting. This is an idea for which Indian culture, of the kind Gandhi admired, has no place.

In the *Ramayana* Prince Rama is deprived of his heritage and goes to live in the forest with his wife Sita and his faithful brother Lakshman. Sita is abducted by Ravana, a demon king, and the brothers pursue him, destroy his kingdom, and rescue Sita; but because Sita has lived with Ravana, however unwillingly, Rama condemns her to exile, and she unmurmuringly acquiesces to his judgment. Rama, Sita, and Lakshman are incarnations of *dharma,* duty; they therefore are not, to Western eyes, either lifelike or heroic; rather, their charm lies in the elegance of the moral ideal they represent, their impersonal submission to their fate, their religious and aesthetic obedience.

The relation between this and Gandhi's writing can be seen in the naïveté of mood that complements his simplicity of language. I need hardly say that I am using these terms equivocally here. India has a very refined literary culture, and Gandhi is a very subtle thinker; but he and Tulsidas aim at an appearance of naïveté and simplicity—at a naïve and simple style of *being*. In short, they put their subtlety and refinement to work in the service of naïveté. This can make Gandhi seem, to the unready reader, either puerile or hypocritical (indeed, many people have thought him both at the same time).

Put him in the context of works such as the *Ramayana*, however, and we understand both him and the special character of our own literary tradition much better. There are many versions of the story, beginning with Valmiki's, in Sanskrit; but that of Tulsidas (written in Hindi) has been the most popular scripture in North India, including Gandhi's Gujarat, for three hundred years.

Tulsidas's version, which Gandhi preferred, is more devotional. Valmiki's hero is royal, and his arms are like bars of iron, a warrior's; Tulsidas's hero is a divine manifestation, not really human at all, and his character is softened. For instance, Tulsidas does not let Rama send Sita into exile; and when she seems to be captured by Ravana, in fact the real Sita enters into a preserving fire of holiness. Her perfection cannot even be imagined as flawed. When Rama creates the world, Sita is his *sakti*, his female power; Sita is "she by the play of whose eyebrows the world comes into being." Though purely feminine, her charm lies in her transcendence. It is typical of Tulsidas's piety that he glorifies the name of Rama even above the person. The form of the Absolute is unknown until revealed in a Name, and thereafter even the mechanical repetition of that Name may bring deliverance. (Again, Gandhi was devoted to the Ramanama, the repetition of Rama's name, a devotion like the recitation of the Hail Mary by Christians.)

Morally, Tulsidas was as severe and ascetic as Gandhi: "The acts of a saint are good, like the acts of a cotton plant, whose produce is dry and white and threadlike." (There is a pun hidden in the word for "act," *guna*, which can also mean both quality and strand. Thus even in his or her actions, a saint is somehow static—is essential rather than existential.) And this stress on dryness can remind us of something similar in medieval asceticism, for both Christianity and Hinduism have a similar tradition of puritanism (now glossed over by their apologists), a suspicion of entertainments and laughter, of the physical and even the actual. Holiness dries up all the vital fluids,

even tears, finally. The good man's triumphs are not actual but virtual: "The axe cuts down the tree, but the sandal sheds its natural fragrance on the axe." (Gandhi said the true *satyagrahi* always
triumphed, whatever his opponent did, and regardless of whether
anyone else supported him; he had triumphed simply by being a
satyagrahi.)

The triumph, Tulsidas implies, remains with the tree (sandalwood
is a famous Indian fragrance). We, from our Western perspective, are
likely to protest, "But it got cut down, killed." But from Tulsidas's
and Gandhi's point of view it is the fragrance that matters, transitory,
impalpable, and unrecorded as that is.

Now in politics Gandhi was an activist and a Westerner. Because
he thought almost anything was possible in politics, he could be
called more of a Westerner than most people of the West. As Erik
Erikson points out in his book *Gandhi's Truth* (New York, 1969), if
you set up Freud against Gandhi, it is Freud's truth that looks con-
templative, and Gandhi's looks and is active. But there was something else in Gandhi that can be called Eastern, and which we can
find hard to swallow. In Tulsidas and in the other stories he was fond
of we can find the influence that made him depict himself in these
autobiographical writings in ways we find disturbing or baffling. I
have called that influence Eastern, but as I have suggested, it could
also be called pre-Renaissance, for there was plenty of writing like
this in the Christian tradition before 1500. Just as Gandhi found in
Europe ideas that took him back to his Hindu heritage, so we can
find in him ideas that will return us to a past that is slipping away
from us.

There are, then, aspects of Gandhi that may seem enigmatic (and
that we may therefore be tempted to call pietistic or hypocritical) because there is a fundamental difference in values—in life-purpose—
between him and us. There are also many facts about his personal
situation at the time he wrote—about India fifty or sixty years ago—
that we need to know in order to grasp what he is saying, what he is
replying to or choosing between. The chronologies supply a broad
outline of those situations and should help to make the contexts
clear. It is hoped that the chronologies and this introduction set
Gandhi in a light that eliminates disfiguring shadows and blotches
and brings out those features which make him one of the magisterial
men of the twentieth century.

MEMBERS OF THE GANDHI FAMILY
MENTIONED IN TEXT

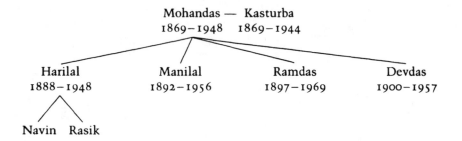

Mohandas — Kasturba
1869–1948   1869–1944

Harilal   Manilal   Ramdas   Devdas
1888–1948   1892–1956   1897–1969   1900–1957

Navin   Rasik

GANDHI IN INDIA

CHRONOLOGY I
1920–1924

   This four-year period of Gandhi's life begins where the Autobiography *leaves off, with Gandhi suddenly and dizzyingly established as supreme national leader—after only four years' political activity in India, and despite a good dozen other contenders for that position who had more impressive credentials. Such people as B. G. Tilak, Annie Besant, Surendrananth Banerji, Lala Lajpat Rai, and Motilal Nehru had deep roots in Indian politics, or powerful alliances, or well-established constituencies, and above all represented current political thinking much better than Gandhi did. His only political patron was G. K. Gokhale, who died within a year of Gandhi's return, after which Gokhale's organization, the Servants of India Society, did not welcome Gandhi.*
   Gandhi was, by their definition and by his own serene admission, eccentric and peripheral. And yet, by 1920, he had moved to the center of Indian politics. His Non-Cooperation campaign swept the country and might, according to some modern historians, have driven the British out of power then and there, had Gandhi been willing to employ or even allow violence.
   He was not willing. Because of the violence at Chauri Chaura in 1922, he suspended the civil disobedience he was then leading; and when he was sent to jail he discontinued his political activities. One may say that he moved out of the political center again. But the power of his performance was such that the center, the focus, the spotlight, followed him. Even in jail, and later in retirement, he was the center of India's political life, as journalists often said. This remained true as long as the British were in power and Indian politics were so much a matter of agitation.

1920

Gandhi was still concerned with the Amritsar massacre of 1919, during which the British authorities in the Punjab had fired on a mass meeting, killing hundreds. He was in Amritsar at the beginning of the year, appealed for donations to the Jallianwala Bagh Memorial Fund, and wrote the Congress Report on the massacre.

He also worked for the Muslim Khilafat Movement, which put pressure on the British government to restore the holy places of Islam to the rule of the caliph. He was trying to unify Indians by making the Hindus support the Muslims in this matter; he wanted to go to England to represent the latter's case. His major activity was the Non-Cooperation Movement, which he inaugurated on August 1 (the third Khilafat day). Its aim was to induce the nation to boycott the institutions of British rule—the army, the law courts, the schools, the universities, the administration—to give up any career in such institutions, and to set up their own institutions to replace them. Thus on November 15, in Ahmedabad, he became Chancellor of Gujarat Vidyapith, the Indian "university" set up in his native province. On September 8, both the Congress (which was predominantly Hindu) and the All India Khilafat Committee passed his resolutions on noncooperation.

1921

On April 13, Gandhi recommended the adoption of a national flag "to live and die for"; and in a speech at Ahmedabad declared "We want a swaraj which should be Ramarajya"; that is, the Western ideal of nationalism combined with the Hindu legend of peace and justice.

On July 31, he began his campaign for swadeshi *(to bring economic and therefore cultural independence to India) with a bonfire of foreign cloth in Bombay. He had appealed to cloth merchants to stop the import of cloth and to keep the price of Indian cloth down. In October he began to spin for half an hour every day before his second meal.*

On August 21, military law was imposed in Malabar, because Muslim Moplahs had rioted and looted the homes and property of Hindus, as well as destroying symbols of British administration.

On December 11, Harilal, Gandhi's alienated son, was arrested for his part in a Gandhian protest.

1922

On January 29, Gandhi began a civil disobedience movement in Bardoli.

On February 4, at Chauri Chaura in the United Provinces, rioting took place in connection with Gandhi's movement; twenty-one policemen and watchmen were killed. Six days later, Gandhi announced that, in consequence, civil disobedience was to be suspended. On February 12, he began a five-day fast in penance. On March 10, he was arrested and charged with promoting disaffection by his writings in Navajivan and Young India. On March 18, he pleaded guilty and was condemned to six years in jail. Two days later he was taken to Yeravda Prison.

1923

Gandhi spent all of this year in jail and out of public life. Some satyagrahi from Mulsi Peta who were in the same jail were flogged for refusing to do the work assigned them; Gandhi intervened on their behalf. In November, he began to write The History of Satyagraha in South Africa.

Meanwhile, the circulation of his newspapers fell off, and his political movement was in disarray. Many of those close to him rebelled against noncooperation; they wanted to enter the councils set up by the British in order to continue their careers of protest from within them. Gandhi refused to discuss such issues while he was a prisoner.

1924

On January 12, Gandhi was operated on for appendicitis, and on February 4 he was released from jail so that he could convalesce. At the end of March, he held discussions about entry into the councils with Malaviya, Motilal Nehru, and Lala Lajpat Rai. In April he again became editor of Young India and Navajivan.

In the selections from this period we see Gandhi introducing himself to India in Indian terms, indeed, specifically in the terms of Gujarat, his home province. He explains his relations to Western culture and reassures his readers that he is still firmly rooted in Gujarat. We also see him locating himself on the map of current politics, choosing Gokhale, and rejecting the more militant Tilak, as his guru. He takes occasion to mention his Muslim friends, Mohammed and Shaukat Ali, who were then his allies in his attempt to *overcome Hindu-Muslim hostility. All of these tactics—explaining himself, quoting criticism, dramatizing his friendships, showing himself both to be simply Indian and to cross cultural barriers—were to remain highly characteristic of Gandhi.*

1. Gandhi Presents Himself to India

(vol. XIX, pp. 176-81)

I happened, by chance, to read the open letter to me addressed by the renowned scholar of Gujarat, Shri Narasinhrao.[1] I find little time for newspapers and rarely get any when I am touring. It is likely, therefore, that I miss many such writings.

I could ill-afford to miss this letter. Shri Narasinhrao has written it with love and in all sincerity. I can see that my present activities have pained him. Reading his letter, others also may have felt like him. I would be happy if I could satisfy their doubts and reassure them. I shall, therefore, try to answer his letter.

Shri Narasinhrao's letter, I can see, rests on one belief. He does not see today the same moral and religious fervour which he did in 1915 and after. He thinks that I am lost in the sea of politics and have been overcome by *moha.*

My soul bears witness that I am the same man that I was in 1915. In fact, my concern for dharma and justice has become more urgent.

I am afraid Shri Narasinhrao is ignorant of my past life. I have spent my entire life in politics and do not regard dharma as something apart from politics. I have always believed in Gokhale's principle of "spiritualizing politics" and tried to act upon it to the best of my ability.

During the satyagraha in South Africa, I used the same epithets which I apply to the Government, but I have never thought that my reason was clouded at that time. Some English friends indeed thought so, but afterwards they felt sorry for that. One of them was the late Mr. Escombe, a Natal minister, and, another, General Smuts, the present [Prime] Minister of South Africa.

The sweet music of *Premal Jyoti*[2] still reverberates in my ears.

1. 1859-1937; Gujarati poet and man of letters; professor of Gujarati, Elphinstone College, Bombay.
2. A verse-translation in Gujarati, by Narasinhrao, of Cardinal Newman's hymn, "Lead Kindly Light."

Even today its message is the goal of my striving. Even now I pray every moment of my life for God's grace and inspiration.

Nevertheless, I had even then called on people to turn their back on Western civilization. It was in 1908 that I clearly saw that imitating it would be the ruin of India. I first shared my views with a British peer[3] and, the same year (1908) on my return to South Africa from England I published them[4] in the columns of *Indian Opinion* and later brought them out in book form under the title *Hind Swaraj*.[5] May I request Shri Narasinhrao to read it in the original or in translation? These pages will give him a clear insight into many of my present activities.

But, by rejection of Western civilization I never meant, nor do I mean even today, shunning everything English or hating the British. I revere the Bible. Christ's Sermon on the Mount fills me with bliss even today. Its sweet verses have even today the power to quench my agony of soul. I can still read with love some of the writings of Carlyle and Ruskin. Even now, the tunes and the verses of many English hymns are like *amrit* to me. Even so, I think that we would be well-advised to reject Western civilization, that it is our dharma to do so.

By Western civilization I mean the ideals which people in the West have embraced in modern times and the pursuits based on these ideals. The supremacy of brute force, worshipping money as God, spending most of one's time in seeking worldly happiness, breathtaking risks in pursuit of worldly enjoyments of all kinds, the expenditure of limitless mental energy on efforts to multiply the power of machinery, the expenditure of crores on the invention of means of destruction, the moral righteousness which looks down upon people outside Europe,—this civilization, in my view, deserves to be altogether rejected.

And yet I clung to British rule because, in my ignorance, I attributed to it strength for undertaking the great task of smashing this civilization. But now I see that British rule is perhaps more Satanic than what Germany does. Even if I am mistaken in this comparison, the two are at any rate equal.

All the characteristics of *Ravanarajya* described by Tulsidas are to be found in British rule and that is why I describe it by that name.

---

3. Presumably Lord Ampthill, whom Gandhi met in England in 1909; *vide* Vol. IX.
4. This should be 1909. Gandhi was in England from about the middle of July to November 13 of that year as member of a deputation on behalf of Indians in South Africa.
5. In January 1910. An English translation, by Gandhi himself, was published in March of the same year.

There is no anger in this, nor "righteous indignation." It is a conclusion which I have reached in all calmness of mind. It is not my intention to suggest that every Englishman or English officer is a devil. Every officer, however, works as part of a Satanic machine and, therefore, whether intentionally or unintentionally, becomes an instrument of injustice, deception and repression. If, holding this belief, I were to conceal it, I would be betraying truth. It is not bad manners to call a thief a thief or a sinner a sinner, nor is it abuse in the manner of an uncultured peasant. On the contrary, if the words have been uttered with sincerity, they can be an expression of love.

If in my life I have tried to practise anything with unswerving devotion it is non-violence, truth and *brahmacharya*. I alone know how difficult it is to practise these. I believe that I have succeeded fairly well in following all the three in action and speech. To say that I have had no angry thought would be untrue, and I would be sinning if I said that I have never felt the urge of desire. I believe, nonetheless, that keeping the three vows in action, speech and thought has so potent a virtue that, if I had acquired the strength to follow them perfectly, the doubt which has occurred to Shri Narasinhrao would never have occurred to him at all. Having said this, I can say on oath that I do not wish ill to General Dyer in any way, that I have not the least desire to see him punished. Were he to fall ill, I would nurse him with love. But I certainly would not pay him a pension out of my money and so have a share in his sin. I would not gloss over the wickedness of his action. I have no doubt that his action was monstrous. The British people, by describing it as an error of judgment, have taken his sin upon themselves.

When Jesus described his times as a generation of vipers, it was not out of anger. At a time when everyone was afraid of telling the truth, Jesus risked his life, described hypocrisy, pride and lying in plain terms for what they were and so put innocent and simple folk on their guard, and saved them. When the Buddha, with the lamb on his shoulder, went up to the cruel Brahmins who were engaged in an animal-sacrifice, it was in so soft language that he spoke to them; he was, however, all love at heart. Who am I in comparison with these? Even so, I aspire to be their equal in love in this very life. Let the reader not think me presumptuous on this account. The highest ideal I have set before myself is a Mehta[6] of Gujarat, Shri Narasinhrao's namesake. His love was no less than that of the Buddha.

6. Narasinh Mehta.

It is quite possible that I am making a mistake, that I am doing injustice to the British, that I have misread history, but it is certainly not true that my present activities are conceived in a spirit of retaliation or that they are less religious in inspiration. I request those friends who would save me from error to know me first. I make an effort to be and to remain pure; I am full of error, but ever ready to correct myself. There is nothing in my life which I wish to conceal. Whatever I think I speak out immediately. But, being one who takes most careful thought before doing anything, I do not easily abandon my views. I should not be surprised to know that my co-workers too think me autocratic. It is my humble belief that I am no autocrat. An autocrat has simply no patience for what others may have to say. So far as my memory goes, I listen even to children and have learnt much from them. There is a great deal, indeed, I have learnt from cowherds and peasants.

I have used the term "co-workers" above. Shri Narasinhrao has unwittingly done me an injustice by taking my statement, "I have no followers; there may be persons who follow my ideas," to be a mere play on words. I have not accepted anyone as my dharma-guru[7] and I don't think myself, either, to be worthy of the honour of being such [to anyone else]. So long as I have not acquired the strength to follow the rules of *yama-niyama* perfectly in thought, word and deed, I am liable to commit errors, any number of them. Such a person is not entitled to accept anyone as his disciple. I made the mistake, some years ago, of regarding just one friend as my disciple at his urging, and burnt my fingers in consequence. My role of a guru simply did not work. I had judged wrongly.

I think it very dangerous, in this age, for anyone to accept another as a guru or be another's guru. We attribute perfection to a guru. By accepting an imperfect man as our guru, we are led into no end of error. That is why I have deliberately said that I welcome people being followers of my ideas but I want no one to be my follower. Following ideas requires understanding; in following a person, faith is the chief thing. I do not want to be an object of the devotion which such faith expresses, but I certainly want people to follow my ideas with devotion. They can do this, of course, only if they understand them. I know, however, that at present many persons follow my ideas simply out of blind regard for me. I accept no responsibility for their sin, since I do not look upon them as my followers. Between a per-

7. Spiritual mentor.

son's being my follower and his being a follower of my ideas there is the same difference which there is, according to Gladstone, between calling a man a fool and describing his ideas as foolish.

This is not all. Shri Narasinhrao sees in me another weakness which "gurus" are especially prone to. How is it that I do not offer satyagraha against people touching my feet out of reverence—do not condemn it—but permit the thing? I respectfully submit to my friend that this does not fall within the scope of satyagraha. Touching a man's feet in reverence is not in itself wrong or sinful so that it calls for satyagraha against it. Moreover, is it possible for anyone, all at once, to persuade the multitude of simple-hearted, loving peasants, who are used to the practice of touching a man's feet, to give it up? I assure Shri Narasinhrao that I am weary of this touching of my feet and these cries of *jai*.[8] My friend Shaukat Ali tries hard to save me from these assaults on my person which take the form of touching my feet, and numbers of volunteers are busy to the same end, but so far I have not escaped these attentions. I do not have the courage, nor the desire, to offer satyagraha against the practice by going on a fast or refusing to speak to the people. The cries of *jai* vex me so much that often I literally plug my ears with cottonwool. I assure Shri Narasinhrao that I shall not be blinded by adoration and will not forsake my duty, either, because of people's scorn.

Shri Narasinhrao invites me to Bandra Point.[9] My only desire in wanting to go there was to call on that good man, Dayaram Gidumal.[10] I heard of him in Hyderabad through members of his family. It was also my desire to compliment Shri Narasinhrao on the courage he has shown in keeping him as an honoured guest of the family. Owing to my preoccupations, however, I have not been able to fulfil this desire.

I do not believe that Bandra Point will give me peace of mind or that I shall have there a clearer vision of the "Kindly Light." I had an occasion years ago to decide whether I would go and stay in Bandra and I deliberately decided not to go. The Bombay slaughter-house is in Bandra. I feel a stab in the heart whenever I pass it. There may be any number of beautiful spots in that place but to me they all seem dyed with the blood of innocent creatures and, therefore, it hurts my soul to have to go there. Another place where I find it painful to stay is Calcutta. There, countless goats are killed in the name of Hinduism and I find this unbearable. I will, therefore, certainly try to go

8. Victory.
9. In Bombay. Narasinhrao lived there at this time.
10. 1857–1939; social reformer; founder of Seva Sadan, Bombay.

to Bandra, but only with the first desire as explained above. As for the "Kindly Light," I get a vision of it in the temple of my heart whenever this is radiant with perfect self-control and the vision invariably gives me the experience of transcendent peace.

[From Gujarati]
Navajivan, 29-12-1920

2. My Teacher

(vol. XX, pp. 369-71)

A strange anonymous letter has been received by me, admiring me for having taken up a cause that was dearest to Lokamanya's heart, and telling me that his spirit was residing in me and that I must prove a worthy follower of his. The letter, moreover, admonishes me not to lose heart in the prosecution of the swaraj programme, and finishes off by accusing me of imposture in claiming to be politically a disciple of Gokhale. I wish correspondents will throw off the slavish habit of writing anonymously. We who are developing the swaraj spirit must cultivate the courage of fearlessly speaking out our mind. The subject-matter of the letter, however, being of public importance, demands a reply. I cannot claim the honour of being a follower of the late Lokamanya. I admire him like millions of his countrymen for his indomitable will, his vast learning, his love of country, and above all, the purity of his private life and great sacrifice. Of all the men of modern times, he captivated most the imagination of his people. He breathed into us the spirit of swaraj. No one perhaps realized the evil of the existing system of Government as Mr. Tilak did. And, in all humility, I claim to deliver his message to the country as truly as the best of his disciples. But I am conscious that my method is not Mr. Tilak's method. And that is why I have still difficulty with some of the Maharashtra leaders. But I sincerely think that Mr. Tilak did not disbelieve in my method. I enjoyed the privilege of his confidence. And his last word to me in the presence of several friends was, just a fortnight before his death, that mine was an excellent method if the people could be persuaded to take to it. But he said he had doubts. I know no other method. I can only hope that, when the final test comes, the country will be proved to have assimilated the method of non-violent non-co-operation. Nor am I unaware of my other limitations. I can lay no claim to scholarship. I have not his powers of organization, I have no compact disciplined party to lead, and having been an exile for twenty-three years, I cannot claim the experience that the Lokamanya had of India. Two things we had in common to the fullest measure—love of country and the steady pursuit of swaraj. I can, therefore, assure the anonymous writer that, yielding to none in my reverence for the memory of the deceased, I will march side by side with the foremost of the Lokamanya's disciples in the pursuit of swaraj. I know that the only offering acceptable to him is the quickest attainment of swaraj by India. That and nothing else can give his spirit peace.

Discipleship, however, is a sacred personal matter. I fell at Dadabhai's feet in 1888,[1] but he seemed to be too far away from me. I could be as son to him, not disciple. A disciple is more than son. Discipleship is a second birth. It is a voluntary surrender. In 1896 I met almost all the known leaders of India in connection with my South African mission. Justice Ranade awed me. I could hardly talk in his presence. Badruddin Taiyabji fathered me, and asked me to be guided by Ranade and Pherozeshah. The latter became a patron. His will had to be law. "You must address a public meeting on the 26th September, and you must be punctual." I obeyed. On the 25th evening I was to wait on him. I did.

"Have you written out your speech?" he inquired.

"No, sir."

"That won't do, young man. Can you write it out tonight? Munshi, you must go to Mr. Gandhi and receive the manuscript from him. It must be printed overnight and you must send me a copy." Turning to me, he added, "Gandhi, you must not write a long speech, you do not know Bombay audiences cannot stand long addresses." I bowed.

The lion of Bombay taught me to take orders. He did not make me his disciple. He did not even try.

I went thence to Poona. I was an utter stranger. My host first took me to Mr. Tilak. I met him surrounded by his companions. He listened, and said, "We must arrange a meeting for you. But perhaps you do not know that we have unfortunately two parties. You must give us a non-party man as chairman. Will you see Dr. Bhandarkar?" I consented and retired. I have no firm impression of Mr. Tilak, except to recall that he shook off my nervousness by his affectionate familiarity. I went thence, I think, to Gokhale, and then to Dr. Bhandarkar. The latter greeted me, as a teacher his pupil.

"You seem to be an earnest and enthusiastic young man. Many

1. This was when Gandhi was studying for the Bar in London; *vide An Autobiography*, Part I, Ch. XXV.

people do not come to see me at this the hottest part of the day. I
never nowadays attend public meetings. But you have recited such a
pathetic story that I must make an exception in your favour."

I worshipped the venerable doctor with his wise face. But I could
not find for him a place on that little throne. It was still unoccupied.
I had many heroes, but no king.

It was different with Gokhale, I cannot say why. I met him at his
quarters on the college ground.[2] It was like meeting an old friend, or,
better still, a mother after a long separation. His gentle face put me
at ease in a moment. His minute inquiries about myself and my
doings in South Africa at once enshrined him in my heart. And as I
parted from him, I said to myself, "You are my man." And from that
moment Gokhale never lost sight of me. In 1901 on my second return from South Africa, we came closer still.[3] He simply 'took me in
hand,' and began to fashion me. He was concerned about how I
spoke, dressed, walked and ate. My mother was not more solicitous
about me than Gokhale. There was, so far as I am aware, no reserve
between us. It was really a case of love at first sight, and it stood the
severest strain in 1913.[4] He seemed to me all I wanted as a political
worker—pure as crystal, gentle as a lamb, brave as a lion and chiv-
alrous to a fault. It does not matter to me that he may not have been
any of these things. It was enough for me that I could discover no
fault in him to cavil at. He was and remains for me the most perfect
man in the political field. Not, therefore, that we had no differences.
We differed even in 1901 in our views on social customs, e.g., widow
remarriage. We discovered differences in our estimate of Western civilization. He frankly differed from me in my extreme views on non-
violence. But these differences mattered neither to him nor to me.
Nothing could put us asunder. It were blasphemous to conjecture
what would have happened if he were alive today. I know that I would
have been working under him. I have made this confession because
the anonymous letter hurt me when it accused me of imposture
about my political discipleship. Had I been remiss in my acknowledgment to him who is now dumb? I thought I must declare my
faithfulness to Gokhale, especially when I seemed to be living in a
camp which the Indian world calls opposite.

Young India, 13-7-1921

2. Of Fergusson College, Poona.
3. Gandhi stayed with Gokhale for about a month at the time of the Calcutta session of the Indian National Congress; *vide An Autobiography*, Part III, Chs. XVII,
XVIII and XIX.
4. This was when Gandhi decided to launch passive resistance.

3. Collecting Funds
(vol. XX, pp. 272–76)

Madhuri and Pushpa are girls of six or seven. It was my greedy hunt for contributions to the Tilak Swaraj Fund that had taken me to the family.

While I sat surrounded by the men and women members of the family, all full of love for me, Madhuri came up, walking with slow, hesitant steps. I called her to me. Unfortunately, they had given me a chair, tables and chairs being the normal thing in the family. Seated in a chair, how could I take up Madhuri? So I drew her to me and put her head on my lap.

"I have cheated you."

"Elders may cheat me, not kids. You cannot have cheated me."

I replied with a smile, observing Madhuri's features the while.

"But I have really cheated you; I gave you only a rupee and a half," she said with courage.

"Then, I must say, I have been really cheated. With so many orna-ments on you, you gave me only a rupee and a half?" I said, and took Madhuri's little hand in mine. Her bangle danced in my palm. I continued:

"You should then do expiation. Kids should be perfectly innocent. They never cheat anybody. To expiate means to wash off one's sin, to cleanse oneself. You ought to do so now."

"How is it possible to be cleansed now? The fact remains that I have cheated you."

"There is an easy way. You have realized that you ought to have given me your ornaments. That is what made you say you had cheated me. You should now give me all your ornaments and your sin will be washed off."

Madhuri's face, bright till now, fell somewhat. I saw this and resumed:

"What should kids have to do with ornaments? We appear hand-some through our actions. Besides, ornaments may be lost. Better give them to help some good cause. And you seem to be a good girl! You confess your error too. You should willingly give your orna-ments. I shall utilize them to supply spinning-wheels to the homes of the poor, and to educate children like yourself. Other little girls like you have also given their ornaments."

I paused.

There were two little ruby pendants on Madhuri's ears and on her

wrists a pair of bangles with strips of gold and another pair of glass
bangles. She whispered:

"Will it be all right if I give these glass bangles?"

I wondered what reply I could give to this child. Shall I take her
with me and adopt her as my daughter? But, then, I thought, I have
so many daughters like her! And, for the present, I am but a miserly
Bania, who knows only grabbing. So I said:

"I can get money even for your bangles. But I want all your ornaments. Surely, it should not be so very difficult to part with them!
For one thing, your sin will be washed off and, for another, they will
come in useful to me. Your ornaments will help us in winning
swaraj. Won't you give me all?"

"I shall not give my gold bangle at any rate. Will you accept these
(pointing to her pendants)?"

"Now that is something. How nice it would be, though, if you gave
me these bangles as well?"

Madhuri felt somewhat unhappy. I kissed her and said, "All right,
give me your pendants."

She ran away, returning in a minute. While she was removing the
pendants, I said: "But have you obtained mother's permission?"

"Yes, she has given her permission."

"She told me to give everything, but I don't like to part with my
bangles."

Madhuri removed the pendants and dropped them into my hands.
A tiny gold link had fallen on to the ground. She looked for it carefully, found it and handed it to me.

Do what I might, though, I could not overcome my greed. My eyes
would not turn away from the bangles. I did not yet know the girl's
name, nor whose daughter she was. I now asked and learnt her name,
recognized the worthy gentleman who was her father, and said:

"Really, Madhuri, what do you see in these bangles that you love
them so much? What should an innocent girl like you do with ornaments? Won't you give your bangles too?"

Madhuri softened. With her own hands, she removed a bangle and
put it into my hand. This was a victory for me, I thought.

But the victory was on Madhuri's side. That little girl had stolen
my heart. I envied her parents. "May all parents have such children,"
I prayed from my heart. My faith in the success of our struggle for
swaraj grew stronger. I said to Madhuri:

"You have been so wonderful. I will not accept the other bangle
even if you give it. But is it willingly that you have given me what
you have? You can take them back, if you wish to."

As I said this, I held out the ornaments before her.

"I gave them quite willingly and do not want them back."

The answer brought fresh blood to me.

I went into another room to see the female members of the family. Some other kids had been following the conversation between Madhuri and me.

2

Pushpa, a neighbour's daughter, removed her bangle and put it into my hand.

"Have you obtained your mother's permission?"

"Yes, Sir. It is with her permission that I give this bangle to you."

"And do you know my terms for accepting all these articles? Little girls who give ornaments must not ask their parents to replace them before we have won swaraj. If they have some others, they may wear them; but, for some time, they must not ask for new ones to be made."

"I have got another such bangle with me. I won't ask for a new one. I have given my bangle to you quite willingly."

Madhuri was looking on. She was also discussing something with her mother. She removed the glass bangles and the remaining gold one, and put them both into my hand!

"I accept this glass bangle. But I told you I would not accept your gold bangle even if you offered it. Please, therefore, do not give it. As it is, you have given much."

"So far as I am concerned, I have given it away to you. I do not want it at all. I have given it willingly. Kindly keep it."

Madhuri scored a victory over me. I broke my word and accepted the other bangle. With wrists and ears bare, Madhuri looked more handsome, to me at any rate. I hugged her to my heart.

Overcome with joy, I offered thanks to God.

Madhuri now addressed herself to a task. She set to work to see other girls' wrists stripped bare. Her efforts met with indifferent success.

Will God, however, judge her from the outcome of her attempt? He has said, in truth: "Do your work; leave the result entirely to Me."

For her part, Madhuri did her "work," not for show but for the satisfaction of the great *atman* inhabiting her little frame.

After exhorting Madhuri and Pushpa to wear khadi and ply the spinning-wheel and after securing a promise from the ladies of the family in regard to both, I left, all admiration in my heart for Madhuri and Pushpa.

If we do not get swaraj this very year, even through the sacrifice of such innocent ones, how great must have been the burden of sin accumulated by us, the so-called elders!

May God ever send into the world children like Madhuri and Pushpa! Let us, men and women alike, salute the stainless *atmans* of such children and learn from them.

I have written down this conversation thirty hours after it took place. I have reproduced it as well as I remember it. Even the children's words are given as they were actually spoken, without any embellishment. I noted all the time that they spoke faultlessly.

[From Gujarati]
Navajivan, 26-6-1921

4. Our Fallen Sisters

(vol. XXI, pp. 104-6)

The first occasion I had of meeting those women who earn their livelihood out of their shame was at Coconada in the Andhra province. There it was a few moments' interview with only half a dozen of them. The second occasion was at Barisal. Over one hundred of them met by appointment. They had sent a letter in advance, asking for an interview and telling me that they had become members of the Congress and subscribed to the Tilak Swaraj Fund, but could not understand my advice not to seek office in the various Congress Committees. They wound up by saying, that they wished to seek my advice as to their future welfare. The gentleman who handed me the letter did so with great hesitation, not knowing whether I would be offended or pleased with the receipt of the letter. I put him at ease by assuring him, that it was my duty to serve these sisters if I could in any way.

For me the two hours I passed with these sisters is a treasured memory. They told me that they were over 350 in the midst of a population of about 20,000 men, women and children. They represent the shame of the men of Barisal, and the sooner Barisal gets rid of it, the better for its great name. And what is true of Barisal is true, I fear, of every city. I mention Barisal, therefore, as an illustration. The credit of having thought of serving these sisters belongs to some young men of Barisal. Let me hope that Barisal will soon be able to claim the credit, too, of having eradicated the evil.

Of all the evils for which man has made himself responsible, none is so degrading, so shocking or so brutal as his abuse of the better half of humanity to me, the female sex, not the weaker sex. It is the nobler of the two, for it is even today the embodiment of sacrifice, silent suffering, humility, faith and knowledge. A woman's intuition has often proved truer than man's arrogant assumption of superior knowledge. There is method in putting Sita before Rama and Radha before Krishna. Let us not delude ourselves into the belief, that this gambling in vice has a place in our evolution because it is rampant and in some cases even state-regulated in civilized Europe. Let us not also perpetuate the vice on the strength of Indian precedents. We should cease to grow the moment we cease to discriminate between virtue and vice, and slavishly copy the past which we do not fully know. We are proud heirs to all that was noblest and best in the by-gone age. We must not dishonour our heritage by multiplying past errors. In a self-respecting India, is not every woman's virtue as much every man's concern as his own sister's? Swaraj means ability to re-gard every inhabitant of India as our own brother or sister.

And so, as a man I hung my head in shame before these hundred sisters. Some were elderly, most were between twenty and thirty, and two or three were girls below twelve. Between them all, they told me, they had six girls and four boys, the eldest of whom was married to one of their own class. The girls were to be brought up to the same life as themselves, unless something else was possible. That these women should have considered their lot to be beyond repair, was like a stab in the living flesh. And yet they were intelligent and modest. Their talk was dignified, their answers were clean and straight. And for the moment their determination was as firm as that of any satya-grahi. Eleven of them promised to give up their present life and take to spinning and weaving from the following day, if they received a helping hand. The others said they would take time to think, for they did not wish to deceive me.

Here is work for the citizens of Barisal. Here is work for all true servants of India, men as well as women. If there are 350 unhappy sisters in a population of 20,000, there may be 5,250,000 in all India. But I flatter myself with the belief that four fifths of the population of India, which live in the villages and are purely agricultural, are not touched by the vice. The lowest figure for all India would therefore be 1,050,000 women living on the sale of their own honour. Before these unfortunate sisters could be weaned from their degradation, two conditions have to be fulfilled. We men must learn to control our passions, and these women should be found a calling that would enable them to earn an honourable living. The movement of non-co-operation is nothing, if it does not purify us and restrain our evil passions. And there is no occupation but spinning and weaving which all can take up without overcrowding. These sisters, the vast majority of them, need not think of marriage. They agreed that they could not. They must therefore become the true *sannyasinis* of India. Having no cares of life but of service, they can spin and weave to their heart's content. One million fifty thousand women diligently weaving every day for eight hours means that number of rupees per day for an impoverished India. These sisters told me they earned as much as two rupees per day. But then they admitted, that they had many things needed to pander to man's lust, which they could discard when they took to spinning and weaving, reverting to a natural life. By the time I had finished with my interviews, they knew without my telling them, why they could not be office-bearers in Congress Committees if they did not give up their sinfulness. None could officiate at the altar of swaraj, who did not approach it with pure hands and a pure heart.

Young India, 15-9-1921

5. My Loin-Cloth

(vol. XXI, pp. 225–27)

[October 2, 1921]

All the alterations I have made in my course of life have been effected by momentous occasions; and they have been made after such a deep deliberation that I have hardly had to regret them. And I did them, as I could not help doing them. Such a radical alteration—in my dress,—I effected in Madura.

I had first thought of it in Barisal. When, on behalf of the famine-stricken at Khulna, I was twitted that I was burning cloth utterly regardless of the fact that they were dying of hunger and nakedness, I felt that I should content myself with a mere loin-cloth and send on my shirt and dhoti to Dr. Roy, for the Khulna people. But I restrained my emotion. It was tinged with egotism. I knew that the taunt was groundless. The Khulna people were being helped, and only a single zemindar could have sent all the relief necessary. I needed therefore nothing to do there.

The next occasion came when my friend Maulana Mahomed Ali

was arrested before my very eyes. I went and addressed a meeting soon after his arrest. I thought of dispensing with my cap and shirt that moment, but then I restrained myself fearing that I might create a scene.

The third occasion came during my Madras tour. People began to tell me that they had not enough khadi to start with and that if khadi was available, they had no money. "If the labourers burn their foreign clothing where are they to get khadi from?" That stuck into my heart. I felt there was truth in the argument. The plea for the poor overpowered me. I expressed grief to Maulana Azad Sobhani, Mr. Rajagopalachariar, Doctor Rajan and others, and proposed that I should thenceforth go about with a loin-cloth. The Maulana realized my grief and entirely fell in with my idea. The other co-workers were uneasy. They felt that such radical change might make people uneasy, some might not understand it; some might take me to be a lunatic, and that all would find it difficult if not impossible, to copy my example.

For four days I revolved these thoughts, and ruminated the arguments, I began telling people in my speeches: "If you don't get khadi, you will do with mere loin-cloth but discard foreign clothing." But I know that I was hesitating whilst I uttered those words. They lacked the necessary force, as long as I had my dhoti and my shirt on.

The dearth of swadeshi in Madras, also continued to make me uneasy. The people seemed to be overflowing with love but it appeared to be all froth.

I again turned to my proposal, again discussed with friends. They had no new argument to advance and September was very nearly closing. What should I do to complete the boycott before the close of September? That was what was for ever troubling me.

Thus we reached Madura on the night of the 22nd. I decided that I should content myself with only a loin-cloth until at least the 31st of October. I addressed a meeting of the Madura weavers early next morning in loin-cloth. Today is the third day.

The Maulana has liked the idea so much that he has made as much alteration in his dress as the *Shariat* permits. Instead of the trousers, he puts on a *lungi*, and wears a shirt of which the sleeves do not reach beyond the elbow. Only at the time of the prayers, he wears a cap, as it is essential. The other co-workers are silently watching. The masses in Madras watch me with bewilderment.

But if India calls me a lunatic, what then? If the co-workers do not copy my example, what then? Of course this is not meant to be copied by co-workers. It is meant simply to hearten the people, and to make my way clear. Unless I went about with a loin-cloth, how might I advise others to do likewise? What should I do where millions have to go naked? At any rate why not try the experiment for a month and a quarter? Why not satisfy myself that I left not a stone unturned?

It is after all this thinking that I took this step. I feel so very easy. For eight months in the year, you do not need a shirt here. And so far as Madras is concerned, it may be said that there is no cold season at all, and even the respectable class in Madras wears hardly anything more than a dhoti.

The dress of the millions of agriculturists in India is really only the loin-cloth, and nothing more. I have seen it with my own eyes wherever I have gone.

I want the reader to measure from this the agony of my soul. I do not want either my co-workers or readers to adopt the loin-cloth. But I do wish that they should thoroughly realize the meaning of the boycott of foreign cloth and put forth their best effort to get it boycotted, and to get khadi manufactured. I do wish that they may understand that swadeshi means everything.

The Hindu, 15-10-1921

6. Women's Contribution
(vol. XXII, pp. 185–88)

Women must make their full contribution in this struggle. They served as volunteers and made the Congress session a great success. This was the first experiment of its kind in the history of the Congress. It is a matter of joy for Gujarat that this good fortune fell to its women. The experiment was a complete success and created a good impression on all. If women start contributing their share in every field of service which is safe for them, our capacity for work will be doubled.

We also know that the Government will not, as far as possible, arrest women. Men, of course, are to get themselves arrested. Women, therefore, will have to take over much of the men's work.

Need for Fearlessness

All that is needed for this purpose is fearlessness. Only those who are pure can possess it. Our minds have become so corrupt that we are always apprehensive about women's purity. In acting thus, we defame all people in the world. We regard woman as so weak that we think she is incapable of preserving her virtue, and man so fallen that his attitude towards woman can be only lustful. Both these notions are disgraceful. If our men and women are really what we think them to be, then we must confess that we are entirely unfit for swaraj. We have no reason to assume that Englishmen and women observe no restraints. Englishwomen do all kinds of work by way of service, whereas if we require a nurse, we find it difficult to get anyone who will do the work.

If swaraj is really drawing nearer, women will daily become more capable of protecting their honour. They must shed their fear. The notion that a woman is incapable of preserving her virtue is false. It is contrary to experience and a matter of shame for both men and women. There certainly are brutish men in the world who commit such crimes, but that man does not exist nor will he ever be born who can force himself upon a woman who values her chastity. It has, of course, to be admitted that not every woman possesses this spiritual strength and purity. We ourselves have brought this about. From the very start, we train our girls in such a way that they become incapable of protecting themselves. By the time the girl has become a woman, the false teaching has taken firm hold of her and she is convinced that a woman is utterly helpless before a man, whoever he may be. If, however, there is such a thing as truth and purity in the world, I wish to state categorically that woman has within her sufficient strength to preserve her chastity. The woman who calls upon Rama when in danger will surely be protected by Him. Which evil man will dare to approach a woman who is prepared to die? Her very eyes will shine with such light that any vicious man will be unnerved by it.

The power to die everyone has but few desire to use it. When someone wishes to dishonour a woman, when a man is in danger of being overmastered by lust, such a man and woman have a right to commit suicide. It is indeed their duty to do so. Those who have the necessary strength of mind can do it with ease. Even in the grip of no matter how strong a person, any man or woman can kill himself or herself by biting off the tongue or, if the hands are free, by pressing the wind-pipe. If a person is prepared to risk death, no matter how securely he or she is tied,—tied to a tree—he can struggle himself free provided he does not mind broken bones. The strong overpower the weak because the latter cling to life and, therefore, do not resist to the point of death. A black ant sitting on a lump of jaggery will rather let its leg be broken than allow itself to be dragged away from it. If a child pulls very hard, its parents let go of its hand for fear that the arm may get dislocated. Every person has the strength necessary to let any limb of his be broken, but he cannot endure the resulting pain, the pain of dying. It is, however, the duty of every man or woman fighting for freedom to be ready to suffer this pain. If we pray to God daily for such strength, we shall surely receive it. I urge every sister to pray thus on arising every morning: "O God, keep me pure, give me strength to preserve my chastity, strength to preserve it even at the cost of my life. With Thee as my Protector, whom need I fear?" Such a prayer made with a pure mind will surely protect every woman.

But What about Men?

As I discuss this matter, I feel ashamed of being a man. Is man, who was born of woman, whose mother carried him for nine months, for whom she suffered pain, who slept only after putting him to sleep and ate only after she had fed him,—is man born an enemy of that mother's kind that they should live in fear of him? A woman does not run away from a tiger; she runs away only from man's lust. I have already pleaded with women. I wish to plead with men as well. Is not a man bound to remove the fears of women, of whom his mother was one? Should he not always pray: "Take my life before I cast lustful eyes upon any woman. If I ever incline to immorality, give me the strength to kill myself. Remove from me all uncleanliness so that no woman will fear me but will feel safe with me as with a brother"? I pray to God that, as long as our men are incapable of protecting our women, He should keep us in slavery. If in a country the men do not protect the women, they are not men at all and are fit only to remain slaves.

My Hope

But I am confident that in India both men and women know the limits they should observe. Both have tasted the sweetness of purity. The girl volunteer whom I saw was without fear. I was filled with joy to see a girl standing fearlessly near the Ellis Bridge and selling khadi

caps. Did she fear anyone? She knew that all men were her brothers.
If one is good oneself, so is the world. The women who flocked in
their thousands to the Congress *pandal* went there without fear. If,
therefore, women refrain from taking part in activities which are
safe for them, it will be because of men's selfishness or the women's
laziness or ignorance. If a woman is not allowed freedom from household chores or if she wastes her time in decking herself up or in gos-
siping, what service can she do to her country?

[From Gujarati]
Navajivan 15-1-1922

7. Experiences in Assam—On the Brahmaputra

(vol. XXI, pp. 84–85)

The ship is sailing on the river. The days of my third-class travel
came to an end long ago. We are all sitting at the moment on the first-
class deck. Whenever I think about the third-class, I feel ashamed of
travelling by first or second class. But I know that, in a strenuous tour
like this, where I am constantly on the move, my health cannot stand
the strain of a journey by third-class. I believe that we should be
sturdy enough to be able to travel by third-class, that our bodies
should be sufficiently trained for the purpose. So long as we fight shy
of travelling third-class, conditions in this class will not improve and
its hardships will not disappear. If all the hundreds of public workers
start travelling by first or second class, public funds will be exhausted
in travelling and our ship of swaraj will make no progress. It is necessary for us every moment to pause and think before spending public
funds. I say this, being ill at ease because of a remark which one rich
gentleman, a public worker, made before me. The moment I brought
up the subject of khadi, he said: "You cannot understand our plight.
You can get a car whenever you want, you will get ten glasses of
goat's milk if you ask for one, everyone gives you khadi; but others,
even a wealthy person like me, will find public service an expensive
job if I have to pay each time taxi and hotel fares and for all the khadi
that I require." This gentleman is a member of the All-India Congress Committee; he does not hesitate to spend money; but I realize
that his daily expenses in Bombay could not have amounted to less
than twenty rupees. I do feel that there is a good deal of substance in
his argument. However, I am helpless in my present situation. I

know that my weakness has reduced my capacity to serve. I do not now have the courage to ask everyone to go walking. Because I myself am weak, I imagine others to be so and often unnecessarily take pity on them. Otherwise, one who wishes to serve the public does not have to spend overmuch. Third-class fares are not so high that one cannot afford the expense and, moreover, one should make it a point to spend nothing on transport at any place one visits. One should eat simple food and dress simply. But we have pampered ourselves so much that we think we cannot do what hundreds of thousands of other people do every day.

I had wanted to describe the river but came out instead, with what has been troubling my mind. The river looks as vast as the sea. Far away in the distance, on the two sides, one sees the banks. The river is about two miles broad, or even more. The journey will take 15 hours. The peace on the river fills the heart with a sense of grandeur. The moon, hidden behind the clouds, is shining with a faint gleam on the water. The ship's propellers make a gentle sound as they cut through water. Except for this, there is peace all round. And yet I find it difficult to have peace of mind. Neither the river nor the ship is mine. It is through the favour of that same power whose tyranny has disillusioned me, whose operations have inflicted wounds on the country, enfeebled it and reduced it to a state of penury, that I sail on the river and go in this ship—this thought disturbs me in the midst of all this peace. Nevertheless, I cannot blame the Government. Why should I blame the Government if thirty crores of Indians do not understand their duty? Should I blame the usurer who charges me excessive interest, or myself for paying it? It is the business man's nature to trade with me. It is for me however to choose whether or not to trade with him. Why do I trade with him? Who can force foreign cloth on me if I do not want it? Realizing that it is my weakness to blame the power behind the trader, I recover my peace and get absorbed in my duty, aware that my work lies with the people.

Narajivan, 11-9-1921

8. The Crime of Chauri Chaura
(vol. XXII, pp. 415–21)

God has been abundantly kind to me. He has warned me the third time that there is not as yet in India that truthful and non-violent atmosphere which and which alone can justify mass disobedience which can be at all described as civil, which means gentle, truthful, humble, knowing, wilful yet loving, never criminal and hateful.

He warned me in 1919 when the Rowlatt Act agitation was started. Ahmedabad, Viramgam, and Kheda erred; Amritsar and Kasur erred. I retraced my steps, called it a Himalayan miscalculation, humbled myself before God and man, and stopped not merely mass civil disobedience but even my own which I knew was intended to be civil and non-violent.

The next time it was through the events of Bombay that God gave a terrific warning. He made me eyewitness of the deeds of the Bombay mob on the 17th November. The mob acted in the interest of non-co-operation. I announced my intention to stop the mass civil disobedience which was to be immediately started in Bardoli. The humiliation was greater than in 1919. But it did me good. I am sure that the nation gained by the stopping. India stood for truth and non-violence by the suspension.

But the bitterest humiliation was still to come. Madras did give the warning, but I heeded it not. But God spoke clearly through Chauri Chaura. I understand that the constables who were so brutally hacked to death had given much provocation. They had even gone back upon the word just given by the Inspector that they would not be molested, but when the procession had passed the stragglers were interfered with and abused by the constables. The former cried out for help. The mob returned. The constables opened fire. The little ammunition they had was exhausted and they retired to the *Thana* for safety. The mob, my informant tells me, therefore set fire to the *Thana*. The self-imprisoned constables had to come out for dear life and as they did so, they were hacked to pieces and the mangled remains were thrown into the raging flames.

It is claimed that no non-co-operation volunteer had a hand in the brutality and that the mob had not only the immediate provocation but they had also general knowledge of the high-handed tyranny of the police in that district. No provocation can possibly justify the brutal murder of men who had been rendered defenceless and who had virtually thrown themselves on the mercy of the mob. And when India claims to be non-violent and hopes to mount the throne of Liberty through non-violent means, mob-violence even in answer to grave provocation is a bad augury. Suppose the "non-violent" disobedience of Bardoli was permitted by God to succeed, the Government had abdicated in favour of the victors of Bardoli, who would control the unruly element that must be expected to perpetrate inhumanity upon due provocation? Non-violent attainment of self-government presupposes a non-violent control over the violent elements in the country. Non-violent non-co-operators can only succeed when they have succeeded in attaining control over the hooligans of India, in other words, when the latter also have learnt patriotically or religiously to refrain from their violent activities at least whilst the campaign of non-co-operation is going on. The tragedy at Chauri Chaura, therefore, roused me thoroughly.

"But what about your manifesto to the Viceroy and your rejoinder to his reply?" spoke the voice of Satan. It was the bitterest cup of humiliation to drink. "Surely it is cowardly to withdraw the next day after pompous threats to the Government and promises to the people of Bardoli." Thus Satan's invitation was to deny Truth and therefore Religion, to deny God Himself. I put my doubts and troubles before the Working Committee and other associates whom I found near me. They did not all agree with me at first. Some of them probably do not even now agree with me. But never has a man been blessed, perhaps, with colleagues and associates so considerate and forgiving as I have. They understood my difficulty and patiently followed my argument. The result is before the public in the shape of the resolutions of the Working Committee. The drastic reversal of practically the whole of the aggressive programme may be politically unsound and unwise, but there is no doubt that it is religiously sound, and I venture to assure the doubters that the country will have gained by my humiliation and confession of error.

The only virtue I want to claim is Truth and Non-violence. I lay no claim to superhuman powers. I want none. I wear the same corruptible flesh that the weakest of my fellow beings wears and am therefore as liable to err as any. My services have many limitations, but God has up to now blessed them in spite of the imperfections.

For, confession of error is like a broom that sweeps away dirt and leaves the surface cleaner than before, I feel stronger for my confession. And the cause must prosper for the retracing. Never has man reached his destination by persistence in deviation from the straight path.

It has been urged that Chauri Chaura cannot affect Bardoli. There is danger, it is argued, only if Bardoli is weak enough to be swayed by Chauri Chaura and is betrayed into violence. I have no doubt whatsoever on that account. The people of Bardoli are in my opinion the most peaceful in India. But Bardoli is but a speck on the map of India. Its effort cannot succeed unless there is perfect co-operation from the other parts. Bardoli's disobedience will be civil only when the other parts of India remain non-violent. Just as the addition of a grain of arsenic to a pot of milk renders it unfit as food so will the civility of Bardoli prove unacceptable by the addition of the deadly poison from Chauri Chaura. The latter represents India as much as Bardoli.

Chauri Chaura is after all an aggravated symptom. I have never imagined that there has been no violence, mental or physical, in the places where repression is going on. Only I have believed, I still believe and the pages of *Young India* amply prove, that the repression is out of all proportion to the insignificant popular violence in the areas of repression. The determined holding of meetings in prohibited areas I do not call violence. The violence I am referring to is the throwing of brickbats or intimidation and coercion practised in stray cases. As a matter of fact in civil disobedience there should be no excitement. Civil disobedience is a preparation for mute suffering. Its effect is marvellous though unperceived and gentle. But I regarded a certain amount of excitement as inevitable, certain amount of unintended violence even pardonable, i.e., I did not consider civil disobedience impossible in somewhat imperfect conditions. Under perfect conditions disobedience when civil is hardly felt. But the present movement is admittedly a dangerous experiment under fairly adverse conditions.

The tragedy of Chauri Chaura is really the index finger. It shows the way India may easily go if drastic precautions be not taken. If we are not to evolve violence out of non-violence, it is quite clear that we must hastily retrace our steps and re-establish an atmosphere of peace, re-arrange our programme and not think of starting mass civil disobedience until we are sure of peace being retained in spite of mass civil disobedience being started and in spite of Government provocation. We must be sure of unauthorized portions not starting mass civil disobedience.

As it is, the Congress organization is still imperfect and its instructions are still perfunctorily carried out. We have not established Congress Committees in every one of the villages. Where we have, they are not perfectly amenable to our instructions. We have not probably more than one crore of members on the roll. We are in the middle of February, yet not many have paid the annual four-anna subscription for the current year. Volunteers are indifferently enrolled. They do not conform to all the conditions of their pledge. They do not even wear hand-spun and hand-woven khaddar. All the Hindu volunteers have not yet purged themselves of the sin of untouchability. All are not free from the taint of violence. Not by their imprisonment are we going to win swaraj or serve the holy cause of the Khilafat or attain the ability to stop payment to faithless servants. Some of us err in spite of ourselves. But some others among us sin wilfully. They join Volunteer Corps well knowing that they are not and do not intend to remain non-violent. We are thus untruthful even as we hold the Government to be untruthful. We dare not enter the kingdom of Liberty with mere lip homage to Truth and Non-violence.

Suspension of mass civil disobedience and subsidence of excitement are necessary for further progress, indeed indispensable to prevent further retrogression. I hope, therefore, that by suspension every Congressman or woman will not only not feel disappointed but he or she will feel relieved of the burden of unreality and of national sin.

Let the opponent glory in our humiliation or so-called defeat. It is better to be charged with cowardice and weakness than to be guilty of denial of our oath and sin against God. It is a million times better to *appear* untrue before the world than to *be* untrue to ourselves.

And so, for me the suspension of mass civil disobedience and other minor activities that were calculated to keep up excitement is not enough penance for my having been the instrument, however involuntary, of the brutal violence by the people at Chauri Chaura.

I must undergo personal cleansing. I must become a fitter instrument able to register the slightest variation in the moral atmosphere about me. My prayers must have much deeper truth and humility about them than they evidence. And for me there is nothing so helpful and cleansing as a fast accompanied by the necessary mental co-operation.

I know that the mental attitude is everything. Just as a prayer may be merely a mechanical intonation as of a bird, so may a fast be a mere mechanical torture of the flesh. Such mechanical contrivances are valueless for the purpose intended. Again, just as a mechanical chant may result in the modulation of voice, a mechanical fast may result in purifying the body. Neither will touch the soul within.

But a fast undertaken for fuller self-expression, for attainment of the spirit's supremacy over the flesh, is a most powerful factor in one's evolution. After deep consideration, therefore, I am imposing on myself a five days' continuous fast, permitting myself water. It commenced on Sunday evening; it ends on Friday evening. This is the least I must do.

I have taken into consideration the All-India Congress Committee meeting in front of me. I have in mind the anxious pain even the five days' fast will cause many friends; but I can no longer postpone the penance nor lessen it.

I urge co-workers not to copy my example. The motive in their case will be lacking. They are not the originators of civil disobedience. I am in the unhappy position of a surgeon proved skill-less to deal with an admittedly dangerous case. I must either abdicate or acquire greater skill. Whilst the personal penance is not only necessary but obligatory on me, the exemplary self-restraint prescribed by the Working Committee is surely sufficient penance for everyone else. It is no small penance and, if sincerely carried out, it can become infinitely more real and better than fasting. What can be richer and more fruitful than a greater fulfilment of the vow of non-violence in thought, word, and deed or the spread of that spirit? It will be more than food for me during the week to observe that comrades are all, silently and without idle discussion, engaged in fulfilling the constructive programme sketched by the Working Committee, in enlisting Congress members after making sure that they understand the Congress creed of truth and non-violence for the attainment of swaraj, in daily and religiously spinning for a fixed time, in introducing the wheel of prosperity and freedom in every home, in visiting "untouchable" homes and finding out their wants, in inducing national schools to receive "untouchable" children, in organizing social service specially designed to find a common platform for every variety of man and woman, and in visiting the homes which the drink curse is desolating, in establishing real *panchayats* and in organizing national schools on a proper footing. The workers will be better engaged in these activities than in fasting. I hope, therefore, that no one will join me in fasting, either through false sympathy or an ignorant conception of the spiritual value of fasting.

All fasting and all penance must as far as possible be secret. But my fasting is both a penance and a punishment, and a punishment has to be public. It is penance for me and punishment for those whom I try to serve, for whom I love to live and would equally love to die. They have unintentionally sinned against the laws of the Congress though they were sympathizers if not actually connected with it. Probably they hacked the constables—their countrymen and fellow beings—with my name on their lips. The only way love punishes is by suffering. I cannot even wish them to be arrested. But I would let them know that I would suffer for their breach of the Congress creed. I would advise those who feel guilty and repentant to hand themselves voluntarily to the Government for punishment and make a clean confession. I hope that the workers in the Gorakhpur district will leave no stone unturned to find out the evil-doers and urge them to deliver themselves into custody. But whether the murderers accept my advice or not, I would like them to know that they have seriously interfered with swaraj operations, that in being the cause of the postponement of the movement in Bardoli, they have injured the very cause they probably intended to serve. I would like them to know, too, that this movement is not a cloak or a preparation for violence. I would, at any rate, suffer every humiliation, every torture, absolute ostracism and death itself to prevent the movement from becoming violent or a precursor of violence. I make my penance public also because I am now denying myself the opportunity of sharing their lot with the prisoners. The immediate issue has again shifted. We can no longer press for the withdrawal of notifications or discharge of prisoners. They and we must suffer for the crime of Chauri Chaura. The incident proves, whether we wish it or no, the unity of life. All, including even the administrators, must suffer. Chauri Chaura must stiffen the Government, must still further corrupt the police, and the reprisals that will follow must further demoralize the people. The suspension and the penance will take us back to the position we occupied before the tragedy. By strict discipline and purification we regain the moral confidence required for demanding the withdrawal of notifications and the discharge of prisoners.

If we learn the full lesson of the tragedy, we can turn the curse into a blessing. By becoming truthful and non-violent, both in spirit and deed, and by making the swadeshi i.e., the khaddar programme complete, we can establish full swaraj and redress the Khilafat and the Punjab wrongs without a single person having to offer civil disobedience.

Young India, 16-2-1922

 # CHRONOLOGY II
1924–1928

In this four-year period Gandhi was out of jail and renewed his political activity. This activity could be called cultural rather than political, if by the latter we only mean Indian demands for autonomy from the British. Gandhi was concerned with Hindu-Muslim hostility, with caste Hindus' treatment of untouchables, with national education (that is, schools run by and for Indians, as opposed to government schools), and with the home spinning and weaving of cloth. In strictly political matters he demonstrated again his willingness to retreat. In August 1924, he resolved a conflict within the nationalist movement by asking those who followed him to surrender to those who did not; and in January 1926, he announced his withdrawal for a year from what he called public work.

In 1927 and 1928, on the other hand, he was very active in politics in the narrower sense, and indeed was aggressive. He supported the boycott of the Simon Commission, which came out from England to investigate affairs in India, and he welcomed the Nehru Report, when it recommended Dominion status and self-government for India, though he was instrumental in the narrow defeat at the Calcutta Congress in December 1928 of a resolution calling for complete independence.

Thus we see the same pattern as before, of advance into and retreat from political activity. In 1926 he had devoted himself to the affairs of his ashram, a primarily religious community of people devoted to prayer, asceticism, and salvation; and these were the people always closest to his heart. From Gandhi's point of view, of course, there was no sharp division between activities aimed at in-

dividual or religious salvation, and those aimed at national or political salvation. Perhaps it is better to describe his pattern not as
"advance-and-retreat" but as "in transition"; weaving the seamless
cloth of his life, Gandhi moved to and fro across the area most
people called politics.

1924

At the end of August, Gandhi resolved the conflict between those
loyal to him and those who wanted to enter the councils by asking
the former for "an act of perfect surrender."

On September 17, he began a twenty-one day fast in the house of
his Muslim ally, Maulana Mohammed Ali. At its end, on October 8,
the latter presented Gandhi with a cow that he had saved from the
butcher—a symbol of Muslim sympathy with the Hindus' reverence for the cow.

On December 27, he spoke at a conference on untouchability.
The cause of the untouchables was one of his constant concerns.

1925

On February 15, he began a tour of Kathiawar, the part of Gujarat
in which he was born. He inaugurated another national school and
declared his basic program, which was to eliminate untouchability
and to replace foreign cloth with khadi, which was the main example of swadeshi, the fostering of home industries.

On September 24, he founded the All India Spinners' Association
(A.I.S.A.) to promote khadi, and thus the home spinning and weaving of cloth.

Madeline Slade came out from England to be his disciple and
took the Hindu name of Mirabehn.

On November 24, he began a seven-day fast because of moral
lapses at the ashram.

1926

His friend Andrews was in South Africa, at Gandhi's request, to
represent the Indians there.

On January 3, he decided to retire for a year from public work in
order to attend to the affairs of the ashram.

On October 10, he executed his will, declaring that he owned no
property; to the Satyagraha Ashram he bequeathed what might,
after his death, be declared to be his.

On December 23, Swami Shraddhanand was assassinated by a
Muslim, a severe blow to the hopes for Hindu-Muslim unity.

1927

On February 2, he began a tour of the Central Provinces.

In March he fell ill, and his doctors said he must give up his program of activities during the hot weather.

In July he became active again.

On August 24, he began a tour of the south of India.

On November 2, he met the viceroy.

On November 7, he left for Ceylon.

On December 1, he returned to Madras.

1928

On January 24, he laid the foundation stone of a temple for untouchables at Vartej.

On February 3, a Statutory Commission from England, under the leadership of Sir John Simon, landed in Bombay. Gandhi supported the boycott of that commission observed by most Indians.

On August 16, he welcomed the Nehru Report, which unanimously recommended Dominion status and self-government for India.

On November 17, Lala Lajpat Rai died from injuries suffered during an encounter with the police.

On December 28, Gandhi attended the Calcutta Congress.

The greater part of the selections from this period is composed of a series of six essays titled "My Jail Experiences," which form a much more detailed counterpart to Gandhi's remarks on South African jails in his Autobiography. His experience of imprisonment, like his experience of fasting, was part of Gandhi's glamour; but he described these things not only to meet his readers' interest but to prepare them imaginatively for similar hardships that they would meet as satyagrahi—to wean them from their middle-class gentility of mind. (Gandhi in fact wrote eleven such essays, but only six of them are included here because of space constraints.) In addition to Gandhi's descriptions of jail and announcements of fasts, we see him debating with a Communist revolutionary and confessing to his very painful relations with his eldest son, Harilal.

9. My Language

(vol. XXIII, pp. 495–98)

Prompted by his love for me as well as for the Gujarati language, a learned friend writes to me with utmost frankness, as follows:[1]

In this interesting letter, there are some English sentences and words in Gujarati script, and two English words are in Roman script. This will shock many Gujarati brothers and sisters who do not know English. I tender my apology to them. Had I made any alterations, the sweetness and the subtle humour in that letter would have disappeared. Even those not knowing English will not find it difficult to understand the substance of the letter.

The reader will readily understand that this letter was not meant for publication. I think the portion I have quoted above came to be written by chance as part of the letter dealing with some private matter. But since the comments therein are reasonable and since my associates as well as I have something to learn from them, I have published an extract.

About five years ago, a learned well-wisher had commented that my Gujarati was "weaker even than a raw matriculate's." A friend who had heard the comment did not like it. When he reported it to me, I said that the comment was correct and was prompted by no hatred towards me but by love of language. What I had said then about that criticism holds good even today.

I know that my knowledge of Gujarati is not profound. I have not been as mindful of grammar as I should like to be. I have not become a writer to serve the cause of the language, but I have had to carry on my work as a journalist with the sort of language I know. I do not say this to have my errors of language condoned. To commit errors knowingly and to ask to be pardoned for them is not only inexcusable, but adding one fault to another. I wish to share with the world a very valuable thing which I have discovered. Maybe there is *moha*,[2] ignorance or vanity in my desire, but this is what it is. Language is a great instrument in my work. A skilful artisan makes do with whatever tool he has. I have had to do the same. We labour under a false notion. A person who is supreme in one respect is often considered to be the same in other respects also. To add to this, if the person is

1. In this letter, not translated here, the correspondent refers to some words and phrases wrongly used by Gandhi in the *History of Satyagraha in South Africa*, serially published in *Navajivan* during 1924–25.
2. Infatuation.

looked upon as a mahatma, is there anything which the people will not credit him with? He is accepted as the greatest of all. In order that no one may be deceived about my language on account of such a superstition, I admit my mistakes by publishing the criticism contained in the letter above. I certainly regard myself as competent in respect of satyagraha, the economic policies needed in India from the point of view of the poor and some other kindred matters. But I consider my language to be plainly rustic and one that violates the rules of spelling and grammar. Therefore, it is not my wish at all that others should imitate it.

The several mistakes pointed out by the friend sitting on the top of the Himalayas ought to have been corrected. The imperfections of my language pain me, but they do not put me to shame. There are some mistakes which could have been easily avoided. I feel ashamed of such mistakes. I consider it better to close down a newspaper than to continue to run it in spite of such mistakes. If a newspaper editor remains indifferent to language, he becomes an offender. The use of the words *murshid* and *amanush*[3] is inexcusable. I cannot guess how those words happened to creep in. I went on dictating, another person took it down and a third transcribed it. My poor knowledge of Urdu and Sanskrit or the copyist's may have been responsible for the mistakes. The real fault is mine first and, then, that of my colleague. Swami Anand cannot pay attention to *Navajivan*'s language, being busy with the work of promoting the circulation of the paper in Gujarat. Mahadev Desai can see no fault in me, just as a lover can see none in his beloved. If he had his way, he would have justified the use even of *murshid* and *amanush*. The learned one has taken his seat on the peak of the Himalayas. None among the three thinks of the injustice likely to be done to the readers. The poor language is an innocent cow and we four have become ready to put her to the knife. The remedy lies in the hands of readers who are lovers of the language. I advise them to serve notices on Swami Anand, Mahadev Desai and others to the effect that if Himalayan blunders of language appear in *Navajivan* hereafter, they will not only stop buying the paper without further intimation, but also set up, if necessary, a "*Navajivan* Boycott Association." If such an association starts a non-violent satyagraha, I shall certainly join it and have a dispute in my own house. I also suggest to the language-lovers that they should write an open letter to "Summit-dweller" that he should take up

---

3. Incorrectly used for *murid*—meaning admirer, adorer, or idolator—and *atima-nush*—meaning superhuman.

every week the maximum of half a page in *Navajivan* to list the errors in the use of Gujarati found in the previous issue. Thus, if the readers of *Navajivan* would take effective steps, they would serve the cause of the language and prove that *Navajivan* enjoys their patronage.

Now, a few words by way of criticism of the critic himself. Since we have learnt English, we consciously or unconsciously reproduce in our Gujarati writing the style and idioms of English despite our efforts to avoid them. I have been regarded as an enemy of the English language. As a matter of fact, I have respect for that language and for the Englishmen who speak it. But I am not prepared to accept the domination of either. I am willing to do without both. I firmly believe that a Gujarati with command over all the resources of his mother-tongue can bring into his writing all the beauties of English, without knowing a single word of English. As I have no prejudice against the English language or the Englishman, I can assimilate the best from both, and this leads to some imitation without any conscious effort on my part. "The bowels of the earth"[4] is an expression used unwittingly. "The womb of the earth"[5] is a very sweet collocation of words. Had I remembered it at the time of dictating, I would have used it by preference. But I do not consider "bowels of the earth" to be an expression which should be avoided. We do have in Gujarati the expression "twisting the mouth"; then, can we not allow the English usage of "twisting the nose"? I have doubts about it, though; while trying to twist the nose, I could not do it, but my mouth got twisted in the process. The Gujarati in me felt happy at this. But can all usage be thus tested? I leave the doubts there for the moment. After we attain swaraj, I shall certainly invite Narasinharaobhai[6] as well as Khabardar,[7] who is quite a match for the former, to a duel before me and try to place some samples of their art before the readers of *Navajivan*. At present, we have no time even to enjoy that innocent fun. I do not believe that the indirect construction is banned in Gujarati. By saying this, I do not intend to belittle the comments of my critic. I have given the extract from the letter in order to ask my linguist friends to keep watch over my language and to oblige me, even as some other friends have been keeping watch over my moral conduct.

Whether the construction of the last sentence is permissible or

4. *Prithvina antardan.*
5. *Prithvinu udar.*
6. Narasinharao B. Divetia (1859–1937).
7. Ardeshar Framji Khabardar (1881–1954); Parsi poet of Gujarat.

not, I, on behalf of the readers, openly invite "Summit-dweller" to say.

[From Gujarati]
Navajivan, 27-4-1924

10. My Jail Experiences—1

(vol. XXIII, pp. 446–49)

The reader knows that I am a hardened criminal. It was not for the first time that I found myself a prisoner in the March of 1922. I had three previous South African convictions to my credit, and as I was regarded at the time by the South African Government as a danger-ous criminal, I was moved from jail to jail and was able, therefore, to gather much experience of jail life. I had, before the Indian convic-tion, passed through six prisons and had come in touch with as many Superintendents and many more jailors. When, therefore, during the beautiful night of the 10th of March I was taken to the Sabarmati Jail together with Mr. Banker, I did not feel any awkwardness which al-ways attends upon a strange and new experience. I almost felt I was going from one home to another in order to make more conquests of love. The preliminaries were more like being taken to a pleasure-trip than to jail. The courteous Superintendent of Police, Mr. Healy, would not even enter the Ashram, but sent Anasuyabai with a mes-sage that he had a warrant for my arrest and that a car awaited me at the Ashram Gate. I was to take whatever time I needed for getting ready. Mr. Banker, who was on his way back to Ahmedabad, was met by Mr. Healy on the way and already arrested. I was not at all un-prepared for the news that Anasuyabai brought. As a matter of fact, after having waited long enough for the coming of the warrant which everybody thought was imminent, I had given instructions that all should retire and I was myself about to lay myself to bed. I had re-turned that evening from Ajmer after a fatiguing journey where most reliable information was given to me that a warrant had been sent to Ajmer for my arrest, but the authorities would not execute the warrant, as the very day that the warrant reached Ajmer, I was going back to Ahmedabad. The real news of the warrant, therefore, came as a welcome relief. I took with me an extra *kuchh* (loin-cloth), two blankets, and five books: *Bhagavad Gita*, *Ashram Hymn Book*, *Ramayana*, Rodwell's translation of the Koran, a presentation copy of the *Sermon on the Mount* sent by schoolboys of a high school in California with the hope that I would always carry it with me. The Superintendent, Khan Bahadur N. R. Wacha, received us kindly, and we were taken to a separate block of cells situated in a spacious, clean compound. We were permitted to sleep on the verandah of the cells, a rare privilege for prisoners. I enjoyed the quiet and the utter silence of the place. The next morning we were taken to the Court for preliminary examination. Both Mr. Banker and I had decided not only not to offer any defence but in no way to hamper the prosecution, but rather to help it. The preliminary examination was, therefore, quickly over. The case was committed to the Sessions, and as we were prepared to accept short service, the trial was to take place on the 18th of March. The people of Ahmedabad had risen to the occasion. Mr. Vallabhbhai Patel had issued strict instructions that there should be no crowds gathering near the Court-house and that there should be no demonstration of any kind whatsoever. There were, therefore, in the Court-house only a select body of visitors, and the police had an easy time of it, which I could see was duly appreciated by the authorities.

The week before the trial was passed in receiving visitors who were generally permitted to see us without restriction. We were allowed to carry on correspondence so long as it was harmless and submitted to the Superintendent. As we willingly carried out all the Jail regulations, our relations with the Jail officials were smooth and even cordial during the week that we were in Sabarmati. Khan Bahadur Wacha was all attention and politeness, but it was impossible not to notice his timidity in everything he did. He seemed to apologize for his Indian birth and unconsciously to convey that he would have done more for us had he been a European. Being an Indian, even in allowing facilities which the regulations permitted, he was afraid of the Collector and the Inspector-General of Prisons and every official who was at all superior to him. He knew that, if it came to a struggle between himself and the Collector or the Inspector-General of Prisons, he had nobody to back him up at the Secretariat. The notion of inferiority haunted him at every step. What was true outside was equally true, if not truer, inside the Jail. An Indian official would not assert himself, not because he could not, but because he lived in mortal fear of degradation, if not dismissal. If he was to retain his post and obtain promotion, he must please his superiors even to the point of [rigour] and even at the sacrifice of principles. The contrast became terrible when we were transferred to Yeravda. The European

Superintendent had no fear of the Inspector-General of Prisons. He could claim just as much influence at the Secretariat as the latter. The Collector for him was almost an interloper. His Indian superiors he held cheap and, therefore, he was not afraid to do his duty when he wished and was equally unafraid to neglect it, when discharge of duty was an onerous task. He knew that, as a rule, he was always safe. This sense of safety enables young European officers often to do the right thing in spite of opposition either from the public or from the Government, and he has also often driven coach and six through all regulations, all instructions and defied public opinion.

Of the trial and the sentence I need say nothing as the reader knows all about it, except to acknowledge the courtesy which was extended to us by all the officials including the Judge and the Advocate-General. The wonderful restraint that was observed by the small crowd of people that was seen in and about the Court, and the great affection showed by them can never be effaced from memory. The sentence of six years' simple imprisonment I regarded as light. For, if Section 124 A of the Penal Code did really constitute [my action] a crime and the Judge administering the laws of the land could not but hold it as a crime, he would be perfectly justified in imposing the highest penalty. The crime was repeatedly and wilfully committed, and I can only account for the lightness of the sentence by supposing not that the Judge took pity on me, for I asked for none, but that he could not have approved of Section 124 A. There are many instances of judges having signified their disapproval of particular laws by imposing the minimum sentence, even though the crime denoted by them might have been fully and deliberately committed. He could not very well impose a lighter sentence seeing that the late Lokamanya was sentenced to six years' imprisonment for a similar offence.

The sentence over, we were both taken back to the prison, this time as fully convicted prisoners, but there was no change in the treatment accorded to us. Some friends were even permitted to accompany us. Leave-taking in the Jail was quite jovial. Mrs. Gandhi and Anasuyabai bore themselves bravely as they parted. Mr. Banker was laughing all the time and I heaved a sigh of relief, thanking God that all was over so peacefully and that I would be able to have some rest and still feel that I was serving the country, if possible more than when I was travelling up and down addressing huge audiences. I wish I could convince the workers that imprisonment of a comrade does not mean so much loss of work for a common cause. If we believe, as we have so often proclaimed we do, that unprovoked suffering is the

surest way of remedying a wrong in regard to which the suffering is
gone through, surely it follows as a matter of course that imprisonment of a comrade is no loss. Silent suffering undergone with dignity
and humility speaks with an unrivalled eloquence. It is solid work
because there is no ostentation about it. It is always true because
there is no danger of miscalculation. Moreover, if we are true workers, the loss of a fellow-worker increases our zest and, therefore, capacity for work. And so long as we regard anybody as irreplaceable,
we have not fitted ourselves for organized work. For organized work
means capacity for carrying it on in spite of depletion in the ranks.
Therefore, we must rejoice in the unmerited suffering of friends or
ourselves and trust that the cause, if it is just, will prosper through
such suffering.

Young India, 17-4-1924

11. My Jail Experiences—2
'Political' Prisoners
(vol. XXIV, pp. 1–4)

"We do not make any distinction between political and other prisoners. Surely you do not want any such distinction to be made in
your favour?" Thus said Sir George Lloyd[1] when he visited the
Yeravda Jail about the end of the last year. He said that in reply to an
inadvertent use made by me of the adjective 'political.' I ought to
have known better. For I was fully aware of the Governor's distaste
for that word. And yet, strange to say, the history tickets of most of
us were marked 'political.' When I remarked upon the anomaly, I was
told by the then Superintendent that the distinction was private and
was intended only for the guidance of the authorities. We, the prisoners, were to ignore it, for we could not base any claim upon it.

I have reproduced Sir George Lloyd's language word for word so far
as I can remember. There is a sting about what Sir George Lloyd said.
And it was so gratuitous. For he knew that I was asking for no favours
and no distinction. Circumstances had brought about a general discussion. But the idea was to tell me, "You are no better than the rest
in the eye of the law and the administration." And yet the painful

1. Governor of Bombay.

inconsistency was that the very time that the distinction was, without any occasion for it, combated in theory, it was made in practice. Only, in the majority of cases, it was made against the political prisoners.

As a matter of fact, it is impossible to avoid making distinctions. If the human factor were not ignored, it would be necessary to understand a prisoner's habits of life, and model his life accordingly in the prisons. It is not a question of distinguishing between rich men and poor men or educated and uneducated, but between modes of life these antecedents have developed in them. As against the inevitable recognition of the existing fact, it has been urged that the men who commit crimes should know that the law is no respecter of persons, and that it is the same to the law whether a rich man or a graduate or a labourer commits theft. This is a perversion of a sound law. If it is really the same to the law as it should be, each will get the treatment according to his capacity for suffering. To give thirty stripes to a delicately-built thief and as many to an able-bodied one would be not impartiality but vindictiveness towards the delicate one and probably indulgence to the able-bodied. Similarly to expect, say, Pandit Motilalji to sleep on a rough coir-mat spread on hard floor is additional punishment, not equality of treatment.

If the human factor was introduced into the administration of the jails, the ceremony on admission would be different from what it is today. Finger-impressions would undoubtedly be taken, a record of past offences would find its place in the register. But there will be, in addition, particulars about the prisoner's habits and mode of life. Not distinction but classification is perhaps the word that better describes the necessary method which the authorities, if they would treat prisoners as human beings, must recognize. Some kind of classification there already is. For instance, there are circles wherein prisoners are housed in batches in long cells. Then there are the separate single cells intended for dangerous criminals. There are solitary cells where prisoners undergoing solitary confinement are locked. There are, again, the condemned cells in which are locked prisoners awaiting the gallows. Lastly, there are cells for under-trial prisoners. The reader will be surprised to find that political prisoners were mostly confined in the separate division or the solitary. In some cases, they were confined in condemned cells. Let me not do an injustice to the authorities. Those who do not know these divisions and cells may form the impression that the condemned cells, for instance, must be specially bad. Such, however, is not the case. The cells are all well-constructed and airy so far as Yeravda Jail is concerned. What is, however, open to strong objection is the association about these cells.

The classification being, as I have shown, inevitable and in existence, there is no reason why it should not be scientific and human. I know that revision of classification according to my suggestion means a revolution in the whole system. It undoubtedly means more expense and a different type of men to work the new system. But additional expense will mean economy in the long run. The greatest advantage of the proposed revolution would no doubt be a reduction in the crimes and reformation of the prisoners. The jails would then be reformatories representing to society sinners as its reformed and respectable members. This may be a far-off event. If we were not under the spell of a long-lived custom, we should not find it a difficult task to turn our prisons into reformatories.

Let me quote here a pregnant remark made by one of the jailors. He once said:

When I admit[,] search or report prisoners, I often ask myself whether I am a better man than most of them. God knows I have been guilty of worse crimes than what some have come here for. The difference is that these poor men have been detected whereas I am not.

Is not what the good jailor confessed true of many of us? Is it not true that there are more undetected than detected crimes? Society does not point the finger of scorn at them. But habit has made us look askance at those who are not smart enough to escape detection. Imprisonment often makes them hardened criminals.

The animal treatment commences on arrest. The accused are in theory assumed to be innocent unless they are found guilty. In practice the demeanour of those in charge of them is one of haughtiness and contempt. A convicted man is lost to society. The atmosphere in the prison inures him to the position of inferiority.

The political prisoners do not as a rule succumb to this debilitating atmosphere, because they, instead of responding to the depressing atmosphere, act against it and, therefore, even refine it to a certain extent. Society, too, refuses to regard them as criminals. On the contrary, they become heroes and martyrs. Their sufferings in the jail are exaggerated by the public. And such indulgence in many cases even demoralizes the political prisoners. But unfortunately, exactly in proportion to the indulgence of the public, is the strictness, most unwarranted, of the officials. The Government regard the political prisoners as more dangerous to society than the ordinary prisoner. An official seriously contended that a political prisoner's crime placed the whole society in danger whereas an ordinary crime harmed only the criminal.

Another official told me that the reason why the political prisoners were isolated and denied newspapers, magazines, etc., was to bring the guilt home to them. Political prisoners, he said, seemed to glory in 'imprisonment.' The deprivation of the liberty, while it afflicted the ordinary criminal, left the political prisoner unmoved. It was, therefore, he added, but natural that the Government should devise some other method of punishment; hence, he said, the denial of facilities which otherwise such prisoners should undoubtedly have. The remarks were made in connection with my request for *The Times of India* weekly, or the *Indian Social Reformer*, or the *Servant of India* or *Modern Review* or *Indian Review*. Let the reader not regard this deprivation as a light penalty for those who regard the newspaper as a necessity in no way inferior to breakfast. I dare say that Mr. Majli would not have suffered mental derangement if he had been allowed the use of newspapers. It is equally depressing for one who is not, like me, a reformer for all occasions, to be put up together with dangerous criminals as almost all the political prisoners were put in Yeravda. It is no light thing to be in the company of those who never speak but to utter foul language or whose conversation is as a rule indecent. I could understand political prisoners being put in such surroundings, if the Government sanely took them in their confidence and used them to exercise a wholesome influence on the ordinary criminal. This however is, I admit, not a practical proposition. My contention is that placing of political prisoners in unwholesome surroundings is an additional and an unwarranted punishment. They ought to be put in a separate division and given a treatment in keeping with their antecedents.

I hope civil resisters will not misunderstand this or any other chapter in which I have advocated reforms of prisons. It would ill become a civil resister to resent whatever inconvenience he may be subjected to. He is out to put up with the roughest treatment. If the treatment is humane, it is well; but it is also well if it be otherwise.

Young India, 8-5-1924

12. My Jail Experiences—3
Ethics of Fasting
(vol. XXIV, pp. 95–99)

When the incidents related in the last chapter[1] took place, my cell was situated in a triangular block containing eleven cells. They were also part of the separate division, but the block was separated from the other separate blocks by a high massive wall. The base of the triangle lay alongside the road leading to the other separate blocks. Hence, I was able to watch and see the prisoners that passed to and fro. In fact, there was constant traffic along the road. Communication with the prisoners was therefore easy. Some time after the flogging incident, we were removed to the European yard. The cells were better ventilated and more roomy. There was a pleasant garden in front. But we were more secluded and cut off from all contact with the prisoners whom we used to see whilst we were in the 'separate.' I did not mind it. On the contrary, the greater seclusion gave me more time for contemplation and study. And the 'wireless' remained intact. It was impossible to prevent it so long as it was necessary for a single other prisoner or official to see us. In spite of effort to the contrary, someone of them would drop a remark resulting in our knowing the happenings in the jail. So one fine morning we heard that several Mulshi Peta prisoners were flogged for short task and that, as a protest against the punishment, many other Mulshi Peta prisoners had commenced a hunger-strike. Two of these were well known to me. One was Dev, and the other Dastane. Mr. Dev had worked with me in Champaran, and had proved one of the most conscientious, sober and honest among the co-workers whom I had the privilege of having in Champaran. Mr. Dastane of Bhusaval is known to everybody. The reader may therefore imagine my pain when I heard that Dev was among the party flogged and that he was also one of the hunger-strikers. Messrs Indulal Yagnik[2] and Manzar Ali Sokta were at this time my fellow-prisoners. They were agitated equally with me. Their first thought was to declare a sympathetic hunger-strike. We discussed the propriety of such a strike and came to the conclusion that it would be wrong to do so. We were neither morally nor in any other way responsible for the floggings or the subsequent hunger-strike. As satyagrahis we were to be prepared for and to suffer cheer-

1. Omitted here.
2. Then secretary, Gujarat Provincial Congress Committee; after 1957, member of Parliament.

fully the rigours of jail life and even injustices including flogging. Such hunger-strike, therefore, with a view to preventing future punishment would be a species of violence done to the jail officials. Moreover, we had no right to sit in judgment upon the action of the authorities. That would be an end to all prison discipline. And even if we wished to judge the authorities, we had not and could not get sufficient data to warrant an impartial judgment. If the fast was to be out of sympathy with the hunger-strikers, we had no data to enable us to judge whether their action was justified or not. Any one of these grounds was sufficient to show that the proposed fast would be wholly premature. But I suggested to my friends that I should try to find out the true facts through the Superintendent, and endeavour as before to get into touch with the hunger-strikers. I felt that we as human beings could not possibly remain uninterested in such matters although we were prisoners, and that under certain circumstances even a prisoner was entitled to claim a hearing in the matter of general jail administration when it was likely to result in the perpetration of gross injustice bordering on inhumanity. So we all decided that I should approach the authorities in the matter. The letter of 29th June, 1923, published in *Young India* of March 6, 1924, will give the reader further details about the matter. There was a great deal of correspondence and negotiation which, being of a confidential nature, I do not wish to publish. I can however say that the Government recognized that I had no desire to interfere with the prison administration and that my proposal to be permitted to see the two leaders among the hunger-strikers was dictated by purely humanitarian motives. They, therefore, permitted me to see Messrs Dastane and Dev in the presence of the Superintendent and Mr. Griffiths, the Inspector-General of Police. It was to me a rare pleasure and a matter of pride to see these two friends walking unaided and with a steady step after full thirteen days' unbroken fast. They were as cheerful as they were brave. I could see that they were terribly reduced in body, but their spirit had waxed strong in exact proportion to the reduction of the body. As I hugged them and greeted them with the question, "Are you nearly dead?" they rang out, "Certainly not," and Dastane added, "We are able to prolong the fast indefinitely, if need be, for we are in the right." "But if you are in the wrong?" I asked. "We shall then like men admit our mistake and abandon the fast," was the reply. By their brightness they made me forget that they were suffering from pangs of hunger. I wish I had leisure to reproduce the whole of the ethical discourse we held. Their ground for fasting was that the punishment inflicted by the Superintendent was unjust and that, therefore, unless the Superintendent admitted his mistake and apologized, they must go on with the fast. I pleaded that this was not a correct attitude. Whilst I was discussing the moral basis of their action, the Superintendent voluntarily and out of his usual good nature intervened and said, "I tell you, if I felt that I had done wrong, I should surely apologize. I know that I do make mistakes. We all do. I may have erred even in this case, but I am not conscious of it." I continued my pleading. I told my friends that it was improper to expect an apology from the Superintendent unless he could be convinced that he was wrong. Their fast could carry no conviction to him of the wrongness of the punishment. Such conviction could be brought about only by reasoning. And, in any case, as satyagrahis who were out for suffering, how could they fast against injustices whether done to them or their co-prisoners? My friends appreciated the force of my argument and Major Jones's generous statement did the rest. They agreed to break the fast and to persuade the others to do likewise. I asked for the Major's permission to give them a portion of my milk which he readily granted. They accepted the milk but said they would first take their bath and then take the milk in the company of the other hunger-strikers. The major ordered milk and fruit diet for the strikers during the period of recuperation. A hearty handshake between us all terminated the meeting. For the moment the officials were not officials and we were not prisoners. We were all friends engaged in solving a knotty problem and glad that it was solved. Thus ended this eventful hunger-strike. The Major admitted that this was the cleanest hunger-strike he had witnessed. He had taken extraordinary precautions to see that no food was passed to the prisoners surreptitiously and he was satisfied that none was passed. Had he known the stuff of which these strikers were made, he need not have taken any precautions at all.

One permanent result of the incident was that the Government passed orders that, except in cases of the gravest provocation and insult offered to the officials, flogging should not be administered without the previous sanction of the superior authority. The precaution was undoubtedly necessary. Whilst, in some matters, widest discretion must be given to the Superintendents of Jails, in matters such as punishments which cannot be recalled, the wisest of Superintendents must be subject to salutary checks.

There can be no doubt that the hunger-strike of Messrs Dastane and Dev and the other satyagrahis produced startling results of a beneficial character. For the motive, though mistaken, was excellent and the action itself purely innocent. But though the result attained was good, the fast must be condemned. The good result was not a direct result of the fast but of repentance and admission of mistaken motive and consequent abandonment of the fast. Fasting by a satyagrahi can only be justified when it is a shame to eat and live. Thus, still confining my attention to a prisoner's conduct, it would be a shame to eat and live if I was deprived of religious liberty or degraded as a human being, as when food is thrown at me instead of being given to me in a courteous manner. It should be unnecessary to say that religious objection should be really so and discourtesy should be such as would be felt by an ordinary prisoner. The caution is necessary because a religious necessity is often pretended merely in order to embarrass, and discourtesy is often felt where none is meant. I may not insist on keeping or bringing the *Bhagavad Gita* for the purpose of stealing in prohibited correspondence. I may not resent as discourtesy the ordinary search which every prisoner must undergo. In satyagraha there is no room for shams. But I would have been bound to fast, say, if the Government had not given me the opportunity of seeing the hunger-strikers merely with a view to understand their view-point and dissuade them from their error, if I found them to be erring. I could not afford to eat to live, when I knew that it was possible to prevent starvation if my keepers recognized the ordinary rules of humanity.

"But," say some friends, "why should you draw these fine distinctions? Why should we not embarrass the jail officials as we embarrass officials outside? Why should we co-operate as you co-operated with the jail authorities? Why should we not non-violently resist them? Why should we obey any regulations at all, save for our own convenience? Have we not a perfect right, is it not our duty, to paralyse the prison administration? If we make the officials' position uncomfortable without using any violence, the Government will find it difficult to arrest a large number and will thus be obliged to sue for peace." This argument has been seriously advanced. I must therefore devote the next chapter to its consideration.

Young India, 22-5-1924

13. My Jail Experiences—4
Jail Economics
(vol. XXIV, pp. 224–26)

Everyone who has any experience of jails knows that they are the most starved of all departments. The hospitals are comparatively the most expensive of public institutions. In the jails everything is of the simplest and the crudest type. In them there is extravagance in the spending of human labour, there is miserliness in the spending of money and materials. In hospitals it is just the reverse. And yet both are institutions designed to deal with human diseases—jails for mental and hospitals for physical. Mental diseases are regarded as a crime and therefore punishable; physical diseases are regarded as unforeseen visitations of nature to be indulgently treated. As a matter of fact, there is no reason for any such distinction. Mental as well as physical diseases are traceable to the same causes. If I steal, I commit a breach of laws governing healthy society. If I suffer from stomachache, I still commit a breach of laws governing a healthy society. One reason why physical diseases are treated lightly is because the so-called higher classes break the laws of physical health—perhaps more frequently than the lower classes. The higher classes have no occasion for committing crude thefts and, as their lives would be disturbed if thefts continued, they being generally law-givers, punish gross stealing, knowing all the while that their swindles which pass muster are far more harmful to society than the crude thefts. It is curious, too, that both institutions flourish because of wrong treatment. Hospitals flourish because patients are indulged and humoured, jails flourish because the prisoners are punished as if they were beyond recall. If every disease, mental or physical, were regarded as a lapse, but every patient or prisoner were to be treated kindly and sympathetically, not severely or indulgently, both jails and hospitals would show a tendency to decrease. A hospital no more than a jail is a necessity for a healthy society. Every patient and every prisoner should come out of his hospital or jail as a missionary to preach the gospel of mental and physical health.

But I must stop the comparison at this stage. The reader will be surprised to learn that the parsimony in prisons is exercised on the ground of economy. Although all labour is taken from prisoners, e.g., drawing water, grinding flour, cleaning roads and closets, cooking food, the prisoners are not only not self-supporting, but they do not even pay for their own food. And in spite of all their labour, the prisoners do not get the food they would like nor the manner of cooking they would appreciate; this for the simple reason that the prisoners who do the cooking, etc., are not as a rule interested in their work. It is for them a task to be performed under unsympathetic supervision. It is easy enough to see that, if the prisoners were philanthropists and, therefore, felt interested in the welfare of their fellow-prisoners, they would not find themselves in prisons. If, therefore, a more rational and more moral system of administration was adopted, the prisons would easily become self-supporting reformatories instead of, as they are now, expensive penal settlements. I would save the terrible waste of labour in drawing water, grinding flour, etc. If I was in charge, I would buy flour from outside, I would draw water by machinery and, instead of having all kinds of odd jobs, I would devote the prisons to agriculture, hand-spinning and hand-weaving. In the small jails only spinning and weaving may be kept. Even now weaving there is in most of the central prisons. All that is necessary is to add carding and hand-spinning. All the cotton needed can be easily grown in connection with many jails. [sic] This will popularize the national cottage industry and make the prisons self-supporting. The labour of all the prisoners will be utilized for remunerative and yet not for competitive purposes, as is now the case in some respects. There is a printing press attached to the Yeravda Jail. Now this press is largely worked by convict labour. I regard this as unfair competition with the general printing presses. If the prisons were to run competitive industries, they would easily be made even profitable. But my purpose is to show that they can be made self-supporting without entering into such competition and, at the same time, teach the inmates a home industry which on their discharge would give them an independent calling, thus providing for them every incentive to live as respectable citizens.

I would moreover provide for the prisoners as homely an atmosphere as is consistent with public safety. I would thus give them all facility for seeing their relatives, getting books and even tuition. I would replace distrust by reasonable trust. I would credit them with every bit of work they might do and let them buy their own food, cooked or raw.

I would make most of the sentences indeterminate, so that a prisoner will not be detained a moment longer than is necessary for the protection of society and for his own reform.

I know that this requires a thorough reorganization and the employing of a different kind of warders from the ex-military men that most of them are now. But I know, too, that the reform can be initiated without much extra cost.

At the present moment, the prisons are rest-houses for rogues and torture-houses for ordinary simple prisoners which the majority are. The rogues manage to get all they want, the simple untutored prisoners do not get even what they need. Under the scheme which I have endeavoured to sketch in its barest outline, the rogues will have to be straight before they feel comfortable, and the simple innocent prisoners will have as favourable an atmosphere as is possible to give them in the circumstances. Honesty will be remunerative and dishonesty at a discount.

By making the prisoners pay for their food in work, there will be little idleness. And by having only agriculture and cotton manufacture, including what handicrafts may be required for these two industries, the expensive supervision will be considerably lessened.

Young India, 12-6-1924

14. My Jail Experiences—5
Some Convict-warders
(vol. XXIV, p. 289–92)

I have already dealt with the system of appointing convicts as officers or warders. I hold the system to be thoroughly bad and demoralizing. The prison officials know it. They say it is due to economy. They think that the jails cannot be efficiently administered with the present paid staff without supplementing it with convict-officers. There is no doubt that, unless the reform suggested by me in the last chapter is inaugurated, it is not possible to do away with the system of entrusting convicts with responsible duties without a very large increase in the prison expenditure.

However, it is not my purpose in this chapter to deal any further with prison reform. I simply wish to relate my happy experiences of the convict officers who were appointed to watch over and look after us.

When Mr. Banker and I were transferred to the Yeravda Central Prison, there was one warder and one *bardasi*. The latter is what the name implies, a mere servant. The convict warder whose acquaintance we first made was a Hindu from the Punjab side. His name was Harkaran. He was convicted of murder. The murder according to him was not premeditated but due to a fit of anger. By occupation he was a petty merchant. His sentence was fourteen years, of which he had almost served nine years. He was fairly old. The prison life had told on him. He was always brooding and most anxious to be discharged. He was therefore morose and peevish. He was conscious of his high dignity. He was patronizing to those who obeyed and served him. He bullied those who crossed his path. To look at him, no one would think he could be guilty of murder. He could read Urdu fluently. He was religiously minded and was fond of reading *bhajans* in

Urdu. The Yeravda library has a few books for prisoners in several Indian languages, e.g., Hindi, Urdu, Marathi, Gujarati, Sindhi, Canarese, Tamil. Harkaran was not above keeping and hiding trifles in defiance of jail regulations. He was in the majority. It would be regarded snobbish and foolish not to steal trifles. A prisoner who did not follow this unwritten law would have a bad time of it from his fellows. Ostracism would be the least punishment. If the whole of the jail yard were to be dug up twelve inches deep, it would yield up many a secret in the shape of spoons, knives, pots, cigarettes, soap and such like. Harkaran, being one of the oldest inmates of Yeravda, was a sort of purveyor-general to the prisoners. If a prisoner wanted anything, Harkaran was the supplier. I wanted a knife for cutting my bread and lemons. Harkaran could procure it if I would have it through him. If I wanted to go through the elaborate process of asking the superintendent, that was my business. I must be prepared for a snubbing. When we became friends, he related all his wonderful exploits; how he dodged officials, how he procured for himself and others dainties, what skilful tricks were employed by prisoners to obtain what they wanted and how it was almost impossible (in his opinion) not to resort to these tricks, was described in minute detail and with much gusto. He was horrified to discover that I was neither interested in the exploits nor was I minded to join the trade. He endeavoured subsequently somewhat to repair the indiscretion he had let himself into, and to assure me that he had seen my point and that he would thenceforth refrain from the irregularities. But I have a suspicion that the repentance was put on. The reader, however, must not run away with the idea that the jail officials do not know these irregularities. They are all an open secret. They not only know them, but often sympathize with the prisoners who do these tricks to make themselves happy and comfortable. They (the officials) believe in the doctrine of 'live and let live.' A prisoner, who behaves correctly in the presence of his superiors, obeys their orders, does not quarrel with his fellows and does not inconvenience officials, is practically free to break any regulation for the sake of procuring greater comfort.

Well, the first acquaintance with Harkaran was not particularly happy. He knew that we were 'important' prisoners. But so was he in a way. After all, he was an officer with a long and honourable record of service behind him. He was no respecter of persons. Mr. Banker was torn away from me the very next morning. Harkaran allowed the full force of his authority to descend upon me. I was not to do this or that. I was not to cross the white line referred to in my letter to Hakimji. But I had not the faintest idea of retaliating or resenting what he said or did. I was too engrossed in my own work and studies even to think of Harkaran's simple and childish instructions. It gave me momentary amusement. Harkaran discovered his error. When he saw that I did not resent his officiousness, nor did I pay any attention to it, he felt non-plussed. He was unprepared for such an emergency. He therefore took the only course that was left open to him and that was to recognize my dissimilarity and respond to me when I refused to respond to him. My non-violent non-co-operation led to his co-operation. All non-violent non-co-operation, whether among individuals or societies, or whether between governments and the governed, must lead ultimately to hearty co-operation. Anyway Harkaran and I became perfect friends. When Mr. Banker was returned to me, he put the finishing touch. One of his many businesses in the jail was to boom me for all I was worth. He thought that Harkaran and others had not sufficiently realized my greatness. In two or three days time I found myself elevated to the position of a baby in woollens. I was too great to be allowed to sweep my own cell or to put out my own blankets for drying. Harkaran was all attention before, but now he became embarrassingly attentive. I could not do anything myself, not even wash a handkerchief. If Harkaran heard me washing it, he would enter the open bath-room and tear the kerchief away from me. Whether it was that the authorities suspected that Harkaran was doing anything unlawful for us or whether it was a mere accident, Harkaran was, to our sorrow, taken away from us. He felt the separation more perhaps than we did. He had a royal time with us. He had plenty of eatables and that openly from our rations, supplemented as they were with fruit that friends sent from outside. And as our fame was 'noised abroad,' Harkaran's association with us had given him an added status with the other prisoners.

When I was given the permission to sleep on the cell verandah, the authorities thought that it was too risky to leave me with one warder only. Probably, the regulations required that a prisoner whose cell was kept open should have two warders to watch over him. It might even be that the addition was made for my protection. Whatever the cause, another warder was posted for night duty. His name was Shabaskhan. I never inquired about the cause, but I thought that a Mohammedan was chosen to balance the Hindu Harkaran. Shabaskhan was a powerful Baloochi. He was Harkaran's contemporary. Both knew each other well. Shabaskhan too was convicted of murder. It resulted from an affray in the clan to which he belonged. Shabaskhan was as broad as he was tall. His build always reminded me of Shaukat Ali. Shabaskhan put me at ease the very first day. He said,

'I am not going to watch you at all. Treat me as your friend and do exactly as you like. You will never find me interfering with you. If you want anything done, I shall be only too happy if I can do it for you.' Shabaskhan was as good as his word. He was always polite. He often tempted me with prison delicacies and always felt genuinely sorry that I would not partake of them. 'You know,' he would say, 'if we do not help ourselves to these few things, life would be intolerable, eating the same things day in and day out. With your people, it is different. You come for religion. That fact sustains you, whereas we know that we have committed crimes. We would like to get away as soon as ever we can.' Shabaskhan was the jailor's favourite. Growing enthusiastic over him, he once said, 'Look at him. I consider him to be a perfect gentleman. In a fit of temper he has committed murder for which he truly repents. I assure you there are not many men outside who are better than Shabaskhan. It is a mistake to suppose that all prisoners are criminals. Shabaskhan I have found to be most trustworthy and courteous. If I had the power, I would discharge him today.' The jailor was not wrong. Shabaskhan was a good man, and he was by no means the only good prisoner in that jail. Let me note in passing that it was not the jail that had made him good. He was good outside.

It is customary in the jails never to keep a convict officer on the same duty for any length of time. Transfers constantly take place. It is a necessary precaution. Prisoners cannot be allowed, under the existing system, to develop intimate relations. We had, therefore, a most varied experience of convict officers. After about two months, Shabaskhan was replaced by Adan. But I must introduce this warder to the reader in the next chapter.

Young India, 26-6-1924

15. My Jail Experiences—6
Some Convict-warders (2)
(vol. XXIV, pp. 366–70)

Adan was a young Somali soldier who was sentenced to ten years' hard labour for desertion from the British Army, which he had joined during the War. He was transferred by the Aden Jail authorities. Adan had served four years when we were admitted. He was practically illiterate. He could read the Koran with difficulty, but could

not copy it correctly, if at all. He was able to speak Urdu fairly fluently and was anxious to learn Urdu. With the permission of the Superintendent, I tried to teach him, but the learning of the alphabet
proved too great a strain upon him and he left it. With all that he was
quick-witted and sharp as a needle. He took the greatest interest in
religious matters. He was a devout Mussalman, offered his prayers
regularly including the midnight one, and never missed the *Ramzan*
fast. The rosary was his constant companion. When he was free, he
used to recite selections from the Koran. He would often engage me
in a discussion on complete fasts according to the Hindu custom as
also on ahimsa. He was a brave man. He was very courteous, but
never cringing. He was of an excitable nature and, therefore, often
quarrelled with the *bardasi* or his fellow-warder. We had, therefore,
sometimes to arbitrate between them. Being a soldier and amenable
to reason, he would accept the award, but he would put his case
boldly and cogently. Adan was the longest with us. I treasure Adan's
affection. He was most attentive to me. He would see to it that I got
my food at the appointed time. He was sad if I ever became ill and
anticipated all my wants. He would not let me exert myself for anything. He was anxious to be discharged or at least to be transferred to
Aden. I tried hard. I drew up petitions for him. The Superintendent
too, tried his best. But the decision rested with the Aden authorities.
Hope was held out to him that he would be discharged before the end
of last year. I do hope he is already discharged. The little service I
rendered gave rise to deep personal attachment. It was a sad parting
when Adan was transferred to another part of the prison. I must not
omit to mention that, when I was organizing spinning and carding in
the jail, Adan, though one of his hands was disabled, helped most
industriously at making slivers. He became very proficient in the art
which he had come to like.

As Shabaskhan was replaced by Adan, Harkaran was replaced by
Bhiwa. Much to our agreeable surprise, Bhiwa was a Mahar from Maharashtra and, therefore, an untouchable. Of all the warders we met
he was perhaps the most industrious. The reader will be surprised to
find that the canker of untouchability has not left even the jails untouched. Poor Bhiwa! He would not enter our cells without considerable hesitation. He would not touch our pots. We quickly set him at
rest by telling him that we had not only no prejudices against untouchables, but that we were trying our best to do away with the
curse. Shankerlal Banker specially befriended him and made him
feel perfectly at home with us. He permitted Bhiwa to be so familiar
with him that the former would resent an angry word from Mr.

Banker and the latter would even apologize. He induced Bhiwa to apply himself to studies and taught him also spinning. The result was that Bhiwa became, in an incredibly short space of time, an accomplished spinner and began so to like it that he thought of learning weaving, and earning his living through that occupation when he went out. I cultivated in the jail the habit of drinking hot water and lemon at 4.15 a.m. When I protested against Mr. Banker doing it for me, he initiated Bhiwa into the mystery. Prisoners, though they get up early enough, do not like to leave their matting (which is their bed) at that early hour. Bhiwa, however, immediately responded to his friend's suggestion. But it was Mr. Banker's business always to wake up Bhiwa at 4 o'clock. When Bhiwa went (he was discharged under special remission), Adan undertook the duty. He will not listen to my doing it myself. And the tradition was kept up even after Mr. Banker's discharge, each outgoing warder initiating the incoming one into all the mysteries. Needless to say, this morning duty was no part of the prison task. Indeed, convicts when they became warders were not expected to do any labour at all. Theirs is but to order.

Even as the best of friends must part some day, Bhiwa bade goodbye. He was permitted to receive from Mr. Banker khaddar caps, khaddar dhotis, khaddar vests and a khaddar blanket. He promised to wear nothing but khaddar outside. Let me hope good Bhiwa, wherever he may be, is keeping the promise.

Bhiwa was followed by Thamu. He too belonged to Maharashtra. Thamu was a mild-mannered warder. He had not much 'go' in him. He would do what he was asked, but did not believe in specially exerting himself. He and Adan, therefore, did not get on quite well together. But Thamu, being timid, always yielded to Adan in the end. He had such a royal time (all had) with us that Thamu did not want to be separated from us. He, therefore, preferred to bear Adan's hard yoke to being transferred. Thamu having come to us a considerable time after Adan, the latter was Thamu's senior with us. It is remarkable how these fictitious seniorities spring up in little places like jails. Yeravda was to us a whole world or, better still, the whole world. Every squabble, every little jar, was a mighty event commanding sustained interest for the day and sometimes even for days. If the jail authorities permitted a jail newspaper to be conducted by the prisoners and for them, it would have a cent per cent circulation, and such toothsome news as properly-cooked dal, well-dressed vegetables, and sensational items as war of words between prisoners, sometimes even resulting in blows and consequent *khatla* (trial) before the Superintendent, would be as eagerly devoured by the prisoners as the news of big dinner parties and great wars are devoured by the public outside. I make the present of a suggestion to enterprising members of the Assembly that, if they desire fame, they cannot do better than introduce a bill requiring Superintendents of jails to permit the publishing and editing of newspapers by prisoners exclusively for their own use and under strict censorship by the authorities.

To return to Thamu, though he was flabby, as a man he was otherwise as good as any of his predecessors. He took to the *charkha* like fish to water. In a week's time, he pulled a more even thread than I did. And after a month, the pupil out-distanced the teacher by a long way. So much so that I grew jealous of Thamu's superiority. I saw too from Thamu's rapid progress that my slow progress was a peculiar defect of mine and that an ordinary person could pull a perfect thread in a month at the outside. Everyone of those who were taught by me excelled me in no time. To Thamu as to Bhiwa, the spinning-wheel had become a welcome companion. They were able to drown the sorrows of separation from their nearest in the soft and gentle music of the wheel. Later on, spinning became Thamu's first work in the morning. He span [sic] at the rate of four hours per day.

When we were shifted to the European yard, there were several changes. Among them was a change of warders. Adan was the first to be transferred. Though neither he nor we liked it, we took his transfer bravely. Then came Thamu's turn. Poor fellow, he broke down. He wanted me to try to keep him. I would not do that. I thought it was beyond my province. The authorities had a perfect right to shift whom and where they would. Adan and Thamu were followed by Kunti, a Gurkha, and a Canarese by name Gangappa. The Gurkha was called Goorkha by everybody. He was reserved, but grew 'chummy' later on. For the first few days, he did not know where he was. Probably he thought we would report and involve him on the slightest pretext. But when he saw that we meant no mischief, he came closer to us. But he was soon transferred. Gangappa I have partly described in the introduction to the jail correspondence. He was an elderly man. His almost punctilious observance of rules and his great devotion to duty commanded my admiration. He put his whole soul into whatever he was ordered by the authorities to do. He took up duties which he need not have. He rarely remained idle. He learnt to make and cook chapatis for my companions. His devotion to me personally I shall never forget. No wife or sister could be more unsparing than Gangappa in his attention. He was awake at all times. He took delight in anticipating my wants. He saw to it that all my things were kept spotlessly clean. During my illness, he was my most efficient nurse, because he was the most attentive. When we were transferred to the European yard, Messrs Mansar Ali and Yagnik used to join me at prayer time. Mr. Mansar Ali was transferred to Allahabad for his discharge in due course. Mr. Yagnik, because he needed more intensive and philosophical rather than devotional meditation, dropped out. Gangappa felt that without these friends I would feel lonely at prayer. The very first time that he saw that I was alone at prayer, he quietly took his seat in front of me. Needless to say, I appreciated the delicate courtesy underlying the action. It was so spontaneous, unofficious, and natural for Gangappa. I do not call it religious in the accepted sense of the term, though, according to my conception, it was truly religious. I always hesitate to invite anybody to these prayer meetings of mine. I did not want them to come for my sake. I did not feel lonely. I realized most at that time the companionship of God. If any one came, I wanted him not for keeping company but for sharing the divine companionship. I, therefore, particularly hesitated to invite the warders. I felt they might join merely out of form, whereas I wanted them to join only if they naturally felt like joining. With Gangappa it was a mixture of pity for me in my loneliness and desire to share with me the sacred half-hour, though he could understand not a word of what I sang save, of course, *Ramanama.* Gangappa drew to the prayer meeting another warder, Annappa, also a Canarese, and later, Mr. Abdul Gani felt impelled to join. I imagine that Mr. Abdul Gani was unconsciously influenced by Gangappa's unobtrusive act of joining me.

The reader will see that I had a uniformly happy experience of these convict-warders. I could not have wished for more devoted companions or more faithful attendants. Paid service would but be a patch upon this and that of friends could only equal it. And yet the pity of it is that society treats such men as criminals and outcastes because they had the misfortune to be convicted. I entirely endorse the remark of the Head Jailor, already quoted by me in a previous chapter, that there are in our jails many men who are better than those outside. The reader will now understand why I felt a pang when I heard that I was discharged, and most of the companions who had covered me with so much kindness and whom there was, in my opinion, no occasion to detain any longer in the jails were left behind.

One word more and I must regretfully part with Gangappa. Gangappa always knew his limitations. He would not spin. He said he could not do it. His fingers had not the cunning for it. But he kept the work-room in order, cleaned my wheel and devoted all his spare time to sunning and cleaning the cotton for carding.

Of all the many happy memories of my prison life, I know that those of the company of the convict-warders will perhaps linger the longest.

Young India, 10-7-1924

16. Defeated and Humbled

(vol. XXIV, pp. 334–38)

Reporters are rarely able to interest me, but one of them did succeed the other day in interesting me in him. I therefore gave him, towards the end of the interview[,] more than he had expected. He asked me what I would do if the house was evenly divided. I told him in effect that God would send something to prevent such a catastrophe. I had no idea that my innocent and half-humorous remark was prophetic.[1]

I had a bare majority always for the four resolutions. But it must be regarded by me as a minority. The house was fairly evenly divided. The Gopinath Saha resolution clinched the issue. The speeches, the result and the scenes I witnessed after, was a perfect eye-opener. I undoubtedly regard the voting as a triumph for Mr. Das although he was apparently defeated by eight votes. That he could find 70 supporters out of 148 who voted had a deep significance for me. It lighted the darkness though very dimly as yet.

Up to the point of the declaration of the poll, I was enjoying the whole thing as a huge joke, though I knew all the while that it was as serious as it was huge. I now see that my enjoyment was superficial. It concealed the laceration that was going on within.

After the declaration, the chief actors retired from the scene. And the house abandoned itself to levity. Most important resolutions were passed with the greatest unconcern. There were flashes of humour sandwiched in between these resolutions. Everybody rose on points of order and information. The ordeal was enough to try the patience of any chairman. Maulana Mahomed Ali came through it all unscathed. He kept his temper fairly. He rightly refused to recognize 'points of information.' I must confess that the suitors for fame

1. A short paragraph is omitted here.

most cheerfully obeyed his summary rulings. Let not the reader conclude that there was, at any stage of the proceedings, the slightest
insubordination. I have not known many meetings where there was
so little acrimony or personalities in the debate as in this, even
though feelings ran high and the differences were sharp and serious. I
have known meetings where, under similar circumstances, the chair-
men have found it most difficult to keep order. The president of the
A.I.C.C. commanded willing obedience.

All the same, dignity vanished after the Gopinath resolution. It
was before this House that I had to put my last resolution. As the
proceedings went on, I must have become more and more serious.
Often I felt like running away from the oppressive scene. I dreaded
having to move a resolution in my charge. I would have asked for
postponement of the resolution but for the promise I had made the
meeting that I would suggest a remedy, or failing that, move a resolution for protecting litigants from the operation of the third resolution which requests resignation from members who do not believe in
the principle of the five boycotts, including that of law-courts, and
do not carry them out in their own persons. Protection was intended
for those who might be *driven* to the courts either as plaintiffs or
defendants. The resolution that was adopted by the Working Committee and previously circulated among the members did protect
them. It was substituted by the one actually passed by the A.I.C.C.
As the reader knows, it exempts from its operation those who might
be covered by the Cocanada resolution. In drafting that amendment I
had not protected litigants. I had wished to do so by a separate resolution. I had announced the fact at the time of introducing the resolution. And it was this promised resolution that opened for me a way
out of 'darkness invisible.' I moved it with the preface that it was
in redemption of the morning promise. I mentioned, too, Mr. Gangadharrao Deshpande was an instance in point. I do not believe in
exemptions and as-far-as-possibles. But I know that some of the
strongest non-co-operators have found it difficult to avoid law-courts.
Unscrupulous debtors have refused payment to non-co-operators because of their knowledge that the latter could not sue them. Similarly, I know men who have brought suits against non-co-operators
because they would not defend themselves. The curious will be
agreeably surprised to discover, if they searched among the rank and
file, the numerous cases in which non-co-operators have preferred to
suffer losses to defending themselves or suing. Nevertheless, it is
perfectly true that representatives have not always been able to keep
to the prohibition. The practice, therefore, has been to wink at filing

suits and more often at defending them. The Committee has from time to time also passed rules legalizing the practice to a certain extent. I thought that now when the A.I.C.C. was adopting a rigid attitude regarding the observance of the boycotts, the position of litigants should be clearly defined. Nothing would please me better than for the Congress to have only those representatives on its executive who would carry out all the boycotts to the full. But the exact fulfilment at the present stage of the boycott of law-courts on the part of many is almost an impossibility. Voluntary acceptance of poverty is essential for the purpose. It must take some time before we can hope to man the Congress organizations with such men and women, and run them efficiently. Recognizing the hard fact, I was prepared to incur the odium of having to move the said resolution of exemption. Hardly had I finished reading it, up sprang the brave Harisarvottama Rao to his feet and, in a vigorous and cogent speech, opposed it. He said it was his painful duty to oppose me. I told him the pain was mine in that I had to move a resolution I could not defend. His must be the pleasure of opposing an indefensible resolution and of keeping the Congress organization pure at any cost. I liked this opposition and was looking forward to the voting. But the opposer was followed by Swami Govindanand who raised the technical objection that no resolution designed to affect one previously passed could be moved at the same session of the Committee. The chairman properly rejected the objection, if only because the previous day the very first resolution was amended after it was passed by a majority. But the last straw was unwittingly supplied by Dr. Choithram. I have known him to be a responsible man. A long period of unbroken service lies to his credit. He has embraced poverty for the sake of his country. I was not prepared for a constitutional objection from him in a matter in which the Committee had on previous occasions softened the effect of the boycott resolution. But he thoughtlessly asked whether my resolution was not in breach of the Congress resolution on boycotts. Maulana Mahomed Ali asked me whether the objection was not just. I said of course it was. He therefore felt bound to hold my resolution unconstitutional. Then I sank within me. There was nothing, absolutely nothing, wrong about anybody's speech or behaviour. All were brief in their remarks. They were equally courteous. And, what is more, they were seemingly in the right. And yet it was all hopelessly unreal. The objections were like reading a sermon on the virtue of self-restraint to a hungry man reduced to a skeleton. Each of the actors acted involuntarily, unconsciously. I felt that God was speaking to me through them and seemed to say, 'Thou fool, knowest not thou that thou art impossible? Thy time is up.' Gangadharrao asked me whether he should not resign. I agreed with him that he should do so at once. And he promptly tendered his resignation. The President read it to the meeting. It was accepted almost unanimously. Gangadharrao was the gainer.

Shaukat Ali was sitting right opposite at a distance of perhaps six yards. His presence restrained me from fleeing. I kept asking myself, 'Could right ever come out of wrong? Was I not co-operating with evil?' Shaukat Ali seemed to say to me through his big eyes, 'There is nothing wrong, for all will be right.' I was struggling to free myself from the enchantment. I could not.

The President asked, 'Shall I now dissolve the meeting?' I said, 'Certainly.' But Maulana Abul Kalam Azad, who was evidently watching whatever changes my face was undergoing, was all eyes. He quickly came up and said, 'We cannot disperse without the message you have promised.' I replied, 'Maulana Saheb, it is true I wanted to say about about the future plans. But what I have been witnessing for the last hour, after the Gopinath resolution, has grieved me. I do not know where I stand now and what I should do.' 'Then,' he said, 'say even if it is only that.' I complied and in a short speech in Hindustani laid bare my heart and let them see the blood oozing out of it. It takes much to make me weep. I try to suppress tears even when there is occasion for them. But, in spite of all my efforts to be brave, I broke down utterly. The audience was visibly affected. I took them through the various stages I had passed and told them that it was Shaukat Ali who stood in the way of my flight. For I regarded him as trustee for Hindu honour, as I was proud enough to regard myself as such for Mussalman honour. And then I told them that I was unable to say how I would shape my future course. I would consult him and other workers who were closely associated with me. It was the saddest speech I had ever made. I finished and turned round to look for Maulana Abul Kalam Azad. He had stolen away from me and was standing at the farthest end opposite to me. I told him I would now like to go. He said, 'Not yet, for a while. For we must speak too.' And he invited the audience to speak. Those who spoke did so with a sob. The sight of the hoary-headed Sikh friend who was choked as he was speaking touched me deep. Of course Shaukat Ali spoke and others. All begged pardon and assured me of their unwavering support. Mahomed Ali broke down twice. I tried to soothe him.

I had nothing to forgive for none had done any wrong to me. On the contrary, they had all been personally kind to me. I was sad because we were weighed in the scales of our own making—the Congress creed—and found wanting; we were such poor representatives of the nation! I seemed to be hopelessly out of place. My grief consisted in the doubt about my own ability to lead those who would not follow.

I saw that I was utterly defeated and humbled. But defeat cannot dishearten me. It can only chasten me. My faith in my creed stands immovable. I know that God will guide me. Truth is superior to man's wisdom.

M. K. GANDHI

The foregoing was written on Monday the 30th June. I wrote it, but I was not satisfied nor am I satisfied now with the performance. On reading it I feel I have not done justice to the meeting or myself. Great as the informal meeting was, the one that preceded it, and that stung me to the quick, was not less great. I do not know that I have made it clear that no speaker had any malice in him. What preyed upon my mind was the fact of unconscious irresponsibility and disregard of the Congress creed or policy of non-violence.[2]

Young India, 3-7-1924

17. All About the Fast

(vol. XXV, pp. 199–202)

September 22, 1924

I wish to assure the reader that the fast has not been undertaken without deliberation. As a matter of fact my life has been a[t] stake ever since the birth of non-co-operation. I did not blindly embark upon it. I had ample warning of the dangers attendant upon it. No act of mine is done without prayer. Man is a fallible being. He can never be sure of his steps. What he may regard as answer to prayer may be an echo of his pride. For infallible guidance man has to have a perfectly innocent heart incapable of evil. I can lay no such claim. Mine is a struggling, striving, erring, imperfect soul. But I can rise only by experimenting upon myself and others. I believe in absolute oneness of God and therefore also of humanity. What though we have many bodies? We have but one soul. The rays of the sun are many through refraction. But they have the same source. I cannot therefore detach myself from the wickedest soul (nor may I be denied identity with

2. Incomplete.

the most virtuous). Whether therefore I will or no, I must involve in my experiment the whole of my kind. Nor can I do without experiment. Life is but an endless series of experiments.

I knew that non-co-operation was a dangerous experiment. Non-co-operation in itself is unnatural, vicious and sinful. But non-violent non-co-operation, I am convinced, is a sacred duty at times. I have proved it in many cases. But there was every possibility of mistake in its application to large masses. But desperate diseases call for desperate remedies. Non-violent non-co-operation was the only alternative to anarchy and worse. Since it was to be non-violent, I had to put my life in the scales.

The fact that Hindus and Mussalmans, who were only two years ago apparently working together as friends, are now fighting like cats and dogs in some places, shows conclusively that the non-co-operation they offered was not non-violent. I saw the symptoms in Bombay, Chauri Chaura and in a host of minor cases. I did penance then. It had its effect *pro tanto*. But this Hindu-Muslim tension was unthinkable. It became unbearable on hearing of the Kohat tragedy. On the eve of my departure from Sabarmati for Delhi, Sarojini Devi wrote to me that speeches and homilies on peace would not do. I must find out an effective remedy. She was right in saddling the responsibility on me. Had I not been instrumental in bringing into being the vast energy of the people? I must find the remedy if the energy proved self-destructive. I wrote to say that I should find it only by plodding. Empty prayer is "as sounding brass or a tinkling cymbal." I little knew then that the remedy was to be this prolonged fast. And yet I know that the fast is not prolonged enough for quenching the agony of my soul. Have I erred, have I been impatient, have I compromised with evil? I may have done all these things or none of them. All I know is what I see before me. If real non-violence and truth had been practised by the people who are now fighting, the gory duelling that is now going on would have been impossible. My responsibility is clearly somewhere.

I was violently shaken by Amethi, Shambhar and Gulbarga. I had read the reports about Amethi and Shambhar prepared by Hindu and Mussalman friends. I had learnt the joint finding of Hindu and Mussalman friends who went to Gulbarga. I was writhing in deep pain and yet I had no remedy. The news of Kohat set the smouldering mass aflame. Something had got to be done. I passed two nights in restlessness and pain. On Wednesday I knew the remedy. I must do penance. In the Satyagraha Ashram at the time of morning prayer we ask Siva, God of Mercy, to forgive our sins knowingly or unknowingly committed. My penance is the prayer of a bleeding heart for forgiveness for sins unwittingly committed.

It is a warning to the Hindus and Mussalmans who have professed to love me. If they have loved me truly and if I have been deserving of their love, they will do penance with me for the grave sin of denying God in their hearts. To revile one another's religion, to make reckless statements, to utter untruth, to break the heads of innocent men, to desecrate temples or mosques, is a denial of God. The world is watching—some with glee and some with sorrow—the dogfight that is proceeding in our midst. We have listened to Satan. Religion—call it by what you like—is made of sterner stuff. The penance of Hindus and Mussalmans is not fasting but retracing their steps. It is true penance for a Mussalman to harbour no ill for his Hindu brother and an equally true penance for a Hindu to harbour none for his Mussalman brother.

I ask of no Hindu or Mussalman to surrender an iota of his religious principle. Only let him be sure that it is religion. But I do ask of every Hindu and Mussalman not to fight for an earthly gain. I should be deeply hurt if my fast made either community surrender on a matter of principle. My fast is a matter between God and myself.

I did not consult friends—not even Hakim Sahib who was closeted with me for a long time on Wednesday—not Maulana Mahomed Ali under whose roof I am enjoying the privilege of hospitality. When a man wants to make up with his Maker, he does not consult a third party. He ought not to. If he has any doubt about it, he certainly must. But I had no doubt in my mind about the necessity of my step. Friends would deem it their duty to prevent me from undertaking the fast. Such things are not matters for consultation or argument. They are matters of feeling. When Rama decided to fulfil his obligation, he did not swerve from his resolve either by the weepings and wailings of his dear mother or the advice of his preceptors, or the entreaty of his people, or even the certainty of his father's death if he carried out his resolve. These things are momentary. Hinduism would not have been much of a religion, if Rama had not steeled his heart against every temptation. He knew that he had to pass through every travail, if he was to serve humanity and become a model for future generations.

But was it right for me to go through the fast under a Mussalman roof? Yes, it was. The fast is not born out of ill will against a single soul. My being under a Mussalman roof ensures it against any such interpretation. It is in the fitness of things that this fast should be taken up and completed in a Mussalman house.

And who is Mahomed Ali? Only two days before the fast we had a discussion about a private matter in which I told him, what was mine was his and what was his was mine. Let me gratefully tell the public that I have never received warmer or better treatment than under Mahomed Ali's roof. Every want of mine is anticipated. The dominant thought of every one of his household is to make me and mine happy and comfortable. Doctors Ansari and Abdur Rahman have constituted themselves my medical advisers. They examine me daily. I have had many a happy occasion in my life. This is no less happy than the previous ones. Bread is not everything. I am experiencing here the richest love. It is more than bread for me.

It has been whispered that by being so much with Mussalman friends, I make myself unfit to know the Hindu mind. The Hindu mind is myself. Surely I do not need to live amidst Hindus to know the Hindu mind when every fibre of my being is Hindu. My Hinduism must be a very poor thing, if it cannot flourish under influences the most adverse. I know instinctively what is necessary for Hinduism. But I must labour to discover the Mussalman mind. The closer I come to the best of Mussalmans, the juster I am likely to be in my estimate of the Mussalmans and their doings. I am striving to become the best cement between the two communities. My longing is to be able to cement the two with my blood, if necessary. But, before I can do so, I must prove to the Mussalmans that I love them as well as I love the Hindus. My religion teaches me to love all equally. May God help me to do so. My fast is among other things meant to qualify me for achieving that equal and selfless love.

Young India, 25-9-1924

18. A Contrast of Despair and Hope
(vol. XXV, pp. 273–74)

During my visit to Puri in 1921, I saw many things that I shall not easily forget. But among them all there were two that I shall never forget. One of them haunts me day and night.

In those days Puri had a philanthropic Superintendent of Police. He managed an orphanage. He showed it to me. It had many happy, well-looking, bright children who were engaged in all kinds of industries—mat-weaving, basket-making, spinning, weaving, etc. The Superintendent told me they were all children of famine-stricken parents, some of whom were picked up as mere skin and bone.

He then took me to an open space in the very shadow of the hoary temple where were arranged in rows the famine-stricken people who were living within twelve miles of Puri. Some of these no doubt owed their lives to the charity of the Gujaratis and the loving service of Amritlal Thakkar who doled out to them the rice he bought with the monies supplied by the Gujaratis. The life was ebbing away in them. They were living pictures of despair. You could count every rib. You could see every artery. There was no muscle, no flesh. Parched, crumpled skin and bone was all you could see. There was no lustre in their eyes. They seemed to want to die. They had no interest in anything save the handful of rice they got. They would not work for money. For love, perhaps! It almost seems as if they would condescend to eat and live if you would give them the handful of rice. It is the greatest tragedy I know of—these men and women, our brothers and sisters, dying a slow torturing death. Theirs is an eternal compulsory fast. And as they break it occasionally with rice they seem to mock us for the life we live.

"Why could they not be kept like the orphans?" I asked the Superintendent. "They will not work and will not stay there," was the reply. The Superintendent might also have added that he could not accommodate thousands of starving men and women, even if they were ready to work, in an asylum.

There is on the face of the earth no other country that has the problem that India has, of chronic starvation and slow death—a process of dehumanization. The solution must therefore be original. In trying to find it we must discover the causes of the tremendous tragedy. These people are starving because there is chronic famine in Orissa due to floods or want of rains. They have no other occupation to fall back upon. They are therefore constantly idle. This idleness has persisted for so long that it has become a habit with them. Starvation and idleness are the normal condition of life for thousands of people on Orissa. But what is true of Orissa is to a less extent true of many other parts of India.

We may find remedies to prevent floods. That will take years. We may induce people to adopt better methods of cultivation. That must take still more years. And when we have stopped inundations and have introduced among millions up to date cultivation, there will still be plenty of time left with the peasants if they will only work. But these improvements will take generations. How are the starving millions to keep the wolf from the door meanwhile? The answer is through the spinning-wheel. But how are the people who will not work at all be made to take up even the spinning-wheel? The answer is by us the workers, the educated and the well-to-do people taking up spinning. An ocular and sincere demonstration by thousands who need not spin for themselves cannot fail to move these starving men and women to do likewise. Moreover it will be only when *we* take up spinning that we shall be able to get the requisite number of skilled spinners who can give the necessary preliminary tuition, choose the right kind of wheel, do the repairs, etc. Lastly voluntary spinning by thousands cannot but cheapen khaddar and enable us to produce finer counts. If, therefore, we will identify ourselves with our famishing countrymen, we will not only not cavil at the spinning franchise but would welcome it as the surest way to the solution of the problem of the ever-deepening and distressful poverty of the masses.

Young India, 31-10-1924

19. Two Conversations
(vol. XXVI, pp. 467–70)

A large number of students come and ask me questions on various subjects. Some of them harass me very much, while others go away satisfied after asking me a few questions in a quiet manner. Both these types of conversations took place during the past few days, and as they are interesting I give them below:

First Conversation

During the return journey from Madras, I lay tired and exhausted in the train and was trying to catch up with my writing. The train halted at a station and presently a young man who had just completed studies entered my compartment after asking my permission. He asked me:

"Are you returning from Vykom?"

"Yes."

"What happened there?"

I did not like this question and asked him in return, "Where do you come from?"

"I belong to Malabar."

He carried two newspapers. I asked, "Do you read newspapers?"

"How can I? I have to travel so much, you see."

"I see you are carrying a copy of *The Hindu*. You can get all the news you want of Vykom from it."

"But I want to hear it from you."

"If everyone, like you, starts asking me the news and I have to answer, I would have no time for any other work. Have you thought of that?"

"But you can tell me."

"Do you read *Young India*?"

"No, I do not get time for reading. I read *The Times* though, for I can get it."

"Then I cannot spare any time for you. You do not read *The Hindu*, nor *Young India*. What can I tell you, then, in ten minutes during a chance meeting like this? Please excuse me."

"So you will not tell me?"

"Please excuse me. You do not even wear khadi and are needlessly harassing me."

"But it is your duty to tell me what happened."

"And it is your duty to wear khadi."

"I have no money."

"You are wearing gold buttons. You give them to me and I shall provide you khadi."

"I have a fancy for these buttons and that is why I wear them. Why should I give them to you?"

"Then please excuse me now."

"So you will not tell me anything because I do not wear khadi?"

"Take it that way if you like. But please excuse me."

"Why don't you say that you will not tell me what happened?"

"All right, if you would have it so."

"I shall make this behaviour of yours public."

"You may, with pleasure. But you should now allow me to do my work."

"I have been doing what I can. I had even collected something like a hundred rupees for the Malabar Fund."

"And yet you will not wear khadi which is woven by poor people."

"When people die of starvation, you think of asking people to spin—do I not know that?"

"Let us not discuss that subject."

"Should I go away then?"

"Please do, now."

I am afraid, I could not make this friend see that he should not waste my time, which is people's time, by asking me about things he can easily learn from newspapers. After he had left, I felt that had I, instead of being serious with him, talked to him good-humouredly, I could have converted him, though I should certainly have had to spend more time on him. I fear that my seriousness and the consequent stiffness lost me a public worker. Truly, how difficult is the path of non-violence! One has always to be vigilant, however busy one may be, and must constantly try to enter the heart of the person with whom one is talking and that of the bystanders. Those who follow the path of non-violence can have no time of their own and cannot think of their convenience. Whether or not they are in a position to attend to a thing or can spare the necessary time, they are servants who have sold themselves to the world for its service. I saved my time, looked to my convenience, tried to become a teacher and, seeking to instruct, lost the pupil. Tulsidas and other saints have rightly said that a person without discrimination is a brute.

Second Conversation

The one whom I wanted to teach had proved to be my teacher. I had learnt the lesson and did not wish to lose another worker. I was, therefore, vigilant. This student was from the Punjab. The Punjabis whom I have met were all of them courteous people. This student, too, was extremely polite and so I had no occasion to exercise vigilance and restrain myself.

"I have been trying for five years," he said, "to be able to see you. My ambition has been fulfilled today."

"You are welcome. Do you have anything in particular to ask me?"

"With your permission, Sir, I should like to ask you a question or two in regard to my studies."

"You are welcome to do that."

"Do you believe that I can make a living from the spinning-wheel?"

"No. I have never recommended spinning as a means of livelihood for people like you. You can take it up only as a form of *yajna*.

"What should I do then?"

"If I can persuade you, I would ask you to take up carding and weaving as a means of livelihood. These crafts can be easily learnt."

"Will they help me to maintain my family?"

"Yes, if all your famiy members help you in the work."

"That is impossible for a family like mine. As you see, I wear khadi. I also spin. I believe in spinning. But how can I create the same faith in my family members? And even if I succeed in doing so, they will not agree to do this work."

"I can well understand your difficulty, but a good many of us will have to change our way of living; otherwise there is nothing but despair in store for the seven lakh villages of our country."

"I understand the idea, but I do not have the strength to follow it in practice today. I want your blessings so that I may have it, but till then what should I do?"

"That is for you and your elders to think out. I have placed before you what I believe to be the ideal."

"Should I learn some craft like pottery?"

"It is certainly useful. You can make a living from it and, if you have some capital to invest and start a factory, you will also help a few others to earn their livelihood. But you must admit that in that case you will have to exploit the labourers, for you will be keeping more for yourself and pay them less."

"That is true. But, being used to city life, I think I cannot do anything else, for the present at any rate. I shall, however, never forget what you have told me. I hope I have your blessings?"

"Every student has my blessings in all good undertakings."

[From Gujarati]
Navajivan, 5-4-1925

20. My Friend, the Revolutionary

(vol. XXVI, pp. 486–92)

The revolutionary whom I endeavoured to answer some time ago, has returned to the charge and challenges me to answer certain questions that arise out of my previous answers to him. I gladly do so. He seems to me to be seeking light, even as I am, and argues fairly and without much passion. So long as he continues to reason calmly, I promise to continue the discussion. His first question is:

Do you really believe that the revolutionaries of India are less sacrificing, less noble or less lovers of their country than the Swarajists, Moderates and the Nationalists? May I challenge you to keep before the public the names of some Swarajists, Moderates or Nationalists who have embraced the death of a martyr for the sake of the motherland? Can you be bold, nay, arrogant enough to deny it in the face of historical facts that the revolutionaries have sacrificed more for their country than any other party which professes to serve India? You are ready to make compromises with other parties, while you abhor our party and describe the[ir] sentiments as poison. Will you not tremble to use the same word of intolerance for the sentiments of any other party which is decidedly inferior in the eyes of God and men to us? What makes you shrink from calling them misguided patriots or venomous reptiles?

I do not regard the revolutionaries of India to be less sacrificing, less noble or less lovers of their country than the rest. But I respectfully contend that their sacrifice, nobility and love are not only a waste of effort, but being ignorant and misguided, do and have done more harm to the country than any other activity. For, the revolutionaries have retarded the progress of the country. Their reckless disregard of the lives of their opponents has brought on repression that has made those that do not take part in their warfare more cowardly than they were before. Repression does good only to those who are prepared for it. The masses are not prepared for the repression that follows in the trail of revolutionary activities and unwittingly strengthen the hands of the very Government which the revolutionaries are seeking to destroy. It is my certain conviction that had the Chauri Chaura murders not taken place the movement attempted at Bardoli would have resulted in the establishment of swaraj. Is it, therefore, any wonder that, with such opinion I call the revolutionary a misguided and therefore, dangerous patriot? I would call my son a misguided and dangerous nurse who, because of his ignorance and blind love, fought at the cost of his own life the physicians whose system of medicine no doubt did me harm but which I could not escape for want of will or ability. The result would be that I would lose a noble son and bring down upon my head the wrath of the physicians who, suspecting my complicity in the son's activities, might seek to punish me in addition to continuing their harmful course of treatment. If the son had attempted to convince the physicians of their error, or me of my weakness in submitting to the treatment, the physicians might have mended their way, or I might have rejected the treatment, or would, at least, have escaped the wrath of the physicians. I do make certain compromises with the other parties because, though I disagree with them, I do not regard their activities as positively harmful and dangerous as I regard the revolutionaries'. I have never called the revolutionaries "venomous reptiles." But I must refuse to fall into hysterics over their sacrifices, however great they may be, even as I must refuse to give praise to the sacrifice of my misguided son for his sacrifice in the illustration supposed by me. I feel sure that those who through insufficient reasoning or false sentiment, secretly or openly, give praise to the revolutionaries for their sacrifices, do harm to them and the cause they have at heart. The writer has asked me to quote instances of non-revolutionary patriots who gave their lives for the country. Well, two completed cases occur to me as I write these notes. Gokhale and Tilak died for their country. They worked in almost total disregard of their health and died much earlier than they need have. There is no necessary charm about death on the gallows; often such death is easier than a life of drudgery and toil in malarious tracts. I am quite satisfied that among the Swarajists and others there are men who will any day lay down their lives if they felt convinced that their death would bring deliverance to the country. I suggest to my friend, the revolutionary, that death on the gallows serves the country only when the victim is a "spotless lamb."

"India's path is not Europe's." Do you really believe it? Do you mean to say that warfare and organization of army was not in existence in India, before she came in contact with Europe? Warfare for fair cause—Is it against the spirit of India? *Vinashaya cha dushkritam*—Is it something imported from Europe? Granted that it is, will you be fanatic enough not to take from Europe what is good? Do you believe that nothing good is possible in Europe? If conspiracy, bloodshed and sacrifice for fair cause are bad for India, will they not be bad as well for Europe?

I do not deny that India had armies, warfare, etc., before she came in contact with Europe. But I do say that it never was the normal course of Indian life. The masses, unlike those of Europe, were untouched by the warlike spirits. I have already said in these pages that I ascribe to the *Gita*, from which the writer has quoted the celebrated verse, a totally different meaning from that ordinarily given. I do not regard it as a description of, or an exhortation to, physical warfare. And, in any case, according to the verse quoted it is God the All Knowing Who descends to the earth to punish the wicked. I must be pardoned if I refuse to regard every revolutionary as an all-knowing God or an avatar. I do not condemn everything European. But I condemn, for all climes and for all times, secret murders and unfair methods even for a fair cause.

"India is not Calcutta and Bombay." May I most respectfully put it before your Mahatmaship that the revolutionaries know the geography of India enough to be able to know this geographical fact easily. We hold this fact as much as we hold that a few spinners do not form the Indian nation. We are entering villages and have been successful everywhere. Can you not believe that they, the sons of Shivaji, Pratap and Ranjit, can appreciate our sentiments with more readiness and depth than anything else? Don't you think that armed and conspired resistance against something satanic and ignoble is infinitely more befitting for any nation, especially Indian, than the prevalence of effortlessness and philosophical cowardice? I mean the cowardice which is pervading the length and breadth of India owing to the preaching of your theory of non-violence or more correctly the wrong interpretation and misuse of it. Non-violence is not the theory of the weak and helpless, it is the theory of the strong. We want to produce such men in India, who will not shrink from death—whenever it may come and in whatever form—will do the good and die. This is the spirit with which we are entering the villages. We are not entering the villages to extort votes for councils and district boards, but our object is to secure co-martyrs for the country who will die and a stone will not tell where his poor corpse lies. Do you believe like Mazzini that ideas ripen quickly, when nourished by the blood of martyrs?

It is not enough to know the geographial difference between Calcutta and the villages outside the railways. If the revolutionaries knew the organic difference between these, they would, like me, become spinners. I own that the few spinners we have, do not make India. But I claim that it is possible to make all India spin as it did before, and so far as sympathy is concerned, millions are even now in sympathy with the movement, but they never will be with the revolutionary. I dispute the claim that the revolutionaries are succeeding with the villagers. But if they are, I am sorry. I shall spare no pains to frustrate their effort. Armed conspiracies against something satanic is like matching satans against Satan. But since one Satan is one too many for me, I would not multiply him. Whether my activity is effortlessness or all efforts, remains perhaps to be seen. Meanwhile, if it has resulted in making two yards of yarn spun where only one was spinning, it is so much to the good. Cowardice, whether philosophical or otherwise, I abhor. And if I could be persuaded that revolutionary activity has dispelled cowardice, it will go a long way to soften my abhorrence of the method, however much I may still oppose it on principle. But he who runs may see that owing to the non-violent movement, the villagers have assumed a boldness to which only a few years ago they were strangers. I admit that non-violence is a weapon essentially of the strong. I also admit that often cowardice is mistaken for non-violence.

My friend begs the question when he says a revolutionary is one who "does the good and dies." That is precisely what I question. In my opinion, he does the evil and dies. I do not regard killing or assassination or terrorism as good in any circumstances whatsoever. I do believe that ideas ripen quickly when nourished by the blood of martyrs. But a man who dies slowly of jungle fever in service bleeds as certainly as the one on the gallows. And if the one who dies on the gallows is not innocent of another's blood, he never had ideas that deserved to ripen.

One of your objections against the revolutionaries is that their movement is not mass movement, consequently the mass at large will be very little benefited by the revolution, for which we are preparing. That is indirectly saying that we shall be most benefitted by it. Is it really what you mean to say? Do you believe that those persons who are ever ready to die for their country—those mad lovers of their country—I mean the revolutionaries of India in whom the spirit of *nishkama karma*[1] reigns, will betray their motherland and secure privileges for a life—this trifling life? It is true that we will not drag the mass just now in the field of action, because we know that it is weak, but when the preparation is complete, we shall call them in the open field. We profess to understand the present Indian psychology full well, because we daily get the chance of weighing our brethren along with ourselves. We know that the mass of India is after all Indian, it is not weak by itself but there is want of efficient leaders; so when we have begot the number of leaders required by constant propaganda and preaching, and the arms, we shall not shrink from calling, and if necessary, dragging the mass in the open field to prove that they are the descendants of Shivaji, Ranjit, Pratap and Govind Singh. Besides we have been constantly preaching that the mass is not for the revolution but the revolution is for the mass. Is it sufficient to remove your prejudice in this connection?

I neither say nor imply that the revolutionary benefits if the masses do not. On the contrary, and as a rule, the revolutionary never benefits in the ordinary sense of the word. If the revolutionaries succeed in attracting, not "dragging," the masses to them, they will find that the murderous campaign is totally unnecessary. It sounds very pleasant and exciting to talk of "the descendants of Shivaji, Ranjit, Pratap and Govind Singh." But is it true? Are we all descendants of these heroes in the sense in which the writer understands it? We are their countrymen, but their descendants are the military classes. We may, in future, be able to obliterate caste, but today it persists and therefore the claim put up by the writer cannot in my opinion be sustained.

Last of all, I shall ask you to answer these questions: Was Guru Govind Singh a misguided patriot because he believed in warfare for noble cause? What will you like to say about Washington, Garibaldi and Lenin? What do you think of Kamal Pasha and De Valera? Would you like to call Shivaji and Pratap, well-meaning and sacrificing physicians who prescribed arsenic when they should have given fresh grape-juice? Will you like to call Krishna Europeanized because he believed also in the *vinasha* of *dushkritas!*

This is a hard or rather awkward question. But I dare not shirk it. In the first instance Guru Govind Singh and the others whose names are mentioned did not believe in secret murder. In the second, these patriots knew their work and their men, whereas the modern Indian revolutionary does not know his work. He has not the men, he has not the atmosphere, that the patriots mentioned had. Though my

1. Effort without desire, the principal teaching of the *Gita*.

views are derived from my theory of life I have not put them before the nation on that ground. I have based my opposition to the revolutionaries on the sole ground of expedience. Therefore, to compare their activities with those of Guru Govind Singh or Washington or Garibaldi or Lenin would be most misleading and dangerous. But by test of the theory of non-violence, I do not hesitate to say that it is highly likely that had I lived as their contemporary and in the respective countries, I would have called everyone of them a misguided patriot, even though a successful and brave warrior. As it is, I must not judge them. I disbelieve history so far as details of acts of heroes are concerned. I accept broad facts of history and draw my own lessons for my conduct. I do not want to repeat it in so far as the broad facts contradict the highest laws of life. But I positively refuse to judge men from the scanty material furnished to us by history. *De mortuis nil nisi bonum.*[2] Kamal Pasha and De Valera too I cannot judge. But for me, as a believer in non-violence out and out they cannot be my guides in life in so far as their faith in war is concerned. I believe in Krishna perhaps more than the writer. But my Krishna is the Lord of the universe, the creator, preserver and destroyer of us all. He may destroy because He creates. But I must not be drawn into a philosophical or religious argument with my friends. I have not the qualifications for teaching my philosophy of life. I have barely qualifications for practicing the philosophy I believe. I am but a poor struggling soul yearning to be wholly good—wholly truthful and wholly non-violent in thought, word and deed, but ever failing to reach the ideal which I know to be true. I admit, and assure my revolutionary friends, it is a painful climb but the pain of it is a positive pleasure for me. Each step upward makes me feel stronger and fit for the next. But all that pain and the pleasure are for me. The revolutionaries are at liberty to reject the whole of my philosophy. To them I merely present my own experiences as a co-worker in the same cause even as I have successfully presented them to the Ali Brothers and many other friends. They can and do applaud whole-heartedly the action of Mustafa Kamal Pasha and possibly De Valera and Lenin. But they realize with me that India is not like Turkey or Ireland or Russia and that revolutionary activity is suicidal at this stage of the country's life at any rate, if not for all time in a country so vast, so hopelessly divided and with the masses so deeply sunk in pauperism and so fearfully terror-struck.

Young India, 9-4-1925

2. Of the dead say nothing but good.

21. Torments on Tour

(vol. XXVI, pp. 574–75)

[April 30, 1925]

These notes are being written during the trying journey to Calcutta. This being my first passage through the Central Provinces after my discharge from prison, people are embarrassingly attentive at every station and there is no rest for the wearied limbs. The discarding of khaddar is most noticeable. Instead of a forest of white khaddar caps, I see everywhere the provoking black foreign caps on almost every head. A friend sadly remarked to me that there was hardly one in a thousand who wore khaddar habitually. I am witnessing all along the route a striking demonstration of the fact. All honour then to the one per thousand who remain faithful to khaddar against heavy odds. My faith in khaddar rises as I find this indifference to if not revolt against khaddar.

The demonstration of the painful truth became complete at Nagpur—the centre that re-affirmed the Calcutta resolution of non-violent non-co-operation. There was a vast crowd at the station. The Congress officials had even arranged a meeting just outside the station. The hot sun was beating overhead. The din was terrific. Nobody heard anybody, much less listened to anybody. There were volunteers but there was no discipline. No way was kept for me to pass through. I insisted on a way being made if I was to go to the meeting place during the half hour that the train was to stop at the station. The way was made with difficulty. I waded through it in the best manner I could. [It] took me over five minutes to reach the platform. Without the crowd pressing from all sides, I could have reached it in half a minute. I took no more than one minute to deliver my message. It took me longer to return to the train than it took to reach the platform, for the crowd had now lost its head completely. The intoxication of affection was now at its height. The shouts of "——ki jai" rent the sky. I was ill able to bear the din and the dust and the suffocation. "O God! deliver me from this affection" was the silent prayer that went up to the Great White Throne. I reached the train in safety. It was provokingly late going. I stood in the doorway wishing and hoping to talk to the crowd if it would keep still for a while. The Congress officials tried, a big Akali tried, to silence the crowd. It was no use. It had come to have *darshan*. That it was having with delirious joy. Its joy was my pain. My name on the lips and black caps on the heads,—what a terrible contrast! What a lie! I could not fight the battle of swaraj with that crowd. And yet, I know that Maulana Shaukat Ali would say there was hope so long as there was that affection, blind though it was. I am not so sure and therefore I was in agony.

At last, I got a hearing. I demanded the black caps. The response was instantaneous but not generous. From that vast crowd I do not think more than one hundred caps were thrown, four of which were thrown not by the owners. They were claimed and promptly returned. This sight had a double lesson for me. With proper organized work, people could be induced to discard foreign or mill-made cloth. That was one lesson; but there was another. People there were who were yet ready to remove the neighbour's cap, just the preliminary to coercion. But there should be no coercion in khaddar wearing or in anything else. Those who wear it must do so voluntarily or not at all.

Young India, 7-9-1925

22. A Domestic Chapter

(vol. XXVII, pp. 259–62)

A *vakil* from Lyallpur sends the following letter addressed to the Editor, *Young India:*

About three or four years ago, a company, "All-India Stores Ltd.," was started at Calcutta with Mr. H. M. Gandhi, son of our Mahatmaji, as one of the directors, as advertised by a representative of the said company at Rawalpindi. A client of mine was persuaded to pay certain sums to the said representative and also to the company in pursuance of his having been so persuaded to become a shareholder. I have written to the known and notified address, 22 Amratalla Street, Calcutta, of the company and so has my client. My client fears that perhaps it was a bogus affair and he has been done out of his money. In the interests of your (Mahatma's) good name and the economic welfare of this poor country, I fondly hope and wish and even pray, my client's fears may be unfounded. The post office has returned all our letters back through the Dead Letter Office. So, some ground at least exists for my client's suspecting that the company is no more. Is it a fact that Mahatmaji's son was a Director in it, and is it a fact that such a company came into being and is still existing, and where?

Please excuse my writing to you about it. My client who is a Mohammedan gentleman and whose respect for Mahatmaji led him to become a shareholder in the company, wants to verify these facts. Hence the query.

But for some important principles involved in the letter, I would have satisfied myself with a private reply, though the letter is meant for publication. It was necessary to publish it also, because it is highly likely that many shareholders feel like the *vakil*'s client. They too should have such satisfaction as I could render to them. I do indeed happen to be the father of Harilal M. Gandhi. He is my eldest boy, is over 36 years old and is father of four children, the eldest being 19 years old. His ideals and mine having been discovered over fifteen years ago to be different, he has been living separately from me and, since 1915 has not been supported by or through me. It has been my invariable rule to regard my boys as my friends and equals as soon as they completed their sixteen years. The tremendous changes that my outer life has undergone from time to time were bound to leave their impress on my immediate surroundings,—especially on my children. Harilal who was witness to all the changes, being old enough to understand them, was naturally influenced by the Western veneer that my life at one time did have. His commercial undertakings were totally independent of me. Could I have influenced him, he would have been found associated with me in my several public activities and earning, at the same time, a decent livelihood. But he chose, as he had every right to do, a different and independent path. He was and is still ambitious. He wants to become rich and that too, easily. Possibly he has a grievance against me that, when it was open to me to do so, I did not equip him and my other children for careers that lead to wealth and fame that wealth brings. He started the Stores in question without any the least assistance of any kind whatsoever from me. I did not lend my name to them. I never recommended his enterprise to anybody either privately or openly. Those who helped him did so on the merits of the enterprise. No doubt his sonship must have helped him. As long as the world lasts, and in spite of its protests against *varnashrama*, it will give credit to heredity. Being my son, he must be good and straight, cautious in his pecuniary affairs and as reliable as his father. So must many have argued. They have my sympathy, but beyond that nothing more. I must disclaim all responsibility, moral or otherwise, for the doings of even those who are nearest and dearest to me except those wherein they act with me or, I permit them to act in my name or with my certificate. I have enough to be responsible for myself. I alone know my sorrows and my troubles in the course of the eternal duel going on within me and which admits of no truce. I ask the reader to believe me when I say that it taxes all my energy, and if I feel as a rule stronger for the combat, it is only because I remain wide awake. I make the reader a present of the thought that even my swaraj activity has a bearing on that duel. It is for the supreme satisfaction of my soul that I engage in it. "This is selfishness double distilled," said a friend once to me. I quickly agreed with him.

I do not know Harilal's affairs. He meets me occasionally, but I never pry into his affairs. I do not know that he is a Director in his Company. I do not know how his affairs stand at present, except that they are in a bad way. If he is honest, limited or unlimited though his Stores were, he will not rest till he has paid all the creditors in full. That is my view of honest trade. But he may hold different views and seek shelter under the law of insolvency. Sufficient for me to assure the public that nothing crooked will have countenance from me. For me, the law of satyagraha, the law of love, is an eternal principle. I co-operate with all that is good. I desire to non-co-operate with all that is evil,—whether it is associated with my wife, son or myself. I have no desire to shield any of the two. I would like the world to know the whole of the evil in us. And in so far as I can, with decency, I let the world into all the domestic secrets so-called. I never make the slightest attempt to hide them, for I know that concealment can only hurt us.

There is much in Harilal's life that I dislike. He knows that. But I love him in spite of his faults. The bosom of a father will take him in as soon as he seeks entrance. For the present, he has shut the door against himself. He must still wander in the wilderness. The protection of a human father has its decided limitations. That of the Divine Father is ever open to him. Let him seek it and he will find it.

Let the *vakil* and his client know that my good name is not worth keeping, if it suffers because of the errors of a grown-up boy who has no encouragement from me in them. "The economic welfare of this poor country" will be fairly safe in spite of failures of private firms, if the President for the time being of the Congress and the members of the various organizations remain true to their trust and never mishandle a single pice. I pity the client who, out of respect for me, became a share-holder in a concern whose constitution he evidently never cared to study. Let the client's example be a warning against people being guided by big names in their transactions. Men may be good, not necessarily their children. Men may be good in some respects, not necessarily, therefore, in all. A man who is an authority on one matter is not, therefore, an authority on all matters. *Caveat emptor.*

Young India, 18-6-1925

 # CHRONOLOGY III
1928–1932

In this four-year period, Gandhi made a striking return to the effectiveness he experienced in 1920, taking the center of the Indian political stage with his Salt March of 1930. This was political effectiveness in every sense, for he put great pressure on the British government, commanding both the participation of Hindus en masse and the admiring attention of the outside world, without compromising his faith in nonviolence.

In the immediate sequel, and in terms of immediate political advantage, the British outmaneuvered him, both in the Gandhi-Irwin Pact, which ended the civil disobedience, and at the Round Table Conference held in London in 1931. But if we use the terms of a larger politics, we see that Gandhi had reestablished himself with Indians and with the whole world as India's political leader and that he ended this period with greater power than he had ever had before.

His letter to Lord Irwin, the viceroy, before the march both sets forth Gandhi's reasons and exemplifies his strategy of personalizing an issue. He always tried to establish a personal relationship with his opponents. One might say he addressed them in such a way as to make them read his letters alone, not in conference or in official uniform. This gave his letters a tone others called sanctimonious but also provided an ad hominem thrust—as, for instance, in his discussion of Lord Irwin's salary. We should also note his employment of a young Englishman to deliver the letter to Irwin (and the later quotation of this young man's criticism of Gandhi), and the religious, indeed Christian, symbolism of the march, whose par-

ticipants were pilgrims dressed in white, led by a saint carrying a staff.

1929

On March 4, Gandhi advised a boycott of foreign cloth and was arrested when a bonfire followed his speech.

On June 2, he founded the Goseva Sangh, for the protection of cows.

On April 8, two young revolutionaries, Bhagat Singh and Batu-keswar Dutt, threw two bombs into the Assembly at Delhi.

On June 12, both were sentenced to transportation for life. Many students were angry with Gandhi for his disapproval of their actions (mixed with admiration though that was.)

On December 23, he, together with Motilal Nehru, M. A. Jinnah, T. B. Sapru, and Vithalbhbhai Patel, met the viceroy to ask for promises of political change, which they did not receive.

On December 31, at the meeting of Congress, he introduced the Resolution for Complete Independence, which was passed.

1930

On January 26, a Pledge of Independence was taken all over India.

On February 15, the Congress Working Committee, meeting at Ahmedabad, authorized Gandhi and his associates to launch civil disobedience "as and when they desire and to the extent they decide." Gandhi retired to the ashram to think about what form it should take.

On March 2, he wrote to the viceroy that he would break the salt laws unless the government initiated reforms. (Salt was taxed, and people were forbidden to procure it free, as on ocean beaches.)

On March 12, at 6:30 a.m., he set out leading a band of seventy-eight ashramites from Sabarmati toward Dandi, two hundred miles away on the coast of Kathiawar. In Young India he refuted the charge by Maulana Shaukat Ali (his former ally) that his movement was not for swaraj but for Hindu raj—and therefore was against the Muslims' interest.

On March 18, at Borsad, on his way to Dandi, he said that he was out to destroy the British system of government in India, which had brought moral, material, spiritual, and cultural ruin.

On April 6, after a night of fasting and prayer, he bathed in the sea at Dandi and collected contraband salt on the beach in order to break the salt law. This was the signal for others to do likewise at

Dandi and all over the country. Altogether, sixty thousand Indians were to go to jail in this campaign.

On May 3, he wrote to the viceroy to announce his intention to lead a raid on the government saltworks at Dharsana.

On May 4, he was arrested and taken to Yeravda Jail.

In July and August, he was visited in prison by Indian liberals, who tried in vain to establish a compromise between the government and Congress.

1931

On January 26, Gandhi was released from prison.

On February 5, he went to Lucknow with Motilal Nehru, who was very ill. Nehru died there the next day.

On February 17, he went to meet the viceroy; and on March 4, the Gandhi-Irwin Agreement was issued, thereby settling the disputes over the recent civil disobedience and promising Congress participation in the upcoming Round Table Conference in London.

On March 19, he tried to convince the viceroy to repeal the death sentence passed on Bhagat Singh.

On March 24, Bhagat Singh was executed. Groups of angry young people demonstrated against Gandhi.

On April 6, he said that the Hindus ought to surrender to the claims of the Muslims and the Sikhs for separation, if those claims were made unanimously.

On August 25, he went to Simla, together with Jawaharlal Nehru and Abdul Ghaffar Khan (the leader of the Pathans), to consult with the viceroy.

On August 27, he signed a new agreement and promised to go to London as the only representative of Congress at the conference.

On September 12, he reached London and went to stay at Kingsley Hall, a settlement house in the East End. The conference was frustrating for him, but he had some success with other groups of Englishmen. On December 5, he left England for France and Switzerland, where he visited Romain Rolland, the writer who had introduced Gandhian ideas to Europe.

On December 15, he sailed from Brindisi. He reached Bombay on December 28.

On December 29, after meeting with the Working Committee and discussing civil disobedience, he sent a wire to the viceroy, asking for an interview.

1932

On January 2, the viceroy refused to see him while the threat of
civil disobedience was in the air.
 On January 4, he and Sardar Patel were arrested.

The selections from this period reflect Gandhi's concerns with his
family and his ashram, in addition to political events. Maganlal
and Chaganlal Gandhi, two of his relatives who had been part of
his innermost circle from his earliest days in South Africa, both figure tragically—Maganlal because of his death, and Chaganlal because of his disgrace. Along with Chaganlal's moral failure, Gandhi
announced Kasturba's; and in her case especially, the delinquency
will seem petty to modern readers, who will be forced to confront
Gandhi's puritanism. A warmer severity makes itself felt in his remarks when Rasik Gandhi, his grandson, died. (Rasik was the son
of Harilal but the disciple of his grandfather.) In the affairs of the
ashram, there were crises over the killing of a sick calf (Gandhi put
it out of its pain, despite the holiness of the cow to Hindus) and the
driving away of mischievous monkeys. And in the background we
glimpse the figure of his principal English disciple at the ashram,
Mirabehn, with whom his relationship was complex, intense, and
often painful.

23. My Best Comrade Gone

(vol. XXXVI, pp. 261–63)

He whom I had singled out as heir to my all is no more. Maganlal
K. Gandhi, a grandson of an uncle of mine had been with me in my
work since 1904. Maganlal's father has given all his boys to the
cause. The deceased went early this month to Bengal with Seth Jamnalalji and others, contracted a high fever whilst he was on duty
in Bihar and died under the protecting care of Brijkishore Prasad in
Patna after an illness of nine days and after receiving all the devoted
nursing that love and skill could give.

Maganlal Gandhi went with me to South Africa in 1903 in the hope
of making a bit of fortune. But hardly had he been store-keeping for
one year, when he responded to my sudden call to self-imposed poverty, joined the Phœnix settlement and never once faltered or failed

after so joining me. If he had not dedicated himself to the country's service, his undoubted abilities and indefatigable industry would have made him a merchant prince. Put in a printing press he easily and quickly mastered the secrets of the art of printing. Though he had never before handled a tool or a machine, he found himself at home in the engine room, the machine room and at the compositor's desk. He was equally at ease with the Gujarati editing of the *Indian Opinion*. Since the Phœnix scheme included domestic farming, he became a good farmer. His was I think the best garden at the settlement. It may be of interest to note that the very first issue of *Young India* published in Ahmedabad bears the marks of his labours when they were much needed.

He had a sturdy constitution which he wore away in advancing the cause to which he had dedicated himself. He closely studied and followed my spiritual career and when I presented to my co-workers *brahmacharya* as a rule of life even for married men in search of Truth, he was the first to perceive the beauty and the necessity of the practice and, though it cost him to my knowledge a terrific struggle, he carried it through to success, taking his wife along with him by patient argument instead of imposing his views on her.

When satyagraha was born, he was in the forefront. He gave me the expression which I was striving to find to give its full meaning to what the South African struggle stood for, and which for want of a better term I allowed to be recognized by the very insufficient and even misleading term "passive resistance." I wish I had the very beautiful letter he then wrote to me giving his reasons for suggesting the name सदाग्रह which I changed to सत्याग्रह . He argued out the whole philosophy of the struggle step by step and brought the reader irresistibly to his chosen name. The letter I remember was incredibly short and to the point as all his communications always were.

During the struggle he was never weary of work, shirked no task and by his intrepidity he infected everyone around him with courage and hope. When everyone went to jail, when at Phœnix courting imprisonment was like a prize to be won at my instance, he stayed back in order to shoulder a much heavier task. He sent his wife to join the women's party.

On our return to India, it was he again who made it possible to found the Ashram in the austere manner in which it was founded. Here he was called to a newer and more difficult task. He proved equal to it. Untouchability was a very severe trial for him. Just for one brief moment his heart seemed to give way. But it was only for a second. He saw that love had no bounds and that it was necessary to live down the ways of 'untouchables,' if only because the so-called higher castes were responsible for them.

The mechanical department of the Ashram was not a continuation of the Phœnix activity. Here we had to learn weaving, spinning, carding, and ginning. Again I turned to Maganlal. Though the conception was mine, his were the hands to reduce it to execution. He learnt weaving and all the other processes that cotton had to go through before it became khadi. He was a born mechanic.

When dairying was introduced in the Ashram he threw himself with zeal in the work, studied dairy literature, named every cow and became friends with every animal on the settlement.

And when tannery was added, he was undaunted and had proposed to learn the principles of tanning as soon as he got a little breathing time. Apart from his scholastic training in the High School at Rajkot, he learnt the many things he knew so well in the school of hard experience. He gathered knowledge from village carpenters, village weavers, farmers, shepherds and such ordinary folk.

He was the Director of the Technical Department of the Spinners' Association, and during the recent floods in Gujarat, Vallabhbhai put him in charge of building the new township Vithalpur.

He was an exemplary father. He trained his children—one boy and two girls, all unmarried still—so as to make them fit for dedication to the country. His son Keshu is showing very great ability in mechanical engineering, all of which he has picked up like his father from seeing ordinary carpenters and smiths at work. His eldest daughter Radha, eighteen years old, recently shouldered a difficult and delicate mission to Bihar in the interest of women's freedom. Indeed he had a good grasp of what national education should be and often engaged the teachers in earnest and critical discussion over it.

Let not the reader imagine that he knew nothing of politics. He did, but he chose the path of silent, selfless constructive service.

He was my hands, my feet and my eyes. The world knows so little of how much my so-called greatness depends upon the incessant toil and drudgery of silent, devoted, able and pure workers, men as well as women. And among them all Maganlal was to me the greatest, the best and the purest.

As I am penning these lines, I hear the sobs of the widow bewailing the death of her dear husband. Little does she realize that I am more widowed than she. And but for a living faith in God, I should become a raving maniac for the loss of one who was dearer to me than my own sons, who never once deceived me or failed me, who was a personification of industry, who was the watchdog of the Ashram in all its aspects—material, moral and spiritual. His life is an inspiration for me, a standing demonstration of the efficacy and the supremacy of the moral law. In his own life he proved visibly for me not for a few days, not for a few months, but for twenty-four long years—now alas all too short—that service of the country, service of humanity and self-realization or knowledge of God are synonymous terms.

Maganlal is dead, but he lives in his works whose imprints he who runs may read on every particle of dust in the Ashram.

Young India, 26-4-1928

24. Soul of the Ashram

(vol. XXXVI, pp. 279–81)

When Shri Vallabhbhai received the news of Maganlal Gandhi's death, he wired: "The soul of the Ashram has departed." There was no exaggeration in this. I cannot imagine the existence of Satyagraha Ashram without Maganlal. Many of my activities were started because I knew that he was there. If ever there was a person with whom I identified myself, it was Maganlal. We often have to consider whether certain matters will hurt another person, even if that person be one's own son or wife. I never had to entertain such fear with regard to Maganlal. I never hesitated to set him the most difficult tasks. I very often put him in embarrassing situations and he silently bore with them. He regarded no work as too mean.

If I were fit to be anyone's guru, I would have proclaimed him my first disciple.

In all my life I gave only one person the freedom to regard me as his guru and I had my fill of it. The fault was not his, as I could see; only I had imperfections. Anyone who becomes a guru should possess the power of conferring on the pupil the capacity to carry out whatever task is assigned to him. I had not that power and still do not have it.

But if Maganlal was not a disciple, he was certainly a servant. I am convinced that no master could possibly find a servant better or more loyal than Maganlal. This may be a conjecture, but I can assert from my experience that I have not found another servant like him. It has been my good fortune always to have found co-workers, or servants if you like, who were faithful, virtuous, intelligent and industrious. Still, Maganlal was the best of all these co-workers and servants.

The three streams of knowledge, devotion and action continuously flowed within Maganlal and, by offering his knowledge and his devotion in the *yajna* of action, he demonstrated before everyone their true form. And because in this way each action of his was full of awareness, knowledge and faith, his life attained the very summit of sannyasa. Maganlal had renounced his all. I never saw an iota of self-interest in any of his actions. He showed—not once, not for a short time but time after time for twenty-four years incessantly— that true sannyasa lay in selfless action or action without desire for reward.

Maganlal's father entrusted all his four sons to me one after another for serving the country. Maganlal was entrusted to me in 1903. He accompanied me to South Africa to earn a living. In 1904, I invited him along with other friends to embrace poverty in order to serve the country. He heard me calmly and embraced poverty. From that time on until his death, his life was an uninterrupted flow.

With each day I realize more and more that my mahatmaship, which is a mere adornment, depends on others. I have shone with the glory borrowed from my innumerable co-workers. However, no one has done more to add to this glory than Maganlal. He co-operated with me fully and with intelligence in all my activities—physical or spiritual. I see no better instance than Maganlal of one who made a tremendous effort to act as he believed. Maganlal was awake all the twenty-four hours establishing unity of thought and action. He used up all his energy in this.

If I have not exaggerated, consciously or unconsciously, in this sketch, one can say that a country in which dharma can be so embodied must triumph and so must its dharma. Hence I wish that every servant of the country should study Maganlal's life and if it commends itself to him imitate it with determination. What was possible for Maganlal is possible for every man who makes the effort. Maganlal could become a true leader because he was a true soldier and I find those who could put up with his fire weeping around me now.

This country, as also the world, is in need of true soldiers. Service of the country, service of the world, self-realization, vision of God— these are not separate things but different aspects of the same thing. Maganlal realized the truth of this in his own life and made others do so. Those who are curious can study his life and find this out.

[From Gujarati]
Navajivan, 29-4-1928

25. 'The Fiery Ordeal'
(vol. XXXVII, pp. 310–315)

> The killing of an ailing calf in the Ashram under circumstances
> described below having caused a great commotion in certain circles
> in Ahmedabad and some angry letters having been addressed to
> Gandhiji on the subject, Gandhiji has critically examined the
> question in the light of the principle of non-violence in an article
> in *Navajivan*, the substance of which is given below.   P.

I. When Killing May Be Ahimsa

An attempt is being made at the Ashram to run a small model dairy
and tannery on behalf of the Goseva Sangha. Its work in this connection brings it up, at every step, against intricate moral dilemmas that
would not arise but for the keenness to realize the Ashram ideal of
seeking Truth through the exclusive means of Ahimsa.

For instance some days back a calf having been maimed lay in agony in the Ashram. Whatever treatment and nursing was possible
was given to it. The surgeon whose advice was sought in the matter
declared the case to be past help and past hope. The suffering of the
animal was so great that it could not even turn [on] its side without
excruciating pain.

In these circumstances I felt that humanity[1] demanded that the
agony should be ended by ending life itself. I held a preliminary discussion with the Managing Committee most of whom agreed with
my view. The matter was then placed before the whole Ashram. At
the discussion a worthy neighbour vehemently opposed the idea of
killing even to end pain and offered to nurse the dying animal. The
nursing consisted in co-operation with some of the Ashram sisters in
warding the flies off the animal and trying to feed it. The ground of
the friend's opposition was that one has no right to take away life
which one cannot create. His argument seemed to me to be pointless
here. It would have point if the taking of life was actuated by self-
interest. Finally in all humility but with the clearest of convictions I
got in my presence a doctor kindly to administer the calf a quietus
by means of a poison injection. The whole thing was over in less
than two minutes.

I knew that public opinion especially in Ahmedabad would not approve of my action and that it would read nothing but *himsa* in it.

1. The Gujarati original has "ahimsa."

But I know too that performance of one's duty should be independent of public opinion. I have all along held that one is bound to act according to what to one appears to be right even though it may appear wrong to others. And experience has shown that that is the only correct course. I admit that there is always a possibility of one's mistaking right for wrong and *vice versa* but often one learns to recognize wrong only through unconscious error. On the other hand if a man fails to follow the light within for fear of public opinion or any other similar reason he would never be able to know right from wrong and in the end lose all sense of distinction between the two. That is why the poet has sung:

> The pathway of love is the ordeal of fire,
> The shrinkers turn away from it.

The pathway of ahimsa, that is, of love, one has often to tread all alone.

But the question may very legitimately be put to me: Would I apply to human beings the principle I have enunciated in connection with the calf? Would I like it to be applied in my own case? My reply is yes; the same law holds good in both the cases. The law of आत्मा पिंडे आत्मा ब्रह्मांडे (as with one so with all) admits of no exceptions, or the killing of the calf was wrong and violent. In practice however we do not cut short the sufferings of our ailing dear ones by death because as a rule we have always means at our disposal to help them and because they have the capacity to think and decide for themselves. But supposing that in the case of an ailing friend I am unable to render any aid whatever and recovery is out of the question and the patient is lying in an unconscious state in the throes of fearful agony, then I would not see any *himsa* in putting an end to his suffering by death.

Just as a surgeon does not commit *himsa* but practises the purest ahimsa when he wields his knife on his patient's body for the latter's benefit, similarly one may find it necessary under certain imperative circumstances to go a step further and sever life from the body in the interest of the sufferer. It may be objected that whereas the surgeon performs his operation to save the life of the patient, in the other case we do just the reverse. But on a deeper analysis it will be found that the ultimate object sought to be served in both the cases is the same, *viz.*, to relieve the suffering soul within from pain. In the one case you do it by severing the diseased portion from the body, in the other you do it by severing from the soul the body that has become an instrument of torture to it. In either case it is the relief of the soul within from pain that is aimed at, the body without the life within being incapable of feeling either pleasure or pain. Other circumstances can be imagined in which not to kill would spell *himsa*, while killing would be ahimsa. Suppose for instance, that I find my daughter—whose wish at the moment I have no means of ascertaining—is threatened with violation and there is no way by which I can save her, then it would be the purest form of *ahimsa* on my part to put an end to her life and surrender myself to the fury of the incensed ruffian.

But the trouble with our votaries of ahimsa is that they have made of ahimsa a blind fetish and put the greatest obstacle in the way of the spread of true ahimsa in our midst. The current (and in my opinion, mistaken) view of ahimsa has drugged our conscience and rendered us insensible to a host of other and more insidious forms of *himsa* like harsh words, harsh judgments, ill-will, anger and spite and lust of cruelty; it has made us forget that there may be far more *himsa* in the slow torture of men and animals, the starvation and exploitation to which they are subjected out of selfish greed, the wanton humiliation and oppression of the weak and the killing of their self-respect that we witness all around us today than in mere benevolent taking of life. Does anyone doubt for a moment that it would have been far more humane to have summarily put to death those who in the infamous lane of Amritsar were made by their torturers to crawl on their bellies like worms? If anyone desires to retort by saying that these people themselves today feel otherwise, that they are none the worse for their crawling, I shall have no hesitation in telling him that he does not know even the elements of ahimsa. There arise occasions in a man's life when it becomes his imperative duty to meet them by laying down his life; not to appreciate this fundamental fact of man's estate is to betray an ignorance of the foundation of ahimsa. For instance, a votary of truth would pray to God to give him death to save him from a life of falsehood. Similarly a votary of ahimsa would on bent knees implore his enemy to put him to death rather than humiliate him or make him do things unbecoming the dignity of a human being. As the poet has sung:

> The way of the Lord is meant for heroes,
> Not for cowards.

It is this fundamental misconception about the nature and scope of ahimsa, this confusing about the relative values, that is responsible for our mistaking mere non-killing for ahimsa and for the fearful amount of *himsa* that goes on in the name of ahimsa in our country. Let a man contrast the sanctimonious horror that is affected by the so-called votaries of ahimsa, at the very idea of killing an ailing animal to cut short its agony with their utter apathy and indifference to countless cruelties that are practised on our dumb cattle world. And he will begin to wonder whether he is living in the land of ahimsa or in that of conscious or unconscious hypocrisy.

It is our spiritual inertia, lack of moral courage—the courage to think boldly and look facts squarely in the face that is responsible for this deplorable state of affairs. Look at our pinjrapoles and go-shalas, many of them represent today so many dens of torture to which as a sop to conscience we consign the hapless and helpless cattle. If they could only speak they would cry out against us and say, "Rather than subject us to this slow torture give us death." I have often read this mute appeal in their eyes.

To conclude then, to cause pain or wish ill to or to take the life of any living being out of anger or a selfish intent is *himsa*. On the other hand after a calm and clear judgment to kill or cause pain to a living being with a view to its spiritual or physical benefit from a pure, selfless intent may be the purest form of ahimsa. Each such case must be judged individually and on its own merits. The final test as to its violence or non-violence is after all the intent underlying the act.

II. When Killing Is Himsa

I now come to the other crying problem that is confronting the Ashram today. The monkey nuisance has become very acute and an immediate solution has become absolutely necessary. The growing vegetables and fruit trees have become a special mark of attention of this privileged fraternity and are now threatened with utter destruction. In spite of all our efforts we have not yet been able to find an efficacious and at the same time non-violent remedy for the evil.

The matter has provoked a hot controversy in certain circles and I have received some angry letters on the subject. One of the correspondents has protested against the "killing of monkeys and wounding them by means of arrows in the Ashram." Let me hasten to assure the reader that no monkey has so far been killed in the Ashram, nor has any monkey been wounded by means of "arrows" or otherwise as imagined by the correspondent. Attempts are undoubtedly being made to drive them away and harmless arrows have been used for the purpose.

The idea of wounding monkeys to frighten them away seems to

me unbearable though I am seriously considering the question of killing them in case it should become unavoidable. But this question is not so simple or easy as the previous one.

I see a clear breach of ahimsa even in driving away monkeys, the breach would be proportionately greater if they have to be killed. For any act of injury done from self-interest whether amounting to killing or not is doubtless *himsa*.

All life in the flesh exists by some *himsa*. Hence the highest religion has been defined by a negative word ahimsa. The world is bound in a chain of destruction. In other words *himsa* is an inherent necessity for life in the body. That is why a votary of ahimsa always prays for ultimate deliverance from the bondage of flesh.

None, while in the flesh, can thus be entirely free from *himsa* because one never completely renounces the will to live. Of what use is it to force the flesh merely if the spirit refuses to co-operate? You may starve even unto death but if at the same time the mind continues to hanker after objects of the sense, your fast is a sham and a delusion. What then is the poor helpless slave to the will to live to do? How is he to determine the exact nature and the extent of *himsa* he must commit? Society has no doubt set down a standard and absolved the individual from troubling himself about it to that extent. But every seeker after truth has to adjust and vary the standard according to his individual need and to make a ceaseless endeavour to reduce the circle of *himsa*. But the peasant is too much occupied with the burden of his hard and precarious existence to have time or energy to think out these problems for himself and the cultured class instead of helping him chooses to give him the cold shoulder. Having become a peasant myself, I have no clear-cut road to go by and must therefore chalk out a path for myself and possibly for fellow peasants. And the monkey nuisance being one of the multitude of ticklish problems that stare the farmer in the face, I must find out some means by which the peasant's crops can be safeguarded against it with the minimum amount of *himsa*.

I am told that the farmers of Gujarat employ special watchmen whose very presence scares away the monkeys and saves the peasant from the necessity of killing them. That may be but it should not be forgotten that whatever efficacy this method might have, it is clearly dependent upon some measure of destruction at some time or other. For these cousins of ours are wily and intelligent beings. The moment they discover that there is no real danger for them, they refuse to be frightened even by gun shots and only gibber and howl the more when shots are fired. Let nobody therefore imagine that the

Ashram has not considered or left any method of dealing with the nuisance untried. But none of the methods that I have known up to now is free from *himsa*. Whilst therefore I would welcome any practical suggestions from the readers of *Navajivan* for coping with this problem, let the intending advisers bear in mind what I have said above and send only such solutions as they have themselves successfully tried and cause the minimum amount of injury.

Young India, 4-10-1928

26. Sunset at Morning

(vol. XL, pp. 28–30)

There have been letters and telegrams of condolence on the death of my grandson Rasik. Instead of replying individually I have thought it proper to express my gratitude to all of them through *Young India* and *Navajivan*. Those who have sent messages will forgive me for not being able to reply to them individually.

It was not my intention to notice this death, but as the news appeared in the newspapers and people have written to me, it seems proper for me to take some note of it.

As for me, the death of friends and relatives does not hurt as much as it used to. All religions forbid fear of death or grief over death. Yet we are afraid of death and grieve over the death of a dear one. And if someone dies in the prime of youth, there is greater grief. Truly speaking, death is God's eternal blessing. The body which is used up falls and the bird within flies away. So long as the bird does not die, the question of grief does not arise.

When despite this there is grief on the death of a relative, it only shows our selfishness and delusion. For the past many years, I have been trying to rid myself of this delusion. Hence the shock on hearing news of Rasik's death was not severe. What shock there was, was due to selfishness.

Rasik was seventeen years of age. He had been under my care from childhood and, like other boys, he was being given training in national service. He was an active, clever and bright boy. He was sturdy and brave. He was always first in taking up work that called for courage. During the past one year his boisterousness was turning into strength. He was a student of the *Gita*. He was an expert carder and spinner. Once or twice he took to spinning continuously for twenty-four hours—and did it successfully.

My youngest son Devdas is working at the Jamia Millia in Delhi. He teaches spinning and Hindi to the students there. About four months back, he had asked for the services of Rasik and another grandson of mine, Navin, to teach carpentry and weaving. Both Rasik and Navin had gone to Delhi and were doing good work there. Earlier, because of his keen desire to serve, Rasik had gone to Bardoli. He became popular wherever he went. The selfish thought that Providence took away such a promising worker made me grieve; but then I thought that Providence is always just and is therefore kind and it would get work out of Rasik. By this faith I have been consoled.

After going to Delhi, Rasik turned a devotee. When I was on my way back *via* Delhi after the Congress session, Rasik had told me that he had entered his seventeenth year. At that time, like many other boys, he took certain vows: first to eat only three things at a meal; secondly, to have only three meals a day, and thirdly, to complete within two years the study of the *Ramayana* with commentary. Knowing his restless temperament, I had warned him. But he told me that he found nothing difficult in this and that he liked to read the *Ramayana*. I was pleased.

With reference to these vows, Rasik wrote to me the following letter,[1] on the 18th of January. On the 8th of February he passed away.

Very few get the care that Rasik received. He was a dear nephew and student of Devdas and had received his matchless service. Dr. Ansari was not merely his physician; he was like a father to him. Dr. Sharma was always at his beck and call. Two nurses were appointed by the doctors to nurse him. Muslim friends from the Jamia left nothing to be desired so far as nursing him was concerned. The Hindus who learnt of his illness were at his service, day and night. I am indebted to all of them. Rasik had realized at such an early age the value of service and duty and engrossed himself in it; taken difficult vows, regarded them as easy to fulfil and read the *Gita* with enthusiasm having vowed to finish study of the *Ramayana* in two years' time. He met death while cherishing such noble sentiments and receiving unsurpassed care. Everyone will envy such a death. And if a grandfather like me feels grieved at this, it is purely selfishness and infatuation.

[From Gujarati]
Navajivan, 24-2-1929

1. Not translated here.

27. Letter to Chhaganlal Joshi
(vol. XXXIX, pp. 434–35)

Larkana,
Saturday [February 9, 1929]

Chi. Chhaganlal,

I have no letter from you today. Rasik has passed away. As I came out after finishing my bath and was preparing to sit down for my meal, I got a telegram from Devdas. I read the telegram and sat down for the meal. Work is going on as usual. I feel grief at Rasik's passing away, but see plainly that it is the result of selfishness. I had entertained hopes of getting much work done through his body and certainly, therefore, I am suffering today as we suffer for selfish reasons when a machine breaks down. If we think of the one within who was driving the machine, we should, on the contrary, be happy, for the cage had become old, was decaying and the swan flew away. There is no cause in this for mourning. I know this and that is why, suppressing my selfish grief, I go on with my work. When one machine breaks down, the rest of us should improve our own machines, make them work more and thus make up for the loss of the one that has broken down.

I shall reach Hyderabad on Wednesday evening. I shall leave the place on Friday morning to go to Mirpurkhas. From there I shall take a train to Delhi.

Let me say one thing. After the death of Maganlal and Rasik, I put increasingly greater value on Ashram work, that is, on ordinary activities. I feel that, if we had served the bodies of these two, they would not have perished. This does not imply any want in the service rendered to them at Patna or Delhi, but has reference to the scientific method of service in the Ashram. Their destiny, however, took them to distant places and they received royal service at those places.

Blessings from
BAPU

28. The Ethics of Burning
(vol. XL, pp. 84–85)

[March 5, 1929]

It will be as late as March 17 before this article is in the reader's hand. I write this on the steamer on my way from Calcutta to Rangoon, so that the spectacle of what took place on March 4 in Shraddhanand Park is still fresh in my mind. I hope that the lathis of hundreds of thousands of policemen will not be able to extinguish the fire that was kindled in that park on that day.

For dharma will not be extinguished by anyone trying to do so. Once it manifests itself in a man's heart, it does not perish even when his body perishes. The fire of dharma lit by the world's men of destiny, prophets, and Hindu and Muslim saints has continued to burn even after their bodies have perished.

But some may ask: Can burning of clothes be dharma? It is my humble opinion that the dharma of burning clothes can be proved. We burn or bury a body from which life has departed. We burn the things which have been contaminated. He who discards liquor will throw it away. However costly the liquor, when one has given up drinking, one will not commit the sin of selling it to another. If costly things are contaminated by the plague, they are burnt. It has been regarded as a dharma to do so. The Johannesburg Municipality did not feel hurt in burning down the expensive building of the market and the provisions contained in it when the plague broke out in Johannesburg. It considered it a duty to do so. There may well be a difference of opinion on the necessity of consigning these things to the flames. But even those opposed to it will concede that burning may become a dharma for those who believe that it is necessary to do so.

Likewise, it is my humble view that it is the dharma of every Indian to burn foreign cloth. After the insolent and cruel performance of the Calcutta police, that dharma has acquired a new urgency. Those who before that event had doubts about the need to burn foreign cloth should have none after it.

No one will doubt that it is our dharma to boycott foreign cloth which has impoverished our country and through which over 60 crores of rupees are drained out of India every year. If this is conceded, what are we to do with the boycotted cloth if not burn it? Some say that it should be given away to the poor. Those who make this suggestion do not see that thereby they insult both themselves and the poor. They insult the poor when they consider them inferior to themselves, and insulting the poor they insult themselves. Do not the poor have self-respect? Do they not want swaraj? Why should we give to the poor a thing which we regard as infected? We do have the mean habit of offering to the poor left-overs from our plates. Shall we add to that meanness by giving them the clothes which we ourselves have discarded?

Let us consider what sort of clothes they are. The clothes I have burnt till today comprised handkerchiefs, clean or unclean black caps, neckties, collars, socks, thin long shirts, blouses, fine saris, etc. What clothes out of these could one give to the poor? And how strange would it be to create in the poor a fondness for them? If we do so, how shall we seek to boycott foreign cloth?

And, finally, no one can doubt the necessity of the bonfire after that scene at Shraddhanand Park. I had told the police that there was no intention of breaking the law for the purpose of burning foreign cloth. Only after the lawyers had given their opinion that the police had not correctly interpreted the section of law on the basis of which the order prohibiting the burning was issued, was it decided to burn clothes in that park. Despite this when the police attempted fruit-lessly to put out the fire merely to annoy the people, the latter were certainly agitated and then started burning at many spots in the park. And that led to some exchange of blows between the police and the people. I believe it will be a gross insult to India if, even after such insolence, foreign cloth is not burnt in every home in every village. After this action of the police, people should have confidence in place of whatever doubt they may have had about the success of the boycott.

[From Gujarati]
Navajivan, 17-3-1929

29. My Shame and Sorrow

(vol. XL, pp. 209–12)

I have been greatly exercised in my mind as to whether or not to write on this topic. But after fullest consideration I have come to the conclusion that not to write would constitute a grave dereliction of duty. Many friends look upon the Satyagraha Ashram, the present Udyoga Mandir, as a sacred institution and send donations on the death of dear ones in respect of its manifold activities which I have thankfully accepted.

Recently some lapses of a serious character have been brought to light on the part of some members of this institution. I have freely spoken about them to the inmates of the Mandir at prayer times. But I do not consider this publicity sufficient. My relations with the readers of *Navajivan* are not commercial, but have a strictly moral base. They are naturally founded on the assumed purity of myself and the institution. I have time and again written on the sin of secrecy. Personally I have no secrets. It is, therefore, necessary for me to take the reader into my confidence. If he has assumed me and the institution to be pure it is but meet that he should know our impurity also.

Chhaganlal Gandhi, elder brother of the late Maganlal Gandhi, is a cousin of mine. He has been like a son to me and was brought up by me under my care from his youth. He has been discovered to be engaged in a series of petty larcenies over a number of years. I should not have felt the aberration so much if the repentance had been voluntary, but as it was the thing was detected quite accidentally and brought to light by a namesake, the vigilant Secretary of the Mandir. Indeed Chhaganlal Gandhi even made an unsuccessful attempt to conceal the guilt. He is now apparently consumed with remorse and is shedding bitter tears. He has, further, of his own accord left the Mandir, but I have hopes that he will one day return to the Mandir completely purified and the Mandir will then welcome him back to its fold with open arms. His larcenies seem to have been of a very trivial character involving very inconsiderable sums of money on the whole. I am inclined to treat the lapse in the nature of a disease. So far as one can see these thefts have not meant any pecuniary loss to the Mandir.

Chhaganlal Gandhi had laid up an amount of about ten thousand from his savings. I do not wish here to enter into the history of these savings. This amount he made over to the Mandir only a few months ago at my suggestion not from any impulse of generosity but from a sense of the duty pointed out. Private possession of wealth being inconsistent with principles of the Mandir, this ownership of not an inconsiderable sum of money jarred on me and I intimated to him accordingly. After holding consultations with his wife and two sons, none of whom desired its use for their sakes, Chhaganlal made it over unconditionally to the Udyoga Mandir. So far as I am aware Chhaganlal at present owns no property whatever except his share in the ancestral property. When I think of Chhaganlal Gandhi's record of thirty years of service and his artlessness and simplicity on the one hand and these lapses on the other, I am perplexed and take refuge in the reflection that the working of the Law of Karma is inscrutable. This is but one chapter of the story of my shame and sorrow.

Now for the second chapter. I have lavished unstinted praise on Kasturbai (Mrs. Gandhi) in my *Autobiography*. She has stood by me in the changes of my life. I believe hers to have been an immaculate life. It is true that her renunciation has not been based on an intelligent appreciation of the fundamentals of life, but from a blind wifely devotion. At any rate she has never hindered me in my progress towards my ideals. By her exemplary care and nursing during my illness she has easily commanded a patient's gratitude. I have spared her no ordeals. She has been a tower of strength to me in my self-imposed vow of *brahmacharya*. But the white surface of these virtues is not without the glaringly dark spots. Although impelled by her sense of wifely devotion she has renounced so far as the world knows earthly possessions, longing for them has persisted. As a result, about a year or so ago she had laid up a sum of about a couple of hundred rupees for her own use out of the small sums presented to her by various people on different occasions. The rule of the Mandir, however, is that even such personal presents may not be kept for private use. Her action, therefore, amounted to theft. Fortunately for her and the Mandir, thieves broke into her room about two years ago. This incident resulted in the discovery of the foregoing misappropriation. For a moment her remorse appeared to be genuine. Events have proved, however, that it was only momentary. Evidently it did not root out the desire for possession. Recently some unknown visitors to the Mandir brought her a sum of four rupees. Instead of handing over this sum, according to the Mandir rules, to the Secretary she kept it with her. A tried inmate of the Mandir was present when the donation was made. It was his obvious duty to put Kasturbai on her guard; but impelled by a false sense of courtesy he remained instead a helpless witness of the wrong. After Chhaganlal's episode the members of the Udyoga Mandir became suddenly vigilant.

The witness of Kasturbai's lapse informed Chhaganlal Joshi about it. Joshi courageously, though in fear and trembling, went to Kasturbai and demanded the money. Kasturbai felt the humiliation and quickly returned four rupees and promised never to repeat the offence. I believe her remorse to be genuine. She has agreed to withdraw herself from the institution should any other previous aberration be discovered against her or in case she should lapse into such conduct again. Her penitenance has been accepted by Udyoga Mandir and she will remain there just as before and accompany me in my tours.

Now for the third chapter. Three years ago a widow was living in the Ashram. All believed her to be pure. About the same time a young man brought up in an orphanage too was living in the Ashram. His conduct appeared to be correct. He was at that time unmarried. He seduced the widow. This is comparatively old history now. But the lapse was discovered only recently. That such immorality should have occurred in the institution that imposes *brahmacharya* on its inmates is a serious tragedy. Alas for the Mandir!

If those who have believed in me and the Mandir desert us after these revelations it will serve two purposes at a stroke. Both they and myself will be extricated from the false position and I would welcome the relief and the lightening of my burden it will bring me. If all good men in the Mandir left it in disgust the problem would again be readily solved. Equally handy would the solution be if all bad men left the Mandir. Lastly, if I could bring myself to flee from the Mandir that too would be a solution. But life's riddles are not solved quite so easily. None of these things will happen. Nature's processes work mysteriously.

I hold the manifestation of the corruption in the Mandir to be merely the reflection of the wrong in myself. Nothing has been further from my thoughts in writing the above lines than to arrogate to myself superior virtue. On the contrary, I sincerely believe that the impurity of my associates is but the manifestation of the hidden wrong within me. I have never claimed perfection for myself. Who knows my aberrations in the realm of thought have reacted on the environment round me. The epithet of "Mahatma" has always galled me and now it almost sounds to me like a term of abuse.

But what am I to do? Should I flee or commit suicide or embark on an endless fast or immure myself alive in the Mandir or refuse to handle public finance or public duty? I can do none of these things mechanically. I must wait for the voice within. I am an incorrigible optimist. I have the hope of attaining swaraj even through the purification of the Mandir. But I must first try, discover and remove my own shortcomings. Therefore in spite of the full knowledge of the grave shortcomings and failures of the Udyoga Mandir, I still live on the hope that it will one day justify its existence and reconvert itself into the Satyagraha Ashram.

It seems to me therefore that for the present I must go on with it, even though I have to proclaim its shortcomings to the world again and again. An activity commenced in God's name may be given up only at His bidding. And when He wishes this activity of mine to be brought to a close He will surely prompt society to hound me out of its pale and I hug to myself the hope that even in that dread hour of retribution I shall still have power to declare my faith in Him. Let me once more reiterate my opinion about the Mandir. Imperfect as it always has been, full of corruption as it has been discovered to be, this institution is my best creation. I hope to see God through its aid. I wish to be judged by the measure of its soundness. Revelations put me on my guard; they make me search within; they humble me. But they do not shake my faith in it. This may be a gross delusion on my part. If so I can say with the immortal Tulsidas that even as one who sees silver in the mother of pearl or water in mirage till his ignorance is dispelled so will my delusion be a reality to me till the eyes of my understanding are opened.

The Bombay Chronicle, 8-4-1929

30. Letter to Chhaganlal Joshi

(vol. XL, pp. 347–49)

6.25 a.m., Silence Day, May 6, 1929

Chi. Chhaganlal,

Your recent letters make me feel a little worried. I feel that you are forcing yourself to do what is beyond your strength. Do nothing out of false regard for me. I know that you find it difficult to stand alone. Do not believe that the dairy, or for that matter even the weaving factory, should run in any circumstances. I have made it my profession in life to break up homes and have felt no wrench in the heart at any time while doing so. I started doing this in the year 1891; that is, ever since I became independent, I have been doing nothing but that. I set up a home in Bombay and broke it up; did the same in Rajkot, broke it up and went to Bombay at a mere suggestion by Kevalram.[1] Then I broke up the home in India to go to South Africa for one year only. The books remained unused, the furniture and other household things became useless, the dress became useless and I had to buy everything new. I had built up the home in Natal with much thought,

1. Kevalram Mavji Dave, a Rajkot lawyer who encouraged Gandhi to go to London to study law.

had exercised much care in buying furniture of my liking. I had furnished a room as a gymnasium. I threw up all this in a moment. I gave away many of the things, something to this friend and something to another. I returned to Bombay and set up a home in Girgaum. Manilal fell ill there and was at death's door. I decided that we could not live in that air. After hunting for a house everywhere, I chose the "Viller Villa." I got a rent-note drawn up and signed it. Revashanker, too, came to live with us. I took out a first-class season ticket, and rented an office in Bombay in Payne Gilbert's chambers. At last, I felt, I had settled down. Just then came a cable: 'Come to South Africa.' I left Ba under the care of Chhaganlal and went to South Africa, accompanied by some youths who cared to come with me. There was the same story there. I cannot tell now how much money I must have wasted on furniture. But I do not remember having ever felt a wrench in the heart in all these wild adventures. I felt lighter every time and convinced that that was God's will and the change was for my good. I shall, then, feel no wrench in my heart in breaking up this Ashram and building a new one. Yes, I crave for one thing—sincerity. Only those of you who can live sincerely may remain. I would not say that those who remain out of a false sense of shame or under pressure from others are sincere in what they do. Sincerity may sometimes appear cruel. You should not shrink from appearing to be cruel to me. Be sincere at any cost. Do not act unnaturally even for a minute. Please understand the meaning of the word *kritrim* here; it does not mean "making false show," but means "unnatural."[2] Do what your conscience bids you do. That will be for your good and through that you will prosper in the end. This is what you can learn from me; though, to be sure, few have learnt it. You will be surprised when I tell you that Maganlal earned the certificate of having done so. You will remember how he used to oppose me in meetings. Sometimes he saw that I had felt upset. He would, on such occasions, come and tell me the next morning. "Bapu, haven't you taught me to oppose you whenever I do not agree with you?" I would then smile at him and calm down. Once we had an argument about spinning. I took one side and he another. He did not understand what I was saying and all the time I was burning with misery. He saw the expression on my face and he, too, felt miserable. But he did not give up his stand. I saw in the end that my argument was not based on experience. The matter was trivial, but Maganlal felt that he would be doing no service to me by yielding to my whims. I recollect many

2. Gandhi uses the English word.

such incidents. There was a reason, too, why he clung to me. He himself explained it in one of his letters. I did not remember the matter at all.

What more shall I write and how may I reassure you so that you may have no fear? You should be as fearless as I am. That requires only faith in God. Who are we? A mere imaginary point such as cannot be drawn on a board. He is the only Reality and is all that exists. Doesn't the *Gita* say, "*Sarvata eva sarva*"? Why should we, then, form all kinds of plans in our minds? We should do, to the best of our understanding, the task that lies at hand and live with our hearts for ever light.

Blessings from
BAPU

[PS.]

I have written this letter to you after writing a similar letter to Mirabehn. She has also made me feel worried. She has asked for permission to come to Nellore and join me. I have had to send a wire to her saying "No." And so I have written a letter to soothe her.

I have not read this letter after finishing it.

From a photostat of the Gujarati

31. 'Food Faddists'

(vol. XLI, pp. 34–36)

I have been known as a crank, faddist, mad man. Evidently the reputation is well deserved. For wherever I go, I draw to myself cranks, faddists and mad men. Andhra has its fair share of all these. They often find their way to Sabarmati. No wonder then that I found these specimens in abundance during my Andhra tour. But I propose to introduce to the reader only one fellow crank who by his living faith in his mission compelled my admiration and induced me to plunge into a dietetic experiment which I had left unfinished at the age of 20 when I was a student in London. This is Sundaram Gopalrao of Rajahmundry. The ground was prepared for him by a survey superintendent whom I met at Vizagapatam and who told me he was practically living on raw food. Gopalrao has a nature-cure establishment in Rajahmundry, to which he devotes the whole of his time. He said to me, "The hip-baths and other kindred appliances are good so far as they go. But even they are artificial. To be rid of disease it is necessary to do away with fire in the preparation of foods. We must take everything in its vital state even as animals do."

"Would you advise me to adopt entirely raw diet?," I asked.

"Certainly, why not? I have cured cases of chronic dyspepsia in old men and women through a balanced diet containing germinating seeds," was Gopalrao's reply.

"But surely there should be a transition stage," I gently remonstrated.

"No such stage is necessary," rejoined Gopalrao. "Uncooked food, including uncooked starch and proteid are any day more digestible than cooked. Try it and you will feel all the better for it."

"Do you take the risk? If the cremation ceremony takes place in Andhra, the people will cremate your body with mine," I said.

"I take the risk," said Gopalrao.

"Then send me your soaked wheat. I commence from today," I said.

Poor Gopalrao sent the soaked wheat. Kasturbai, not knowing that it could possibly be meant for me, gave it to the volunteers who finished it. So I had to commence the experiment the following day—9th May. It is therefore now a month when I am writing these notes.

I am none the worse for the experiment. Though I have lost over five pounds in weight, my vitality is unimpaired. During the last eight days the weight has shown a decided tendency to increase.

Fellow faddists should know what I am doing.

I take generally eight *tolas* of germinating wheat, eight *tolas* of sweet almonds reduced to a paste, eight *tolas* of green leaves spinach or pounded [sic], six sour lemons, and two ounces of honey. Wheat is replaced twice or thrice during the week by an equal quantity of germinating gram. And when gram is taken in the place of wheat, cocoanut milk replaces almond paste. The food is divided into two parts, the first meal is taken at 11 a.m., the second at 6.15 p.m. The only thing touched by fire is water. I take in the morning and once more during the day boiling water, lemon and honey.

Both wheat and gram germinate in 36 hours. The grain is soaked in water for twenty-four hours. The water is then strained. The grain is then left in a piece of wet khadi overnight. You find it sprouting in the morning ready for use. Those who have sound teeth need not pound the grain at all. For cocoanut milk a quarter of the kernel is grated fine and you squeeze the milk through a piece of stout khadi.

It is unnecessary to enter into further details. What I have given is enough for diet reformers to help me with their suggestions. I have lived for years on uncooked fruits and nuts but never before beyond a fortnight on uncooked cereals and pulses. Let those therefore who know anything of unfired food favour me with literature or their own experiences.

I publish the facts of this experiment because I attach the greatest importance to it. If it succeeds it enables serious men and women to make revolutionary changes in their mode of living. It frees women from a drudgery which brings no happiness but which brings disease in its train. The ethical value of uncooked food is incomparable. Economically this food has possibilities which no cooked food can have. I therefore seek the sympathetic help of all medical men and laymen who are interested in reformed dietetics.

Let no one blindly copy the experiment. I have not Gopalrao's faith. I do not claim success for it yet. I am moving cautiously. The facts are published so as to enable me to compare notes with fellow food reformers.

Young India, 13-6-1929

32. Letter to Mirabehn
(vol. XLI, pp. 78–79)

June 24, 1929

Chi. Mira,

It is well you do not want me to speak to you tomorrow on the incident. But I did want, after witnessing the exhibition, to reduce to writing my thoughts. I do that now.

The exhibition is proof of the correctness of my statement. None else would have felt like committing suicide over a simple innocent remark of mine. You want to be with me in my tours occasionally, it is true; you want to come to the Ashram leaving your work at least every four months. You recognize these desires as limitations. I make allowance for them. But why feel disturbed when I tell you what I feel to be the truth that they are not themselves the disease, but they are symptoms of a deep-seated disease which has not been touched. If you were not what I have described you to be, you would rejoice over my drawing attention to the disease and courageously strive to overcome it. Instead, you simply collapsed, much to my grief and anxiety.

This disease is idolatry. If it is not, why hanker after my company! Why touch or kiss the feet that must one day be dead cold? There is nothing in the body. The truth I represent is before you. Experience and effort will unravel it before you, never my association in the manner you wish. When it comes in the course of business you will, like others, gain from it and more because of your devotion. Why so helplessly rely on me? Why do everything to please me? Why not independently of me and even in spite of me? I have put no restrictions on your liberty, save those you have welcomed. Break the idol to pieces if you can and will. If you cannot, I am prepared to suffer with you. But you must give me the liberty to issue warnings.

My diagnosis may be wrong. If so, it is well. Strive with me cheerfully instead of being nerve-broken. Everyone but you takes my blows without being unstrung.

If your effort has hitherto failed, what does it matter? You have hitherto dealt mechanically with symptoms. There you have had considerable success. But if I say you have not been able to touch the root, why weep over it? I do not mind your failures. They are but stepping-stones to success. You must rise from this torpor never to fall into it again.

I have done. May God be with you.

Love.

BAPU

33. Unfired Food

(vol. XLI, pp. 306–7)

Instead of hopeful progress I have to report a tragedy this week. In spite of great carefulness in experimentation along an unbeaten track, I have been laid low. A mild but persistent attack of dysentery has sent me to bed and not only to cooked food but also to goat's milk. Dr. Harilal Desai used all his skill and patience to save me from having to go back to milk, which I had left last November in the hope of not having to go back to it, but he saw that he could not reduce the mucus and the traces of blood that persistently appeared in the bowels without making me take curds. At the time of writing this therefore I have had two portions of curds, with what effect I shall note at the foot of this article which is being written on Sunday night.

It appears that I was not digesting the raw foods I was taking, and what I had mistaken for good motions were precursors of dysentery. The other conditions including vitality being good, I had no cause to suspect any evil.

My companions too have one after another fallen off, except four, of whom one has been on raw food for nearly a year with great success as he thinks.

The companions have left off because they were feeling weak and were losing weight week by week.

Thus Sjt. Gopalrao's claim that unfired food is suitable for any stomach and can be taken with impunity by young and old, sick and healthy, is to say the least of it 'unproven.' This apparent failure should serve as a warning to the zealots that they should move most cautiously and be scrupulously exact in their statements and careful in their deductions.

I call the failure apparent, because I have the same faith in unfired food today that I first had nearly forty years ago. The failure is due to my gross ignorance of the practice of unfired food and of right combinations. Some of its good results are really striking. No one has suffered seriously. My dysentery has been painless. Every doctor who has examined me has found me otherwise in better health than before. For my companions I have been a blind guide leading the blind. I have sadly missed the guidance of someone who has known the virtue of unfired food and who would have the patience of a scientist.

But if I regain my health and have a little leisure, I hope to revert to the experiment with better hope in that I shall know what mistakes to avoid. As a searcher for Truth I deem it necessary to find the perfect food for a man to keep body, mind and soul in a sound condition. I believe that the search can only succeed with unfired food, and that in the limitless vegetable kingdom there is an effective substitute for milk, which, every medical man admits, has its drawbacks and which is designed by nature not for man but for babies and young ones of lower animals. I should count no cost too dear for making a search which in my opinion is so necessary from more points of view than one; therefore I still seek information and guidance from kindred spirits. To those who are not in sympathy with this phase of my life and who out of their love for me are anxious about me, I give my assurance that I shall not embark upon any experiment that would endanger my other activities. I am of opinion that though I have been making such experiments since the age of 18, I have not often suffered from serious illness and have been able to preserve tolerably good health. But I would also like them to feel with me that so long as God wants me for any work on this earth, He will preserve me from harm and prevent me from going too far.

Those who are making the experiment must not give it up because of the temporary check I have received. Let them learn from the causes of my failure.

1. If there is the slightest danger of insufficient mastication, let the ingredients be finely pulverized and dissolved in the mouth instead of being swallowed.

2. If there is an undissolved residue in the mouth, it must be put out.

3. Grains and pulses should be used sparingly.

4. Green vegetables should be well washed and scraped before being used and should also be used sparingly.

5. Fresh and dried fruits (soaked) and nuts should be the staples at least in the beginning stages.

6. Milk should not be given up till the unfired foods have been taken without any harm for a sufficiently long period. All the literature I have read points to fruits and nuts with only a small quantity of green vegetables as a perfect food.

(I am able to report on Tuesday morning that diluted curds are working well.)

Young India, 22-8-1929

34. Some Thoughts on U.P. Tour

(vol. XLII, pp. 220–21)

The long awaited U.P. tour was by the grace of God finished on 24th instant. Friends had feared a breakdown in my health but the wall of protection that Acharya Kripalani and the other companions had erected round me ensured for me as much comfort and rest as was necessary and possible in the circumstances. The brunt of this protection however fell upon the broad shoulders of Acharya Kripalani who was sometimes really angry and more often feigned anger when leaders of places visited wanted more time and more appointments or when people insisted on seeing me or crowding into my car. The result was that he came in some places to be regarded as a fiend without feeling, and without consideration for others. He quietly pocketed all these epithets and went about his way. But as we parted at Agra, his message to me was, "I have neither the heart nor the aptitude for offering apologies. I do my duty as I know how and there my task ends. You should offer all the necessary apologies for me." Acharya Kripalani when I first met him in 1915 was already a seasoned warrior. He was then earning Rs. 400 per month but was a *brahmachari* taking only Rs. 40 for himself and sending the balance to Dr. Choithram who was conducting a *brahmacharya* ashram at Hyderabad. He became my most efficient door-keeper in Champaran[1] when I was besieged by crowds of eager and pressing ryots.

In utter disregard of consequences he threw himself in the thick of the non-co-operation fight and from professor became a khadi hawker and organizer. When the call came from Sardar Vallabhbhai, he responded and gave a new lease of life to the Vidyapith. And now surrounded by a band of faithful workers he is conducting khadi ashrams in the U.P. with a zeal which any young man may well envy. For the sake of his country he has exiled himself from Sind and is equally at home with Biharis as with U.P. men. At the pressing instance of the A.I.S.A. he has become its co-agent with Pandit Jawaharlal Nehru for the U.P. And it was in this capacity that he supervised the tour. I am sure that those who came under his lash will forgive him his quick temper. I wish we had more workers of the Kripalani type. Their quick temper would be forgotten in the quick and sure invigorating change that their solid work will bring about in our enervating surroundings.

Even the hopes that Acharya Kripalani had to disappoint, I know, sprang from affection of which I had as much abundance in U.P. as in Andhra and elsewhere. Indeed the attention received by me and my companions was often embarrassing. Where one volunteer was wanted, ten were ready. The hospitality was imprudently lavish. And I regret to have to confess that we were not always insistent on refusing such as was unnecessary. My own experience is that a gentle but firm refusal to accept what is not strictly needed for creature comforts is never mistaken for rudeness.

My advice to workers is:

1. Do not waste volunteers. It is no sign of hospitality, it is sign of want of organizing ability.

2. Take national workers at their word. If, for instance, they say they do not need sweets, believe them and do not provide sweets to them. Know that every rupee spent on unnecessary things is so much taken away from the mouths of the semi-starved millions.

1. In 1917.

3. Keep your appointments rigidly to the minute.

4. Having made promises fulfil them at the cost of your life. Let your word even in small matters be as good as your bond.

There was too much dilatoriness and loose talk among organizers. The result was loss of time, disappointments and vexation of spirit.

I must postpone a consideration of the provincial service and one or two other matters to the next issue.

Young India, 28-11-1929

35. When I Am Arrested
(vol. XLII, pp. 496–98)

It must be taken for granted that, when civil disobedience is started, my arrest is a certainty. It is, therefore, necessary to consider what should be done when the event takes place.

On the eve of my arrest in 1922 I had warned co-workers against any demonstration of any kind save that of mute, complete non-violence, and had insisted that constructive work which alone could organize the country for civil disobedience should be prosecuted with the utmost zeal. The first part of the instructions was, thanks be to God, literally and completely carried out—so completely that it has enabled an English noble contemptuously to say, 'Not a dog barked.' For me when I learnt in the jail that the country had remained absolutely non-violent, it was a demonstration that the preaching of non-violence had had its effect and that the Bardoli decision[1] was the wisest thing to do. It would be foolish to speculate what might have happened if 'dogs' had barked and violence had been let loose on my arrest. One thing, however, I can say, that in that event there would have been no independence resolution at Lahore, and no Gandhi with his confidence in the power of non-violence left to contemplate taking the boldest risks imaginable.

Let us, however, think of the immediate future. This time on my arrest there is to be no mute, passive non-violence, but non-violence of the activest type should be set in motion, so that not a single believer in non-violence as an article of faith for the purpose of achieving India's goal should find himself free or alive at the end of the

1. Of February 1922 to suspend the civil disobedience movement; *vide* Vol. XXII, pp. 377–81.

effort to submit any longer to the existing slavery. It would be, therefore, the duty of everyone to take up such civil disobedience or civil
resistance as may be advised and conducted by my successor, or as
might be taken up by the Congress. I must confess, that at the
present moment, I have no all-India successor in view. But I have sufficient faith in the co-workers and in the mission itself to know that
circumstances will give the successor. This peremptory condition
must be patent to all that he must be an out and out believer in the
efficacy of non-violence for the purpose intended. For without that
living faith in it he will not be able at the crucial moment to discover
a non-violent method.

It must be parenthetically understood that what is being said here
in no way fetters the discretion and full authority of the Congress.
The Congress will adopt only such things said here that may commend themselves to Congressmen in general. If the nature of these
instructions is to be properly understood, the organic value of the
charter of full liberty given to me by the Working Committee should
be adequately appreciated. Non-violence, if it does not submit to any
restrictions upon its liberty, subjects no one and no institution to
any restriction whatsoever, save what may be self-imposed or voluntarily adopted. So long as the vast body of Congressmen continue to
believe in non-violence as the only policy in the existing circumstances and have confidence not only in the *bona fides* of my successor and those who claim to believe in non-violence as an article of
faith to the extent indicated but also in the ability of the successor
wisely to guide the movement, the Congress will give him and them
its blessings and even give effect to these instructions and his.

So far as I am concerned, my intention is to start the movement
only through the inmates of the Ashram and those who have submitted to its discipline and assimilated the spirit of its methods. Those,
therefore, who will offer battle at the very commencement will be
unknown to fame. Hitherto the Ashram has been deliberately kept
in reserve in order that by a fairly long course of discipline it might
acquire stability. I feel that if the Satyagraha Ashram is to deserve the
great confidence that has been reposed in it and the affection lavished upon it by friends, the time has arrived for it to demonstrate
the qualities implied in the word satyagraha. I feel that our self-
imposed restraints have become subtle indulgences, and the prestige
acquired has provided us with privileges and conveniences of which
we may be utterly unworthy. These have been thankfully accepted in
the hope that some day we would be able to give a good account of
ourselves in terms of satyagraha. And if at the end of nearly 15 years

of its existence, the Ashram cannot give such a demonstration, it and I should disappear, and it would be well for the nation, the Ashram and me.

When the beginning is well and truly made I expect the response from all over the country. It will be the duty then of everyone who wants to make the movement a success to keep it non-violent and under discipline. Everyone will be expected to stand at his post except when called by his chief. If there is spontaneous mass response, as I hope there will be, and if previous experience is any guide, it will largely be self-regulated. But everyone who accepts non-violence whether as an article of faith or policy would assist the mass movement. Mass movements have, all over the world, thrown up unexpected leaders. This should be no exception to the rule. Whilst, therefore, every effort imaginable and possible should be made to restrain the forces of violence, civil disobedience once begun this time cannot be stopped and must not be stopped so long as there is a single civil resister left free or alive. A votary of satyagraha should find himself in one of the following states:

1. In prison or in an analogous state; or
2. Engaged in civil disobedience; or
3. Under orders at the spinning-wheel, or at some constructive work advancing swaraj.

Young India, 27-2-1930

36. Letter to Lord Irwin
(vol. XLIII, pp. 2–8)

Satyagraha Ashram, Sabarmati,
March 2, 1930

Dear Friend,

Before embarking on civil disobedience and taking the risk I have dreaded to take all these years, I would fain approach you and find a way out.

My personal faith is absolutely clear. I cannot intentionally hurt anything that lives, much less fellow human beings, even though they may do the greatest wrong to me and mine. Whilst, therefore, I hold the British rule to be a curse, I do not intend harm to a single Englishman or to any legitimate interest he may have in India.

I must not be misunderstood. Though I hold the British rule in India to be a curse, I do not, therefore, consider Englishmen in general to be worse than any other people on earth. I have the privilege of claiming many Englishmen as dearest friends. Indeed much that I have learnt of the evil of British rule is due to the writings of frank and courageous Englishmen who have not hesitated to tell the unpalatable truth about that rule.

And why do I regard the British rule as a curse?

It has impoverished the dumb millions by a system of progressive exploitation and by a ruinously expensive military and civil administration which the country can never afford.

It has reduced us politically to serfdom. It has sapped the foundations of our culture. And, by the policy of cruel disarmament, it has degraded us spiritually. Lacking the inward strength, we have been reduced, by all but universal disarmament, to a state bordering on cowardly helplessness.

In common with many of my countrymen, I had hugged the fond hope that the proposed Round Table Conference might furnish a solution. But, when you said plainly that you could not give any assurance that you or the British Cabinet would pledge yourselves to support a scheme of full Dominion Status, the Round Table Conference could not possibly furnish the solution for which vocal India is consciously, and the dumb millions are unconsciously, thirsting. Needless to say there never was any question of Parliament's verdict being anticipated. Instances are not wanting of the British Cabinet, in anticipation of the Parliamentary verdict, having pledged itself to a particular policy.

The Delhi interview[1] having miscarried, there was no option for Pandit Motilal Nehru and me but to take steps to carry out the solemn resolution of the Congress arrived at in Calcutta at its Session in 1928.

But the Resolution of Independence[2] should cause no alarm, if the word Dominion Status mentioned in your announcement had been used in its accepted sense. For, has it not been admitted by responsible British statesmen that Dominion Status is virtual Independence? What, however, I fear is that there never has been any intention of granting such Dominion Status to India in the immediate future.

But this is all past history. Since the announcement many events have happened which show unmistakably the trend of British policy.

1. Which took place on December 23, 1929.
2. The resolution referred to is the Congress resolution passed at Lahore in 1929.

It seems as clear as daylight that responsible British statesmen do not contemplate any alteration in British policy that might adversely affect Britain's commerce with India or require an impartial and close scrutiny of Britain's transactions with India. If nothing is done to end the process of exploitation India must be bled with an ever increasing speed. The Finance Member regards as a settled fact the 1/6 ratio which by a stroke of the pen drains India of a few crores. And when a serious attempt is being made through a civil form of direct action, to unsettle this fact, among many others, even you cannot help appealing to the wealthy landed classes to help you to crush that attempt in the name of an order that grinds India to atoms.

Unless those who work in the name of the nation understand and keep before all concerned the motive that lies behind the craving for independence, there is every danger of independence coming to us so changed as to be of no value to those toiling voiceless millions for whom it is sought and for whom it is worth taking. It is for that reason that I have been recently telling the public what independence should really mean.

Let me put before you some of the salient points.

The terrific pressure of land revenue, which furnishes a large part of the total, must undergo considerable modification in an independent India. Even the much vaunted permanent settlement benefits the few rich zamindars, not the ryots. The ryot has remained as helpless as ever. He is a mere tenant at will. Not only, then, has the land revenue to be considerably reduced, but the whole revenue system has to be so revised as to make the ryot's good its primary concern. But the British system seems to be designed to crush the very life out of him. Even the salt he must use to live is so taxed as to make the burden fall heaviest on him, if only because of the heartless impartiality of its incidence. The tax shows itself still more burdensome on the poor man when it is remembered that salt is the one thing he must eat more than the rich man both individually and collectively. The drink and drug revenue, too, is derived from the poor. It saps the foundations both of their health and morals. It is defended under the false plea of individual freedom, but, in reality, is maintained for its own sake. The ingenuity of the authors of the reforms of 1919 transferred this revenue to the so-called responsible part of dyarchy, so as to throw the burden of prohibition on it, thus, from the very beginning, rendering it powerless for good. If the unhappy minister wipes out this revenue he must starve education, since in the existing circumstances he has no new source of replacing that revenue. If the weight of taxation has crushed the poor from above, the destruction of the central supplementary industry, i.e., hand-spinning, has undermined their capacity for producing wealth. The tale of India's ruination is not complete without reference to the liabilities incurred in her name. Sufficient has been recently said about these in the public Press. It must be the duty of a free India to subject all the liabilities to the strictest investigation, and repudiate those that may be adjudged by an impartial tribunal to be unjust and unfair.

The iniquities sampled above are maintained in order to carry on a foreign administration, demonstrably the most expensive in the world. Take your own salary. It is over Rs. 21,000 per month, besides many other indirect additions. The British Prime Minister gets £5,000 per year, i.e., over Rs. 5,400 per month at the present rate of exchange. You are getting over Rs. 700 per day against India's average income of less than annas 2 per day. The Prime Minister gets Rs. 180 per day against Great Britain's average income of nearly Rs. 2 per day. Thus you are getting much over five thousand times India's average income. The British Prime Minister is getting only ninety times Britain's average income. On bended knees I ask you to ponder over this phenomenon. I have taken a personal illustration to drive home a painful truth. I have too great a regard for you as a man to wish to hurt your feelings. I know that you do not need the salary you get. Probably the whole of your salary goes for charity. But a system that provides for such an arrangement deserves to be summarily scrapped. What is true of the Viceregal salary is true generally of the whole administration.

A radical cutting down of the revenue, therefore, depends upon an equally radical reduction in the expenses of the administration. This means a transformation of the scheme of government. This transformation is impossible without independence. Hence, in my opinion, the spontaneous demonstration of 26th January, in which hundreds of thousands of villagers instinctively participated. To them independence means deliverance from the killing weight.

Not one of the great British political parties, it seems to me, is prepared to give up the Indian spoils to which Great Britain helps herself from day to day, often, in spite of the unanimous opposition of Indian opinion.

Nevertheless, if India is to live as a nation, if the slow death by starvation of her people is to stop, some remedy must be found for immediate relief. The proposed Conference is certainly not the remedy. It is not a matter of carrying conviction by argument. The matter resolves itself into one of matching forces. Conviction or no conviction, Great Britain would defend her Indian commerce and interests by all the forces at her command. India must consequently evolve force enough to free herself from that embrace of death.

It is common cause that, however disorganized and, for the time being, insignificant it may be, the party of violence is gaining ground and making itself felt. Its end is the same as mine. But I am convinced that it cannot bring the desired relief to the dumb millions. And the conviction is growing deeper and deeper in me that nothing but unadulterated non-violence can check the organized violence of the British Government. Many think that non-violence is not an active force. My experience, limited though it undoubtedly is, shows that non-violence can be an intensely active force. It is my purpose to set in motion that force as well against the organized violent force of the British rule as [against] the unorganized violent force of the growing party of violence. To sit still would be to give rein to both the forces above mentioned. Having an unquestioning and immovable faith in the efficacy of non-violence as I know it, it would be sinful on my part to wait any longer.

This non-violence will be expressed through civil disobedience, for the moment confined to the inmates of the Satyagraha Ashram, but ultimately designed to cover all those who choose to join the movement with its obvious limitations.

I know that in embarking on non-violence I shall be running what might fairly be termed a mad risk. But the victories of truth have never been won without risks, often of the gravest character. Conversion of a nation that has consciously or unconsciously preyed upon another, far more numerous, far more ancient and no less cultured than itself, is worth any amount of risk.

I have deliberately used the word "conversion." For my ambition is no less than to convert the British people through non-violence, and thus make them see the wrong they have done to India. I do not seek to harm your people. I want to serve them even as I want to serve my own. I believe that I have always served them. I served them up to 1919 blindly. But when my eyes were opened and I conceived non-cooperation, the object still was to serve them. I employed the same weapon that I have in all humility successfully used against the dearest members of my family. If I have equal love for your people with mine it will not long remain hidden. It will be acknowledged by them even as the members of my family acknowledged it after they had tried me for several years. If the people join me as I expect they will, the sufferings they will undergo, unless the British nation sooner retraces its steps, will be enough to melt the stoniest hearts.

The plan through civil disobedience will be to combat such evils as I have sampled out. If we want to sever the British connection it is because of such evils. When they are removed the path becomes easy. Then the way to friendly negotiation will be open. If the British commerce with India is purified of greed, you will have no difficulty in recognizing our independence. I respectfully invite you then to pave the way for immediate removal of those evils, and thus open a way for a real conference between equals, interested only in promoting the common good of mankind through voluntary fellowship and in arranging terms of mutual help and commerce equally suited to both. You have unnecessarily laid stress upon the communal problems that unhappily affect this land. Important though they undoubtedly are for the consideration of any scheme of government, they have little bearing on the greater problems which are above communities and which affect them all equally. But if you cannot see your way to deal with these evils and my letter makes no appeal to your heart, on the 11th day of this month,[3] I shall proceed with such co-workers of the Ashram as I can take, to disregard the provisions of the salt laws. I regard this tax to be the most iniquitous of all from the poor man's standpoint. As the independence movement is essentially for the poorest in the land the beginning will be made with this evil. The wonder is that we have submitted to the cruel monopoly for so long. It is, I know, open to you to frustrate my design by arresting me. I hope that there will be tens of thousands ready, in a disciplined manner, to take up the work after me, and, in the act of disobeying the Salt Act to lay themselves open to the penalties of a law that should never have disfigured the Statute-book.

I have no desire to cause you unnecessary embarrassment, or any at all, so far as I can help. If you think that there is any substance in my letter, and if you will care to discuss matters with me, and if to that end you would like me to postpone publication of this letter, I shall gladly refrain on receipt of a telegram to that effect soon after this reaches you.[4] You will, however, do me the favour not to deflect me from my course unless you can see your way to conform to the substance of this letter.

3. The march, however, started on March 12.
4. The viceroy's reply was simply an expression of regret that Gandhi should be "contemplating a course of action which is clearly bound to involve violation of the law and danger to the public peace."

This letter is not in any way intended as a threat but is a simple and sacred duty peremptory on a civil resister. Therefore I am having it specially delivered by a young English friend who believes in the Indian cause and is a full believer in non-violence and whom Providence seems to have sent to me, as it were, for the very purpose.

I remain,
Your sincere friend,
M. K. GANDHI

H. E. Lord Irwin
Viceroy's House
New Delhi-3

Young India, 12-3-1930

37. About That Letter

(vol. XLIII, pp. 14–16)

My letter to the Viceroy went on the 2nd instant as anticipated by the newspapers. Forecasts have been published of its contents which are largely untrue. I wish these correspondents and the news agencies will, instead of making the publication of news a matter merely of making money, think of the public good. If there had been anything to give to the public, surely Pandit Jawaharlal Nehru would have given it. But it was thought advisable to wait for an acknowledgment from Delhi before publishing the letter. I am not intent on a fight. I am leaving no stone unturned to avoid it. But I am ready for it the moment I find that there is no honourable way out of it. Premature publication of news indirectly obtained by means not always straight ought not to be the function of journalists. I know that the newspaper said to be the greatest in the world makes it a boast to obtain by secret methods news which no other agency can. It makes it a boast to publish news which the keepers are most anxious often in the public interest to withhold for the time being. But the English public submits to the treatment, because moneyed and influential men conduct *The Times*. We have blindly copied the rulers' code of manners without discrimination in the matter of publication of news as in many others of still greater importance. I know that mine is a voice in the wilderness, though I speak with the authority of an unbroken experience of practical journalism for over twenty years, if successful conducting of four weeklies[1] can be regarded as such. Be that as it may, the imminent fight includes among the points of attack this slavish habit of copying everything English. No one will accuse me of any anti-English tendency. Indeed I pride myself on my discrimination. I have thankfully copied many things from them. Punctuality, reticence, public hygiene, independent thinking and exercise of judgment and several other things I owe to my association with them. But never having had the slightest touch of slave mentality in me and never having even a thought of materially benefiting myself through contact, official or otherwise, with them, I have had the rare good fortune of studying them with complete detachment. On the eve of battle therefore I would warn fellow journalists against copying the English method of obtaining and publishing news. Let them study my original method which was introduced long before I became a Mahatma and before I had acquired any status of importance in the public life of India. It was a hard struggle, but I found in the field of journalism as in many others that the strictest honesty and fair dealing was undoubtedly the best policy. Any shorter cut is longer at least by double the length sought to be saved. For there must be a retracing. I say all this not for the sake of reading a lesson to fellow-journalists but for the sake of the struggle in which I would value the co-operation of journalists whether they approve of or oppose my methods of political warfare. Let them not add to the risks I am already taking. The rule I would like them to observe is never to publish any news without having it checked by someone connected with me and having authority.

With this long preface I may inform the reader that the letter was sent through a special messenger to be personally delivered to the Private Secretary to His Excellency the Viceroy. The messenger selected was a young English friend Reginald Reynolds who came to India some months ago and who has identified himself completely with the Indian cause. For me the sending of the letter was a religious act as the whole struggle is. And I selected an English friend as my messenger, because I wanted to forge a further check upon myself against any intentional act that would hurt a single Englishman. If I have any sense of honour in me, this choice should prove an automatic restraint even upon unconscious error. It pleases me also to have the unselfish and unsolicited association of a cultured, well-read, devout Englishman in an act which may, in spite of all my effort to the contrary, involve loss of English life.

1. *Indian Opinion, Young India, Navajivan* and *Hindi Navajivan.*

As for the letter itself, when the reader has the text before him he will see that it is not an ultimatum, but it is a friendly, if also a frank, communication from one who considers himself to be a friend of Englishmen. But the reader must hold himself in patience for a while.

Young India, 6-3-1930

38. The Departure

(vol. XLIII, pp. 83–85)

Thousands of Ahmedabad citizens, both men and women, kept vigil on the night of the 11th. Thousands flocked to the Ashram. One heard rumours all through the night. "Here is some news," someone with a grave face twice whispered into my ear! "Reliable news has been received that a special train is arriving this evening and will take you away to be borne to Mandalay." As it is the same to me whether I am in jail or outside, the news had no effect on me and I went to bed in perfect peace. But the sight of the mill-workers and mill-owners around me could not but make me happy. Though eagerly expected, "they" did not come, and at the appointed hour and minute God gave us the send-off. We walked on between rows of people who had come to see us set out, the rows extending to as far as the Chandola lake. I can never forget the scene. For me, this was the form in which God's blessing descended on me. In the face of such a spectacle, how could I believe that there was no prospect of success in this struggle? Both the rich and the poor were present in proportion to their numbers in the population. If the spectacle has any meaning, it is this, at any rate, that all people want freedom and they want it through peaceful means. In the eyes of men lining the road from the Ashram to Ellis Bridge I saw not poison but nectar. I saw in their eyes no anger against British rule or rulers, but I saw there the joy born of the confidence that complete freedom was now at hand.

The authorities on their part had acted wisely. Not one policeman was to be seen. What business could the police have where people had come together for a festive occasion? What would the police do there?

May the self-confidence displayed by the citizens of Ahmedabad last for ever! Let that confidence spread all over the country, and complete freedom will be ours without much effort. If such freedom is our birthright, how much time should we need to win that right? To breathe is my birthright, and breathing therefore proceeds with ease. It is the long history of slavery that has given us the illusion that slavery is our natural state. The truth is that it is not the natural state of any man whatever. If three hundred million men and women are determined to win freedom, you may take it that it is theirs. The scene on the 12th was a sign of that determination.

But I am not a man to be easily taken in by appearances. All over the world, the common mass of men move like sheep following one another. It was so on the 12th too. Many had come out just because others had done so. For many others, this coming out for the festival was the beginning and the end of their self-sacrifice. If that was the truth, their coming out was no sign of the approach of freedom. If a hundred thousand men oppress three hundred million and the latter come together to struggle to get rid of the oppression, they will win their freedom from slavery with very little effort and sacrifice. But some sacrifice there has to be. Winning freedom is not child's play. It requires the labour of thoughtful men, so that if the three hundred million would not become khadi-wearers, at any rate three million must come forward to offer civil disobedience. If many join in this sacrifice for swaraj they would share the labour. If the number of such people is small, they will have to bear a greater burden, for the labour needed for winning freedom will always be the same. The only question, therefore, is who should bear this burden and how. The immediate burden of bringing success to the present march falls on the Gujaratis. Bringing success to the march does not mean only providing regular meals and rendering other services to the party. The mahajans at the various places are doing that with love. To bring success to the march means men and women coming out in large numbers to join the struggle. People should get ready for civil disobedience of the salt law as soon as the marching party reaches Jalalpur. Every village should get ready its own quota of civil law-breakers so that at the proper time they plunge into the fight.

[From Gujarati]
Navajivan, 16-3-1930

39. Turning the Searchlight Inward [1]
(vol. XLIII, pp. 146–49)

March 29, 1930

I have been asked to deliver a sermon. I have little fitness for the task. But tonight I propose to make a confession and turn the searchlight inward. You may call this introspection a sermon if you like.

India in general and you in particular are acquainted with one part of my nature. Moreover, more than in any other part of Gujarat, in this district are concentrated workers who have come in closest touch with me. They know this habit of mine from personal experience.

I am plain-spoken. I have not hesitated to describe the mountain-high faults of the Government in appropriate language. And I have not hesitated often to picture as mountain-high our faults appearing to us as trifling. You know, the common rule is to see our own big lapses as tiny nothings. And when we do realize our blemishes somewhat, we at once pass them on to the broad shoulders of God and say He will take care of them; and then with safety thus assured we proceed from lapse to lapse. But as you know I have disregarded this rule for years. So doing, I have hurt the feelings of many friends and even lost some of them. Tonight I have to repeat the painful operation.[2]

Only this morning at prayer time I was telling my companions that as we had entered the district in which we were to offer civil disobedience, we should insist on greater purification and intenser dedication. I warned them that as the district was more organized and contained many intimate co-workers, there was every likelihood of our being pampered. I warned them against succumbing to their pampering. We are not angels. We are very weak, easily tempted. There are many lapses to our debit. God is great. Even today some were discovered. One defaulter confessed his lapse himself whilst I was brooding over the lapses of the pilgrims. I discovered that my warning was given none too soon. The local workers had ordered milk from Surat to be brought in a motor lorry and they had incurred other expenses which I could not justify. I therefore spoke strongly

1. This appeared in *Young India* with the following note from Gandhi: "At Bhatgam (Dist. Surat) on 29th ultimo I delivered an introspective speech which moved both the audience and me deeply. As it turned out to be an important speech, I give a free and somewhat condensed translation below."
2. The paragraph that follows has been omitted.

about them. But that did not allay my grief. On the contrary it increased with the contemplation of the wrongs done.[3]

Therefore in your hospitality towards servants like us, I would have you to be miserly rather than lavish. I shall not complain of unavoidable absence of things. In order to procure goat's milk for me you may not deprive poor women of milk for their children. It would be like poison if you did. Nor may milk and vegetables be brought from Surat. We can do without them if necessary. Do not resort to motor-cars on the slightest pretext. The rule is, do not ride if you can walk. This is not a battle to be conducted with money. It will be impossible to sustain a mass movement with money. Anyway it is beyond me to conduct the campaign with a lavish display of money.

Extravagance has no room in this campaign. If we cannot gather crowds unless we carry on a hurricane expensive propaganda, I would be satisfied to address half a dozen men and women.

It will be said that in that case reports will not appear in newspapers. I wish to tell you once and for all that this campaign will not succeed through newspaper reports, but with the assistance of Shri Rama. And, no light is necessary when we are near Him; neither are pen and ink and such other accessories required, nor even speech. An appeal can be made to Him even if one has lost one's limbs.

We may not consider anybody low. I observed that you had provided for the night journey a heavy kerosene burner mounted on a stool which a poor labourer carried on his head. This was a humiliating sight. This man was being goaded to walk fast. I could not bear the sight. I therefore put on speed and outraced the whole company. But it was no use. The man was made to run after me. The humiliation was complete. If the weight had to be carried, I should have loved to see someone among ourselves carrying it. We would then soon dispense both with the stool and the burner. No labourer would carry such a load on his head. We rightly object to *begar* (forced labour). But what was this if it was not *begar*? Remember that in swaraj we would expect one drawn from the so-called lower class to preside over India's destiny. If then we do not quickly mend our ways, there is no swaraj such as you and I have put before the people.

From my outpouring you may not infer that I shall weaken in my resolve to carry on the struggle. It will continue no matter how co-workers or others act. For me there is no turning back whether I am alone or joined by thousands. I would rather die a dog's death and

3. Five paragraphs have been omitted here.

have my bones licked by dogs than that I should return to the Ashram a broken man.[4]

I admit that I have not well used the money you have given out of the abundance of your love. You are entitled to regard me as one of those wretches described in the verses sung in the beginning. Shun me.

Young India, 3-4-1930

40. Letter to Narandas Gandhi
(vol. XLIII, pp. 449–51)

Yeravda Mandir,
June 30, 1930

Chi. Narandas,

I have now received all your letters.

We have thought long about the trouble being given by the Bharwads. To me our dharma is plain. It is the same towards the entire world. We should win over the Bharwads by love, and at the same time try to protect what it is our duty to protect. That can be done only by giving our lives to the Bharwads. In other words, we should lay down our lives in protecting our things but should never attack the Bharwads in doing so. However, I do not wish to blame anyone for what has happened. We can follow dharma only within the limits of our capacity, otherwise we would be guilty of artificiality. We should, therefore, do what the impulse of the moment dictates. That impulse is the measure of our strength. As for the future, I have no doubt that our dharma is what I have stated it to be. But before and after adopting that course for protecting our things, we should discharge two other duties. I have been observing and saying for the last fifteen years that we have not mixed with our neighbours. What pains me is that I myself did not follow that path. I tried to persuade Maganlal to follow it. Some kind of a start was made. There were, however, difficulties in the way and the attempt was abandoned. We are now paying for our indifference. But recalling the past is of no value except for drawing lessons from it. Let us look to the present.

4. Gandhi here says: "Turning to the women, I concluded and nearly broke down as I finished the last sentences."

Just now, therefore, we should discuss the problem with the Bharwads. We should ourselves try to plead with them in the presence of persons who know them. We should also tell them what we wish. If they want to graze their cattle [on our land], they should pay us something. If, however, we have no land we should explain that to them. We should also appeal to our neighbours to plead with the Bharwads. We should render them whatever other service we can, and should continue to do so irrespective of their behaviour. We should explain to them why the Ashram has been established and what it aims at doing. Even if we do all this, it is possible that they will occasionally raid the Ashram. If they do, those of us who can, may lay down their lives and let the Bharwads take away what they will after killing them. If we do not have the will and the strength for this, you may do what seems best to all of you. I have only explained the duty, as I understand it, that is proper to an Ashram. You should, however, put out of consideration what I may write, for beyond expressing my views I can do nothing. Moreover, an opinion expressed from a distance is likely to be erroneous. What I might think if I were present there may very well be different from what I think from here. Moreover, no matter with what detachment a prisoner tries to think, his conclusions are likely to be based on incomplete data. You need not, therefore, attach much weight to my view. I shall be satisfied if it helps you to come to your own decision. In any case it was good that afterwards you treated the Bharwads for injuries.

I am writing to Bhansali; read that letter. Your decisions about Chandrakanta and Giriraj seem all right.

I am getting on well. These days I am also trying to learn by heart verses from the *Gita*. I have completed Chapter XII and done half of Chapter XIII. Does man know what he wants? I liked Kaka's coming, but I also see that it has turned out to be an obstacle. Since his coming my daily study has fallen behind. Without him I would have proceeded faster with the *Gita*. Actually, I tried to prevent his coming, but failed. My reason for doing that was quite different. I did not like that he, too, should be confined within four walls as I was. But the Government had made up its mind to provide me company and did so. I, therefore, tolerate Kaka. And he has to bear separation from the large company at Sabarmati. Thus we find the situation a mixture of all sentiments—there are at least the pathetic, the humorous and the heroic. However, if I have relaxed in one field of my daily study, I have started Marathi. I would have become proud if I had become altogether self-reliant. Now that I have been receiving invisible services from Kakasaheb, they will help me in reminding me of my right place. Besides, the exercise which my reason gets in sweet discussions about the *Gita* and other works is an additional benefit. Thus I get an opportunity of another kind for self-examination. I can, therefore, say that I would have been content if Kaka had not come, and am also content now that he has come. Who can weigh and decide whether his coming is a gain or a loss to me? To him who believes that anything he gets unasked comes from God, every such thing is a benefit—is a gift of His grace. Kaka's coming, therefore, is such a gift. It does not matter if the study of the *Gita* has slowed down.

Convey my greetings to Vallabhbhai. The question of Kaka's diet has been settled. He gets two pounds of cow's milk, ten *tolas* of butter, twenty *tolas* of fresh, uncooked vegetables and twenty *tolas* of chapati. He turns the milk into curds. He is getting on quite well. His weight has increased by one pound. By way of vegetables, he gets brinjals and radishes by turn during the week. He cooks the brinjals and eats the radishes raw.

Blessings from
BAPU

From Gujarati

41. Letter to Narandas Gandhi

(vol. XLIV, pp. 56-59)

July 28/31, 1930

Chi. Narandas,

I got your letter. Kakasaheb remarks that the ink and the paper which you use are such that the ink comes out on the other side of the sheet, and hence it will not do to write on both sides. What he says is correct. In such a case, it is desirable to write on one side only.

This time the letters were properly packed. I preserve the envelopes and will use them when I need them. I have already told you in my previous letter that I had received the cotton. I could card some of it only today. The air was very moist because of the rains. It is not the spinning which tires me out, but the sitting for long hours. I shall discover some way by and by. I will not readily accept defeat. There is nothing in this which need cause you concern. Even when I was out of jail, did I ever sit at the spinning-wheel for four or five hours at a stretch?

The injury to Keshu's finger must have healed by now. Can Balkrishna's body stand the strain of night watch? He should not do anything beyond his strength.

Both of us keep good health. On a spring balance Kakasaheb weighed 109 lb. He must be walking about 8 miles a day, including the walking he does for exercise and during work. The exertion of spinning is in addition to this. His diet is still the same.

If there are any men or women to whom I have not written and who expect letters from me, let me know their names. I should have had a letter from Ramabehn (Ranchhodbhai's). She must have received mine.

Now about ahimsa.

Tuesday morning

The commencement of this discourse is both comic and painful. We two had a discussion on how to economize in the use of cloth-lined envelopes and save the same envelopes for use again and again. The question was whether to paste a blank sheet on the whole side of the envelope or paste only slips over portions where something was written. This was a futile discussion. We wasted on it 15 minutes of beautiful time after prayers, demonstrating our foolishness thereby. In doing this we violated truth and ahimsa and displayed lack of discrimination. Truth was violated, because the discussion was not inspired by an ardent desire for its search. Ahimsa was shamed, because I, who ought to give every moment of my time to discover the sufferings of the people and in thinking about the ways of ending them, wasted 15 priceless minutes in a futile discussion. We displayed lack of discrimination, because if we had thought about the utility of the discussion, it would not have lasted even a minute. After we had stolen 15 minutes from people's time, we realized our foolishness and thanked God for opening our eyes.

I have purposely given this introduction.

The path of Truth is as narrow as it is straight. Even so is that of ahimsa. It is like balancing oneself on the edge of a sword. By concentration an acrobat can walk on a rope. But the concentration required to tread the path of Truth and ahimsa is far greater. The slightest inattention brings one tumbling to the ground. One can realize Truth and ahimsa only by ceaseless striving.

But it is impossible for us to realize perfect truth so long as we are imprisoned in this mortal frame. We can only visualize it in our imagination. We cannot, through the instrumentality of this ephemeral body, see face to face truth which is eternal. That is why in the last resort we must depend on faith.

It appears that the impossibility of full realization of truth in this mortal body led some ancient seeker after truth to the appreciation of ahimsa. The question which confronted him was: "Shall I bear with those who create difficulties for me, or shall I destroy them?" The seeker realized that he who went on destroying others did not make headway but simply stayed where he was, while the man who suffered those who created difficulties marched ahead and at times even took the others with him. The first act of destruction taught him that the truth which was the object of his quest was not outside himself but within. Hence the more he took to violence, the more he receded from truth. For in fighting the imagined enemy without, he neglected the enemy within.

We punish thieves because we think they harass us. They may leave us alone; but they will only transfer their attentions to another victim. This other victim, however, is also a human being, ourselves in a different form, and so we are caught in a vicious circle. The trouble from thieves continues to increase, as they think it is their business to steal. In the end we see that it is better to tolerate the thieves than to punish them. The forbearance may even bring them to their senses. By tolerating them we realize that thieves are not different from ourselves, they are our brethren, our friends, and may not be punished. But whilst we may bear with the thieves, we may not endure the infliction. That would only induce cowardice. So we realize a further duty. Since we regard the thieves as our kith and kin, they must be made to realize the kinship. And so we must take pains to devise ways and means of winning them over. This is the path of ahimsa. It may entail continuous suffering and the cultivating of endless patience. Given these two conditions, the thief is bound in the end to turn away from his evil ways and we shall get a clearer vision of truth. Thus step by step we learn how to make friends with all the world; we realize the greatness of God, of Truth. Our peace of mind increases in spite of suffering; we become braver and more enterprising; we understand more clearly the difference between what is everlasting and what is not; we learn how to distinguish between what is our duty and what is not. Our pride melts away and we become humble. Our worldly attachments diminish and likewise the evil within us diminishes from day to day.

Ahimsa is not the crude thing it has been made to appear. Not to hurt any living thing is no doubt a part of ahimsa. But it is its least expression. The principle of ahimsa is hurt by every evil thought, by undue haste, by lying, by hatred, by wishing ill of anybody. It is also violated by our holding on to what the world needs. But the world needs even what we eat day by day. In the place where we stand there are millions of micro-organisms to whom the place belongs and who are hurt by our presence there. What should we do then? Should we commit suicide? Even that is no solution, if we believe, as we do, that so long as the spirit is attached to the flesh, on every destruction of the body it weaves for itself another. The body will cease to be only when we give up all attachment to it. This freedom from all attachment is the realization of God as Truth. Such realization cannot be attained in a hurry. Realizing that this body does not belong to us, that it is a trust handed over to our charge, we should make the right use of it and progress towards our goal.

I wished to write something which would be easy for all to understand, but I find that I have written a difficult discourse. However, no one who has thought even a little about ahimsa should find any difficulty in understanding what I have written.

It is perhaps clear from the foregoing that without ahimsa it is not possible to seek and find Truth. Ahimsa and Truth are so intertwined that it is practically impossible to disentangle and separate them. They are like the two sides of a coin, or rather of a smooth unstamped metallic disc. Who can say which is the obverse and which is the reverse? Nevertheless, ahimsa is the means and Truth is the end. Means to be means must always be within our reach, and so ahimsa becomes our supreme duty and Truth becomes God for us. If we take care of the means, we are bound to reach the end sooner or later. If we resolve to do this, we shall have won the battle. Whatever difficulties we encounter, whatever apparent reverses we sustain, we should not lose faith but should ever repeat one *mantra:* "Truth exists, it alone exists. It is the only God and there is but one way of realizing it; there is but one means and that is ahimsa. I will never give it up. May the God that is Truth, in whose name I have taken this pledge, give me the strength to keep it."

Blessings from
BAPU

[P.S.]
There are 57 letters.

From a microfilm of the Gujarati

42. Letter to Narandas Gandhi
(vol. XLIV, pp. 147–50)

Yeravda Mandir,
September 14/16, 1930

Chi. Narandas,

I got your letter. I follow your hint concerning the women. Read my letter to Chhaganlal Joshi. You or Gangabehn should keep in correspondence with the women who have settled down for work in different places outside the Ashram. If it seems necessary and if she can find time, Gangabehn should even pay visits to some of those places. Lapses will occur in some of them, but we need not be afraid about them. We should remain, and see that others, too, remain, sufficiently vigilant and leave the result to God. What indeed is our *tapashcharya* in comparison to the degree of self-control we expect from and wish to see in others? Whatever that is, we wish to follow no other path. We wish to uphold the fullest freedom for women. It does not matter if we miss the path on our way, if we stumble, are pricked by thorns or fall down. I gave the letter on Tuesday as usual, but it must have been posted late by the office here either deliberately or through negligence. I have not complained. You should, of course, write to me whenever you do not get the letters in time. It is good that Punjabhai has returned. Have you appointed anyone from the Ashram to look after him? I am writing to Manibhai[1] about the money for honouring the memory of the poet which is lying with Revashankerbhai. Tell Mrs. Zaulinger that I am awaiting her reply. She may write to me anything she wishes to without any hesitation. You have acted rightly in regard to Kamalabehn Lundy. For the present it is best that she should say or write nothing. There is plenty of silent service she can do. Balbhadra has done fine work indeed in carding. This shows that, if we refuse to regard a person as too dull-minded for a particular thing and go on encouraging him, the result is bound to be good.

I am getting on all right just now. As usual I take milk and curds. Instead of raisins and dates, I eat daily seven or eight tomatoes, four or five big-sized, baked sweet potatoes and about six spoons of cabbage or any other vegetable that is available. This helps me in passing stools. I drink at 7.30 in the morning the juice of one lemon with hot water and salt. In the afternoon, I take the juice of one lemon

1. Rajchandra.

with soda bicarb. If this regimen suits me, it will solve the problem of constipation and effect considerable economy. I get the vegetables from what grows in the garden here. If we count the expenditure, I don't think it exceeds two annas daily, whereas raisins and dates probably cost every day not less than six annas. Those who suffer from constipation may try this diet. I cannot say that it will benefit all. About myself, too, I cannot yet say that the good effect will last. If this experiment is followed, any other food should be avoided. The baked sweet potatoes should be eaten by themselves and chewed well. They should not be dipped in milk or curds. Probably it will do no harm if one eats the skin. I do eat some. Because of my delicate stomach I am afraid to eat all. Anybody else who has a similar stomach and who tries this experiment should also avoid the skin. I would be really happy if you could find my sandals. Kusum is bound to know about them. She may have entrusted them to Premabehn. If you have not yet sent the cotton send it even by post in the last resort. Both the belts, one of six strings and the other of eight strings, were found to be too thin. They come off the pulley and go on revolving without moving the latter. Do not send me new ones in their place. Some are ready with me and I will somehow manage to make others. I asked you to let me know a simpler method because such a method would save my time.

September 15, 1930

My silence ended a little while ago and Kakasaheb read out to me Ramdas's letter to him. Ramdas says in it that he wrote a letter to me which I have not received. I was very happy that Ramdas gave in the letter to Kakasaheb detailed information about his health and studies. When he is released from jail, we shall be able to write to each other. I shall then get any letter written by him if I can keep up this correspondence. I send you the letters in cloth-lined envelopes now. I have with me only the envelopes received from you. I retain their size when returning them, so that you may be able to use them again. Otherwise I could have made them smaller and used them.

Tuesday morning, September 16, 1930

I read in papers about Ba having been harassed in Surat by the police. Is there any truth in the report?

The law, that to live man must work, first came home to me upon reading Tolstoy's writings on bread labour. But even before that I had begun to pay homage to it after reading Ruskin's *Unto This Last.* The phrase 'jatmahenat' is a translation of the English expression 'bread labour.' Literally it means labour for *roti.* The divine law that man must earn his bread by labouring with his own hands was first stressed, not by Tolstoy but by an obscure Russian writer named T. M. Bondoref. Tolstoy took it from him and gave it wider publicity when he accepted it. In my view, the same principle has been set forth in Chapter III of the *Gita* where we are told that he who eats without offering sacrifice eats stolen food. Sacrifice here can only mean bread labour. Be that as it may, that verse is the origin of our observance.

Reason, too, leads us to an identical conclusion. How can a man who does not do body labour have the right to eat? "In the sweat of thy brow shalt thou eat thy bread," says the Bible. A millionaire cannot carry on for long, and will soon get tired of his life, if he rolls in his bed all day long and is even helped to his food. He, therefore, induces hunger by exercise and helps himself to the food he eats. If everyone, whether rich or poor, has thus to take exercise in some shape or form, why should it not assume the form of productive labour, i.e., bread labour? No one asks the cultivator to inhale fresh air, or to use his muscles. And more than nine-tenths of humanity lives by tilling the soil. How much happier, healthier and more peaceful would the world become if the remaining tenth followed the example of the overwhelming majority at least to the extent of labouring enough for their food. And many hardships connected with agriculture would be easily redressed if such people took a hand in it. Again, invidious distinctions of rank would be abolished if everyone wthout exception acknowledged the obligation of bread labour. At present these distinctions have invaded even the varna system in which there was not a trace of it originally. There is a worldwide conflict between capital and labour, and the poor envy the rich. If all worked for their bread, distinctions of rank would be obliterated; the rich would still be there, but they would deem themselves only trustees of their property and would use it mainly in the public interest. Bread labour is a veritable blessing to one who would observe non-violence, worship Truth and make the observance of *brahmacharya* a natural act. This labour can truly be related to agriculture alone. But at present at any rate everybody is not in a position to take to it. A person can, therefore, spin or weave, or take up carpentry or smithery, instead of tilling the soil, always regarding agriculture, however, to be the ideal. Everyone must be his own scavenger. Evacuation is as necessary as eating; and the best thing would be for everyone to dispose of his own waste. If this is impossible, each family should see to its own scavenging. I have felt for years that there must be something radically wrong where scavenging has been made the concern of a separate class in society. We have no historical record of the man who first assigned the lowest status to this essential sanitary service. Whoever he was, he did us no good. We should, from our very childhood, have the idea impressed upon our minds that we are all scavengers, and the easiest way of doing so is for everyone who has realized this to commence bread labour as a scavenger. Scavenging, thus intelligently taken up, will help one to understand religion in a different and truer light. If children, the old and those disabled by illness do not do bread labour, that should not be regarded as violation of the law of bread labour.

The child is, as it were, included in the mother. If nature's laws were not violated, the old would not be disabled and there would be no disease.

Blessings from
BAPU

[P.S.]

Tell Khurshedbehn that, if she requires money, she should have no hesitation in obtaining it from the Ashram. If she got it from any other source, it would pain me.

There are 55 letters.

From the Gujarati.

43. Letter to Narandas Gandhi

(vol. XLIV, pp. 189–90)

Tuesday morning, September 30, 1930

As I told you in my letter last week, I have translated into English the discourse on Equality of Religions and send the translation herewith. If Valjibhai has translated it and if his translation has already been printed, he should read the translation which I am sending. Anybody else who wishes to read it may do so and the last person should hand it over to Mirabehn. If Valjibhai's translation has not been printed, he should carefully go through my translation and then publish whichever he likes. Do you intend to publish the discourses in Gujarati only or their English translations also?

This subject is so important that I dwell a little further on it.

My meaning will perhaps become clearer if I describe here some of my experiences. In Phœnix we had our daily prayers in the same way as in Sabarmati, and Mussalmans as well as Christians attended them along with Hindus. The late Sheth Rustomji and his children too attended the prayer meetings. Rustomji Sheth very much liked the Gujarati *bhajan.* "Dear, dear to me is the name of Rama." If my memory serves me right, Maganlal or Kashi was once leading us in singing this hymn, when Rustomji Sheth exclaimed joyously "Say the name of Hormazd instead of the name of Rama." His suggestion was readily taken up, and after that whenever the Sheth was present, and sometimes even when he was not, we put in the name of Hormazd in place of Rama. The late Husain, son of Daud Sheth, often stayed at the Phœnix Ashram, and enthusiastically joined our prayers. To the accompaniment of an organ, he used to sing in a very sweet voice the song *"Hai bahare bagh,"* "The garden of this world has only a momentary bloom." He taught us all this song, which we also sang at prayers. Its inclusion in our *Bhajanavali* is a tribute to truth-loving Husain's memory. I have never met a young man who practised Truth more devotedly than Husain. Joseph Royeppen often came to Phœnix. He was a Christian, and his favourite hymn was *"Vaishnava jana."* He loved music and once sang this hymn saying "Christian" in place of "vaishnava." The others accepted his reading with alacrity, and I observed that this filled Joseph's heart with joy.

When I was turning over the pages of the sacred books of different faiths for my own satisfaction, I became sufficiently familiar for my purpose with Christianity, Islam, Zoroastrianism, Judaism and Hinduism. In reading these texts, I can say that I felt the same regard for all these faiths although, perhaps, I was not then conscious of it. Reviving my memory of those days, I do not find I ever had the slightest desire to criticize any of those religions merely because they were not my own, but read each sacred book in a spirit of reverence and found the same fundamental morality in each. Some things I did not understand then, as I did not in Hindu scriptures. I do not understand those things even now, but experience has taught me that it is a mistake hastily to imagine that anything that we cannot understand is necessarily wrong. Some things which I did not understand first have since become as clear as daylight. Equimindedness helps us to solve many difficulties and even when we criticize anything, we express ourselves with a humility and courtesy which leave no sting behind them.

One difficulty still remains. As I stated last time, the acceptance of the doctrine of Equality of Religions does not abolish the distinction between religion and irreligion. We do not propose to cultivate tolerance for irreligion. That being so, some people might object that there would be no room left for equimindedness, if everyone took his own decision as to what was religion and what was irreligion. Such a question may be raised and one may even make a mistake in deciding what is religion and what is irreligion. If, however, we follow the law of love, we shall not bear any hatred towards the irreligious brother. On the contrary, though we see that he follows irreligion, we shall love him and, therefore, either we shall bring him to see the error of his ways or he will convince us of our error, or each will tolerate the other's difference of opinion. If the other party does not observe the law of love, he may be violent to us. If, however, we cherish real love for him, it will overcome his bitterness in the end. All obstacles in our path will vanish, if only we observe the golden rule that we must not be impatient with those whom we may consider to be in error, but must be prepared, if need be, to suffer in our own person.

As I have stated earlier in this letter, I think I will omit the subject of swadeshi. I have yet to think on what subject I shall write next.

Blessings from
BAPU

[P.S.]
There are 70 letters.
From the Gujarati.

44. Under the Canopy of Heaven [1]
(vol. XLV, pp. 347-52)

March 26, 1931

The first speech in the Congress pandal, or the inauguration address if I may so call it, was delivered by Gandhiji on the 26th, when a vast audience listened to him spellbound.

By the executions the Government have given the nation grave cause for provocation. It has shocked me too inasmuch as my negotiations and talks had made me entertain a distant hope that Bhagat Singh, Rajguru and Sukhdev might be saved. I am not surprised that young men are angry with me for not having been able to save them. But I have no reason to be angry with them. For one thing, this is not

1. Only parts are reproduced.

the first occasion of its kind in my life. It is the duty of him who claims to serve humanity not to be angry with those whom he is serving. As for myself non-violence being my creed, I cannot afford to be angry with anybody. But even if it is not his creed, it is the duty of a genuine servant not to be angry with his masters. Anger ought to be taboo with him. But if he cannot help being angry, he must abdicate his function as servant of humanity. I for one do not want to do so and therefore I said they had a right to be angry, not I. But I must tell them I had been serving the peasants and workers long before the young men were born. I have lived amongst them, cast my lot with them. Ever since I took the pledge of service, I have dedicated my head to humanity. It is the easiest thing in the world to chop off my head, it does not take the slightest preparation or organization. And outside protection I have never sought. In fact it is futile to think of protecting me for I know that God Almighty is the only Protector. Having said this, let me declare that the demonstrations[2] of the young men yesterday far from making me angry delighted me, inasmuch as there was no discourtesy about them. They might have laid hands on me; instead, they formed my bodyguard and escorted me to my car. I must confess that when I saw them, I felt that my experiences in South Africa, where I was mobbed and assaulted, were going to be repeated.

But there was no cause for apprehension. The young men were simply shouting, "Gandhi go back," "Down with Gandhism." They had a right to do so inasmuch as they thought that I had not done everything in my power to save Bhagat Singh, or that being a believer in ahimsa, I had simply neglected Bhagat Singh and his comrades. But they had no intention to molest me or for the matter of that anyone else. They allowed everyone to pass, and then a young man handed to me flowers made of black cloth. They might have thrown them on me and insulted me, but they had no such intention. Flowers are given me everywhere, I am usually indifferent about them, even when they are received from dear sisters and sometimes even chide them for wasting the flowers on me. But these I seized and have treasured them. I shall also tell you what I want to do with them. If the young men come and tell me that they should not have been angry and that their suspicions about me were groundless and that therefore they want the flowers returned to them, I shall gladly give them back. But if they do not do so, they will be sent to the Ashram to be preserved as heirlooms.

2. On Gandhi's arrival at Malir station.

Those young men wanted to proclaim to the world that however great the Mahatma may be, they were sure that he was doing harm to India. I think they had a right to expose me, if they felt that I was betraying the country. I want you to understand my attitude. I cannot behave otherwise with these young men inasmuch as I want to win them over by love. Having flung aside the sword, there is nothing except the cup of love which I can offer to those who oppose me. It is by offering that cup that I expect to draw them close to me. I cannot think of permanent enmity between man and man, and believing as I do in the theory of rebirth, I live in the hope that if not in this birth, in some other birth I shall be able to hug all humanity in friendly embrace.

I have dwelt at length on this little episode, in order that you may not think ill of the young men. Do not seek to protect me. The Most High is always there to protect us all. You may be sure that when my time is up, no one, not even the most renowned physician in the world, can stand between Him and me.

And now a message for the young men. If you want my service, do not disown me; come and understand everything from me. You must know that it is against my creed to punish even a murderer, a thief or a dacoit. There can be therefore no excuse for suspicion that I did not want to save Bhagat Singh. But I want you also to realize Bhagat Singh's error. If I had had an opportunity of speaking to Bhagat Singh and his comrades, I should have told them that the way they pursued was wrong and futile. I declare that we cannot win swaraj for our famishing millions, for our deaf and dumb, for our lame and crippled, by the way of the sword. With the Most High as witness I want to proclaim this truth that the way of violence cannot bring swaraj, it can only lead to disaster. I wish to tell these young men with all the authority with which a father can speak to his children that the way of violence can only lead to perdition. I shall explain to you why. Do you think that all the women and the children who covered themselves with glory during the last campaign would have done so if we had pursued the path of violence? Would they have been here today? Would our women known as the meekest on earth, would women like Gangabehn, who stood the lathi-blows until her white sari was drenched in blood, have done the unique service they did if we had violence in us? With God's name on their lips she and her sisters hurled defiance at their oppressors, without anger in their hearts. And our children—our *vanarasena* (monkey-army). How could you have had these innocent ones, who renounced their toys, their kites and their crackers, and joined as soldiers of swaraj—how could you

have enlisted them in a violent struggle? We were able to enlist as
soldiers millions of men, women and children because we were
pledged to non-violence. I beseech the young men to have patience
and self-control. Anger cannot take us forward. We need not consider
the Englishmen as our enemies. I have used satyagraha against them
but have never thought of them as enemies. I want to convert them
and the only way is the way of love. Rowdy demonstrations cannot
help us. Could they call Bhagat Singh back to life? They can only
retard the advent of swaraj. I agree that the Government has given
sufficient cause for provocation, but I want the impatient youth in
the name of God, in the name of our dear Motherland, to throw
themselves heart and soul in the non-violent struggle. I ask them to
trust my unbroken experience of forty years of the practice of non-
violence.

But if they will not, they might kill me but they cannot kill
Gandhism. If Truth can be killed Gandhism can be killed. If non-
violence can be killed Gandhism can be killed. For what is Gandhism
but winning swaraj by means of truth and non-violence? Will they
refuse swaraj attained through truth and non-violence? I ask them
therefore not to mar the wonderful work done by the workers of
Sind. The workers have in the course of three weeks created this
Congressnagar, so that swaraj for the peasant, the labourer, the scavenger—all of whom have worked cheek by jowl in creating this city
of huts—the lame and the blind, the starving and the well-fed, the
wretch and the poor, may soon be a living reality. I beseech you not
to mar the beautiful work they have done.

This leads me to the events in Cawnpore which has been a scene
of carnage. This is due largely to the violence we had harboured
against one another. It is the handwriting on the wall. Though we
have shown ourselves capable of limited non-violence, we have harboured violence in our hearts, we have been guilty of using coercion.
The papers allege that Cawnpore Hindus went mad over Bhagat
Singh's martyrdom and started with intimidating the Mussalmans
who would not close their shops in Bhagat Singh's honour. You know
the sequel. I am quite sure that if the spirit of Bhagat Singh is watching what is happening in Cawnpore today, he would feel deeply hu-
miliated and ashamed. I say this for I have heard him described as a
man of honour. And what havoc we have done! Women insulted!
Children done to death! Let no Hindu comfort himself with the
thought that they were Mussalman children; let no Mussalman feel
happy in the knowledge that it is Hindu children who have been
killed. I do not know their religion. Let it be recognized that both

Hindus and Mussalmans had lost their senses. They were all children of the soil, children of our common Motherland.

I have felt deeply ashamed of these deeds of blood, and to whoever my voice may reach I wish to declare that such things may any day prove more than I can bear. How can we, with Hindus and Mussalmans slaughtering one another, continue to assert that we have been non-violent? How can I, a votary of truth, hug the belief that we as a nation are non-violent if the mischief spreads? If I did so, I would be untrue to myself and to my Maker. With carnage going on about me I cannot bear to live unconcerned. Let me declare, that as soon as I feel that life is unbearable, I should hope to have the courage to fast myself to death rather than witness these blood feuds. You know by this time that I cannot bear denial of pledges solemnly and voluntarily undertaken. I would sooner be dead than see merchants and others break their pledged word, than see those calling themselves Congressmen and swearing by the creed of the Congress break it in their hearts or openly. If I can witness this contradiction with equanimity, with what face can I stand before the world and my Maker? He will tell me I have been living a life of falsehood, a life of sham and fraud. I may not deceive myself and the world. Every moment of my existence is dedicated to the winning of swaraj by means of truth and non-violence.

I know you will say that that sort of thing has been going on all these years, and I have done nothing to stop it. Penances with me are no mechanical acts. They are done in obedience to the inner voice. I am telling you what has been going on within me all these days. The crisis may never come, either because I am unnecessarily agitated, or because I have lost courage to face reality. I must be true to my Maker, and the moment I feel that life is unsupportable for me, I hope not to be found wanting. What better reparation can I do than willing surrender of the body that has ceased to evoke response and may be a hindrance to the discovery of the true way?

As he was about to close, the question[3] mentioned above was asked him not by one who wanted to be cantankerous but by one who wanted everything to be known to the public. He replied:

Well, I was not on my defence, and so I did not bother you with the details of what I did to save Bhagat Singh and his comrades. I pleaded with the Viceroy as best I could. I brought all the persuasion at my command to bear on him. On the day fixed for the final interview

3. Given as subtitle in the source, which read: "What Did You Do to Save Bhagat Singh?"

with Bhagat Singh's relations I wrote a personal letter to the Viceroy on the morning of 23rd. I poured my whole soul into it, but to no avail. I might have done one thing more, you say. I might have made the commutation a term of the settlement. It could not be so made. And to threaten withdrawal would be a breach of faith. The Working Committee had agreed with me in not making commutation a condition precedent to truce. I could therefore only mention it apart from the settlement. I had hoped for magnanimity. My hope was not to materialize. But that can be no ground for breaking the settlement.

And it was not I alone who did what was humanly possible. The revered friend Panditji and Dr. Sapru tried their best. But why should that failure worry us? Success is in God's hands. Our failure should spur us to greater effort. That effort lies in being true to ourselves, in Hindus and Mussalmans determining to live as brothers in heart unity, in merchants and others keeping their voluntary pledges, in workers eschewing violence in thought, word and deed. May God help us to mend our ways. May He help us to be strong enough to be true to ourselves and to Him.

Young India, 2-4-1931

45. Bhagat Singh

(vol. XLV, pp. 359–61)

Brave Bhagat Singh and his two associates have been hanged. Many attempts were made to save their lives and even some hopes were entertained, but all was in vain.

Bhagat Singh did not wish to live. He refused to apologize; declined to file an appeal. If at all he would agree to live, he would do so for the sake of others; if at all he would agree to it, it would be in order that his death might not provoke anyone to indiscriminate murder. Bhagat Singh was not a devotee of non-violence, but he did not subscribe to the religion of violence; he was prepared to commit murder out of a sense of helplessness. His last letter was as follows: "I have been arrested while waging a war. For me there can be no gallows. Put me into the mouth of a cannon and blow me off." These heroes had conquered the fear of death. Let us bow to them a thousand times for their heroism.

But we should not imitate their act. I am not prepared to believe that the country has benefited by their action. I can see only the harm that has been done. We could have won swaraj long ago if that line of action had not been pursued and we could have waged a purely non-violent struggle. There may well be two opinions on this conjecture of mine. However, no one can deny the fact that if the practice of seeking justice through murders is established amongst us, we shall start murdering one another for what we believe to be justice. In a land of crores of destitutes and crippled persons, this will be a terrifying situation. These poor people are bound to become victims of our atrocities. It is desirable that everyone should consider the consequences of this. Further, we want a swaraj which is theirs and for them. By making a dharma of violence, we shall be reaping the fruit of our own actions.

Hence, though we praise the courage of these brave men, we should never countenance their activities.

By hanging these men, the Government has demonstrated its own brute nature, it has provided fresh proof of its arrogance resulting from its power by ignoring public opinion. From this hanging it may be concluded that it is not the intention of the Government to part with any real power to the people. The Government certainly had the right to hang these men. However, there are some rights which do credit to those who possess them only if they are enjoyed in name only. If a person exercises all his rights on all occasions, in the end they are destroyed. On this occasion, the Government would have brought credit to itself if it had not exercised its rights and this would have been highly useful in maintaining peace.

However, it is obvious that the Government has not to date developed such discretion. It has given a clear reason for the public to get enraged. If the latter shows anger, it will lose the game which it is about to win. Some officials may even hope that the public will give vent to its anger. Whether they do so or not, ours is a straightforward path. While negotiating the settlement, Bhagat Singh's hanging was weighing upon us. We had hoped that the Government would be cautious enough to pardon Bhagat Singh and his associates to the extent of remitting the sentence of hanging. We should not break the pledge we have taken just because our hopes have not been fulfilled, but should bear this blow which has fallen upon us and honour our pledge. By doing so under even such trying circumstances, our strength to get what we desire will increase rather than decrease, while, if we break our pledge or violate the truce, we shall suffer loss of vigour, loss of strength and it will add to our present difficulties in reaching our objective. Hence our dharma is to swallow our anger, abide by the settlement and carry out our duty.

[From Gujarati]
Navajivan, 29-3-1931

46. An Englishman's Dilemma

(vol. XLVI, pp. 3–8)

India knows the Englishman who carried my letter containing the eleven points to the Viceroy and who waged a ceaseless struggle in the face of heavy odds in England whilst the Civil Disobedience was going on. Mr. Reginald Reynolds now writes the following plaintive letter.[1]

I have removed nothing from the letter except domestic and personal references. I publish the letter at Mr. Reynolds's wish. And I do so with pleasure as I know that though by reason of amazing faith in me the Congress endorsed the Pact,[2] there are Indians who share this brave Englishman's views. There must be also some Englishmen, be they ever so few, who are puzzled like Reynolds over my moderation and so-called inconsistency. I must, therefore, attempt to answer Reynolds's complaints for his and their sakes. India will want their active help and sympathy for many a year to come.

The charge of moderation I must admit. Friends who know me have certified that I am as much a moderate as I am an extremist and as much a conservative as I am a radical. Hence perhaps my good fortune to have friends among these extreme types of men. The mixture is due, I believe, to my view of ahimsa.

Inconsistency is only apparent. It appears so to many friends because of my responsiveness to varying circumstances. Seeming consistency may really be sheer obstinacy.

The real point is this. Charges of moderation or extremism or inconsistency ought not to matter. What must count with a public servant is the approbation of his own conscience. He must be like a rudderless vessel who, leaving the infallible solace of his own conscience, ever seeks to please and gain the approbation of the public.

---

1. Omitted.
2. Gandhi-Irwin Pact.

Service must be its own and sole reward. Whether therefore the argument and facts I am about to set forth serve their purpose or not, it must be sufficient for the reader as it is, I am aware, for Reynolds to know that in entering upon and advising the acceptance of the Settlement, I have done what in my opinion was not only right but obligatory.

Now for the facts and the arguments. Reynolds and those who think like him have been led into confusion because he and they have missed the historical perspective. A single new factor may change a whole situation. Reynolds mentions four events: (1) The Delhi Manifesto of November 1929, (2) The Eleven points, (3) The terms given to Mr. Slocombe, (4) The Gandhi-Nehru terms.

The Delhi Manifesto was an answer to Lord Irwin's famous declaration and was therefore just confined to that declaration.

The Eleven-point letter was written as a precursor to Civil Disobedience and set forth the conditions on which Civil Disobedience could be averted. It had therefore to be different from the November Manifesto.

The terms to Mr. Slocombe were given just after the commencement of civil disobedience. There was therefore a slight variation from the Eleven-point letter but no reduction of it.

The Gandhi-Nehru terms were given during the height of the movement and whilst we were all in custody and thus by being shut out of the world at a disadvantage. In all the four stages the Round Table Conference had not been held, the Government policy was not declared.

The Settlement is the natural evolution from the first stage. Whatever the variations between the stages, they are due to the varying situations. Unlike as in the four stages, the Round Table Conference had been held and the Government policy declared before the fifth stage, i.e., the Settlement, was reached.

At no other time was it possible to offer co-operation at the Round Table Conference because the British Government would not declare its policy and the intention of the delegates to the Conference was not known. But at Delhi last March the demand of the Conference delegates was known as was also known the British policy. The demand was Dominion Status. The British policy was a declaration tantamount to the acceptance of the demand.

Not that either the Indian demand for Dominion Status or the British declaration satisfy the Congress requirement, especially as they are hedged in by the so-called safeguards which, according to the Congress notion, certainly are not designed in the interest of India.

Nevertheless this is an unmistakable advance upon the past uncertainty. And when it was ascertained that it was possible for the Congress to press forward its view to the fullest extent, it was felt that the Congress would put itself in the wrong if it had declined to put forth its demand and press for its acceptance at a Round Table. The Congress would have been bound at any stage to enter upon a discussion of its claims after such declaration as has been made by the British Government. A satyagrahi never misses, can never miss, a chance of compromise on honourable terms, it being always assumed that in the event of failure he is ever ready to offer battle. He needs no previous preparation, his cards are always on the table. Suspension or continuation of battle is one and the same thing to him. He fights or refrains to gain precisely the same end. He dare not always distrust his opponents. On the contrary he must grasp the hand of friendship whenever there is the slightest pretext. The pretext here was the unexpectedly unanimous Indian demand, the British response, inadequate though it was, and the utter sincerity running through Lord Irwin's conversations.

I have never claimed any change of heart on the part of the powers that be. That has still to come. When it comes, there will be a settlement not merely provisional but absolutely permanent. Then there will be full surrender on the part of the satyagrahi; for change of heart means surrender to the Indian demand *in toto* and without any mental reservation.

Lastly, throughout all the stages there never has been a lowering of the flag. Dominion Status was given up on 23rd December 1929. It is now Complete Independence, i.e., association if possible with the British on equal terms and with the right to either party to dissolve it at will. That this may not be attained through conference as yet is quite possible; that the so-called safeguards may remain the halters that they are is also highly possible. If so the Congress will not be responsible for failure, but it will come out with enhanced moral prestige and its demand more fully known and equally fully justified. It is true that all the political prisoners are not discharged. Their discharge could not be demanded as part of the *Provisional* Settlement. They will be discharged if full settlement is reached. If it is not reached, those who are temporarily out will then be in and increase the army of political prisoners. For a satyagrahi a prisoner's life is no disability, no unhappiness. Prison for him is the gateway to freedom.

Lastly, let there be no mistake as to what *purna* swaraj means to the Congress. It is full economic freedom for the toiling millions. It is no unholy alliance with any interest for their exploitation. Any alliance must mean their deliverance.

Young India, 16-4-1931

47. A Frank Friend
(vol. XLVII, pp. 406–8)

[Before September 11, 1931][1]

Thus writes an English friend who has known me for years:

No one has for some time told you quite bluntly, and in good English, that you are making an unmitigated fool of yourself, and out of personal vanity and the desire to act the dictator, are descending to lies and subterfuges which even ordinary men, who lay no claim to special sanctity, do not indulge in.

You know full well, that the main reason for your not attending the Round Table Conference is due to your inability to solve the Hindu-Muslim question, and that you have used petty matters as an excuse. Your Congress Committee man at Allahabad, Mr. Sundarlal, has publicly made this statement, and you know full well the text of your motion, moved at the Working Committee meeting, when you were turned down by your Committee. You admitted in that resolution the failure of Hindu-Muslim negotiations and your inability to put forward any political proposals at the Round Table Conference, and that you would confine yourself solely to work for the amelioration of the condition of the masses.

You, who prate of worshipping at the altar of truth, the same altar that I worship at, are by half-truths, cunning words and deliberate deception trying to force the blame of your deliberate pre-arranged determination not to go to the Round Table Conference on the Government.

When, as you now boldly declare, sedition is the creed of Congress and the overthrow of this Government its objectives, are you not, with calculated deliberation, forcing the Government to take action? You may throw dust successfully in the eyes of your followers, but at least you do know that you cannot deceive His eyes. Go and introspect. Call on that inner voice honestly, not as Gandhi the politician, who, without the political guidance of Pandit Motilal Nehru, is making a fool of himself, and forcing events towards an upheaval which will benefit nobody but goondas, but to the other

1. This was written on board the ship. Gandhi reached Marseilles on September 11.

Gandhi, whom millions, and I include myself in that list, respect for his creed of love and the splendid work he is doing for the depressed classes. That Gandhi is overpowered. Your personal pride and autocratic spirit has vanquished the other Gandhi.

I want, every European wants, to see India politically free, and the Round Table Conference is the constitutional means for that purpose. You, however, deliberately seek her freedom through blood, because your pride received an enormous shock when you found that the Conference would go on without you, though you will call it 'passive resistance' and other names. You cannot evade these facts.

Go, I beg of you, and introspect, and after purification come to the altar of truth.

In order that I may not miss his wrath through any mishap, he registered the letter. The letter could be handed to me only on board. The best answer to the letter is that I am writing this on the steamer that is taking me to London. Indeed I might have suppressed the letter. But I did not, as it is typical of many I have received in the course of my life. When I do something that pleases them, my English friends issue embarrassing certificates. And when I do something that displeases them, forgetful of what they said in the past, they swear at me. They will not stop to inquire of me why they see an inconsistency between my past conduct and the present. They will not have the patience to discover the perfect harmony between two seemingly inconsistent acts. When I find such friends, I distrust their praise and its disinterestedness, and hence remain unaffected by their censure. Take the writer of the foregoing elegant censure. Only a few months ago, I was a good man. Now suddenly I have become all that is bad, even a liar, because he suspects that I would not go to London because of my failure to bring about Hindu-Muslim unity. He will not even condescend to ask me for an explanation, and believes a garbled report of my speech at the last A.I.C.C. meeting. Let him and the public know, that I hold in my bag a wire from Pandit Sundarlal, saying that he never made the remark attributed to him. But I suggest that even if Pandit Sundarlal did make the remark attributed to him, that would be no basis for a friend to found an accusation against me. A friendship, that cannot bear the slightest strain and would believe any rumour or report against a friend is not worth much, if anything. Let those English friends who have sent me wires or letters of congratulations, be warned against rushing to unjust judgments, the moment they hear reports about my doings which may displease them. The reports need not always be false, as was the case in the present instance. If the common purpose is well understood, friendships formed to advance that purpose should weather all storms of misunderstandings, misreportings and the like.

I will therefore state the purpose. It is complete freedom from the alien yoke in every sense of the term, and this for the sake of the dumb millions. Every interest therefore, that is hostile to their interest, must be revised, or must subside if it is not capable of revision. This freedom does not, need not, exclude partnership with the English on terms of absolute equality and terminable at the will of either party. Those Englishmen, who sincerely desire the immediate consummation of such an event, will never need to repent of their having issued to me a certificate of merit. The others will see nothing but evil in my most innocent acts.

Young India, 17-9-1931

48. Speech at Prayer Meeting [1]
(vol. XLVII, pp. 393–94)

S.S. "Rajputana",
[September 5, 1931]

Prayer has been the saving of my life. Without it I should have been a lunatic long ago. My autobiography will tell you that I have had my fair share of the bitterest public and private experiences. They threw me into temporary despair, but if I was able to get rid of it, it was because of prayer. Now I may tell you that prayer has not been part of my life in the sense that truth has been. It came out of sheer necessity, as I found myself in a plight when I could not possibly be happy without it. And the more my faith in God increased, the more irresistible became the yearning for prayer. Life seemed to be dull and vacant without it. I had attended the Christian service in South Africa, but it had failed to grip me. I could not join them in prayer. They supplicated God, but I could not do so, I failed egregiously. I started with disbelief in God and prayer, and until at a late

1. This is extracted from Mahadev Desai's account in which he reports: "The morning prayers are too early to attract these friends, but practically all Indians (who number over 40),—Hindus, Mussalmans, Parsis, Sikhs,—and a sprinkling of Europeans attend the evening prayers. At the request of some of these friends a fifteen minutes' talk after prayer and before dinner has become a daily feature. . . . A question is asked each evening, and Gandhi replies to it the next. One of the Indian passengers—a Mussalman youth—asked Gandhi to give his personal testimony on prayer, not a theoretical discourse but a narration of what he had felt and experienced as a result of prayer."

stage in life I did not feel anything like a void in life. But at that stage I felt that as food was indispensable for the body, so was prayer indispensable for the soul. In fact food for the body is not so necessary as prayer for the soul. For starvation is often necessary in order to keep the body in health, but there is no such thing as prayer-starvation. You cannot possibly have a surfeit of prayer. Three of the greatest teachers of the world—Buddha, Jesus, Mahomed—have left unimpeachable testimony that they found illumination through prayer and could not possibly live without it. But to come nearer home. Millions of Hindus and Mussalmans and Christians find their only solace in life in prayer. Either you vote them down as liars or self-deluded people. Well, then, I will say, that this lying has a charm for me, a truth-seeker, if it is 'lying' that has given me that mainstay or staff of life, without which I could not bear to live for a moment. In spite of despair staring me in the face on the political horizon, I have never lost my peace. In fact I have found people who envy my peace. That peace, I tell you, comes from prayer. I am not a man of learning but I humbly claim to be a man of prayer. I am indifferent as to the form. Everyone is a law unto himself in that respect. But there are some well-marked roads, and it is safe to walk along the beaten tracks, trod by the ancient teachers. Well, I have given my practical testimony. Let everyone try and find that as a result of daily prayer he adds something new to his life, something with which nothing can be compared.

Young India, 24-9-1931

49. Interview by *THE NEW YORK TIMES*

(vol. XLVII, pp. 415–17)

Marseilles,
September 11, 1931

Mahatma Gandhi has no intention of visiting the United States because he believes he is "not wanted" there, he said in an interview with The New York Times *when he landed here. . . .*

He explained that he refused to contemplate such a visit unless and until he could feel certain that Americans would receive him as the spokesman for India's cause and not as a social curiosity. His American friends had told him, he added, that this was not now possible.

[In reply to another question he said:]

To climatic conditions I am indifferent. If the political weather is favourable, I will go anywhere where I am needed.

I am afraid there is no hope for India at the Round Table Conference as far as external appearances are concerned. But, as an irrepressible optimist, I hope against hope that something will turn up which will alter the aspect of the horizon. But since such a hope is only based on faith, not on reason, it may prove illusory.

I have come to London with neither a programme nor proposals. I have simply accepted the invitation of the British Government, and I am ready to place myself at their disposal, to answer questions and to give them all the information within my power. I have come expecting to remain in London only two weeks, but I am ready, if necessary, to remain two months.

The only engagement I have made is in the nature of a pilgrimage. I have promised to visit my friend, Romain Rolland, the celebrated French writer, who is lying sick at his home near Territet, Switzerland, and whose sister, Madeleine Rolland, was among the old friends who greeted me on my arrival at Marseilles.

Asked if he believed the recent change in the Government of Great Britain would change the British policy toward India, Mr. Gandhi said unhesitatingly:

No. Besides, the new Government has already given me assurances it will carry out the policy of its predecessor, as far as the India Conference is concerned.

With regard to the critical Hindu-Muslim differences, however . . . the Mahatma admitted:

I fear the Hindu-Muslim question has now become almost insoluble for reasons on which I don't wish to enlarge. But I am still not without hope that a solution may be found. It is open to the Muslims to block the way to a settlement of the future of India as it is equally open to the British Government to make their opposition an excuse for not granting India self-government. But if the British Government is in earnest in its desire to make a friendly settlement with India it should not take shelter behind the Muslims.

I asked Mr. Gandhi if he was fully satisfied that Muslims and other racial or religious minorities would receive justice under a swaraj home-rule government, mainly Hindu, as it would be if appointed on a population basis.

He replied that the claims of the minorities must receive the fullest satisfaction in any future settlement. He himself, he recalled, had frequently urged his fellow-Hindus to accept all the Muslim claims, partly on sentimental grounds and partly because he was convinced some of them were unrealizable in practice. But he said emphatically that Muslim opinion must be conciliated and satisfied before swaraj was possible. He confessed,

*however, that he did not know in the present state of confusion and unrest
how this was to be effected.*

*I then challenged Mr. Gandhi to explain apparent inconsistencies in his
attitude regarding the 60,000,000 out cast Hindu 'untouchables,' certain of
his statements concerning this grave problem having provoked much criticism from his friends, both in India and in America.*

Mr. Gandhi said with the greatest earnestness:

Believe me, my attitude on the question of untouchability has
never wavered in the slightest degree. My position regarding the untouchables is unanswerable. Before my critics were born I defended
the rights of the untouchables. The misunderstanding which arose
regarding my attitude was apparently due to the fact that I rebuked
the leaders of an untouchables' deputation which interviewed me
early last year. But I am always rebuking someone, and usually my
dearest friends.

What I told this deputation was that I refused to declare publicly
that the untouchable classes must be made a 'reserved' subject in
any home-rule settlement. I refused because I did not believe it possible. Nor do I today.

But I believe sincerely that no swaraj government could exist for
twenty-four hours which continued to uphold the principle of untouchability. No untouchable need fear that his interests under
swaraj will be neglected, as they are neglected now. At the present
moment the untouchables cannot be protected by the British Government, since the British cannot afford to offend the various interests interested in maintaining untouchability. But a real Indian government would not be forced to surrender to these interests, for it
would have a much greater interest to serve—that of national unity.

I reaffirm my statement that India's national existence will stand
or fall on the question of the untouchables.

The New York Times, 12-9-1931

50. Speech at Birmingham Meeting[1]
(vol. XLVIII, pp. 187–89)

Q. *You talk of the impoverishment of India as being the result of British
exploitation, but is it not a fact that the real cause of the agriculturists'*

1. Only part of this speech is reproduced.

misery is the rapacity of the Bania and extravagance of expenditure on the occasion of marriages and funerals? Finally, you charge the British Government with extravagance. But what have you to say to the extravagance of the Indian Princes?

A. The Indian Bania is not a patch upon the English Bania and, if we were acting violently, the Indian Bania would deserve to be shot. But then, the British Bania would deserve to be shot a hundred times. The rate of interest charged by the Indian Bania is nothing compared to the loot carried on by the British Bania through the jugglery of currency and merciless exactions of Land Revenue. I do not know of another instance in history of such an organized exploitation of so unorganized and gentle a race. As for the profligacy of the Indian Princes, while I would have little hesitation, if I had the power, in dispossessing them of their insolent palaces, I would have infinitely less in depriving the British Government of New Delhi. The extravagance of the Princes was nothing compared to the heartless squandering of crores of rupees on New Delhi to satisfy the whim of a Viceroy in order to reproduce England in India, when masses of people were dying of hunger.

An amusing question was asked by a friend who quoted a letter from The Manchester Guardian *in which the correspondent questioned Gandhiji's authority to speak for the untouchables, as he belonged to the priestly class which had kept that community depressed so far, and asked whether Gandhiji himself was not a great hindrance in the way of a settlement.*

I never knew that I was a Brahmin, but I do happen to be a Bania, which is certainly regarded as a term of painful reproach. But let me inform the audience that my community excommunicated me when I came to English shores 40 years ago and the work that I have been doing entitles me to be called a farmer, weaver and untouchable. I was wedded to the work for the extinction of untouchability long before I was wedded to my wife. There were two occasions in our joint life when there was a choice between working for the untouchables and remaining with my wife and I would have preferred the first. But thanks to my good wife, the crisis was averted. In my Ashram, which is my family, I have several untouchables and a sweet but naughty girl living as my own daughter. As to whether I am acting as a hindrance to a settlement, I confess, I am for the simple reason that I would not be satisfied with any compromise short of real complete independence for India.

Q. *Sometimes we have found it difficult to reconcile the special form of united protest that you have evolved, with an appeal to reason. What is it that makes you sometimes feel that appeal to reason should be put aside in favour of more drastic action?*

A. Up to the year 1906 I simply relied on appeal to reason. I was a very industrious reformer. I was a good draftsman, as I always had a close grip of facts which in its turn was the necessary result of my meticulous regard for truth. But I found that reason failed to produce an impression when the critical moment arrived in South Africa. My people were excited—even a worm will and does sometimes turn—and there was talk of wreaking vengeance. I had then to choose between allying myself to violence or finding out some other method of meeting the crisis and stopping the rot, and it came to me that we should refuse to obey legislation that was degrading and let them put us in jail if they liked. Thus came into being the moral equivalent of war. I was then a loyalist, because I implicitly believed that the sum total of the activities of the British Empire was good for India and for 'humanity.' Arriving in England soon after the outbreak of the War, I plunged into it and later, when I was forced to go to India as a result of the pleurisy that I had developed, I led a recruiting campaign at the risk of my life, and to the horror of some of my friends. The disillusionment came in 1919 after the passage of the Black Rowlatt Act and the refusal of the Government to give the simple elementary redress of proved wrongs that we had asked for. And so, in 1920, I became a rebel. Since then the conviction has been growing upon me, that things of fundamental importance to the people are not secured by reason alone, but have to be purchased with their suffering. Suffering is the law of human beings; war is the law of the jungle. But suffering is infinitely more powerful than the law of the jungle for converting the opponent and opening his ears, which are otherwise shut, to the voice of reason. Nobody has probably drawn up more petitions or espoused more forlorn causes than I, and I have come to this fundamental conclusion that, if you want something really important to be done, you must not merely satisfy the reason, you must move the heart also. The appeal of reason is more to the head, but the penetration of the heart comes from suffering. It opens up the inner understanding in man. Suffering is the badge of the human race, not the sword.

Young India, 5-11-1931

51. A Retrospect

(vol. XLVIII, pp. 432–36)

[December 23, 1931]

Never since taking up the editorship of *Young India* have I, though not being on a sickbed or in a prison, been unable to send something for *Young India* or *Navajivan*, as I was during my stay in London.

The uninterrupted series of engagements keeping me awake till over midnight made it physically impossible for me to write anything for these journals. Fortunately, Mahadev Desai was with me and though he too was overworked, he was able to send a full weekly budget for *Young India*.

Nevertheless the reader will expect me to give my own impressions of the London visit.

Though I approached the visit in fear and trembling, I am not sorry for having gone there. It brought me in touch with the responsible Englishmen and women as also with the man in the street. This experience will be of inestimable value in future, whether we have to put up a fight again or not. It is no small matter to know with whom you are fighting or dealing.

It was a good thing that Muriel Lester, the soul of Kingsley Hall settlement, invited me to stay at her settlement and that I was able to accept the invitation. The choice lay between Kingsley Hall and Mr. Birla's Arya Bhavan. I had no difficulty in making my choice nor had Mr. Birla. But great pressure was put upon me by Indian friends, and that naturally, to stay at Arya Bhavan. Experience showed that Kingsley Hall was an ideal choice. It is situated among the poor of London and is dedicated purely to their service. Several women and some men, under the inspiration of Muriel Lester, have dedicated themselves to such service. Not a corner of the big building is used for any other purpose. There is religious service, there are entertainments, there are lectures, billiards, reading-room, etc., for the use of the poor. The inmates live a life of severe simplicity. There is no superfluous furniture to be found in all that settlement. The inmates occupy tiny rooms called cells. It was no joke to accommodate five of us in that settlement. But love makes room where there is none. Four settlers vacated their cells which were placed at our disposal. Bedding, etc., had to be borrowed. Fortunately, we had all armed ourselves with sufficient blankets and, being used to squat on the floor, most of the articles borrowed could be returned. But, there was no doubt, my presence at the settlement put a severe tax on its time, space and other resources. But the good people would not hear of my leaving it. And to me it was a privilege to receive the loving, silent and unseen services of the members and a perennial joy to come in vital contact with the poor of the East End of London. Needless to say I was able to live exactly as in India, and early morning walks through the streets of East London are a memory that can never be effaced. During these walks I had most intimate talks with those members who joined me and others whom Muriel allowed. For she was a vigilant guardian of my time whilst I was in the settlement. And she would get easily angry if she heard that my time was being abused by people when she was not by me.

During my stay in East London, I saw the best side of human nature and was able to confirm my intuitive opinion that at bottom there was neither East nor West. And as I received the smiling greetings of the East Enders, I knew that they had no malice in them and they wanted India to regain her independence. This experience has brought me closer to England if such a thing was possible. For me the fight is never with individuals, it is ever with their manners and their measures. But this intimate contact with the simple poor people of the East End, including the little children, will put me still more on my guard against any hasty action.

I may not omit my all too brief experience of Lancashire and its operatives and employers whom, to my agreeable surprise, I found to be so free from prejudice and receptive of new facts and arguments drawn from them. Here, of course, the ground was prepared for me by Charlie Andrews. I must mention too the never-to-be-forgotten visit to Mr. C. P. Scott of the *Manchester Guardian*, the most impartial and the most honest paper in Great Britain. A great British statesman told me the *Guardian* was the sanest and the most honest journal in the world. Nor can I easily forget the communions at Canterbury, Chichester, Oxford, Cambridge and Eton. They gave me an insight into the working of the British mind which I could have got through no other means. These contacts have brought about friendships which will endure for ever. I do not omit the two detectives and their companions and the many constables who were told off to look after me. To me Sergeants Evans and Rogers, the two detectives, were no mere police officers. They became my trusty guides and friends looking after my comforts with the punctilious care of loving nurses. And it was a matter of great joy to me that they were permitted at my request to accompany me as far as Brindisi.

Last, but not least, was my pilgrimage to Romain Rolland, the sage of Villeneuve. Could I have left India just to visit him and his inseparable sister Madeleine, his interpreter and friend, I would have undertaken the voyage. But that could not be. The excuse of the Round Table Conference made this pilgrimage easily possible, and chance threw Rome in my way. And I was able to see something of that great and ancient city and Mussolini, the unquestioned dictator of Italy. And what would not I have given to be able to bow my head before the living image at the Vatican of Christ Crucified! It was not without a wrench that I could tear myself away from that scene of living tragedy. I saw there at once that nations like individuals could only be made through the agony of the Cross and in no other way. Joy comes not out of infliction of pain on others, but out of pain voluntarily borne by oneself.

II

I am, therefore, returning home not filled with disappointment but with hope enriched. This hope is based on the fact that what I saw in England and on the Continent not only did not shake my faith in truth and non-violence, but, on the contrary, strongly confirmed it. I found, too, many more kindred spirits than I had expected.

Of the Round Table Conference there is nothing new I can report. I spoke out plainly what I thought about its composition and its achievements. One thing, however, I would like to say here. It would be wrong to think that the British Ministers are humbugs and that they do not mean what they say. I have come away with the impression that they are honest in their professions but they are labouring under a heavy handicap. The delegates, whilst seemingly unanimous over fundamentals, betrayed amazing differences on details of fundamental importance. The minorities' question became a hopeless tangle, not wholly through the fault of the Ministers. But, after all, this was a temporary handicap. Their greatest handicap lay in their being spoon-fed on one-sided and often hopelessly false statements and anti-nationalist opinions received by them from their agents in India ever since the commencement of the British Raj. For the Ministers this information is generally gospel truth. They, therefore, believe us to be incapable of handling our own Defence and Finance, they believe that the presence of British troops and British civilians is necessary for the well-being of India. Perhaps, there is no nation on earth equal to the British in the capacity for self-deception.

In confirmation of what I am writing, I would commend to the reader the speech delivered by Sir Samuel Hoare at the House of Commons at the debate on the White Paper. In spite of warnings to the contrary, each time I saw the Secretary of State for India I came away with a higher opinion of his honesty and frankness. Of all the British Ministers I found him to be the most straightforward and frank. He is also a strong man, but he is a hard man. I believe him to be capable of advising or approving of ruthless repression and hitting the hardest. And he would honestly think that he was merciful even as a surgeon is merciful who applies the knife when he must with a steady and strong hand. This Secretary of State is a hard-working conscientious man who would slave away even though he might have a temperature. He knows his mind at a given moment. He has behind him all the British parties and the large majority known in modern British history. His speech, therefore, is the best British type. And yet it falls hopelessly short of the Congress demand and is based, as Congressmen would say, on utterly wrong data which unfortunately he believes in common with many honest British statesmen.

How can this British mentality be changed or, in other words, how can power be wrested from such unwilling hands? No argument will carry conviction to these statesmen; they are all seasoned hard-headed soldiers. They like and appreciate facts, deeds. They will understand an open rebellion and, if they cannot suppress it, they will at once admit that we are capable of defending ourselves and administering our own affairs. And I have come away with my view confirmed that they will also understand and perhaps more quickly appreciate a non-violent rebellion. But the unfortunate fact is that they do not believe in our corporate non-violence. And, what is more, they believe that corporate non-violence on a mass scale is impossible. No argument can remove this disbelief. Only actual experience can induce faith.

Nor do they believe that the Congress is really the party that can deliver the goods. Even General Smuts could not convince them that the Congress was such a party. How could he in the teeth of reports to the contrary from their agents in India?

Thus it appears to me that a further fiery ordeal is a necessity of the case. The British mind is not ready for anything radically more than the Prime Minister's declaration.

III

But I can come to no hasty conclusion. This is being written on 23rd December on S.S. *Pilsna* in ignorance of the situation in India. I do not know what possibilities there still are for further negotiation.

Nor do I know how far the situation in Bengal, United Provinces, Gujarat, and the South permits of peaceful negotiations. This much is clearer to me than ever before that our true battleground is not London, it is India. We have to convert not the British Ministers but the British civilians in India. The strongest Secretary of State for India cannot move much beyond the advice of his local agents. India Office is a clog on the wheel of India's progress. The real power resides in the 250 District Collectors, not even in the Viceroy. These Collectors have powers nowhere enjoyed on earth even by real dictators. The latter do not have behind them the machinery of a mighty Government which the Collectors can move at will.

But thus stated the problem becomes incredibly simple. Each district has the key to the situation in its own hands. We have to work out our own salvation in India by negotiation if at all possible, by direct action if it becomes imperatively necessary. I know that I shall not light-heartedly invite the nation to the ordeal, nor shall I hesitate, if I find no way out, to advise action. I shall strain every nerve to discover a way out.

Young India, 31-12-1931

52. The Jesus I Love
(vol. XLVIII, pp. 437–39)

December 25, 1931

I shall tell you how, to an outsider like me, the story of Christ, as told in the New Testament, has struck. My acquaintance with the Bible began nearly forty-five years ago, and that was through the New Testament. I could not then take much interest in the Old Testament, which I had certainly read, if only to fulfil a promise I had made to a friend whom I happened to meet in a hotel. But when I came to the New Testament and the Sermon on the Mount, I began to understand the Christian teaching, and the teaching of the Sermon on the Mount echoed something I had learnt in childhood and something which seemed to be part of my being and which I felt was being acted up to in the daily life around me.

I say it seemed to be acted up to, meaning thereby that it was not necessary for my purpose that they were actually living the life. This teaching was non-retaliation, or non-resistance to evil. Of all the things I read what remained with me for ever was that Jesus came almost to give a new law—though He of course had said He had not come to give a new law, but tack something on to the old Mosaic law. Well, He changed it so that it became a new law—not an eye for an eye, and a tooth for a tooth, but to be ready to receive two blows when one was given, and to go two miles when you were asked to go one.

I said to myself, "This is what one learns in one's childhood. Surely this is not Christianity." For, all I had then been given to understand was that to be a Christian was to have a brandy bottle in one hand and beef in the other. The Sermon on the Mount, however, falsified the impression.

As my contact with real Christians, i.e., men living in fear of God, increased, I saw that the Sermon on the Mount was the whole of Christianity for him who wanted to live a Christian life. It is that Sermon which has endeared Jesus to me.

I may say that I have never been interested in a historical Jesus. I should not care if it was proved by someone that the man called Jesus never lived, and that what was narrated in the Gospels was a figment of the writer's imagination. For the Sermon on the Mount would still be true for me.

Reading, therefore, the whole story in that light, it seems to me that Christianity has yet to be lived, unless one says that where there is boundless love and no idea of retaliation whatsoever, it is Christianity that lives. But then it surmounts all boundaries and book-teaching. Then it is something indefinable, not capable of being preached to men, not capable of being transmitted from mouth to mouth, but from heart to heart. But Christianity is not commonly understood in that way.

Somehow, in God's providence, the Bible has been preserved from destruction by the Christians, so-called. The British and Foreign Bible Society has had it translated into many languages. All that may serve a real purpose in the time to come. Two thousand years in the life of a living faith may be nothing. For though we sang, "All glory to God on high and on the earth be peace," there seems to be today neither glory to God nor peace on earth.

As long as it remains a hunger still unsatisfied, as long as Christ is not yet born, we have to look forward to Him. When real peace is established, we will not need demonstrations, but it will be echoed in our life, not only in individual life, but in corporate life. Then we shall say Christ is born. That to me is the real meaning of the verse we have sung.[1] Then we will not think of a particular day in the year

1. The proceedings had opened with the singing of a hymn celebrating Christ's Nativity: "While shepherds watched their flocks by night."

as that of the birth of Christ, but as an ever-recurring event which can be enacted in every life.

And the more I think of fundamental religion, and the more I think of miraculous conceptions of so many teachers who have come down from age to age and clime to clime, the more I see that there is behind them the eternal truth that I have narrated. That needs no label or declaration. It consists in the living of life, never ceasing, ever progressing towards peace.

When, therefore, one wishes "A Happy Christmas" without the meaning behind it, it becomes nothing more than an empty formula. And unless one wishes for peace for all life, one cannot wish for peace for oneself. It is a self-evident axiom, like the axioms of Euclid, that one cannot have peace unless there is in one an intense longing for peace all round. You may certainly experience peace in the midst of strife, but that happens only when to remove strife you destroy your whole life, you crucify yourself.

And so, as the miraculous birth is an eternal event, so is the Cross an eternal event in this stormy life. Therefore, we dare not think of birth without death on the Cross. Living Christ means a living Cross. Without it life is a living death.

Young India, 31-12-1931

CHRONOLOGY IV
1932–1936

In this four-year period, Gandhi devoted his energies to renewing Hinduism from within. He began by concentrating upon the problem of untouchability. He fasted against a British government plan to promote the interests of untouchables against those of caste Hindus. Gandhi was ready to die to prevent the implementation of that plan, even though a powerful group of untouchables was organized to welcome the British initiative politically. He was determined that Hindus themselves should come to the rescue of untouchables, and that they should do so as an act of religious conscience. They should acknowledge their human guilt as a sin against their religion as well as against their brothers, and they must take the untouchables back into Hinduism. Having defeated the British, he turned upon his coreligionists, both the Brahmin guardians of orthodox Hinduism and the selfish profiteers who exploited the caste hierarchy. He founded a Harijan Association and launched many specific reforms.

Later, at the end of 1934, he founded the All India Village Industries Association, whose aim was to save the Indian village and villager. In India as elsewhere—by the will or neglect of the Indian middle class as well as of the British administration—the interests of villages were being sacrificed to those of the cities. Industry was being promoted at the expense of agriculture. Gandhi's association was designed to make the villagers largely self-sufficient by improving the quality of the goods they themselves produced. He founded the association just a few months after he resigned from Congress, and the two acts together constituted a turn away from political to cultural action.

Some of his most famous fasts occurred in this period. Besides fasting against the British government and its plan, he fasted against Hindus' treatment of untouchables and against his own followers' violence in the cause and sexual license among themselves. Fasting was a mode of discipline as well as a mode of purification and of protest.

1932

On August 18, he wrote to the prime minister, announcing a fast unto death against the British government's Communal Award, which proposed to create separate electorates for untouchables within an Indian system of elected councils. Gandhi wanted Hindus to repent for their treatment of untouchables and to bring the latter back inside the circle of their religion, not to have the untouchables constitute a separate entity outside Hinduism.

On September 20, he began to fast. Dr. Ambedkar, the leader of the untouchables, felt he was being forced to agree with Gandhi by moral blackmail, and he resented it.

On September 24, Gandhi agreed to accept the resolve reached among leaders of all shades of Hindu opinion that "henceforth among Hindus no one shall be regarded as an untouchable by reason of his birth."

On September 26, when the British government also accepted this Poona Settlement, he broke his fast.

In November, he began to issue a series of directives about how to combat untouchability.

1933

On February 11, Gandhi began to publish the weekly Harijan; *this was the word (literally meaning "people of God") that he now began to apply to untouchables.*

On May 8, he began a twenty-one-day fast for the purification of the Harijan cause because sexual license had been discovered among those who worked for it. The government released him from jail. He therefore postponed his civil disobedience campaign for six weeks.

On July 25, he announced the disbanding of his Sabarmati Ashram and the beginning of individual civil disobedience.

On July 31, he was arrested.

On August 4, he was released but was ordered to leave the area of Yeravda and to live in Poona. He broke this order and was rearrested. He asked permission to continue his Harijan work from jail.

On August 16, he began to fast because this request was refused. On August 23, he was released because his life was in danger.

On September 14, he suspended civil disobedience.

On November 7, he began an all-India Harijan tour. He wanted Hindu temples opened to Harijans, access to drinking water guaranteed to them, and the removal of all the penalties imposed on them.

1934

In January, a great earthquake occurred in Bihar, which claimed many lives and threw many people onto relief. Gandhi collected funds on their behalf but said (in March) that the earthquake could be regarded as God's punishment for the sin of untouchability. This angered people such as Rabindranath Tagore, who thought that Indians needed to be educated out of superstition and religiosity. A public debate took place between the two on this issue.

There were demonstrations against him during his Harijan tour, staged by religiously orthodox, or Sanatani, Hindus.

On June 25, a bomb was thrown at him in Poona, a center of Hindu nationalist feeling.

On July 1, he welcomed the formation of a Socialist Party within the Congress.

On July 17, he announced his retirement from Congress, where his leadership involuntarily caused hypocritical behavior on the part of those who did not really agree with him.

On August 7, he began a seven-day fast because of violence engaged in by his followers against the Sanatanis during the tour.

On October 29, he retired from Congress.

On December 15, he founded the All India Village Industries Association (A.I.V.I.A.). He was transferring his activities from politics to cultural change.

1935

On January 2, he laid the foundation stone of the Harijan Colony in New Delhi and opened the Harijan Conference at Narela.

On January 10, he announced the program of the A.I.V.I.A.—to promote the use of unpolished rice and hand-ground flour, the production of gur (rather like molasses), and so on.

From February 1 through 4, he attended the A.I.V.I.A. meeting at Wardha.

1936

In January, Gandhi had some septic teeth removed and was ordered to rest. Around January 17, he was interviewed by Margaret Sanger, who came to India campaigning for contraception and for marriage reform. Gandhi disagreed with her but described his own marital experience.

In April, he moved from Wardha to the poverty-striken village of Segaon, where he set up a new ashram, Sevagram.

The selections that follow reflect life in the ashram as well as his major political and cultural activities. While he was in jail, Gandhi wrote more often than usual to the ashram; and as well as numerous letters to individuals (some interesting examples to Premabehn Kantak are included), he wrote general letters addressed to Narandas Gandhi, the manager of the ashram, but meant for everyone to hear. He also wrote discourses and essays for the people there, including one on the stars, in which he began to take an interest while in jail. We glimpse his concern for alien members of the ashram, such as Mirabehn and Nilla Cram Cook, an American. And at the end of the period we read his interview with Margaret Sanger, to whom he talked about sex and marriage.

53. Letter to Premabehn Kantak

(vol. XLIX, pp. 104–6)

February 19, 1932

Chi. Prema,

Your letter was very good. I was glad that you wrote quite freely.

This is my reply to your criticism.[1] I must hear what the persons concerned have to say in their defence. Only after that can I express my opinion in each case. In a general way, however, I can say that, whenever some freedom was permitted, it was done not as a privilege but as a matter of necessity. I have formed the impression that those who permit themselves any freedom do so not out of lethargy

---

1. Regarding inmates of the ashram allowing themselves freedom from one or other of the ashram rules.

but because their bodies, or say their natures, demand it. We ought not to sit in judgment over others. We may not even be aware of the effort they make [to follow the rules]. This does not mean that such persons have no imperfection in them. If they did not have any, why did they join the Ashram at all? They are not hypocrites. There is a great error in believing that everyone should or can do what one does. If I tried to lift a weight which Hariyomal[2] can, I would die that very moment. Similarly, it would be wrong of him to envy me my weakness.

Many have said that people deceive me. I don't say that no one deceives me, but the number of such persons is certainly not large. I have observed that many persons cannot, when they are away from me, keep up the standard of behaviour which they preserve when I am there. Some even leave me for this reason. There are many such instances and that is why I have been accused of possessing a kind of magnetism.

But this is not likely to satisfy you or others. Nor have I said this to defend myself. I have only explained my attitude. The real position, however, is this, and I have held this belief for many years. The deficiencies of the Ashram reflect my own. I have told many people that they cannot know me by meeting me. When they meet me, I may even impress them as being good. Even if I am not good, people would believe that I was because I am a lover of truth. My love of truth casts a momentary spell over people. In order to know me, people should see the Ashram in my absence. There would be no error and no injustice to me in believing that all its deficiencies are a reflection of my own deficiencies. It is but true that I have drawn the crowd which has gathered in the Ashram. If, though living in the Ashram, they have not been able to overcome their weaknesses but have, on the contrary, developed more, the fault is not theirs but mine. The imperfection of my spiritual striving is responsible for this state of affairs. Nor is it that I do not observe or know about my shortcomings. All that I can say is that they are there despite my best efforts to overcome them. And, moreover, I am convinced that, because I am ceaselessly striving to improve the Ashram, it has not, on the whole, fallen altogether from its ideal. I derive some satisfaction from the thought that every one of the three Ashrams which I established served or has served its immediate aim. I will not, however, deceive myself or anybody else with this comforting thought. I

2. A strong man from Sind who worked on the ashram farm.

wish to travel far and there are hills and valleys to be crossed on the way. I am resolved, however, to continue the journey. And I rest in peace in the knowledge that there is no defeat in the quest for truth.

It is true indeed that the Ashram has not been able to attract the learned class. The reason is that I don't regard myself as a learned man. The few learned men who were drawn to the Ashram joined it not in order to pursue their learned callings but to receive and nurse something else altogether. They [are] seekers after truth. The quest of truth may be undertaken even by the illiterate, by children and by the old, by women and by men. Literary education sometimes serves as the golden lid which covers the face of truth. I do not, by saying this, condemn such education, but only put it in its proper place. It is one of the means [in the pursuit of truth].

We have selected most of the prayers from Sanskrit because it is chiefly Hindus who joined the Ashram. We have no aversion to prayers in other languages. Don't we use such prayers occasionally? If, instead of a large number of Hindus, a large number of Muslims had joined the Ashram, prayers from the Koran would be recited every day and I would even join such prayers.

Does this answer your doubts? Does it satisfy you? If it does not, ask me again and again. I shall not get tired. I wish to satisfy you. Don't get tired.

Blessings from
BAPU

From the Gujarati.

54. Letter to Premabehn Kantak

(vol. XLIX, pp. 156–58)

February 25, 1932

Chi. Prema,

I got your letter.

You want from me inspired utterances which would touch the heart. If I had a safe filled with them, I would open it and send some every week. But I have so such safe. The words which I pen or speak, come to me unsought. Only such words have truth in them, for they are living words. All other statements are insincere. They may seem arresting, but I think they produce no abiding effect on the heart. I can do nothing insincere. During my student days in England, I attempted twice [to make prepared speeches] and failed on both occasions. I never tried again.

And what is true about my speaking is also true about my behaviour to you on all other occasions which you mention. I remember the conversation we had regarding Mirabehn.[1] I must have replied to you as I felt at the moment. I can understand that my words did not produce a good impression on you. That is a measure of the imperfection of my non-violence. I must have said only what I felt, but you might have felt a sting in my words. "One must speak the truth in words which are agreeable" is not only a maxim of practical wisdom but is a moral principle. "Agreeable" here means non-violent. If I had told you gently what I did excitedly, my words would not have left behind them the bitter memory which they have. Truth stated in a spirit of non-violence may hurt at the moment, but its ultimate effect must be as sweet as *amrit*. This is an essential test of non-violence. I am writing this from my own bitter experience. I may have spoken to you vehemently in defence of Mirabehn, but I have not made any man or woman weep as bitterly as I have made her. My hardness of heart, impatience and ignorant attachment were responsible for such conduct. I have felt Mirabehn's self-sacrifice to be beyond praise and, therefore, wish to see her perfect. The moment I see any imperfection in her, my ignorant attachment makes me impatient and I rebuke her sharply. The result is a flood of tears. These instances have opened my eyes to the presence of violence in me and, recalling them, I have been trying to reform myself. I, therefore, welcome your letters. I do not know whether in return I shall be able to give you anything, but personally I benefit from them. I realized this thing—my hard-heartedness—more vividly in England. Mira was the chief person in attendance on me. There, too, I caused her to weep bitterly on the slightest provocation. But I learnt a lesson from that experience. God has never let any delusion of mine last for ever. Even in the political sphere, whenever I have taken a false step God has immediately opened my eyes. Your letters help that process of awakening.

You will now understand my previous letter better. How can we expect perfection from an imperfect being? A blind man has collected a band of other blind folk. But the blind man knows that he is

1. The addressee had been rebuked by Gandhi when she complained against Mirabehn's having blocked a passage; later she quoted this incident as proof of Gandhi's unwillingness to listen to complaints against those whom he trusted.

blind, and also knows the cure for his blindness. Hence, though living with blind people, he is confident that he will not lead them into a pit, nor will he himself fall into it. He walks with a stick in [h]is hand. He feels the path ahead with the stick before taking every step. And, therefore, things have gone well on the whole so far. If, despite his using the stick, the blind man has occasionally strayed from the path, he has immediately realized his error and retraced his steps and led back his co-workers. So long as my blindness remains, even a person like you who loves me will continue to have reasons to criticize me. When the blindness has disappeared, there will be no such grounds for criticism. Meanwhile, let all of us, blind men and women, who are seekers after truth, describe the elephant as we perceive it. Our descriptions will vary, but each will be perfectly true from the person's limited point of view. After all, everyone of us will have but touched the elephant. When our eyes open all of us will dance with joy and shout: 'How blind we were! This is an elephant, about which we had read in the *Gita*. How fortunate it would have been if our eyes had opened earlier.' But why should we worry if their opening is delayed? Time has no meaning for God, or rather He measures it differently. Ignorance, thus, will become transformed into knowledge.

I hope you will get from this an explanation of all the shortcomings you may have observed in me. That does not mean, of course, that you should not put your doubts before me. You may continue to put them and I will reply every time.

Send my blessings to Sushila and Kisan. And also to Dhurandhar if you are permitted to write to him. How is Jamnadas's health? What happened to his school?

Blessings from
BAPU

From the Gujarati.

55. Watching the Heavens—I

(vol. XLIX, pp. 295–99)

A lover of truth feels undiminished joy till the end of his life. He never regards himself as too old to keep on striving for a vision of the God of Truth. He who undertakes every activity in order to see God, also called Truth, who sees Truth in everything [that exists] will not find old age an obstacle [in his quest]. So far as that quest is concerned, the seeker regards himself as immortal and for ever young.

I, for one, have been in this beautiful state of mind for years. I have never felt old age as an obstacle to devoting myself to learning anything which I believed would take me nearer to the God of Truth. A recent example of this is my desire for a study of the heavens. Deep in my heart, I had felt often enough the desire to know something about the stars, but I had assumed that the numerous activities which claimed my attention did not permit me to satisfy it. Maybe my belief was wrong, but so long as I did not myself see the error in it it could not but prevent me from making the necessary effort. I think most probably I myself had prompted Shankerlal, during our imprisonment in 1922 [to take up this study]. Books on the subject were received. Shankerlal picked up enough knowledge to satisfy him. I could find no time!

In 1930-31, I had the good fortune to enjoy Kakasaheb's company [in jail]. He was well versed in this subject. But I did not avail myself of the opportunity, for my desire was not strong enough then. In 1931, I was filled with sudden enthusiasm during the last month of my stay in jail. Why should I not give time to watch that which, to the outward eye, instantaneously reveals the presence of God? How pathetic that one should see like an animal merely with the physical eye without the grand sight penetrating to the sensory nerves behind? How could I let go this fine opportunity to watch the great divine *lila!*[1] I am now quenching the thirst which was awakened then for a knowledge of the heavens, and I have progressed so far that I cannot restrain myself from sharing with inmates of the Ashram the thoughts which fill my mind.

We are taught right from our childhood that our bodies are made of the five great elements—earth, water, *akash*, light and air. We ought to know something about them, but in fact we know very little. At the moment we are concerned with *akash*.

Akash means space. If there were no space in our bodies, we would not be able to live even for a moment. This is true about the universe too. Our earth is surrounded by infinite space. The blue which we see extending over us in all directions is *akash*. The earth has poles. It is a solid sphere, and its axis is 7,900 miles long. But the *akash* is empty space. If we imagine this space to have an axis, we shall have

1. Play, sport.

to imagine it to be of infinite length. In this infinite space, the earth is like a mere particle of sand, and on this particle of sand each one of us is a particle, of such infinitesimal size that it is impossible to explain how small it is. There is, therefore, no exaggeration at all in saying that, as bodies, we are mere ciphers. Our body, as compared with the size of the earth, is a thousand times more insignificant than an ant's is as compared with ours. Why, then, should we feel attached to it? Why should we grieve when a body perishes?

However, though in itself the human body is insignificant, it has indeed great value, for it is the house of the *atman*, in truth of the *Paramatman*, of the God of Truth, if we but realize it.

If this thought sinks deep into our heart, we would never want to make it an instrument of enjoying gross pleasures. And if we fill our imagination with the heavens and, realizing the meaning of their vastness, understand our utter insignificance, all our pride would vanish. If the countless shining divinities in the sky did not exist, we would not have come into existence. In spite of the many discoveries of astronomers, our knowledge about the sky is practically nil. What little we know tells us beyond the shadow of a doubt that if the sun-god rested even for a day from his ever ceaseless *tapascharya*, we would perish. Likewise, if the moon stopped raining down her cool rays, we would meet with the same fate. And we can also infer that the countless stars which we see in the sky at night have some role in maintaining this world in existence. Thus, we are most intimately connected with every living creature in the world and with everything that exists; everything depends for its existence on everything else. Hence we ought to try and know something about our benefactors the shining divinities gliding in the sky.

There is one more reason why we ought to do this. We have a saying among us: "The hills look beautiful from a distance." There is much truth in this saying. The sun, which keeps us alive from a distance, would instantly burn us to ashes if we went near it. This is also true about the other heavenly bodies. Since we know both the beneficial and the harmful properties of the things which surround us on this earth, we may sometimes feel aversion to them and even feel ourselves polluted by physical contact with some of them. Of the divinities in the sky, however, we know only the merits. Hence we never tire of watching them. Knowledge about them can never harm us. Moreover, as we meditate on these divinities, we can raise our imagination with ennobling ideas as high as we wish.

There is no doubt at all that every obstacle which we place between ourselves and the sky harms us physically, mentally and spiritually. If we lived in a natural state, we would live under the sky for all the twenty-four hours of the day. If we cannot do that, we should spend in the open as many hours as we can. We can watch the heavens, i.e., the stars, only at night, and we can do that best lying on our backs. Hence, anybody who wishes to derive the utmost profit from the observation of the stars should sleep in the open directly under the sky. If there are tall buildings or trees near the place where one is sleeping, they will obstruct the view.

Both children and grown-ups love dramas and the spectacular scenes which they present. But no drama composed or acted by human beings can even equal the great spectacle which Nature has arranged for us on the stage of the sky. Moreover, in a theatre we may harm our eyes, breathe unclean air and also run a great risk of our moral sense being weakened. On the other hand, this drama arranged by Nature can do us nothing but good. Watching the stars soothes the eyes; to watch the stars, one must remain outdoors, and this gives fresh air to the lungs; and we have heard of no instance so far of harm having been done to moral character by watching the stars. The more we meditate on this miracle of God, the more we grow spiritually. Anybody who is afflicted by impure thoughts and gets dreams in his sleep should try to sleep in the open and let himself be absorbed in watching the stars. He will soon fall into dreamless sleep. When we are totally absorbed in the grand spectacle in the heavens, we seem to hear those shining bodies in their utter silence, singing the praise of God. Let him, who has eyes to see, watch the ever-changing patterns of this eternal dance. Let him, who has ears to hear, listen to the silent music of these countless *gandharvas*.

Let us now try to learn something about these stars, or rather let me share with all co-workers what little knowledge I have picked up. The better method, of course, would be to learn something about the earth before proceeding to observation of the stars. It is quite likely that the boys and girls in the Ashram who have had the benefit of Kakasaheb's company already know the facts which I am going to describe. I should be happy if that is so. I am writing this for all inmates of the Ashram, children and grown-ups, old and new. Those to whom the subject is interesting will find the study quite easy.

The right time for the study of the sky is immediately after prayer. We need not give it more than twenty minutes at a time. Those who understand the true meaning of this study will regard it as a part of the prayer. Those of the inmates who sleep in the open may spend as much time as they wish, when they are alone, in watching the stars. As they become absorbed in the scene, they will soon fall asleep. If they wake up during the night, they may spend some more time in looking at the sky. Since the sky seems to be moving all the time, the scene keeps changing from second to second.

If we look at the sky at 8 p.m. in the west, we shall see a grand figure.

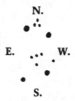

This figure will be in the west. I see it directly opposite me as I lie on my back with my head in the east. No one who sees the figure from this position will ever forget it afterwards. Since this is the bright half of the month, this and other constellations shine with a rather pale light, but even then this particular constellation is so bright that even a novice like me can spot it easily. I shall refer next time to the beliefs which people formerly held about this group both in our country and in the West. Just now, I shall only tell you that from the description of the position of this constellation in the Vedas, Tilak Maharaj was able to ascertain the date of the Vedas. We have in the Ashram library, a copy of the treatise by the late Shri Dikshit which gives plenty of information on this subject. My job is only to arouse interest in this direction. Once that is done, I myself shall learn more about the subject from the inmates of the Ashram. For me, these constellations have become a means of communion with God. May they be so for the inmates of the Ashram too.

> Live as you like,
> But realize Hari somehow, anyhow.

From the Gujarati.

56. Letter to Swami Anand

(vol. L, pp. 124–27)

July 1, 1932

Bhai Anandanand,[1]

You made me wait for a long time. Sardar asked me several times why your letter was still not received. We knew that it was not received. But what can you do? Even if the reason is known, one does hope for a thing which one ardently desires. You will receive this letter or it will come back to me. Many of those who have come in contact with me had similar experience about separation as you have got, though I am near you.[2] You are to draw as much satisfaction therefrom as you can. Kallenbach[3] had laid down a fine standard. His experience was that when he first came in contact with me, he met me daily and took as much of my time as he could; when we came in very close contact and began to live together he had hardly time to talk with me though we lived, ate and slept together. While returning home from office, there were always some people talking with us. So, that became a regular matter of quarrel between us. He applied the rule of three and came to the conclusion that it was his experience that the more one came into contact with me, the more he remained away from me. I supported his statement and added, "You have come so near me because you have understood me. Hence you have no right to take my time now nor have I the right to spare time for you, leaving aside those who have yet to know me." And on this understanding our affairs went on. Is it not that there is some truth underlying such experience, viz., that in the case of associates who are closely united with one another there remains nothing to make inquiries about? If they do so they may be said to fail to that extent in their general duty. And if this is true, associates like you who are near, though living at a distance, have no reason to feel sorrowful about.[4] I did know that your weight had gone down, but I had no fears about your health. The Magan spinning-wheel is not a modi-

1. Swami Anandanand, manager of the Navajivan Press.
2. The addressee had stated in his letter that he would not commit the crime of taking up Gandhi's time when he was free, and was not lucky enough to be his companion in jail. He could, therefore, never hope to be able to live with Gandhi and have an opportunity of discussing things personally with him.
3. Hermann Kallenbach, a German architect; devoted friend and co-worker of Gandhi in South Africa.
4. The following is reproduced from the English rendering of the letter available in Bombay Secret Abstracts.

fied or improved form of the Gandiva wheel. It is a distinct, useful and excellent discovery made by Prabhudas.[5] Its wheel can be worked by foot instead of by hand, and so both the hands being free, two spindles can be worked simultaneously. Hence he who becomes an expert in working it can without doubt spin one and a half times, if not double, of what he can do on a one-spindle wheel. I did want to work the wheel to satisfy Prabhudas. In the mean time the doctors here prohibited me from drawing the yarn or working the wheel with the left hand. So, there was a twofold reason for me to work the Prabhudas wheel. As Maganlal encouraged the making of that wheel and contributed largely to the scientific side of it, it has been named *Magan Rentio*. I am spinning on it at present. The speed has reached about 140 rounds. It will still go up. From the above remarks, I hope you have understood that I have been spinning only on one spindle because, giving complete rest to the left hand, I draw the thread with the right.

The yarn is of 19 counts. There is nothing to fear about the hand. When it is used in doing a particular kind of work, the elbow is aching and doctors persistently believe that the complaint is not due to any internal cause, but it is due to an external cause, viz., due to the drawing of threads daily. So, they are of the opinion that by giving rest to the muscles the complaint will subside by itself. Despite this, that part is treated by [ultra-]violet rays. Hence there is no cause for anxiety. My weight has failed to go up to 112 lb. It has not exceeded 106½ lb. I have been taking milk for the last ten days under pressure from the Superintendent. I am yet unable to say that I have benefited by it. My present weight is 104 lb. Sardar is doing well. His weight may be said to be the same as it was when he came [here]. It can be said that the nose complaint is under slight control. The weight of Mahadev is also good. His health is excellent. Mahadev had been spinning 840 yards of yarn of No. 45 to 50 up to the day before yesterday. He spent about five hours daily on it. As he also felt the effects of exertion, he spins half the amount of yarn for the last two days and is doing carding work, of course, in addition. I spin 200 yards of yarn. I study Urdu, astronomy and books on currency and write the history of the Ashram when I get time. Mahadev is reading on stray subjects. He has, of course, in addition, to write for me. Now the spinning having been reduced, he may, perhaps, begin to write something. Sardar produces wealth from dust, in other words, he has been making envelopes from wastepaper of *badami*[6] and other colours. If

5. Prabhudas Gandhi, eldest son of Chhaganlal Gandhi.
6. Brown.

I were to give you a description of the papers, you will laugh a lot. To whomsoever we have to write a letter, we make use of these envelopes. As we do not differentiate between Government money and ours, we save every cowry where possible. The making of envelopes is undoubtedly an addition to the wealth of India or that of the world, however small it may be. Keeping in mind that everything that is used as Government property is our property, we make use of it. Sardar is spending time also in reading and has thought of acquiring a working knowledge of Sanskrit. He has also called for the *Sanskrit Pathamala* by Satavlekar[7] and intends side by side to be well versed in Hindi too. This is the account of our work. Our family consists of a cat and her two kittens. Though their names are not entered in the history ticket, they share a little of milk, etc.[8]

Mahadevbhaini Diary, Vol. I, pp. 265–7

57. History of the Satyagraha Ashram [1]
(vol. L, pp. 188–225)

[July 11, 1932]

Introduction

Ashram here means a community of men of religion. Looking at the past in the light of the present, I feel that an ashram was a necessary of life for me. As soon as I had a house of my own, my house was an ashram in this sense, for my life as a householder was not one of enjoyment but of duty discharged from day to day. Again, besides the members of my family I always had some friends or others living with me, whose relation with me was spiritual from the first or became such later on. This went on unconsciously till 1904 when I read Ruskin's *Unto This Last*, which made a deep impression on me. I determined to take *Indian Opinion* into a forest where I should live with the workers as members of my family. I purchased 100 acres of land and founded Phœnix Settlement, which neither we nor anyone else called an ashram. It had a religious basis, but the visible object was purity of body and mind as well as economic equality. I did not then consider *brahmacharya* (chastity) to be essential; on the other

7. 1866–1968; renowned scholar and author of several books in Sanskrit.
8. Passage omitted.
1. Only fragments of this history are reproduced here.

hand it was expected that co-workers would live as family men and have children. A brief account of Phœnix will be found in *Satyagraha in South Africa*.

This was the first step.

The second step was taken in 1906. I learnt in the school of experience that *brahmacharya* was a *sine qua non* for a life devoted to service. From this time onward I looked upon Phœnix deliberately as a religious institution. The same year witnessed the advent of satyagraha which was based on religion and implied an unshakable faith in the God of Truth. Religion here should not be understood in a narrow sense, but as that which acts as a link between different religions and realizes their essential unity.

This went on till 1911. All these years the Phœnix Settlement was progressing as an ashram though we did not call it by that name.

We took the third step in 1911. So far only those people lived at Phœnix who were working in the press and the paper. But now as a part of the satyagraha movement we felt the need of an ashram where satyagrahi families could live and lead a religious life. I had already come in contact with my German friend Kallenbach. Both of us were living a sort of ashram life. I was a barrister and Kallenbach an architect. However we led a comparatively very simple life in the sparsely populated country, and were religiously minded. We might commit mistakes out of ignorance, but we were trying to seek the root of every activity in religion. Kallenbach purchased a farm of 1,100 acres and the satyagrahi families settled there. Religious problems confronted us now at every step and the whole institution was managed from a religious standpoint. Among the settlers there were Hindus, Mussalmans, Christians and Parsis. But I do not remember that they ever quarrelled with one another, though each was staunch in his own faith. We respected one another's religion and tried to help everybody to follow his own faith and thus to make spiritual progress. This institution was not known as Satyagraha Ashram but as Tolstoy farm. Kallenbach and I were followers of Tolstoy and endeavoured to practise much of his doctrine. Tolstoy Farm was closed in 1912 and the farmers were sent to Phœnix. The history of Tolstoy Farm will also be found in *Satyagraha in South Africa*.

Phœnix now was no longer meant for the workers of *Indian Opinion* only; it was a satyagraha institution. That was only to be expected, for *Indian Opinion* owed its very existence to satyagraha. Still it was a great change. The even tenor of the lives of the settlers at Phœnix was disturbed, and they had now to discern certainty in the midst of uncertainty like the satyagrahis. But they were equal to the new demands made upon them. As at Tolstoy Farm, so also at Phœnix I established a common kitchen which some joined while others had private kitchens of their own. The congregational prayer in the evening played a large part in our lives. And the final satyagraha campaign was started by the inmates of Phœnix Settlement in 1913. The struggle ended in 1914. I left South Africa in July that year. It was decided that all settlers who wanted to go to India should be enabled to go there. Before going to India I had to meet Gokhale in England. The idea was to found a new institution in India for those who went there from Phœnix. And the community life commenced in South Africa was to be continued in India. I reached India early in 1915 with a view to establish an ashram though I was still unaware that I would call it by that name.

I toured all parts of India for a year, and visited some institutions[2] from which I had much to learn. I was invited by several cities to establish the ashram in their neighbourhood with a promise of assistance in various ways. Ahmedabad was selected at last. This was the fourth, and I imagine the last step. Whether or not it will always be the last is something of which no forecast is possible.[3] How was the new institution to be named? What should be its rules and regulations? On these points I had full discussions and correspondence with friends, as a result of which we decided to call the institution Satyagraha Ashram. It is an appropriate name if we take its object into consideration. My life is devoted to the quest of truth. I would live and, if need be, die in prosecuting it, and of course I would take with me as many fellow-pilgrims as I could get.

The Ashram was established in a rented house at Kochrab on May 25, 1915. Some citizens of Ahmedabad undertood to finance it. At the beginning there were about 20[4] inmates, most of them from South Africa. Of these again the large majority spoke Tamil or Telugu. The chief activity in the Ashram at this time was teaching Sanskrit, Hindi and Tamil to the old as well as the young, who also received some general education. Hand-weaving was the principal industry with some carpentry as accessory to it. No servants were engaged; therefore cooking, sanitation, fetching water—everything was attended to by the Ashramites. Truth and other observances were obligatory on them all. Distinctions of caste were not observed.

2. Servants of India Society, Santiniketan, Gurukul Kangri.
3. Gandhi disbanded the Satyagraha Ashram in 1933. When he shifted to Segaon in April 1936, he had no intention of establishing an ashram there. However, it gradually developed into the Sevagram Ashram.
4. In Vol. XIII, p. 98, however, Gandhi mentions the number as 35.

Untouchability had not only no place in the Ashram, but its eradication from Hindu society was one of our principal objectives. Emancipation of women from some customary bonds was insisted upon from the first. Therefore women in the Ashram enjoy full freedom. Then again it was an Ashram rule that persons following a particular faith should have the same feeling for followers of other faiths as for their co-religionists.

But for one thing I was solely responsible, and I am indebted to the West for it. I refer to my dietetic experiments, which commenced in 1888 when I went to England for studies. I always invite members of my family and other co-workers to join in. The experiments were designed to achieve three objects, viz., (1) to acquire control over the palate as a part of self-control in general; (2) to find out which diet was the simplest and the cheapest so that by adopting it we might identify ourselves with the poor; and (3) to discover which diet was necessary for perfect health, as maintenance of health is largely dependent upon correct diet.

If in England I had not been under a vow to be a vegetarian, I might perhaps never have undertaken experiments in diet. But once I began to experiment, these three objectives took me into deeper waters, and I was led to make various kinds of experiments. And the Ashram too joined in, though these experiments were not a part of Ashram discipline.

The reader has perhaps now seen that the Ashram set out to remedy what it thought were defects in our national life from the religious, economic and political standpoints. As we gathered new experiences we undertook fresh activities. Even now I cannot say that the Ashram has embarked on all possible activities that I can think of. There have been two limitations. First, we were sure we must cut our coat according to our cloth, that is, we must manage with what funds were placed at our disposal by friends without any special effort in collection. Secondly we should not go in search of new spheres of activity, but if any activity naturally suggested itself to our minds, we should go in for it without counting the cost.

These two limitations spring from a religious attitude. This implies faith in God, that is, doing everything in dependence upon and under the inspiration of God. The man of religion conducts such activities as are sent by God with such resources as God places at his disposal. He never lets us see that He Himself does anything; He achieves His aims through men inspired by Him. When help was received from unexpected quarters or from friends without our asking for it, my faith led me to believe that it was sent by God. Similarly when some activity came to us unsought so that not to take it up would have been sheer cowardice, laziness or the like, I thought it was a godsend.

The same principle applies to co-workers as to material resources and to activities. We may have the funds and know how they are to be used, but we can do nothing in the absence of co-workers. Co-workers also should come unsought. We did not merely imagine but had a living faith that the Ashram was God's. If therefore He wished to make the Ashram His instrument as regards any activity, it was for Him to place the requisite men and munitions at the Ashram's disposal. Phœnix, Tolstoy Farm and Sabarmati Ashram have all been conducted more or less according to these principles consciously or unconsciously. Ashram rules were observed at first with some laxity, but the observance has become stricter from day to day.

The Ashram population doubled itself in a few months. Again the Kochrab bungalow was a hardly suitable building for an ashram. It would do for one well-to-do family, but not for sixty men, women and children engaged in various activities and observing *brahmacharya* and other vows. However we had to manage with what building was available. But very soon it became impossible to live in it for a number of reasons. As if God wanted to drive us out of it, we had suddenly to go out in search of a new site and to vacate the bungalow. The curious will look up the *Autobiography* for an account of these events. There was one defect in the Ashram at Kochrab which was remedied after we had removed to Sabarmati. An Ashram without orchard, farm or cattle would not be a complete unit. At Sabarmati we had cultivable land and therefore went in for agriculture at once.

Such is the prehistory and history of the Ashram. I now propose to deal with its observances and activities in so far as I remember them. My diary is not at hand. Even if it is, it takes no note of the personal history of the Ashramites. I therefore depend upon memory alone. This is nothing new for me, as *Satyagraha in South Africa* and the *Autobiography* were written in the same manner. The reader will please bear this limitation in mind, as he goes through these pages.

VII. Swadeshi

At the Ashram we hold that swadeshi is a universal law. A man's first duty is to his neighbour. This does not imply hatred for the foreigner or partiality for the fellow-countryman. Our capacity for service has obvious limits. We can serve even our neighbour with some difficulty. If every one of us duly performed his duty to his neighbour, no one in the world who needed assistance would be left unattended. Therefore one who serves his neighbour serves all the world. As a matter of fact there is in swadeshi no room for distinction between one's own and other people. To serve one's neighbour is to serve the world. Indeed it is the only way open to us of serving the world. One to whom the whole world is as his family should have the power of serving the universe without moving from his place. He can exercise this power only through service rendered to his neighbour. Tolstoy goes further and says that at present we are riding on other people's backs; it is enough only if we get down. This is another way of putting the same thing. No one can serve others without serving himself. And whoever tries to achieve his private ends without serving others harms himself as well as the world at large. The reason is obvious. All living beings are members one of another so that a person's every act has a beneficial or harmful influence on the whole world. We cannot see this, near-sighted as we are. The influence of a single act of an individual on the world may be negligible. But that influence is there all the same, and an awareness of this truth should make us realize our responsibility.

Swadeshi therefore does not involve any disservice to the foreigner. Still swadeshi does not reach everywhere, for that is impossible in the very nature of things. In trying to serve the world, one does not serve the world and fails to serve even the neighbour. In serving the neighbour one in effect serves the world. Only he who has performed his duty to his neighbour has the right to say, 'All are akin to me.' But if a person says, 'All are akin to me,' and neglecting his neighbour gives himself up to self-indulgence, he lives to himself alone.

We find some good men who leave their own place and move all over the world serving non-neighbours. They do nothing wrong, and their activity is not an exception to the law of swadeshi. Only their capacity for service is greater. To one man, only he who lives next door to him is his neighbour. For a second man his neighbourhood is co-extensive with his village and for a third with ten surrounding villages. Thus everyone serves according to his capacity. A common man cannot do uncommon work. Definitions are framed with an eye to him alone, and imply everything which is not contrary to their spirit. When he observes the law of swadeshi, the ordinary man does not think that he is doing service to any others. He deals with the neighbouring producer, as it is convenient for him. But an occasion may arise when this is inconvenient. One who knows that swadeshi is the law of life will observe it even on such occasions. Many of us at present are not satisfied with the quality of goods made in India, and are tempted to buy foreign goods. It is therefore necessary to point out that swadeshi does not simply minister to our convenience but is a rule of life. Swadeshi has nothing to do with hatred of the foreigner. It can never be one's duty to wish or to do ill to others.

Khadi has been conceived as the symbol of swadeshi, because India has committed a heinous sin by giving it up and thus failing in the discharge of her natural duty.

The importance of khadi and the spinning-wheel first dawned on me in 1908,[5] when I had no idea of what the wheel was like and did not even know the difference between the wheel and the loom. I had only a vague idea of the condition of India's villages, but still I clearly saw that the chief cause of their pauperization was the destruction of the spinning-wheel, and resolved that I would try to revive it when I returned to India.

I returned in 1915 with my mind full of these ideas. Swadeshi was one of the observances ever since the Ashram was started. But none of us knew how to spin. We therefore rested content with setting up a handloom. Some of us still retained a liking for fine cloth. No swadeshi yarn of the requisite fineness for women's saris was available in the market. For a very short time therefore they were woven with foreign yarn. But we were soon able to obtain fine yarn from Indian mills.

It was no easy job even to set up the handloom at the Ashram. None of us had the least idea of weaving. We obtained a loom and a weaver through friends. Maganlal Gandhi undertook to learn weaving.

I conducted experiments at the Ashram and at the same time carried on swadeshi propaganda in the country. But it was like *Hamlet* without the Prince of Denmark so long as we could not spin yarn. At last however I discovered the spinning-wheel, found out spinners and introduced the wheel in the Ashram. The whole story has been unfolded in the *Autobiography*.

But that did not mean that our difficulties were at an end. On the other hand they increased, since such of them as were hidden till now became manifest.

Touring in the country I saw that people would not take to the

5. Gandhi wrote on the subject in *Hind Swaraj*.

spinning-wheel as soon as they were told about it. I knew that not much money could be made by spinning, but I had no idea of how little it was. Then again the yarn that was spun would not at once be uniform as well as fine. Many could spin only coarse and weak yarn. Not all kinds of cotton were suitable for spinning. The cotton must be carded and made into slivers, and in carding much depended upon the condition of the cotton. Any and every spinning-wheel would not do. To revive the spinning-wheel thus meant the launching of a big scheme. Money alone could not do the trick. As for man-power too, hundreds of workers would be needed, and these men should be ready to learn a new art, to be satisfied with a small salary and to live out their lives in villages. But even that was not enough. The rural atmosphere was surcharged with idleness and lack of faith and hope. The wheel could make no headway if this did not improve. Thus a successful revival of the wheel could be brought about only with an army of single-minded men and women equipped with infinite patience and strong faith.

VIII. Removal of Untouchability

The real anti-untouchability work carried on in the Ashram is the reformed conduct of the Ashramites. There is no room in the Ashram for any ideas of high and low.

However the Ashram believes that varnas[6] and ashramas[7] are essential elements of Hinduism. Only it puts a different interpretation on these time-honoured terms. Four varnas and four ashramas are an arrangement not peculiar to Hinduism but capable of world-wide application, and a universal rule, the breach of which has involved humanity in numerous disasters. The four ashramas are *brahmacharya, garhasthya, vanaprasthya* and sannyasa. *Brahmacharya* is the stage during which men as well as women prosecute their studies, and should not only observe *brahmacharya* but should also be free from any other burden except that of studies. This lasts till at least the twenty-fifth year, when the student becomes a householder if he wishes. Almost all the students thus become householders. But this stage should close at the age of fifty. During that period the householder enjoys the pleasures of life, makes money, practises a profession and rears a family. From fifty to seventy-five wife and husband should live apart and wholly devote themselves to the service of the people. They must leave their families and try to look upon the

6. The four castes.
7. The four stages of life.

world as a big family. During the last 25 years they should become sannyasis, live apart, set to the people an example of ideal religious life and maintain themselves with whatever the people choose to give them. It is clear that society as a whole would be elevated if many carried out this scheme in their lives.

So far as I am aware, the ashrama arrangement is unknown outside India, but even in India it has practically disappeared at present. There is no such thing now as *brahmacharya*, which is intended to be the foundation of life. For the rest we have sannyasis, most of them such only in name, with nothing of sannyasa about them except the orange robe. Many of them are ignorant, and some who have acquired learning are not knowers of Brahman but fanatics. There are some honourable exceptions but even these well-conducted monks lack the lustre we love to associate with sannyasa. It is possible that some real sannyasis lead a solitary life. But it is obvious that sannyasa as a stage in life has fallen into desuetude. A society which is served by able sannyasis would not be poor in spirit, unprovided even with the necessaries of life, and politically dependent, as Hindu society is at present. If sannyasa were with us a living thing, it would exert a powerful influence on neighbouring faiths, for the sannyasi is a servant not only of Hinduism but of all the faiths of mankind.

But we can never hope to see such sannyasis unless *brahmacharya* is observed in the country. As for *vanaprasthya*, there is no trace of it. The last stage we have to consider is that of the householder. But our householders are given to unregulated self-indulgence. Householders in the absence of the three other ashramas live like brutes. Self-restraint is the one thing which differentiates man from beast, but it is practised no longer.

The Ashram is engaged in the great endeavour to resuscitate the four ashramas. It is like an ant trying to lift a bag of sugar. This effort though apparently ridiculous is part of the Ashram quest of truth. All the inmates of the Ashram therefore observe *brahmacharya*. Permanent members must observe it for life. All the inmates are not members in this sense. Only a few are members, the rest are students. If this effort is crowned with success, we may hope to see a revival of the ashrama scheme of life. The sixteen years during which the Ashram has functioned are not a sufficiently long period for the assessment of results. I have no idea of the time when such assessment will be possible. I can only say that there is nothing like dissatisfaction with the progress achieved up to date.

Ashram Observances in Action; also from the Gujarati in *Satyagrahash-ramno Itihas*

58. Statement to the Press

(vol. LI, pp. 62–65)

September 16, 1932

The fast which I am approaching was resolved upon in the name of God for His work and, as I believe in all humility, at His call. Friends have urged me to postpone the date for the sake of giving the public a chance to organize itself. I am sorry it is not open to me to change even the hour, except for the reason stated in my letter to the Prime Minister.[1]

The impending fast is against those who have faith in me, whether Indians or foreigners, and for those who have it not. Therefore it is not against the English official world, but it is against those Englishmen and women who, in spite of the contrary teaching of the official world, believe in me and the justice of the cause I represent. Nor is it against those of my countrymen who have no faith in me, whether they be Hindus or others; but it is against those countless Indians (no matter to what persuasion they belong) who believe that I represent a just cause. Above all, it is intended to sting the Hindu conscience into right religious action.

The contemplated fast is no appeal to mere emotion. By the fast I want to throw the whole of my weight (such as it is) in the scales of justice pure and simple. Therefore, there need be no undue haste or feverish anxiety to save my life. I implicitly believe in the truth of the saying that not a blade of grass moves but by His will. He will save it if He needs it for further service in this body. None can save it against His will. Humanly speaking, I believe it will stand the strain for some time.

The separate electorate is merely the last straw. No patched-up agreement between caste Hindu leaders and rival "depressed" class leaders will answer the purpose. The agreement to be valid has got to be real. If the Hindu mass mind is not yet prepared to banish untouchability root and branch, it must sacrifice me without the slightest hesitation.

There should be no coercion of those who are opposed to joint electorates. I have no difficulty in understanding their bitter opposition. They have every right to distrust me. Do I not belong to that

1. The reason stated was: "The fast will cease if during its progress, the British Government of its own motion or under pressure of public opinion revise their decision and withdraw their scheme of communal electorates for the 'depressed' classes, whose representatives should be elected by the general electorate under the common franchise no matter how wide it is."

Hindu section miscalled a superior class, or caste Hindus, who have ground down to powder the so-called untouchables? The marvel is that the latter have remained nevertheless in the Hindu fold.

But whilst I can justify this opposition, I believe that they are in error. They will, if they can, separate the "depressed" class entirely from the Hindu society and form them into a separate class—a standing and living reproach to Hinduism. I should not mind if thereby their interest could be really served.

But my intimate acquaintance with every shade of untouchability convinces me that their lives, such as they are, are so intimately mixed with those of the caste Hindus in whose midst and for whom they live, that it is impossible to separate them. They are part of an indivisible family.

Their revolt against the Hindus with whom they live and their apostasy from Hinduism I should understand. But this so far as I can see they will not do. There is a subtle something—quite indefinable—in Hinduism which keeps them in it even in spite of themselves.

And this fact makes it imperative for a man like me, with a living experience of it, to resist the contemplated separation even though the effort should cost life itself.

The implications of this resistance are tremendous. No compromise which does not ensure the fullest freedom for the "depressed classes" inside the Hindu fold can be an adequate substitute for the contemplated separation. Any betrayal of the trust can merely postpone the day of immolation for me and henceforth for those who think with me. The problem before responsible Hindus is to consider whether in the event of social, civic or political persecution of the "depressed" classes they are prepared to face satyagraha in the shape of perpetual fast, not of one reformer like me, but an increasing army of reformers whom I believe to exist today in India and who will count their lives of no cost to achieve the liberation of these classes and therethrough [rid] Hinduism of an age-long superstition.

Let fellow-reformers who have worked with me also appreciate the implications of the fast.

It is either a hallucination of mine or an illumination. If it is the former, I must be allowed to do my penance in peace. It will be the lifting of a dead weight on Hinduism. If it is an illumination, may my agony purify Hinduism and even melt the hearts of those who are at present disposed to distrust me.

Since there appears to be a misunderstanding as to the application of my fast, I may repeat that it is aimed at a statutory separate electorate, in any shape or form, for the "depressed" classes. Immediately that threat is removed once for all, my fast will end. I hold strong views about reservation of seats, as also about the most proper method of dealing with the whole question. But I consider myself unfit as a prisoner to set forth my proposals. I should however abide by an agreement on the basis of joint electorate that may be arrived at between the responsible leaders of caste Hindus and the "depressed" classes and which has been accepted by mass meetings of all Hindus.

One thing I must make clear. The satisfactory ending to the "depressed" classes question, if it is to come, should in no way mean that I would be committed to the acceptance of His Majesty's Government's decision on the other parts of the communal question. I am personally opposed to many other parts of it, which to my mind make the working of any free and democratic constitution well-nigh impossible, nor would a satisfactory solution of this question in any way bind me to accept the constitution that may be framed. These are political questions for the National Congress to consider and determine. They are utterly outside my province in my individual capacity. Nor may I as a prisoner air my individual views on these questions. My fast has a narrow application. The "depressed" classes question being predominantly a religious matter, I regard it as specially my own by reason of my lifelong concentration on it. It is a sacred personal trust which I may not shirk.

The fasting for light and penance is a hoary institution. I have observed it in Christianity and Islam. Hinduism is replete with instances of fasting for purification and penance. But it is a privilege, if it is also a duty. Moreover, to the best of my light, I have reduced it to a science. As an expert, therefore, I would warn friends and sympathizers against copying me blindly or out of false or hysterical sympathy. Let all such qualify themselves by hard work and selfless service of the "untouchables" and they would have independent light if their time for fasting has come.

Lastly, in so far as I know myself this fast is being undertaken with the purest of motives and without malice or anger to any single soul. For me it is an expression of, and the last seal on, non-violence. Those, therefore, who would use violence in this controversy against those whom they may consider to be inimical to me or the cause I represent will simply hasten my end. Perfect courtesy and consideration towards opponents is an absolute essential of success in this case at least if not in all cases.

M. K. GANDHI

From a photostat

59. Interview to the Press
(vol. LI, pp. 116–20)

September 20, 1932

*For the first time in nine months journalists were permitted to see Ma-
hatma Gandhi in Yeravda Jail this evening at 5.30 when they were treated
to one of the most easily delivered and seriously thoughtful interviews
to which it has ever been my fortune to listen. No journalist could see
Mahatma Gandhi today and discuss the position with him five hours
after he had commenced "a fast unto death" without being immensely
impressed. . . .*
When asked if he was hopeful about a happy ending to the affair, he said:

I am an irrepressible optimist. Unless God has forsaken me, I hope
that it will not be a fast unto death.

*Mahatma Gandhi said that he had had many telegrams from people who
had decided or wished to enter upon a fast in sympathy with him.*

I urge everybody not to fast in sympathy. I have undertaken it at
God's call, and, therefore, unless there is a similar definite call to
these people they have no business to fast. For one day, for the sake of
purification or identification with the cause, it is a good thing; but
that is all. Such a fast is both a privilege and a duty, and the privilege
accrues only to those who have disciplined themselves for it.

*The interview then turned to the question of the day, the representation
of the Depressed Classes, or as Mahatma Gandhi calls them, the Suppressed Classes.*
*First of all he expressed surprise that the statement given to the Govern-
ment of Bombay had not been released. That had been given five days ago.
Had he to redraft it today it would be rather different in the light of happenings since then, and he said at the end of the interview that his new statement was supplementary to the other, but not dependent on it. He said:*

My cards are on the table, but, so far as the present instance is concerned, I could say nothing from behind prison bars. Now that the
restrictions are removed, I have answered the first call of the Press.
My fast is only against separate electorates, and not against statutory reservation of seats. To say that I am damaging the cause by uncompromising opposition to statutory reservation of seats is only
partly true. Opposed I was, and am even now, but there was never put
before me for any acceptance or rejection a scheme for statutory reservation of seats. Therefore, there is no question of my having to decide upon that point. When I developed my own idea about that
point, I certainly expressed disappointment, and in my humble opin-

ion, such statutory reservation, short of doing service, may do harm in the sense that it will stop natural evolution. Statutory reservation is like a support to a man. Relying on such support to any extent he weakens himself.

If people won't laugh at me, I would gently put forward a claim, which I have always asserted, that I am a 'touchable' by birth but an untouchable by choice; and I have endeavoured to qualify myself to represent, not the upper ten even among the untouchables, because be it said to their shame there are castes and classes among them, but my ambition is to represent and identify myself with, as far as possible, the lowest strata of untouchables, namely, the 'invisibles' and the 'unapproachables,' whom I have always before my mind's eye wherever I go; for they have indeed drunk deep of the poisoned cup. I have met them in Malabar and in Orissa, and am convinced that if they are ever to rise, it will not be by reservation of seats but will be by the strenuous work of Hindu reformers in their midst, and it is because I feel that this separation would have killed all prospect of reform that my whole soul has rebelled against it; and, let me make it plain, that the withdrawal of separate electorates will satisfy the letter of my vow but will never satisfy the spirit behind it, and in my capacity of being a self-chosen untouchable, I am not going to rest content with a patched-up pact between the 'touchables' and the untouchables.

What I want, what I am living for, and what I should delight in dying for, is the eradication of untouchability root and branch. I want, therefore, a living pact whose life-giving effect should be felt not in the distant tomorrow but today, and, therefore, that pact should be sealed by an all-India demonstration of 'touchables' and untouchables meeting together, not by way of a theatrical show, but in real brotherly embrace. It is in order to achieve this, the dream of my life for the past fifty years, that I have entered today the fiery gates. The British Government's decision was the last straw. It was a decisive symptom, and with the unerring eye of the physician that I claim to be in such matters, I detected the symptom. Therefore, for me the abolition of separate electorates would be but the beginning of the end, and I would warn all those leaders assembled at Bombay and others against coming to any hasty decision.

My life I count of no consequence. One hundred lives given for this noble cause would, in my opinion, be poor penance done by Hindus for the atrocious wrongs they have heaped upon helpless men and women of their own faith. I, therefore, would urge them not to swerve an inch from the path of strictest justice. My fast I want to throw in the scales of justice, and if it wakes up caste Hindus from their slumber, and if they are roused to a sense of their duty, it will have served its purpose. Whereas, if out of blind affection for me, they would somehow or other come to a rough and ready agreement so as to secure the abrogation and then go off to sleep, they will commit a grievous blunder and will have made my life a misery. For, while the abrogation of separate electorates would result in my breaking the fast, it would be living death for me if the vital pact for which I am striving is not arrived at. It would simply mean that, as soon as I called off the fast, I would have to give notice of another in order to achieve the spirit of the vow to the fullest extent.

This may look childish to the onlooker but not so to me. If I had anything more to give, I would throw that in also to remove this curse, but I have nothing more than my life.

I believe that if untouchability is really rooted out, it will not only purge Hinduism of a terrible blot but its repercussions will be world-wide. My fight against untouchability is a fight against the impure in humanity, and, therefore, when I penned my letter to Sir Samuel Hoare I did so in the full faith that the very best in human family will come to my assistance if I have embarked on this thing with a heart, so far as it is possible for a human being to achieve, free of impurity, free of all malice and all anger. You will, therefore, see that my fast is based first of all in the cause of faith in the Hindu community, faith in human nature itself, and faith even in the official world.

In attacking untouchability I have gone to the very root of the matter, and, therefore, it is an issue of transcendental value, far surpassing swaraj in terms of political constitutions, and I would say that such a constitution would be a dead weight if it was not backed by a moral basis, in the shape of the present hope engendered in the breasts of the downtrodden millions that that weight is going to be lifted from their shoulders. It is only because the English officials cannot possibly see this living side of the picture that in their ignorance and self-satisfaction they dare to sit as judges upon questions that affect the fundamental being of millions of people, and here I mean both caste Hindus and untouchables, that is, the suppressor and the suppressed; and it was in order to wake up even officialdom from its gross ignorance, if I may make use of such an expression without being guilty of offence, that I felt impelled by a voice from within to offer resistance with the whole of my being.

He stated that he had made definite suggestions to the deputation from the Emergency Committee whom he received yesterday and he presumed that these would have been communicated to the Press today in Bombay.

*Referring to a possible photograph Mahatma Gandhi made a jocular re-
mark concerning his funeral rites whereupon I asked him if he had made
any preparations for such rites when visited by his son Devdas yesterday if
the very worst happened, and I received a dramatic reply.*

I have asked my son to say in my name at the Bombay Conference
that he as his father's son was prepared to forfeit his father's life
rather than see any injury being done to the Suppressed Classes in
mad haste.

*What did he really think about the possibilities of his fast lasting? He
replied:*

I am as anxious as anyone to live. Water has an infinite capacity for
prolonging life, and I will take water whenever I feel I require it. You
can depend upon me to make a supreme effort to hold myself together so that the Hindu conscience may be quickened as also the
British conscience and this agony may end. My cry will rise to the
throne of the Almighty God.

The Epic Fast, pp. 118–23

60. Statement to the Press
(vol. LI, pp. 143–45)

September 26, 1932

The fast undertaken in the name of God was broken in the presence of Gurudev, and Parachure Shastri, the leper prisoner and a
learned pandit, seated opposite each other, and in the company of
loving and loved ones who had gathered round me. The breaking was
preceded by the Poet singing one of his Bengali hymns, then *mantras* from the Upanishads by Parachure Shastri, and then my favourite hymn *"Vaishnava Jana."*

The hand of God has been visible in the glorious manifestation
throughout the length and breadth of India during the past seven
days. The cables received from many parts of the world blessing the
fast have sustained me through the agony of body and soul that I
passed through during the seven days, but the cause was worth going
through that agony.

The sacrificial fire, once lit, shall not be put out as long as there is
the slightest trace of untouchability still left in Hinduism. If it is
God's will that it does not end with my life, I have the confidence

that there are several thousands of earnest reformers who will lay down their lives in order to purify Hinduism of this awful curse.

The settlement arrived at is, so far as I can see, a generous gesture on all sides. It is a meeting of hearts, and my Hindu gratitude is due to Dr. Ambedkar, Rao Bahadur Srinivasan and their party on the one hand and Rao Bahadur M. C. Raja on the other. They could have taken up an uncompromising and defiant attitude by way of punishment to the so-called caste Hindus for the sins of generations. If they had done so, I at least could not have resented their attitude and my death would have been but a trifling price exacted for the tortures that the outcastes of Hinduism have been going through for unknown generations. But they chose a nobler path and have thus shown that they have followed the precept of forgiveness enjoined by all religions. Let me hope that the caste Hindus will prove themselves worthy of this forgiveness and carry out to the letter and spirit every clause of the settlement with all its implications.

The settlement is but the beginning of the end. The political part of it, very important though it no doubt is, occupies but a small space in the vast field of reform that has to be tackled by caste Hindus during the coming days, namely, the complete removal of social and religious disabilities under which a large part of the Hindu population has been groaning. I should be guilty of a breach of trust if I did not warn fellow reformers and caste Hindus in general that the breaking of the fast carried with it a sure promise of a resumption of it if this reform is not relentlessly pursued and achieved within a measurable period. I had thought of laying down a period, but I feel that I may not do so without a definite call from within.

The message of freedom shall penetrate every untouchable home and that can only happen if reformers will cover every village. Yet, in the wave of enthusiasm and in an inordinate desire to spare me a repetition of the agony, there should be no coercion. We must, by patient toil and self-suffering, convert the ignorant and the superstitious but never seek to compel them by force.

I wish, too, that the almost ideal solution that has been arrived at may be followed by the other communities, and that we might see the dawn of a new era of mutual trust, mutual give and take, and a recognition of the fundamental unity of all communities. I would here single out the Hindu-Muslim-Sikh question. I am the same to the Mussalman today that I was in 1920–22. I should be just as prepared to lay down my life as I was in Delhi[1] to achieve organic unity

1. In September 1924.

and permanent peace between them. I hope and pray that there will be, as a result of this upheaval, a spontaneous move in this direction and then, surely, the other communities can no longer stand out.

In conclusion, I would like to thank the Government and the jail staff and the medical men appointed by the Government to look after me. Extreme care and attention was bestowed upon me. Nothing was left undone. The jail staff worked under terrible pressures, and I observed that they did not grudge this labour. I thank them all from high to low.

I thank the British Cabinet for hastening the decision on the settlement. The terms of the decision sent to me I have not approached without misgivings. It accepts, I suppose very naturally, only that part of the Agreement that refers to the British Cabinet's communal decision. I expect that they had a constitutional difficulty in now announcing their acceptance of the whole Agreement. But I would like to assure my Harijan friends, as I would like henceforth to name them, that so far as I am concerned, I am wedded to the whole of that Agreement, and that they may hold my life as hostage for its due fulfilment, unless we ourselves arrive at any other and better settlement of our own free will.

The Hindu, 27-9-1932, and *The Epic Fast,* pp. 142–45

61. Statement on Untouchability [1]

(vol. LI, pp. 341–45)

November 4, 1932

For reasons over which I had no control I have not been able to deal with the question of untouchability, as I had fully intended to after the breaking of the fast. The Government having now granted me permission to carry on public propaganda in connection with the work, I am able to deal with the numerous correspondents who have been writing to me either in criticism of the Yeravda Pact, or to seek guidance, or to know my views about the different questions that arise in the course of the campaign against untouchability. In this preliminary statement I propose to confine myself to the salient

1. Following the lifting of restrictions by the government on Gandhi's interviews and his carrying on propaganda in connection with anti-untouchability work, Gandhi issued a series of statements to the press. This is the first of them.

questions only, deferring for the time being other questions which do not call for immediate disposal.

I take up first the question of the possibility of my resuming the fast. Some correspondents contend that the fast savours of coercion and should not have been undertaken at all and that, therefore, it should never be resumed. Some others have argued that there is no warrant in Hindu religion, or any religion for that matter, for a fast like mine. I do not propose to deal with the religious aspect. Suffice it to say that it was at God's call that I embarked upon the last fast and it would be at His call that it would be resumed, if it ever is. But when it was first undertaken, it was undoubtedly for removal of untouchability, root and branch. That it took the form it did was no choice of mine. The Cabinet decision precipitated the crisis of my life, but I knew that the revocation of the British Cabinet's decision was to be but the beginning of the end. A tremendous force could not be set in motion merely in order to alter a political decision, unless it had behind it a much deeper meaning, even unknown to its authors. The people affected instinctively recognized that meaning and responded.

Perhaps no man within living memory has travelled so often from one end of India to the other or has penetrated so many villages and come into contact with so many millions as I have. They have all known my life. They have known that I have recognized no barriers between 'untouchables' and 'touchables' or caste and outcaste. They have heard me speak often in their own tongues denouncing untouchability in unmeasured terms, describing it as a curse and a blot upon Hinduism. With rare exceptions, at hundreds of these mass meetings or at private meetings in all parts of India, there has been no protest against my presentation of the case against untouchability. Crowds have passed resolutions denouncing untouchability and pledging themselves to remove it from their midst and they have on innumerable occasions called God as witness to their pledge and asked for His blessing that He may give them strength to carry out their pledge. It was against these millions that my fast was undertaken and it was their spontaneous love that brought about a transformation inside of five days and brought into being the Yeravda Pact. And it will be against them that the fast will be resumed if that Pact is not carried out by them in its fullness. The Government are now practically out of it. Their part of the obligation they fulfilled promptly. The major part of the resolutions of the Yeravda Pact has to be fulfilled by these millions, the so-called caste Hindus, who have flocked to the meetings I have described. It is they who have to embrace the suppressed brethren and sisters as their very own, whom they have to invite to their temples, to their homes, to their schools. The 'untouchables' in the villages should be made to feel that their shackles have been broken, that they are in no way inferior to their fellow-villagers, that they are worshippers of the same God as other villagers and are entitled to the same rights and privileges that the latter enjoy.

But if these vital conditions of the Pact are not carried out by caste Hindus, could I possibly live to face God and man? I ventured even to tell Dr. Ambedkar, Rao Bahadur Raja and other friends belonging to the suppressed group that they should regard me as a hostage for the due fulfilment by caste Hindus of the conditions of the Pact. The fast, if it has to come, will not be for the coercion of those who are opponents of the reform, but it will be intended to sting into action those who have been my comrades or who have taken pledges for the removal of untouchability. If they belie their pledges, or if they never meant to abide by them, and their Hinduism was a mere camouflage, I should have no interest left in life. My fast, therefore, ought not to affect the opponents of reform, nor even fellow-workers and the millions who have led me to believe that they were with me and the Congress in the campaign against untouchability, if the latter have on second thoughts come to the conclusion that untouchability is not after all a crime against God and humanity.

In my opinion, fasting for purification of self and others is an age-long institution and it will subsist so long as man believes in God. It is the prayer to the Almighty from an anguished heart. But whether my argument is wise or foolish, I cannot be dislodged from my position so long as I do not see the folly or the error of it. It will be resumed only in obedience to the inner voice, and only if there is a manifest breakdown of the Yeravda Pact, owing to the criminal neglect of caste Hindus to implement its conditions. Such neglect would mean a betrayal of Hinduism. I should not care to remain its living witness.

There is another fast which is a near possibility and that is in connection with the opening of the Guruvayur temple in Kerala. It was at my urgent request that Sjt. Kelappan suspended his fast for three months, a fast that had well-nigh brought him to death's door. I would be in honour bound to fast with him if on or before the first January next that temple is not opened to the 'untouchables' precisely on the same terms as the 'touchables,' and if it becomes necessary for Sjt. Kelappan to resume his fast. I have been obliged to dwell at some length upon these possible fasts because of the receipt of hot correspondence from two or three quarters. Co-workers, however, should not be agitated over the possibility. To become unnerved over a prospect one would not like to face very often results in its materializing. The best way of averting it is for all affected by it to put forth their whole strength into the work that would render the occurrence impossible.

Correspondents have asked whether inter-dining and intermarriage are part of the movement against untouchability. In my opinion they are not. They touch the caste men equally with the outcastes. It is, therefore, not obligatory on an anti-untouchability worker to devote himself or herself to inter-dining and intermarriage reform. Personally, I am of opinion that this reform is coming sooner than we expect. Restriction on inter-caste dining and intercaste marriage is no part of Hindu religion. It is a social custom which crept into Hinduism when perhaps it was in its decline, and was then meant perhaps to be a temporary protection against disintegration of Hindu society, and emphasis on them has turned the attention of mass mind from the fundamentals which are vital to life's growth. Wherever, therefore, people voluntarily take part in functions where 'touchables' and 'untouchables,' Hindus and non-Hindus are invited to join dinner parties, I welcome them as a healthy sign. But I should never dream of making this reform, however desirable in itself it may be, part of an all-India reform which has been long overdue.

Untouchability in the form we all know it is a canker eating into the very vitals of Hinduism. Dining and marriage restrictions stunt Hindu society. I think the distinction is fundamental. It would be unwise in a hurricane campaign to overweight and thus endanger the main issue. It may even amount to a breach of faith with the masses to call upon them suddenly to view the removal of untouchability in a light different from what they have been taught to believe it to be. On the one hand, therefore, whilst inter-dining may go on where the public is itself ready for it, it should not be part of the India-wide campaign.

I have letters, some of them angrily worded, from those who style themselves sanatanists. For them untouchability is the essence of Hinduism. Some of them regard me as a renegade. Some others consider that I have imbibed notions against untouchability and the like from Christianity and Islam. Some again quote scriptures in defence of untouchability. To these I have promised a reply through this statement. I would venture, therefore, to tell these correspondents that I claim myself to be a sanatanist. Their definition of a sanatanist is obviously different from mine. For me sanatan dharma is

the vital faith handed down from generations belonging even to pre-
historic period and based upon the Vedas and the writings that followed them. For me the Vedas are as indefinable as God and Hinduism. It would be only partially true to say that the Vedas are the four
books which one finds in print. These books are themselves remnants
of the discourses left by the unknown seers. Those of later generations added to these original treasures according to their lights.
There then arose a great and lofty-minded man, the composer of the
Gita. He gave to the Hindu world a synthesis of Hindu religion at
once deeply philosophical and yet easily to be understood by any un-
sophisticated seeker. It is the one open book to every Hindu who
will care to study it, and if all the other scriptures were reduced to
ashes, the seven hundred verses of this imperishable booklet are
quite enough to tell one what Hinduism is and how one can live up
to it. And I claim to be a sanatanist because for forty years I have
been seeking literally to live up to the teachings of that book. Whatever is contrary to its main theme I reject as un-Hindu. It excludes
no faith and no teacher. It gives me great joy to be able to say that I
have studied the Bible, the Koran, Zend Avesta and the other scriptures of the world with the same reverence that I have given to the
Gita. This reverent reading has strengthened my faith in the *Gita*.
They have broadened my outlook and therefore my Hinduism. Lives
of Zoroaster, Jesus and Mohammed, as I have understood them, have
illumined many a passage in the *Gita*. What, therefore, these sanatani friends have hurled against me as a taunt has been to me a
source of consolation. I take pride in calling myself a Hindu because
I find the term broad enough not merely to tolerate but to assimilate
the teachings of prophets from all the four corners of the earth. I find
no warrant for untouchability in this book of life. On the contrary it
compels me, by an appeal to my reason and a more penetrating appeal to my heart, in language that has a magnetic touch about it, to
believe that all life is one and that it is through God and must return
to Him.

According to sanatan dharma taught by that venerable Mother, life
does not consist in outward rites and ceremonial, but it consists in
the uttermost inner purification and merging oneself, body, soul and
mind, in the divine essence. I have gone to the masses in their millions with this message of the *Gita* burnt into my life. And they
have listened to me, I am quite sure, not for any political wisdom or
for eloquence, but because they have instinctively recognized me as
one of them, as one belonging to their faith. And as days have gone
by, my belief has grown stronger and stronger that I could not be

wrong in claiming to belong to sanatan dharma, and if God wills it, He will let me seal that claim with my death.

The Epic Fast, pp. 311–17

62. Letter to Ramdas Gandhi
(vol. LI, pp. 372–75)

November 7, 1932

I am replying to your letter today. I had wanted to reply to it much earlier, but while searching for verses [from the *Gita*] as desired by you, I thought that it would be better if I selected at one time all such verses which you could follow in life without difficulty. I could do that today, and send with this the verses which I have selected. I have mentioned the chapter and number of the verse in each case, so that you can also look up the *Gita* and see where the verse occurs. You will see that all the verses appeal directly to the heart and are easy even for children to understand, and also that the Lord has assured not once but several times that He himself will awaken knowledge in the man who cultivates *bhakti* for Him and will provide his needs. *Bhakti* means selfless service of every living creature, in all of whom dwells the Lord. This includes repetition of Ramanama for one's own peace of mind. Moreover, you will see that even the verses selected from Chapter VI contain what I wish to teach you just now. The verses from Chapter XI are the sublimest part of Arjuna's sublime praise of the Lord. And the last verse of Chapter XVIII explains the reward of studying the *Gita* and of an earnest effort to put its teaching into practice. That is, where there is Shri Krishna, who stands for perfect knowledge, and Arjuna, who stands for action informed with knowledge, everything else will follow. If you meditate over these verses, you will see that one must never worry. A student of the *Gita* ought not to worry any time. We are enjoined to offer up everything as sacrifice to the Lord. Everything means everything without exception. Do you think anybody who does that would carry a load of worries in his head?

You must have discovered by now whether your disturbed digestion is the result of too much thinking and excessive worry, or whether it indicates the necessity of some change in your food. Do not be overambitious, either, in your reading and study. The resolutions which you have formed in your mind will now go on slowly maturing. You will know your strength when you are released. Why should you worry now whether or not you will really know it? There is no need at all to do so. You will find the meanings of the verses in the *Anasaktiyoga*, and in any case Surendra is there with you. You may, on your own or on the advice of Surendra or others like him, add some more to the verses which I have selected. I had made a note of the verses which I wished to select. While doing so in my copy of the *Gita*, I gave them the title "Ramdas Gita." Let us see how much they help you.

I will now tell you about something which will amuse you. Nimu asked me to suggest a name for your son. Sarita has already christened him Kahanji. I suggested Kahandas, thinking that it would go well with your name and would also satisfy Sarita's wish. But I should have known that Nimu would not like a name ending with *das*. She disapproved of Kahandas and asked me to suggest another name, but said that if you approved of Kahandas, she also would accept it. Vasumati, claiming her right, as aunt, to name the child, wrote to me and said that I, being an old man, would naturally suggest a name which an old man would like, but that she would not approve of any such name. She, therefore, asked for a name which would please people in this twentieth century. I have replied to her and told her that it was the exclusive right of an aunt to name a baby and that, therefore, she might give the child any name she liked. I have suggested a few names for her approval such as Fakkadlal, Chhogalashankh, Lakhtarlal, Bardolikar and Sabarmatiwala.[1] In my letter to Nimu, I have suggested Nirmallal, and also told her that, if she did not like the name Kahandas, she was hardly likely to be pleased with the name Ramdas either. I have, therefore, asked her to suggest a new name for you too. I was about to suggest one but checked myself. She should call you Nirmalkant. But we would then be going back to the age of the *Ramayana*, instead of living in the twentieth century, for in that age husbands were known by the names of the wives. Ramachandra was called Sitapati, Krishna was called Lakshmikant and Mahadev was called Parvatipati. We find a number of such instances. If you wish to throw any light on this profound subject, you are welcome to do so.

You ask how I cultivated non-attachment. The thing was very easy for me since everything I did was spontaneous, that is, arose naturally from my devotion to truth. If one is filled with a desire to serve the whole world, one can easily cultivate non-attachment. If I had

1. All these are fanciful and extremely funny names.

chosen to serve only our family, I would certainly have been filled with ignorant love and even developed attachment. I would also have suffered because of illnesses and deaths. But suffering runs away from you if you dedicate yourself to the service of the countless millions. Over whose illness would you worry and over whose death would you grieve? It would be almost impossible to do either. However, non-attachment does not mean insensitivity, or cruelty, for after all one does wish to serve the people, and, therefore, compassion becomes stronger instead of becoming weaker, and one's efficiency and concentration in work also increases. All these are signs of non-attachment. Moreover, the beauty of the thing lies in the fact that by serving the world, one does not cease to serve one's family, for service of the family is included in service of the world. I am perfectly sure in my mind that I have served Ba, you and your brothers and other members of the family no whit less than I could have done otherwise. The service was pure because attachment was replaced by equality of mind. I am sure that none of you has lost anything in consequence and that I myself have gained much. Thus I found non-attachment easy to cultivate. The word *anasakti* occurred to me when, after I had finished the translation of the *Gita*, Kaka asked me to suggest a title. It is not that I started cultivating non-attachment after realizing that, if one wished to serve the whole world, one could do so only with non-attachment. I understood only gradually that I was acting without attachment. Those around me saw that before I did. When I returned to India, people started describing me as a karmayogi. I used to read and study the *Gita* even in South Africa. But I had not then thought about the meaning of karmayogi. But other people saw all that in my life, and afterwards I also felt that their description had truth in it. All cannot have such good fortune. I had it because I think I have always loved truth right from my childhood. But you need not go into these deep waters just now. At present you should try to cultivate non-attachment without attachment even to that aim. That is, you should do with a light and happy heart any service for which you get an opportunity and read and study at the same time whatever you can manage. You need not worry either for Nimu or for the children. You will now see, with the new eyes which "Ramdas Gita" will give you, that God is there to worry for them and for you. You should not only believe this with your reason, but have faith in it and live accordingly. You will then be happy and learn everything you wish to. Fix firmly in your mind the Lord's assurance in Chapter IX, that even the most sinful man will have become a good man if he cultivates single-minded *bhakti* for Him. The entire world might perish, but an assurance by the Lord never proves false. I think I have written enough.

[From Gujarati]
Mahadevbhaini Diary, Vol. II, pp. 214–17

63. Letter to C. Rajagopalachari

(vol. LIII, pp. 42–44)

January 13, 1933

My Dear C. R.,

Vallabhbhai had a battle royal with me last night on your behalf. If a person, an utter stranger to him, had chance to be there, from the vehemence of Vallabhbhai's language, he would have concluded that we must be most quarrelsome persons.

He thought that I was doing violent injustice to you, inasmuch as, without consultation with you, I made proposals that might prove to be utterly embarrassing, as had happened on two occasions.

The cause of our quarrel was my compromise proposal. He thought that I had no right to publish it without consultation with you, and he was quite sure that though you were too good to mention it to me, you had felt very much embarrassed by it, if not also irritated. I told him that you were too good to conceal your embarrassment from me, if you were really embarrassed, and that would be quite unlike you. I even added that in this particular instance you happened even to like my proposal and that even if it was discovered that you did not like it and that you were really embarrassed, it was impossible for me every time to consult you, or such other colleagues on such occasions. I went further and argued that work on such lines would become almost impossible. People act together when there is a general agreement between them on fundamentals and [provided] that their deductions from those fundamentals were, as a rule, identical, and that if, at times, they came to different deductions, a timely confession of error would keep their friendship in tact, as also the common cause. Nothing that I could say, however, would conciliate Vallabhbhai. The curfew bell, mutually agreed upon by us, came to the rescue, and put an end to what promised to be an endless discussion. But I retired to bed with a determination that I would refer the matter to you. Your reply, one way or the other, would bring some consolation to your counsel, and you know that it won't make me disconsolate if you agreed with your counsel on both his propositions, namely, that before giving to the world the compromise proposal which I had given to Pandit Panchanan Tarkaratna I should have consulted you, and that it, as a matter of fact, did embarrass you. You would also add to your opinion on these points, your opinion whether on merits you consider my proposal to be sound or otherwise.

A perfect tragedy was enacted here yesterday. Five pandits and their five advisers came to the jail gate yesterday an hour and a half after the appointed time and took two hours and a half in exchanging brief notes with me, the three notes that they exchanged with me taking all the two hours and a half. And, will you believe it, when I tell you that they would not come in and carry on the discussion because I would not remove one word I had added to their draft, the word being an adjective added to the word 'untouchables.' The adjective applied was 'as at present classified.' Of course it altered the whole scope of their discussion. So they went away. Of course it is not our position that there is no untouchability at all in the Shastras. Our position is that there is no untouchability in the Shastras as we practise it today. They were expected to prove that untouchability as at present practised has sanction in the Shastras. It is an impossible task to perform honestly. No text that has yet been cited on their behalf has proved it. The *Shastris* on our behalf are really very learned men, and also pious men. It is their honest conviction that there is no warrant for the untouchability of the present day in the Shastras. The real untouchability will be there for all time. It is a sound hygienic rule practised all over the world.

Yours sincerely,

From a microfilm

64. Letter to Premabehn Kantak

(vol. LIII, pp. 288–91)

February 13, 1933

Chi. Prema,

It is the morning of the silence day. I got up at three and have taken up your letter to reply to it. I liked it very much indeed. You have given me in it all that I wanted. It fully answers to my imagination of what women can give me. What it gives seems small and unspectacular, but is very useful to a seeker after truth. I learn something from an objective letter like this one, and it helps me to guide you and others.

The Ashram is indeed a dharmashala. But the word has two meanings. It means a place where people can stay free, but it also means a place where one can learn dharma and try to follow it. The Ashram is a dharmashala in this second sense of the word. But dharma means truth. The Ashram, therefore, is a place where one may know the truth and try to follow it, that is, show *agraha*[1] for it, and hence it is Satyagraha Ashram.

In our quest for truth, we wish to cultivate unity with all living creatures. The Ashram, therefore, is an ever-growing family. But it is something more even than that, for it is the means and dharma is the end, and not *vice versa*. It is also a big school, and yet it is not so; for, since it is a family, we cannot mechanically apply there rules of outward behaviour such as are followed for other types of training. The letter of the rule has to be sacrificed in order to save the spirit of the rule.

I will now apply these observations to some specific cases. In bringing up and educating Lakshmi, we, including you, are being tested. What would we do to children in our own family? What would you do to your own sister? If Lakshmi does not observe the rules, the fault is chiefly mine, and then yours. I leave out the others. I leave out Narandas, too, for if we hold him responsible for the behaviour of every person in the Ashram, he will not be able to attend to his own duties. Looking after Lakshmi is a woman's job, and particularly of the woman to whom it is entrusted. The fault is chiefly mine because I am her adopted father and also mother. I did my duty as a father but not as a mother, because I remained away from the Ashram most of the time. I feel now that I should not have accepted Lakshmi at all. But who was I to decide? I am but a servant of God. I did not seek Lakshmi. God sent her. Let Him, then, look after her. She was under the charge of Ba first, then of Santok, then of Gangabehn, and now she is under your charge. None of you asked to have charge of her. It was time and circumstances which put her under the charge of these persons one after another. You should now do the best that you can. Whenever necessary, you may consult me. Do not get tired of your charge or despair. Have faith and bathe her with your love. God will ultimately solve the problem. She has come to us as a representative of Harijans to claim payment of the debt which we owe to them. If she is full of shortcomings and is indolent, the

1. Firmness.

responsibility for that lies on you, me and on the caste Hindus. We reap as we sow. I am trying to get her married off. I have written to Lakshmidas and inquired about Maruti. I have also written to Dudabhai.

You need not get upset because more boys and girls are coming to the Ashram. They will benefit to the extent that they observe the rules. We may let them stay as long as we tolerate their laxity, and ask them to leave when we can do so no longer. People do not stay in a dharmashala permanently. Even near relations do not stay permanently. Those of them who can accommodate themselves to the discipline of the Ashram will stay, and the others will leave. Why should we care either way? Moreover, we cannot adopt any other policy in the present circumstances. As long as we can do so, we should admit people who come unasked and who seem deserving. Most of them will leave on their own. Our rules themselves will drive them away. Everybody who comes must do physical work. They should clean lavatories and eat simple food in the same manner as we swallow medicine. They will not get jaggery, nor wheat as often as they might wish. If we can daily demonstrate more and more clearly by our manner of life that the Ashram is a representative of the starving poor, we shall always be safe and happy. This means that there should be increasing simplicity in our life in the Ashram and the rules should be observed more and more strictly. If fire preserves its nature, creatures which cannot endure it simply cannot live near it. That is the virtue of fire and not its defect. It is because, unlike fire, we are not true to ourselves that all the problems arise. My suggestion about simplicity and strictness in observing the rules concerns ourselves. We should cultivate them in ever greater degree. We seek protection for ourselves in our inner selves and not outside of us— "we" here means all of us who voluntarily stay in the Ashram, you, I and everybody else. And one should not observe only as many rules as the other inmates do. One must observe every rule as strictly as one can. In this lies the secret of the progress of the Ashram. The rule should be, a liberal attitude towards others and strictness towards oneself. Even so, we shall preserve some minimum decency in our attitude to ourselves, for very often our liberal attitude towards others will not be sincere and our strictness towards ourselves will be so only in appearance.

The ideal for girls is a life of inviolate *brahmacharya*. Training for it includes training for ideal married life. Boys and girls do not require to be instructed as to what married life means. That relation is a part of the animal nature of men and women. The institution of marriage was devised as a means of exercising some control on that nature. Its perfect control means *brahmacharya*. Anybody who can observe this perfect control will also be able to observe the limited control of marriage. But those who regard marriage itself as their ideal will not understand the real purpose even of marriage. What training does one require for lust? It will grow of itself. However, the girl who has accepted complete *brahmacharya* as her ideal must learn how to manage a home. She must learn something about child-care. She will not be a nun living in a cave. An unmarried woman marries the whole world, makes herself a mother and a daughter to all people and thereby becomes fit to manage the affairs of the whole society. Maybe there has been no such unmarried woman. Nevertheless that is the ideal. For all girls, therefore, the training should be the same. I think I have explained the idea clearly. If I have not done so, ask me to explain it again.

This will explain your duty towards that Muslim woman.

The real cause of fainting fits and similar ailments in girls lies in our own shortcomings. If we have made fairly satisfactory progress, even the presence of young people among us will not be dangerous to the Ashram. But whenever we see such danger, we should ask the young man or woman to leave. If you wish to stop admitting other young men or women, you may do so.

All my hopes rest on Narandas. If Narandas who is the secretary of the Ashram is the Narandas as I imagine him to be, everything will be well. My faith in him is daily increasing. If he is defeated, some other old inmate of the Ashram will grow and advance, and I am sure, therefore, that everything will be well. There are many residents in the Ashram but only a few inmates. That is why we do not get sufficient workers. In these very imperfect conditions, all of you should do the best that you can.

The Ashram is the measuring rod by which people can judge me. I take it with me wherever I go. Wherever my body may be, my soul is always in the Ashram. All the shortcomings found in the Ashram must be present, visibly or invisibly, in me too. If I have made a mistake in understanding you all, the blame must be mine and nobody else's. If, however, I do not know myself, how can I sit in judgement over all of you? When I think of particular persons, I see that I did not invite anybody except Chhaganlal and Maganlal. All the others were sent to me by God to test me or to help me.

And now another matter. You made a mistake in not going to Dr. Patel yourself. You cannot ask a doctor's advice through a note. Observe complete silence. Show your throat to the doctor and follow his advice. You should not be obstinate in this matter.

BAPU

65. The Schoolmaster Abroad
(vol. LIII, pp. 399–402)

I wrote to the Rt. Hon. Srinivasa Sastri for a message to the *Harijan*. And I received a characteristic reply marked 'private.' The letter seemed to me to be too good to be suppressed. I, therefore, wired for permission to publish it. The reply wire was as characteristic as the letter.

Firstly inappropriate to *Harijan*, secondly, offensive to partisans. Ill requital for your steadfast affection. However if perchance useful please publish.

And here is the letter:

Private   Svagatam, Mylapore,
February 13, 1933

Dear Brother,

Thanks for your affectionate letter, in which you ask for a message to your new baby.

I am going to change towards you. It is necessary in your interest, no matter what effort it costs me.

You live in a difficult world. Waking or dreaming, you are racked by thoughts of sin and penance, confessions and truth-quests, satyagraha and moral self-flagellation. Those that talk to you or correspond with you continually pose doubts and serious problems, only deepening the grimness and suffocation around you. Few bring lightness of talk, familiar expletives, innocent jokes, revealing banter. You badly need a privileged jester in your establishment. Have you read a story called Ardath by Ouida? The hero there has a critic whose business is to expose his errors and bring to light the flaws in his character. Being a professional fault-finder, he overdoes his part in the end and defeats his first object. I shall vary my function from time to time and disappear from the scene every now and then. But I will endeavour to awaken parts of your mind long gone to sleep and to supply elements of nourishment which it has long been without. Of course, you can stop the medicine if it disagrees and you cannot stand it. That would be a sign to me that the disease had gone too far.

You are an extraordinarily correct writer of English. The ordinary reader will not detect any slips on your part. They are not only rare but of a subtle nature. The eye of a schoolmaster, made acute by dwelling on trivialities of grammar, can alone see them. Here are some, all from the first number of the *Harijan* and from the parts bearing your name.

Page 3. "If it is a bye-product of the caste system, it is only in the same sense *that* an ugly growth is of a body." ('That' is fast undergoing a change in English, but this is far in excess of present usage. Better say '*in which* an ugly growth is a bye-product of a body.')

Also read the whole passage again. Don't you say in effect 'if the caste system is a bye-product of the caste system'?

Page 3. "The outcaste-ness, in the sense we understand it, has therefore to be destroyed altogether." (A slip similar to the above. Between 'sense' and 'we' insert 'in which.')

Page 4. "Caste Hindus have to open their temples to Harijans, precisely on the same terms as the other Hindus."

(Say 'the same terms as *to* the other Hindus.' Else, it would mean that the other Hindus opened their temples on certain terms to Harijans.)

Page 7. "Beyond this I may not go, for the reason I have already stated and which the reader should respect." (Insert 'which' after 'reason.' The conjunction 'and' must not be made to connect a suppressed 'which' and an expressed 'which.')

Page 8. "Untouchability has a great deal to answer *for* the insanitation of our streets and our latrines." (Idiomatically, 'for' is part of the verb 'answer,' and cannot govern 'the insanitation.' We must insert 'in' after 'for,' though the sentence becomes inelegant. I would recast it: 'Untouchability is answerable for a great deal of the insanitation etc.')

Page 8. "Therefore, a person who is to attend to scavenging, whether it is a paid Bhangi or an unpaid mother, they are unclean until they have washed themselves clean of their unclean work."

(The looseness is, perhaps, the result of rapid dictation unchecked by subsequent reading. 'A person' is left hanging in the air. The plurals 'they,' 'themselves' and 'their' are justified by the common gender required. Still the discord of a number is apparent to the point of harshness and may be avoided. Read 'A person . . . is unclean until washed clean of the unclean work.')

Let me add a criticism of substance. On page 7 you answer a question under the heading "Seeking or Giving?". The paragraph has gained brevity at the expense of clearness. The difference between giving cooperation and seeking it requires more elucidation. Likewise the analogy of love leading to feeding in one case and starving in another. But you are obscure and even baffling when you say that your policy of non-cooperation with Government allows of your seeking its co-operation whenever your purpose is, in your opinion, 'very sacred and altogether good.' Most sensible people follow this rule in ordinary life, not seeking co-operation when they don't care and seeking it when they care. They don't proclaim it as a policy or give it a grand name.

Ever yours affectionately,
V. S. Srinivasan

I wanted to share this letter with the public, because such a letter would help any publicist and his cause and that in an unexpected manner, more so when written without any thought of publication.

I want also to use the publication of the letter for easing the tension between sanatanists and reformers. Let them learn that closest friendships can subsist between persons of contrary temperaments. As the public know, Sastri and I have opposite views on many important questions. Our mutual regard and affection have never suffered on that account. There is no reason whatsoever why the same rule cannot be extended to parties and groups representing opposite schools of opinion. The sanatanists are out to defend religion as they believe it. I take their claim at its face value and deal with it as such. Why need they impute to me political motives when I solemnly assert that for me, too, the question of untouchability is a matter purely of religion? Would that the affection subsisting between Sastri and me prove so deep and extensive as to reach and affect the whole society!

But enough of this. I almost hear Sastri's spirit whispering to me: 'You are misusing the medicine I prescribed to wean you from your disease of grimness and the like.' Therefore, let me hasten to tell him and the public that I have in my little camp of four a specially privileged jester in Sardar Vallabhbhai Patel. He succeeds in bending me almost double every day with laughter over his unexpected sallies. Gloom hides her fiendish face in his presence. No disappointment, however great, can make him gloomy for long. And he will not let me be serious for two consecutive minutes. He will not spare even my 'saintliness'! It may deceive simple people but never the Sardar or the sanatanists. Both tear down the mask and compel me to see myself as they delight to see me. To be just to the sanatanists, let me admit that Vallabhbhai does not see me quite as sanatanists do. But that is beside the point. The thing that Sastri wants in our little family is there cent per cent. Next time he enters the Assembly or some such place, he must vote special thanks to the Government for putting Vallabhbhai with me or me with him.

But this consoling information does not in any way release Sastri from his self-imposed obligation. For the Sardar will not do what Sastri can be trusted to do mostly. Unlike him, the Sardar has the wretched habit in the end of saying 'ditto' to all I say. And that is bad for anybody.

Let the student note in passing Sastri's love for the language he has mastered as few men have done. He is a purist in everything. We badly need purists in our country. I want only purists as fellow-workers in this glorious campaign of abolition of untouchability.

As to the purity of the language of *Harijan*, whatever faults are found notwithstanding Sastri's warning will be shared with me by Shastri, the Editor, and by Mahadev Desai, who shares with the schoolmaster the weakness for writing correctly in the language which for the moment he is using.

I must leave the reader to find out for himself or herself the many other beauties of Sastri's letter. If he will do so, he must read the letter three or four times and look up all the references in the first issue of *Harijan*.

Harijan, 25-2-1933

66. Letter to Ramdas Gandhi

(vol. LIII, pp. 417–19)

February 25, 1933

Chi. Ramdas,

Khushaldas has passed away. I received both the accompanying letters yesterday evening. I have written to Shantilal and informed him. Khushaldas has indeed been released from the suffering of this life. The truth is that everybody who goes on a journey along that royal road is released from this life. For this life is given to us for repaying our debts, and nobody can leave before he has paid off his. If this idea is correct, death means that the person has paid off his debt partially at least.

He who knows with perfect conviction that this life is given to us for repaying our debts can repay his debts to all, and the ancients described that as attaining *moksha*. *Moksha* means complete freedom from debt and, consequently, end of the cycle of births for the person.

I was pained to see your condition yesterday, your broken health and your mental suffering. I had no remedy for either, and was pained because you attributed to your father more power than he possessed. I felt as Harishchandra had done. He had become ready to sell his only son for the sake of dharma. I have been doing very much the same thing. Though I know the remedy for your poor health, I cannot adopt it because of my concern for dharma, nor can end your mental suffering for the same reason.

If you follow the rule that you cannot avail yourself of facilities which other prisoners who keep bad health would not get, you can do nothing to improve your health. I can understand that you would not like to ask for special facilities for yourself, but it does not seem right to me that you should not avail yourself of facilities which may be offered to you when you explain to the authorities the condition of your health. When you are outside, you enjoy more facilities than the countless millions and never think about the matter. I ask for and enjoy, both in jail and outside, facilities which they can never hope to get, and am fully aware that I do so. But I do not feel that I violate dharma thereby. If an elephant tries to crawl like an ant, he will not suceed in becoming an ant thereby and will cease to be an elephant, which means that he will have lost his true nature. An elephant like me, however, would humbly accept his big size and consume food weighing more than thousands of ants and would also draw, without the least effort, loads which those ants could never draw. An elephant is entitled to consume food which the size of his body requires. Only, he must not waste that food by not giving proportionate service in return. That is, he should carry loads proportionate to his strength. If he does that, he will have consumed as much food and given as much service as an ant. This is communism. If, therefore, you can secure the food which your body requires by legitimate means and without humiliating yourself for the purpose, you should do so and improve your health, and then serve other people to the best of your ability.

But even in trying to serve other people and securing facilities for yourself by legitimate means, you should know and understand your duty as a prisoner. A prisoner has no right except that of preserving his self-respect, for he ceases to be the master of his body as soon as he becomes a prisoner and the jail superintendent becomes its master. Even if the latter does not give the prisoner enough to eat or to drink or sufficient clothes to wear, the prisoner should remain contented and cheerful. Anybody who cannot do so is not a true prisoner. We must admit that in this age the British policy towards prisoners is comparatively more liberal than that of any other government. It is improving day by day. There is certainly room for much more improvement still, but that is another matter. A prisoner may fight to bring about such improvement. If, however, he remembers the general principle stated above, he will not be disappointed if he fails in his attempt—for he has no absolute right to enjoy any facility. If you understand this reasoning fully, I shall be relieved and you will be able to overcome your mental unrest.

I will certainly try to do what I can in regard to everything which you mentioned—but in my own way, and that is bound to take time. The delay will not make me impatient, and I wish that you also should not be. What can you or I do? Certainly we are not masters of the result.

We can only try the best that we can. You have been doing what you can, and I also will do what I can. Even if we don't succeed, you should dance with joy, and so will I.

> Be not moved by joy or sorrow; with the body were they created;
> None can escape them for by the Lord of Raghu were they decreed.

Do you follow all this? Read the letter three or four times, and if you do not follow any point ask me to explain it again.

Keep me informed about the condition of your health.

Blessings from
BAPU

From a photostat of the Gujarati

67. Letter to Narandas Gandhi

(vol. LV, pp. 67–70)

April 29, 1933

Chi. Narandas,

I got your postcard. I will ask Devdas about Manilal's bill. Panditji and Lakshmibehn came and saw me. Narmada also was with them. I was pained to hear about Amina. I will write to her. Read that letter and give it to her if you approve of it. If I cannot write today, I will write later when I get time. Meanwhile, manage as you think best. They told me about Ramabehn also. I intend to write to her too. Show as much love as you can. But human love must have some limit also, for how can we know when love may become *moha?*[1] One's love, therefore, should never be at the cost of one's duty, no matter even if such conduct seems cruel. If anybody who looks at

1. Ignorant attachment.

the matter superficially were to believe that I am being cruel to . . . ,[2] I would not blame him. At present . . .[3] is bound to think me cruel. But what can I do? My regard for dharma will not let me adopt any other course. What is true of me is also true of you. You should, therefore, follow what seems to you to be your dharma even at the risk of being accused of cruelty or inviting my criticism.

I got yesterday your letter about N. It proved that Vallabhbhai's interpretation was correct. I am, therefore, making preparations for sending her. I shall probably be able to send her on Monday. Assuming that she will arrive on that day, send a cart to the station. Probably Dr. Margarete Spiegel also will accompany her. Even if I don't receive your consent about her, I will assume it. At the [Ahmedabad] station they will get into the metre gauge train which connects with the Gujarat Mail. You should remember that both the ladies are to be trained for Harijan work. You must strictly follow the rule that neither they nor any other European whom we may admit should be permitted to have any connection with the civil disobedience movement. I am specially writing to the Government about those two women. They and others who may join the Ashram should strictly follow the Ashram rules and you should see that they do so. If they do not observe the rules or become a source of trouble to you, I don't at all intend that you should still let them remain. If that happens, inform me immediately. The food requirement of both is simple. I very much doubt if they will be able to digest *jowar* and *bajri*. You will have to provide fruit and milk to both in fairly good quantities, otherwise they will not be able to keep up their strength. N. does not include milk and ghee in her diet at present. Both eat with relish thick wheat *rotlas* without ghee or butter, nine inches in diameter and baked twice till they are crisp and without ghee or butter. They eat these *rotlas* and chew them without the help of any liquid. N. does not drink milk or eat ghee at present. Her food is such *rotlas*, papaw, oranges, and uncooked vegetables like cucumber, tomatoes, cabbage, carrots, etc. She will, however, drink milk there if necessary. Her son gets three pounds of milk daily. He also eats toasted *rotli* and fruits. If we coax him very much, he eats a little uncooked vegetable. He doesn't care for sweets at all, but greatly enjoys drinking fresh unboiled milk. He eats every article one by one. I hope nobody will spoil this child by teaching him to drink tea or coffee or eat sweets. His energy is boundless. We have in the Ashram other

2. The name has been omitted.
3. The name has been omitted.

children who are as self-willed as he is, but he does not cling to his mother all the time. He has produced on me the impression that he can live with anybody. It is very desirable that nobody there should, out of false love, tempt him to eat unwholesome things. For the rest, we should trust to his and our fate. I am sending N. there with great hopes. I have cherished her like a daughter for the last three or four months. I have preserved many of her letters. There is nothing in her life which she wishes to hide. I have advised her to bury the memory of all persons who had fallen under her spell. But she has assured me that she does not wish to hide from me a single guilty action or thought of hers, and thereby won my initial confidence. But I can give no guarantee about her future conduct. I am acting on the basis of complete trust in her. Give her suitable work from time to time within her capacity. She has great ability. She is extremely active and wants to do good. If she can reduce herself to a cypher, she will be able to do much. If she becomes proud of her ability or her noble intentions or good work, she will fall. For the present give her such manual work as she can do. Make arrangements to help her to pick up Hindi quickly. Her power of grasping is very good. She already knows a little Hindi.

Margarete is of a different type. She is 35 years old and, therefore, her character is practically formed. She is a woman of great learning and is quick in learning things by heart, but she is not very intelligent. She is obstinate, but her motives are pure. I think her life has been blameless. She has great love for the Ashram. But she has no sense of proportion when she speaks. Ever since she has been here, she has been talking about the Ashram in season and out of season. She has left the country and come to India because of the movement in Germany against her but she has no plan before her. I am sending N. there willingly and with great joy. I don't feel such joy in sending Margarete, but we cannot turn her away. She has come merely with the intention of living in the Ashram. What can we say to her? She will of course do whatever work she is physically capable of. She has been a teacher for some years and so you can immediately give her the work of teaching English. She is eager to do teaching. Even as a teacher, however, N. is more capable. But since she is joining the Ashram to atone for her past life, I feel slightly doubtful whether you should immediately give her such work. If you do wish to give it, you may certainly do so.[4]

From a microfilm of the Gujarati

4. A page and a half has been omitted.

68. Fast for Purification

(vol. LV, pp. 74–75)

[April 30, 1933]

A tempest has been raging within me for some days. I have been struggling against it. On the eve of the 'Harijan Day' the voice became insistent, and said, 'why don't you do it?' I resisted it. But the resistance was vain. And the resolution was made to go on an unconditional and irrevocable fast for twenty-one days, commencing from Monday noon the 8th May and ending on Monday noon the 29th May.

As I look back upon the immediate past, many are the causes too sacred to mention that must have precipitated the fast. But they are all connected with the great Harijan cause. The fast is against nobody in particular and against everybody who wants to participate in the joy of it, without for the time being having to fast himself or herself. But it is particularly against myself. It is a heart-prayer for the purification of self and associates, for greater vigilance and watchfulness. But nobody who appreciates the step about to be taken is to join me. Any such fast will be a torture of themselves and of me.

Let this fast, however, be a preparation for many such fasts to be taken by purer and more deserving persons than myself. During all these months since September last, I have been studying the correspondence and literature and holding prolonged discussions with men and women, learned and ignorant, Harijans and non-Harijans. The evil is far greater than even I had thought it to be. It will not be eradicated by money, external organization and even political power for Harijans, though all these three are necessary. But to be effective, they must follow or at least accompany inward wealth, inward organization and inward power, in other words, self-purification. This can only come by fasting and prayer. We may not approach the God of Truth in the arrogance of strength, but in the meekness of the weak and the helpless.

But the mere fast of the body is nothing without the will behind it. It must be a genuine confession of the inner fast, an irrepressible longing to express truth and nothing but truth. Therefore, those only are privileged to fast for the cause of truth who have worked for it and who have love in them even for opponents, who are free from animal passion and who have abjured earthly possessions and ambition. No one, therefore, may undertake, without previous preparation and discipline, the fast I have foreshadowed.

Let there be no misunderstanding about the impending fast. I have no desire to die. I want to live for the cause, though I hope I am equally prepared to die for it. But I need for me and my fellow-workers greater purity, greater application and dedication. I want more workers of unassailable purity. Shocking cases of impurity have come under my notice. I would like my fast to be an urgent appeal to such people to leave the cause alone.

I know that many of my sanatanist friends and others think that the movement is a deep political game. How I wish this fast would convince them that it is purely religious.

If God has more service to take from this body, He will hold it together despite deprivation of earthly food. He will send me spiritual food. But He works through earthly agents, and everyone who believes in the imperative necessity of removing untouchability will send me the food I need, by working to the best of his or her ability for the due and complete fulfilment of the pledge given to Harijans in the name of caste Hindus.

Let co-workers not get agitated over the coming fast. They should feel strengthened by it. They must not leave their post of duty; and those who have temporarily retired for much-needed rest or for being cured of ailments are as much at the post as healthy workers serving in their respective quarters. No one should come to me unless it be for necessary consultation on matters connected with the movement.

It is, I hope, needless for me to pray to friends that they will not ask me to postpone, abandon or vary the approaching fast in any way whatsoever. I ask them to believe me that the fast has come to me literally as described above. I, therefore, ask friends in India and all the world over to pray for me and with me that I may safely pass through the ordeal and that, whether I live or die, the cause for which the fast is to be undertaken may prosper.

And may I ask my sanatanist friends to pray that, whatever be the result of the fast for me, the golden lid that hides Truth may be removed?

Harijan, 6-5-1933

69. All About the Fast

(vol. LV, pp. 254-58)

It is, perhaps, meet that the very first writing for the Press I should attempt after the fast should be for the *Harijan,* and that in connection with the fast. God willing, I hope now to contribute my weekly quota to the *Harijan* as before the fast. Let no one, however, run away with the idea that I have regained my pre-fast capacity for work. I have still to be very careful how I work. Correspondents will, therefore, have mercy on me. They should know that for a while yet I shall be unable to cope with all their letters. Whatever they may have for my special attention will have still to wait for some time, probably yet another month. Who knows what will happen a month hence? We are short-lived and do not know even what will happen the next moment. Then what can one say about the ambitions of a Harijan worker like myself? To those who buy and read *Harijan-bandhu* in a spirit of service, my advice is that they should not wait for my writings and opinions. The way for rendering service to Harijans is quite clear. The field is vast. *Harijanbandhu* endeavours to give an idea of the week's activities. It also attempts to indicate what needs to be done, what can be done and how it is to be done. From that all could find one or the other way of service. Then where is the need of my writing or opinion? If I am tempted to write about it, it is only for my own satisfaction. I have to write only when I have something to say or explain to the readers. I hope readers won't be disheartened and will maintain their relations with *Harijanbandhu* irrespective of whether I have something to write or not and whether I have the strength and the leisure.

Now for the fast.

The first question that has puzzled many is about the Voice of God. What was it? What did I hear? Was there any person I saw? If not, how was the Voice conveyed to me? These are pertinent questions.

For me the voice of God, of Conscience, of Truth or the Inner Voice or 'the still small Voice' mean one and the same thing. I saw no form. I have never tried, for I have always believed God to be without form. One who realizes God is freed from sin for ever. He has no desire to be fulfilled. Not even in his thoughts will he suffer from faults, imperfections or impurities. Whatever he does will be perfect because he does nothing himself but the God within him does everything. He is completely merged in Him. Such realization comes to one among tens of millions. That it can come I have no doubt at all. I yearn to have such realization but I have not got it yet and I know that I am yet very far from it. The inspiration I had was quite a different thing. Moreover, many get such inspiration quite often or at some time. There is certainly need for a particular type of *sadhana*[1]

---

1. Spiritual effort.

to obtain such inspiration. If some efforts and some *sadhana* are necessary even to acquire the ability to have the commonest thing, what wonder if efforts and *sadhana* are needed to get divine inspiration? The inspiration I got was this: The night I got the inspiration, I had a terrible inner struggle. My mind was restless. I could see no way. The burden of my responsibility was crushing me. But what I did hear was like a Voice from afar and yet quite near. It was as unmistakable as some human voice definitely speaking to me, and irresistible. I was not dreaming at the time I heard the Voice. The hearing of the Voice was preceded by a terrific struggle within me. Suddenly the Voice came upon me. I listened, made certain that it was the Voice, and the struggle ceased. I was calm. The determination was made accordingly, the date and the hour of the fast were fixed. Joy came over me. This was between 11 and 12 midnight. I felt refreshed and began to write the note about it which the reader must have seen.

Could I give any further evidence that it was truly the Voice that I heard and that it was not an echo of my own heated imagination? I have no further evidence to convince the sceptic. He is free to say that it was all self-delusion or hallucination. It may well have been so. I can offer no proof to the contrary. But I can say this—that not the unanimous verdict of the whole world against me could shake me from the belief that what I heard was the true voice of God.

But some think that God Himself is a creation of our own imagination. If that view holds good, then nothing is real, everything is of our own imagination. Even so, whilst my imagination dominates me, I can only act under its spell. Realest things are only relatively so. For me the Voice was more real than my own existence. It has never failed me, and for that matter, anyone else.

And everyone who wills can hear the Voice. It is within everyone. But like everything else, it requires previous and definite preparation.

The second question that has puzzled many is whether a fast in which an army of doctors watch and guide the fasting person, as they undoubtedly and with extraordinary care and attention watched and guided me, when he is coddled in various other ways as I was, could be described as a fast in answer to the call of the Inner Voice. Put thus, the objection seems valid. It would undoubtedly have been more in keeping with the high claim made for the fast, if it had been unattended with all the extraordinary, external aids that it was my good fortune or misfortune to receive.

But I do not repent of having gratefully accepted the generous help that kind friends extended to me. I was battling against death. I accepted all the help that came to me as godsend, when it did not in any way affect my vow.

As I think over the past, I am not sorry for having taken the fast. Though I suffered bodily pain and discomfort, there was indescribable peace within. I have enjoyed peace during all my fasts but never so much as in this. Perhaps, the reason was that there was nothing to look forward to. In the previous fasts there was some tangible expectation. In this there was nothing tangible to expect. There was undoubtedly faith that it must lead to purification of self and others and that workers would know that true Harijan service was impossible without inward purity. This, however, is a result that could not be measured or known in a tangible manner. I had, therefore, withdrawn within myself.

The nature of the fast deserves some more consideration. Was it mere mortification of the flesh? I firmly believe that a fast taken for mortification of the flesh does some good from the medical point of view; apart from that it produces no particular effect. I know my fast was not at all meant for the mortification of the flesh. Nor was I ready for it. The time of the fast was beyond my imagination. From the letters then written to friends it is clear that I did not foresee any immediate fast. For me, this fast was a supplication or prayer to God coming from the depth of my heart. The fast was an uninterrupted twenty-one days' prayer whose effect I can feel even now. I know now more fully than ever that there is no prayer without fasting, be the latter ever so little. And this fasting relates not merely to the palate, but all the senses and organs. Complete absorption in prayer must mean complete exclusion of physical activities till prayer possesses the whole of our being and we rise superior to, and are completely detached from, all physical functions. That state can only be reached after continual and voluntary crucifixion of the flesh. Thus all fasting, if it is a spiritual act, is an intense prayer or a preparation for it. It is a yearning of the soul to merge in the divine essence. My last fast was intended to be such a preparation. How far I have succeeded, how far I am in tune with the Infinite, I do not know. But I do know that the fast has made the passion for such a state intenser than ever.

Looking back upon the fast, I feel it to have been as necessary as I felt it was when I entered upon it. It has resulted in some revelations of impurities among workers of which I had no knowledge whatsoever, and but for the fast I would never have gained that knowledge. All the letters that have come under my notice go to show that it has led to greater purification among the workers. The fast was meant not for the purification of known workers only who had been found wanting, but for all the workers, known and unknown, in the Harijan cause. Nothing probably could have brought home to the workers so well as this fast the fact that the movement is purely religious in the highest sense of the term, to be handled in a religious spirit by workers of character above reproach.

The work of removal of untouchability is not merely a social or economic reform whose extent can be measured by so much social amenities or economic relief provided in so much time. Its goal is to touch the hearts of the millions of Hindus who honestly believe in the present-day untouchability as a God-made institution, as old as the human race itself. This, it will be admitted, is a task infinitely higher than mere social and economic reform. Its accomplishment undoubtedly includes all these and much more. For it means nothing short of a complete revolution in the Hindu thought and the disappearance of the horrible and terrible doctrine of inborn inequality and high-and-lowness, which has poisoned Hinduism and is slowly undermining its very existence. Such a change can only be brought about by an appeal to the highest in man. And I am more than ever convinced that that appeal can be made effective only by self-purification, i.e., by fasting conceived as the deepest prayer coming from a lacerated heart.

I believe that the invisible effect of such fasting is far greater and far more extensive than the visible effect. The conviction has, therefore, gone deeper in me that my fast is but the beginning of a chain of true voluntary fasts by men and women who have qualified themselves by previous preparation for them and who believe in prayer as the most effective method of reaching the heart of things. How that chain can be established I do not know as yet. But I am striving after it. If it can be established, I know that it will touch, as nothing else will, the hearts of Hindus, both the opponents of reform and the Harijans. For the Harijans have also to play their part in the movement no less than the reformers and the opponents. And I am glad to be able to inform the reader that the Harijans have not been untouched by the fast. A number of letters received from abroad suggest that even there many hearts have awakened. If an imperfect fast by a man like me could create such awakening, who could then estimate how great and far-reaching the result would be if innocent men and women unassumingly, without any hope of medical or other aid and without one or the other concession, sacrifice their lives in an unbroken chain of fasts?

Harijan, 8-7-1933

70. Bihar and Untouchability
(vol. LVII, pp. 86–87)

A friendly wire says, "Will you not lay aside untouchability and go to Bihar?" An angry wire says, "Must Mahatma fiddle while Bihar is burning?" Both the wires pay me an undeserved compliment and exaggerate my capacity for service, as they assume that I can do more than my comrades. I have no such hallucination about my capacity. Rajendra Prasad is one of the best among my co-workers. He can command my services whenever he likes. The Harijan cause is as much his as it is mine, even as the cause of Bihar is as much mine as it is his. But God has summoned him to the Bihar relief as He has chosen the Harijan cause for me. When the call comes from Bihar, I hope I shall not be found wanting. Champaran discovered me when I was a mere wanderer. Babu Braj Kishore Prasad and his band of workers gave me their complete allegiance when India was wondering what place I had in her public life. I am tied to Bihar by sacred ties which are indissoluble. Therefore I need no spur to send me to Bihar. Perhaps I am serving her best by remaining at my post for the time being. All the world is directing her attention to the catastrophe.[1] It would be presumption on my part to rush to Bihar when all are ready to assist her. Those also help who know how and when to wait.

But another wire says I must use the Harijan collections for Bihar relief. I think it would be a clear breach of trust on my part if I listened to the advice. We may not afford to be unnerved in the face of great calamities. Not all the riches of the world would restore Bihar to her original condition. Time must elapse before reconstruction takes place and things become normal. What is necessary is that those who have anything to give are induced to give the most, not the least, they can.

But I make bold to suggest that, in reconstructing life in Bihar, if the wisest use is to be made of the help that is being sent, the organizers would have resolutely to set their faces against reproducing evil customs and habits. They may not encourage untouchability or caste divisions unperceivably based on untouchability. Nature has been impartial in her destruction. Shall we retain our partiality— caste against caste, Hindu, Muslim, Christian, Parsi, Jew, against one another—in reconstruction, or shall we learn from her the lesson that there is no such thing as untouchability as we practise it today?

1. An earthquake had occurred in that province of India.

Tremendous responsibility rests both upon the government and the unofficial agency as to how reconstruction is to be undertaken. And as both are working in co-operation for this purpose, it ought not to be difficult to rebuild Bihar on human and sanitary lines.

I share the belief with the whole world—civilized and uncivilized—that calamities such as the Bihar one come to mankind as chastisement for their sins. When that conviction comes from the heart, people pray, repent and purify themselves. I regard untouchability as such a grave sin as to warrant divine chastisement. I am not affected by posers such as 'why punishment for an age-old sin' or 'why punishment to Bihar and not to the South' or 'why an earthquake and not some other form of punishment.' My answer is: I am not God. Therefore I have but a limited knowledge of His purpose. Such calamities are not a mere caprice of the Deity or Nature. They obey fixed laws as surely as the planets move in obedience to laws governing their movement. Only we do not know the laws governing these events and, therefore, call them calamities or disturbances. Whatever, therefore, may be said about them must be regarded as guess work. But guessing has its definite place in man's life. It is an ennobling thing for me to guess that the Bihar disturbance is due to the sin of untouchability. It makes me humble, it spurs me to greater effort towards its removal, it encourages me to purify myself, it brings me nearer to my Maker. That my guess may be wrong does not affect the results named by me. For what is guess to the critic or the sceptic is a living belief with me, and I base my future actions on that belief. Such guesses become superstitions when they lead to no purification and may even lead to feuds. But such misuse of divine events cannot deter men of faith from interpreting them as a call to them for repentance for their sins. I do not interpret this chastisement as an exclusive punishment for the sin of untouchability. It is open to others to read in it divine wrath against many other sins.

Let anti-untouchability reformers regard the earthquake as a Nemesis for the sin of untouchability. They cannot go wrong, if they have the faith that I have. They will help Bihar more and not less for that faith. And they will try to create an atmosphere against reproduction of untouchability in any scheme of reconstruction.

Harijan, 2-2-1934

71. Superstition v. Faith
(vol. LVII, pp. 164–66)

The Bard of Santiniketan is Gurudev for me as he is for the in-mates of that great institution. I and mine had found our shelter there when we returned from our long self-imposed exile in South Africa. But Gurudev and I early discovered certain differences of out-look between us. Our mutual affection has, however, never suffered by reason of our differences, and it cannot suffer by Gurudev's latest utterance on my linking the Bihar calamity with the sin of un-touchability. He had a perfect right to utter his protest when he be-lieved that I was in error. My profound regard for him would make me listen to him more readily than to any other critic. But in spite of my having read the statement three times, I adhere to what I have written in these columns.

When at Tinnevelly I first linked the event with untouchability, I spoke with the greatest deliberation and out of the fulness of my heart. I spoke as I believed. I have long believed that physical phe-nomena produce results both physical and spiritual. The converse I hold to be equally true.

To me the earthquake was no caprice of God nor a result of a meet-ing of mere blind forces. We do not know all the laws of God nor their working. Knowledge of the tallest scientist or the greatest spiritualist is like a particle of dust. If God is not a personal being for me like my earthly father, He is infinitely more. He rules me in the tiniest detail of my life. I believe literally that not a leaf moves but by His will. Every breath I take depends upon His sufferance.

He and His Law are one. The Law is God. Anything attributed to Him is not a mere attribute. He is the Attribute. He is Truth, Love, Law, and a million things that human ingenuity can name. I do be-lieve with Gurudev in "the inexorableness of the universal law in the working of which God Himself never interferes." For God is the Law. But I submit that we do not know the Law or the laws fully, and what appear to us as catastrophes are so only because we do not know the universal laws sufficiently.

Visitations like droughts, floods, earthquakes and the like, though they seem to have only physical origins, are, for me, somehow con-nected with man's morals. Therefore, I instinctively felt that the earthquake was a visitation for the sin of untouchability. Of course, sanatanists have a perfect right to say that it was due to my crime of preaching against untouchability. My belief is a call to repentance and self-purification. I admit my utter ignorance of the working of the laws of Nature. But, even as I cannot help believing in God though I am unable to prove His existence to the sceptics, in like manner I cannot prove the connection of the sin of untouchability with the Bihar visitation even though the connection is instinctively felt by me. If my belief turns out to be ill-founded, it will still have done good to me and those who believe with me. For we shall have been spurred to more vigorous efforts towards self-purification, assuming, of course, the untouchability is a deadly sin. I know fully well the danger of such speculation. But I would be untruthful and cowardly if, for fear of ridicule, when those that are nearest and dearest to me are suffering, I did not proclaim my belief from the house-top. The physical effect of the earthquake will be soon forgotten and even partially repaired. But it would be terrible if it is an expression of the Divine wrath for the sin of untouchability and we did not learn the moral lesson from the event and repent of that sin. I have not the faith which Gurudev has that "our own sins and errors, however enormous, have not got enough force to drag down the structure of creation to ruins." On the contrary, I have the faith that our own sins have more force to ruin that structure than any mere physical phenomenon. There is an indissoluble marriage between matter and spirit. Our ignorance of the results of the union makes it a profound mystery and inspires awe in us, but it cannot undo them. But a living recognition of the union has enabled many to use every physical catastrophe for their own moral uplifting.

With me the connection between cosmic phenomena and human behaviour is a living faith that draws me nearer to my God, humbles me and makes me readier for facing Him. Such a belief would be a degrading superstition, if out of the depth of my ignorance I used it for castigating my opponents.

Harijan, 16-2-1934

72. Statement on Bomb Incident [1]

(vol. LVIII, pp. 108–9)

Poona,
June 25, 1934

I have had so many narrow escapes in my life that this newest one does not surprise me. God be thanked that no one was fatally injured by the bomb, and I hope that those who were more or less seriously injured, will be soon discharged from hospital.

I cannot believe that any sane sanatanist could ever encourage the insane act that was perpetrated this evening. But I would like sanatanist friends to control the language that is being used by speakers and writers claiming to speak on their behalf. The sorrowful incident has undoubtedly advanced the Harijan cause. It is easy to see that causes prosper by the martyrdom of those who stand for them. I am not aching for martyrdom, but if it comes in my way in the prosecution of what I consider to be the supreme duty in defence of the faith I hold in common with millions of Hindus, I shall have well earned it, and it will be possible for the historian of the future to say that the vow I had taken before Harijans that I would, if need be, die in the attempt to remove untouchability was literally fulfilled.

Let those who grudge me what yet remains to me of this earthly existence know that it is the easiest thing to do away with my body. Why then put in jeopardy many innocent lives in order to take mine which they hold to be sinful? What would the world have said of us if the bomb had dropped on me and the party, which included my wife and three girls, who are as dear to me as daughters and are entrusted to me by their parents? I am sure that no harm to them could have been intended by the bomb-thrower.

I have nothing but deep pity for the unknown thrower of the bomb. If I had my way and if the bomb-thrower was known, I should certainly ask for his discharge, even as I did in South Africa in the case of those who successfully assaulted me. Let the reformers not be incensed against the bomb-thrower or those who may be behind him.

---

1. A bomb was thrown on what the assailant believed was the car carrying Gandhi on his way to the Municipal Building. Gandhi arrived at 7:30 p.m. little knowing what had occurred. When informed of the incident, he received the news calmly and agreed to the suggestion that the programme should be carried out. Accordingly the address was presented and Gandhi left the hall at 8:30 p.m. This appeared under the title "Providence Again."

What I should like them to do is to redouble their efforts to rid the country of the deadly evil of untouchability.

Harijan, 29-6-1934

73. Letter to Vallabhbhai Patel

(vol. LVIII, pp. 403–6)

[Before] September [5], 1934[1]

Dear Vallabhbhai,

After much deliberation and discussions with friends who have been to Wardha recently, I have come to the conclusion that the best interests of the Congress and the nation will be served by my completely severing all official or physical connection with the Congress, including the original membership. This does not mean that I cease to take any interest in an organization with which I have been intimately connected since 1920 and which I have worshipped since my youth. In spite of all I have recently said about the corruption that has crept into the organization, it still remains, in my opinion, the most powerful and the most representative national organization in the country. It has a history of uninterrupted noble service and sacrifice from its inception. Its progress has been unbroken and steady. It has weathered storms as no other institution in the country has. It has commanded the largest measure of sacrifice of which any country would be proud. It has today the largest number of self-sacrificing men and women of unimpeachable character.

It is not with a light heart that I leave this great organization. But I feel that my remaining in it any longer is likely to do more harm than good. I miss at this juncture the association and advice of Jawaharlal who is bound to be the rightful helmsman of the organization in the near future. I have, therefore, kept before me his great spirit. And I feel that whilst his great affection for me would want to keep me in the Congress, his reason would endorse the step I have taken. And since a great organization cannot be governed by affections but by

1. Gandhi had been having discussions on his withdrawal from active leadership of the Congress. In his letter of August 20 to the addressee, Gandhi had said that he would "prepare a draft" and send it to him. This letter appears to be a draft of his "Statement to the Press," which was finally released on September 17, 1934.

cold reason, it is better for me to retire from a field where my presence results in arresting full play of reason. Hence in leaving the organization I feel that I am in no sense deserting one who is much more than a comrade and whom no amount of political differences will ever separate from me.

Nor by retiring at this critical juncture am I less true to Babu Rajendra Prasad who will in all probability be the President of the forthcoming Congress, and who unlike Jawaharlal shares most of my ideals and whose sacrifice for the nation, judged whether in quality or quantity, is not to be excelled.

Then there is the Congress Parliamentary Board which would perhaps not have come into being, unless I had encouraged its formation with my whole heart. It supplies a want that was felt by many staunch and true Congressmen. It was necessary, therefore, to bring it into being. Such services as I am capable of rendering will still be at its disposal as at any Congressman's. It must command the full support of all Congressmen who have no insuperable objection to the entry of Congressmen into the existing legislatures. I should be sorry if the Board lost a single vote because of my withdrawal.

I fear none of the consequences dreaded by some friends, for I know my ground. A tree is no more hurt by a ripe fruit falling from it than would the Congress be by my going out of it. Indeed the fruit will be dead weight, if it did not fall when it was fully ripe. Mine is that condition. I feel that I am a dead weight on the Congress now.

There is a growing and vital difference of outlook between many Congressmen and myself. My presence more and more estranges the intelligentsia from the Congress. I feel that my policies fail to convince their reason, though strange as it may appear, I do nothing that does not satisfy my own reason. But my reason takes me in a direction just the opposite of what many of the most intellectual Congressmen would gladly and enthusiastically take, if they were not hampered by their unexampled loyalty to me. No leader can expect greater loyalty and devotion than I have received from intellectually-minded Congressmen even when they have protested and signified their disapproval of the policies I have laid before the Congress. I feel that for me any more to draw upon this loyalty and devotion is to put an undue strain upon them. I wish that those who strongly disapprove of my method would outvote me and compel my retirement. I have tried to reach that position but I have failed. They would cling to me till the end. The only way I can require such loyalty is by voluntary retirement. I cannot work in opposition when there are some fundamental differences between the Congress intelligentsia and me. Ever since my entry into public life I have never acted in that manner. . . .[2]

Then there is the growing group of socialists. Jawaharlal is their undisputed leader. I know pretty well what he wants and stands for. He claims to examine everything in a scientific spirit. He is courage personified. He has many years of service in front of him. He has an indomitable faith in his mission. The socialist group represents his views more or less, though probably their mode of execution is not exactly his. That group is bound to grow in influence and importance. I have welcomed the group. Many of them are respected and self-sacrificing co-workers. With all this, I have fundamental differences with them on the programme published in their authorized pamphlets. But I would not, by reason of the moral pressure I may be able to exert, suppress the spread of the ideas propounded in their literature. My remaining in the Congress would amount to the exercise of such pressure. I may not interfere with free expression of those ideas, however distasteful some of them may be to me. . . .[3]

For me to dominate the Congress in spite of these fundamental differences is almost a species of violence which I must refrain from. Their reason must be set free at any cost. Having discovered this undisputable fact, I would be disloyal to the Congress if, even at the risk of losing all my reputation, I did not leave the Congress.

But there is no danger to my reputation or that of the Congress, if I leave only to serve it better in thought, word and deed. I do not leave in anger or in a huff, nor yet in disappointment. I have no disappointment in me. I see before me a bright future for the country. Everything will go well, if we are true to ourselves. I have no other programme before me save the Congress programme now before the country. . . .[4]

In this and various other ways I would love to serve the Congress in my own humble manner. Thus living in complete detachment, I hope, I shall come closer to the Congress. Congressmen will then accept my services without being embarrassed or oppressed.

One word to those who have given me their whole-hearted devotion in thought, word and deed in the pursuit of the common goal. My physical withdrawal from the Congress is not to be understood to mean an invitation to them to withdraw. They will remain in the

2. Omission as in the source.
3. Omission as in the source.
4. Omission as in the source.

Congress fold so long as the Congress needs them and work out such common ideals as they have assimilated.

Yours,
BAPU

Mahatma, Vol. III, pp. 386–8

74. How to Begin? (I)
(vol. LX, pp. 108–10)

Correspondents have been writing, and friends have been seeing me, to ask me how to begin the village industries work and what to do first.

The obvious answer is, "Begin with yourself and do first that which is easiest for you to do."

This answer, however, does not satisfy the enquirers. Let me, therefore, be more explicit.

Each person can examine all the articles of food, clothing and other things that he uses from day to day and replace foreign makes or city makes by those produced by the villagers in their homes or fields with the simple inexpensive tools they can easily handle and mend. This replacement will be itself an education of great value and a solid beginning. The next step will be opened out to him of itself. For instance, say, the beginner has been hitherto using a tooth-brush made in a Bombay factory. He wants to replace it with a village brush. He is advised to use a *babul* twig. If he has weak teeth or is toothless, he has to crush one end of it, with a rounded stone or a hammer, on a hard surface. The other end he slits with a knife and uses the halves as tongue-scrapers. He will find these brushes to be cheaper and much cleaner than the very unhygienic factory-made tooth-brush. The city-made tooth-powder he naturally replaces with equal parts of clean, finely-ground wood-charcoal and clean salt. He will replace mill-cloth with village-spun khadi, and mill-husked rice with hand-husked, unpolished rice, and white sugar with village-made *gur*. These I have taken merely as samples already mentioned in these columns. I have mentioned them again to deal with the difficulties that have been mentioned by those who have been discussing the question with me. Some say, with reference to rice for instance, 'Hand-husked rice is much dearer than mill-husked rice.'

Others say, 'The art of hand-husking is forgotten, and there are no huskers to be found.' Yet others say, 'We never get mill-husked rice in our parts. We can supply hand-husked rice at 19 seers to the rupee.' All these are right and all are wrong. They are right so far as their own experience in their own district is concerned. All are wrong because the real truth is unknown to them. I am daily gathering startling experiences. All this comes from beginning with oneself. The following is the result of my observations to date.

Whole, unpolished rice is unprocurable in the bazaars. It is beautiful to look at and rich and sweet to the taste. Mills can never compete with this unpolished rice. It is husked in a simple manner. Most of the paddy can be husked in a light *chakki* without difficulty. There are some varieties the husk of which is not separated by grinding. The best way of treating such paddy is to boil it first and then separate the chaff from the grain. This rice, it is said, is most nutritious and, naturally, the cheapest. In the villages, if they husk their own paddy, it must always be cheaper for the peasants than the corresponding mill-husked rice, whether polished or unpolished. The majority of rice found ordinarily in the bazaars is always more or less polished, whether hand-husked or mill-husked. Wholly unpolished rice is always hand-husked and is every time cheaper than the mill-husked rice, the variety being the same.

Subject to further research, the observations so far show that it is because of our criminal negligence that rice-eating millions eat deteriorated rice and pay a heavy price into the bargain. Let the village worker test the truth of these observations for himself. It won't be a bad beginning.

Next week I must take up *gur* and other articles of diet and another part of village work.

Harijan, 25-1-1935

75. How to Begin? (II)
(vol. LX, pp. 150–51)

Last week I dealt with rice. Let us now take up wheat. It is the second most important article of diet, if not the first. From the nutritive stand-point, it is the king of cereals. By itself, it is more perfect than rice. Flour bereft of the valuable bran is like polished rice. That branless flour is as bad as polished rice is the universal testimony of medical men. Whole-wheat flour ground in one's own *chakki* is any day superior to, and cheaper than, the fine flour to be had in the bazaars. It is cheaper because the cost of grinding is saved. Again, in whole-wheat flour there is no loss of weight. In fine flour there is loss of weight. The richest part of wheat is contained in its bran. There is a terrible loss of nutrition when the bran of wheat is removed. The villagers and others who eat whole-wheat flour ground in their own *chakkis* save their money and, what is more important, their health. A large part of the millions that flour mills make will remain in and circulate among the deserving poor when village grinding is revived.

But the objection is taken that *chakki* grinding is a tedious process, that often wheat is indifferently ground and that it does not pay the villagers to grind wheat themselves. If it paid the villagers formerly to grind their own corn, surely the advent of flour mills should make no difference. They may not plead want of time, and when intelligence is allied to labour, there is every hope of improvement in the *chakki*. The argument of indifferent grinding can have no practical value. If the *chakki* was such an indifferent grinder, it could not have stood the test of time immemorial. But to obviate the risk of using indifferently ground whole-wheat flour, I suggest that, wherever there is suspicion, the flour of uneven grinding may be passed through a sieve and the contents may be turned into thick porridge and eaten with or after chapati. If this plan is followed, grinding becomes incredibly simple, and much time and labour can be saved.

All this change can only be brought about by some previous preparation on the part of workers and instruction of villagers. This is a thankless task. But it is worth doing, if the villagers are to live in health and elementary comfort.

Gur[1] is the next article that demands attention. According to the medical testimony I have reproduced in these columns, *gur* is any day superior to refined sugar in food value, and if the villagers cease to make *gur* as they are already beginning to do, they will be deprived of an important food adjunct for their children. They may do without *gur* themselves, but their children cannot without undermining their stamina. *Gur* is superior to bazaar sweets and to refined sugar. Retention of *gur* and its use by the people in general means several crores of rupees retained by the villagers.

But some workers maintain that *gur* does not pay the cost of production. The growers who need money against their crops cannot af-

1. Jaggery.

ford to wait till they have turned cane-juice into *gur* and disposed of it. Though I have testimony to the contrary, too, this argument is not without force. I have no ready-made answer for it. There must be something radically wrong when an article of use, made in the place where also its raw material is grown, does not pay the cost of labour. This is a subject that demands local investigation in each case. Workers must not take the answer of villagers and despair of a remedy. National growth, identification of cities with villages, depend upon the solution of such knotty problems as are presented by *gur*. We must make up our mind that *gur* must not disappear from the villages, even if it means an additional price to be paid for it by city people.

Harijan, 1-2-1935

76. A Renunciation
(vol. LXI, pp. 436–37)

In 1891 after my return from England, I virtually took charge of the children of the family and introduced the habit of walking with them—boys and girls—putting my hands on their shoulders. These were my brothers' children. The practice continued even after they grew old. With the extension of the family, it gradually grew to proportions sufficient to attract attention.

I was unconscious of doing any wrong, so far as I can recollect, till some years ago at Sabarmati an inmate of the Ashram told me that my practice, when extended to grown-up girls and women, offended the accepted notions of decency. But after discussion with the inmates it was continued. Recently two co-workers who came to Wardha suggested that the practice was likely to set a bad example to others and that I should discontinue it on that account. Their argument did not appeal to me. Nevertheless I did not want to ignore the friends' warning. I, therefore, referred it for examination and advice to five inmates of the Ashram. Whilst it was taking shape a decisive event took place. It was brought to my notice that a bright university student was taking all sorts of liberties in private with a girl who was under his influence, on the plea that he loved her like his own sister [and] could not restrain himself from some physical demonstration of it. He resented the slightest suggestion of impurity. Could I mention what the youth had been doing, the reader would unhesitatingly pronounce the liberties taken by him as impure. When I read the correspondence, I and those who saw it came to the conclusion that either the young man was a consummate hypocrite or was self-deluded.

Anyway the discovery set me athinking. I recalled the warning of the two co-workers and asked myself how I would feel if I found that the young man was using my practice in its defence. I may mention that the girl who is the victim of the youth's attentions, although she regards him as absolutely pure and brotherly, does not like them, even protests against them, but is too weak to resist his action. The self-introspection induced by the event resulted, within two or three days of the reading of the correspondence, in the renunciation of the practice, and I announced it to the inmates of the Wardha Ashram on the 12th instant. It was not without a pang that I came to the decision. Never has an impure thought entered my being during or owing to the practice. My act has always been open. I believe that my act was that of a parent and enabled the numerous girls under my guidance and wardship to give their confidences which perhaps no one else has enjoyed in the same measure. Whilst I do not believe in a *brahmacharya* which ever requires a wall of protection against the touch of the opposite sex and will fail if exposed to the least temptation, I am not unaware of the dangers attendant upon the freedom I have taken.

The discovery quoted by me has, therefore, prompted me to renounce the practice, however pure it may have been in itself. Every act of mine is scrutinized by thousands of men and women, as I am conducting an experiment requiring ceaseless vigilance. I must avoid doing things which may require a reasoned defence. My example was never meant to be followed by all and sundry. The young man's case has come upon me as a warning. I have taken it in the hope that my renunciation will set right those who may have erred whether under the influence of my example or without it. Innocent youth is a priceless possession not to be squandered away for the sake of a momentary excitement, miscalled pleasure. And let the weak girls like the one in this picture be strong enough to resist the approaches, though they may be declared to be innocent, of young men who are either knaves or who do not know what they are doing.

Harijan, 21-9-1935

77. Interview to Margaret Sanger

(vol. LXII, pp. 156-60)

[December 3/4, 1935]

Gandhiji poured his whole being into his conversation. He revealed himself inside out, giving Mrs. Sanger an intimate glimpse of his own private life. He also declared to her his own limitations, especially the stupendous limitation of his own philosophy of life—a philosophy that seeks self-realization through self-control, and said that from him there could be one solution and one alone:

[G.] I could not recommend the remedy of birth-control to a woman who wanted my approval. I should simply say to her: My remedy is of no use to you. You must go to others for advice.

Mrs. Sanger cited some hard cases. Gandhiji said:

I agree, there are hard cases. Else birth-control enthusiasts would have no case. But I would say, do devise remedies by all means, but the remedies should be other than the ones you advise. If you and I as moral reformers put our foot down on this remedy and said, 'You must fall back on other remedies,' those would surely be found.

Both seemed to be agreed that woman should be emancipated, that woman should be the arbiter of her destiny. But Mrs. Sanger would have Gandhiji work for woman's emancipation through her pet device, just as believers in violence want Gandhiji to win India's freedom through violence, since they seem to be sure that non-violence can never succeed.

She forgets this fundamental difference in her impatience to prove that Gandhiji does not know the women of India. And she claims to prove this on the ground that he makes an impossible appeal to the women of India—the appeal to resist their husbands. Well, this is what he said:

My wife I made the orbit of all women. In her I studied all women. I came in contact with many European women in South Africa, and I knew practically every Indian woman there. I worked with them. I tried to show them they were not slaves either to their husbands or parents, not only in the political field but in the domestic as well. But the trouble was that some could not resist their husbands. The remedy is in the hands of women themselves. The struggle is difficult for them, and I do not blame them. I blame the men. Men have legislated against them. Man has regarded woman as his tool. She has learned to be his tool and in the end found it easy and pleasurable to be such, because when one drags another in his fall the descent is easy. . . .[1] I have felt that during the years still left to me if I can drive home to women's minds the truth that they are free, we will have no birth-control problem in India. If they will only learn to say 'no' to their husbands when they approach them carnally! I do not suppose all husbands are brutes and if women only know how to resist them, all will be well. I have been able to teach women who have come in contact with me how to resist their husbands. The real problem is that many do not want to resist them. . . . No resistance bordering upon bitterness will be necessary in 99 out of 100 cases. If a wife says to her husband, 'No, I do not want it,' he will make no trouble. But she hasn't been taught. Her parents in most cases won't teach it to her. There are some cases, I know, in which parents have appealed to their daughters' husbands not to force motherhood on their daughters. And I have come across amenable husbands too. I want woman to learn the primary right of resistance. She thinks now that she has not got it. . . .

Mrs. Sanger raises the phantasmagoria of "irritations, disputes, and thwarted longings that Gandhiji's advice would bring into the home." . . . She cited cases of great nervous and mental breakdowns as a result of the practice of self-control. Gandhiji spoke from a knowledge of the numerous letters he receives every mail, when he said to her:

The evidence is all based on examination of imbeciles. The conclusions are not drawn from the practice of healthy-minded people. The people they take for examples have not lived a life of even tolerable continence. These neurologists assume that people are expected to exercise self-restraint while they continue to lead the same ill-regulated life. The consequence is that they do not exercise self-restraint but become lunatics. I carry on correspondence with many of these people and they describe their own ailments to me. I simply say that if I were to present them with this method of birth-control they would lead far worse lives.

He told her that when she went to Calcutta she would be told by those who knew what havoc contraceptives had worked among unmarried young men and women. But evidently for the purpose of the conversation, at any rate, Mrs. Sanger confined herself to propagation of knowledge of birth-control among married couples only. . . . The distinction that Gandhiji drew between love and lust will be evident from the following excerpts from the conversation:

When both want to satisfy animal passion without having to suffer the consequences of their act it is not love, it is lust. But if love is

1. Omissions as in the source.

pure, it will transcend animal passion and will regulate itself. We have not had enough education of the passions. When a husband says, 'Let us not have children, but let us have relations,' what is that but animal passion? If they do not want to have more children they should simply refuse to unite. Love becomes lust the moment you make it a means for the satisfaction of animal needs. It is just the same with food. If food is taken only for pleasure it is lust. You do not take chocolates for the sake of satisfying your hunger. You take them for pleasure and then ask the doctor for an antidote. Perhaps you tell the doctor that whisky befogs your brain and he gives you an antidote. Would it not be better not to take chocolates or whisky?

MRS. S. *No. I do not accept the analogy.*

G. Of course you will not accept the analogy because you think this sex expression without desire for children is a need of the soul, a contention I do not endorse.

MRS. S. *Yes, sex expression is a spiritual need and I claim that the quality of this expression is more important than the result, for the quality of the relationship is there regardless of results. We all know that the great majority of children are born as an accident, without the parents having any desire for conception. Seldom are two people drawn together in the sex act by their desire to have children. . . . Do you think it possible for two people who are in love, who are happy together, to regulate their sex act only once in two years, so that relationship would only take place when they wanted a child? Do you think it possible?*

G. I had the honour of doing that very thing and I am not the only one.

Mrs. Sanger thought it was illogical to contend that sex union for the purpose of having children would be love and union for the satisfaction of the sexual appetite was lust, for the same act was involved in both. Gandhiji immediately capitulated and said he was ready to describe all sexual union as partaking of the nature of lust.

I know, from my own experience that as long as I looked upon my wife carnally, we had no real understanding. Our love did not reach a high plane. There was affection between us always, but we came closer and closer the more we or rather I became restrained. There never was want of restraint on the part of my wife. Very often she would show restraint, but she rarely resisted me although she showed disinclination very often. All the time I wanted carnal pleasure I could not serve her. The moment I bade good-bye to a life of carnal pleasure our whole relationship became spiritual. Lust died and love reigned instead. . . .

Mrs. Sanger is so impatient to prove that Gandhiji is a visionary that she forgets the practical ways and means that Gandhiji suggested to her. She asked:
Must the sexual union take place only three or four times in an entire lifetime?

G. Why should people not be taught that it is immoral to have more than three or four children and that after they have had that number they should sleep separately? If they are taught this it would harden into custom. And if social reformers cannot impress this idea upon the people, why not a law? If husband and wife have four children, they would have had sufficient animal enjoyment. Their love may then be lifted to a higher plane. Their bodies have met. After they have had the children they wanted, their love transforms itself into a spiritual relationship. If these children die and they want more, then they may meet again. Why must people be slaves of this passion when they are not of others? When you give them education in birth-control, you tell them it is a duty. You say to them that if they do not do this thing they will interrupt their spiritual evolution. You do not even talk of regulation. After giving them education in birth-control, you do not say to them, 'thus far and no further.' You ask people to drink temperately, as though it was possible to remain temperate. I know these temperate people. . . .

And yet as Mrs. Sanger was so dreadfully in earnest Gandhiji did mention a remedy which could conceivably appeal to him. That method was the avoidance of sexual union during unsafe periods confining it to the "safe" period of about ten days during the month. That had at least an element of self-control which had to be exercised during the unsafe period. Whether this appealed to Mrs. Sanger or not I do not know. But therein spoke Gandhiji the truth-seeker. Mrs. Sanger has not referred to it anywhere in her interviews or her Illustrated Weekly *article. Perhaps if birth-controllers were to be satisifed with this simple method, the birth-control clinics and propagandists would find their trade gone. . . .*

Harijan, 25-1-1936

78. Nothing Without Grace

(vol. LXII, pp. 210-12)

By the grace of medical friends and self-constituted gaolers, Sardar Vallabhbhai and Jamnalalji, I am now able by way of trial to resume to a limited extent my talks with the readers of *Harijan*. The restrictions that they have put on my liberty and to which I have agreed, are that, for the time being at any rate, I shall not write for *Harijan* more than I may consider to be absolutely necessary and that, too, not involving more than a few hours' writing per week. I shall not carry on private correspondence with reference to correspondents' personal problems or domestic difficulties, except those with which I have already concerned myself, and I shall not accept public engagements or attend or speak at public gatherings. There are positive directions about sleep, recreation, exercise and food, with which the reader is not concerned and with which therefore I need not deal. I hope that the readers of *Harijan* and correspondents will co-operate with me and Mahadev Desai, who has in the first instance to attend to all correspondence, in the observance of these restrictions.

It will interest the reader to know something about the origin of the breakdown and the measures taken to cope with it. So far as I have understood the medical friends, after a very careful and painstaking examination of my system they have found no functional derangement. Their opinion is that the breakdown was most probably due to deficiency of proteins and carbohydrates in the form of sugar and starches, coupled with overstrain for a prolonged period involving long hours and concentration on numerous taxing private problems in addition to the performance of daily public duty. So far as I can recollect I had been complaining for the past twelve months or more that, if I did not curtail the volume of ever-growing work, I was sure to break down. Therefore when it came, it was nothing new to me. And it is highly likely that the world would have heard little of it but for the over-anxiety of one of the friends who, on seeing me indisposed, sent a sensational note to Jamnalalji who gathered together all the medical talent that was available in Wardha and sent messages to Nagpur and Bombay for further help.

The day I collapsed I had a warning on rising in the morning that there was some unusual pain about the neck, but I made light of it and never mentioned it to anybody. I continued to go through the daily programme. The final stroke was a most exhausting and serious conversation I had with a friend whilst I was having the daily evening stroll. The nerves had already been sufficiently taxed during the preceding fortnight with the consideration and solution of problems which for me were quite as big and as important as, say, the paramount question of swaraj.

Even if no fuss had been made over the collapse, I would have taken nature's peremptory warning to heart, given myself moderate rest and tided over the difficulty. But looking back upon the past I

feel that it was well that the fuss was made. The extraordinary precautions advised by the medical friends and equally extraordinary
care taken by the two 'gaolers' enforced on me the exacting rest
which I would not have taken and which allowed ample time for introspection. Not only have I profited by it but the introspection has
revealed vital defects in my following out of the interpretation of the
Gita as I have understood it. I have discovered that I have not approached with adequate detachment the innumerable problems that
have presented themselves for solution. It is clear that I have taken
many of them to heart and allowed them to rouse my emotional
being and thus affect my nerves. In other words they have not, as
they should have in a votary of the *Gita*, left my body or mind untouched. I verily believe that one who literally follows the prescription of the eternal Mother need never grow old in mind. Such a one's
body will wither in due course like leaves of a healthy tree, leaving
the mind as young and as fresh as ever. That seems to me to be the
meaning of Bhishma delivering his marvellous discourse to Yudhishthira though he was on his death-bed. Medical friends were never
tired of warning me against being excited over or affected by events
happening around me. Extra precautions were taken to keep from me
news of a tragic character. Though, I think, I was not quite so bad a
devotee of the *Gita* as their precautions lead me to suppose, there
was undoubtedly substance behind them. For I discovered with what
a wrench I accepted Jamnalalji's conditions and demand that I should
remove from Maganwadi to Mahila Ashram. Anyway I had lost
credit with him for detached action. The fact of the collapse was for
him eloquent enough testimony for discrediting my vaunted detachment. I must plead guilty to the condemnation.

The worst however was to follow. I have been trying to follow
brahmacharya consciously and deliberately since 1899. My definition of it is purity not merely of body but of both speech and thought
also. With the exception of what must be regarded as one lapse, I can
recall no instance, during more than thirty-six years' constant and
conscious effort, of mental disturbance such as I experienced during
this illness. I was disgusted with myself. The moment the feeling
came I acquainted my attendants and the medical friends with my
condition. They could give me no help. I expected none. I broke
loose after the experience from the rigid rest that was imposed upon
me. The confession of the wretched experience brought much relief
to me. I felt as if a great load had been raised from over me. It enabled
me to pull myself together before any harm could be done. But what
of the *Gita*? Its teaching is clear and precise. A mind that is once

hooked to the Star of stars becomes incorruptible. How far I must be from Him, He alone knows. Thank God, my much-vaunted Mahatmaship has never fooled me. But this enforced rest has humbled me as never before. It has brought to the surface my limitations and imperfections. But I am not so much ashamed of them, as I should be of hiding them from the public. My faith in the message of the *Gita* is as bright as ever. Unwearied ceaseless effort is the price that must be paid for turning that faith into rich infallible experience. But the same *Gita* says without any equivocation that the experience is not to be had without divine grace. We should develop swelled heads if Divinity had not made that ample reservation.

Harijan, 29-2-1936

CHRONOLOGY V
1936–1940

In this four-year period, Congress appealed to Gandhi to help it decide whether to cooperate with the British government's new administrative reforms—whether to run candidates in elections for office in provincial governments. This issue was like that of "Council Entry" fifteen years before, when Gandhi had been opposed to all such cooperation. But this time, to the surprise of nearly everyone, he declared himself in favor, provided that the British guaranteed freedom of action to the elected officials. The explanation for this change was perhaps that Gandhi by 1936 felt himself more detached from Congress than he had before, and that his interests and the Congress's were now more different. What was best for it was rarely what would have been best for him and his satyagrahis. For himself, he asked Congress to represent the villagers of India, and to protect them by conserving their culture by promoting home-spinning and prohibition of alcohol and so on.

The success of the Congress candidates in those elections meant, among other things, that Muslims found themselves directly ruled by Hindus for the first time; and the consequent irritations were inflamed by leaders of the Muslim League such as M. A. Jinnah. From this time on, the course of Hindu-Muslim relations ran more steeply downhill toward disaster. Gandhi's main hope for improving them lay in his alliance with Abdul Ghaffar Khan, a leader of the Pathans who had been converted to Gandhian nonviolence. But the Pathans belonged to the Northwest Province, on the border with Afghanistan, and were out of touch with the majority of Indian Muslims.

In the pursuit of his political interests, Gandhi ran into moral difficulties of a new kind during this period. He took part in an in-

effective satyagraha *by the people of Rajkot against their ruler in 1939. He accepted a settlement suggested by the British and then admitted his opponents' charge that by so doing he had broken the rules of* satyagraha. *Though these opponents were more deeply in the wrong than some of his other enemies, he conceded the moral victory to them. And in a conflict over the leadership of Congress, he suffered a comparable moral defeat. He distrusted the man elected to the presidency (Subhas Chandra Bose) and, unable to carry his point by persuasion, intervened to force that man out.*

1936

In May, Harilal Gandhi was converted to Islam, with a great deal of publicity, which was implicitly anti-Gandhian.

On September 8, Gandhi was put into Wardha Hospital for fever, a disease almost unavoidable in Segaon.

On December 27, he addressed the open session of Congress after Nehru's address as president for the year. He asked Congress to take a vow to hold all its future sessions in villages and to carry out his program of spinning, prohibition, and untouchability reform.

1937

In the early part of this year, Gandhi was involved in the controversy over whether congressmen should stand for election to administrative offices newly created by the British government—a limited measure of self-rule. Gandhi surprised his followers by favoring such candidacy.

On April 28, his draft resolution on the constitutional deadlock was adopted by the Congress Working Committee.

On June 3, he declared that he was anxious that congressmen should take office, but only if the government was willing to give guarantees that they should have freedom of action.

On July 14, the first Congress ministry was formed in the Central Provinces; other such ministries were formed elsewhere during the second half of the month.

On August 17, he attended the Working Committee meeting at Wardha, where directives were sent out to Congress ministers.

1938

In January 1938, Subhas Chandra Bose (a Bengali politician whom Gandhi distrusted) was nominated to be the next president of Congress. On February 2 and 13, Bose and Gandhi met to exchange views.

On *February 15*, he advised the Congress ministries in Bihar and the United Provinces to resign if the governors there would not agree to the release of political prisoners.

On *April 29*, he set off to tour the Northwest Frontier Province, where Khan Abdul Ghaffar Khan was preaching Gandhian non-violence to the Pathans, who were both Muslim and one of India's most famous "martial races." Gandhi had long wanted to visit this province (which was always full of violence and unrest) but had been denied a visa by the central government.

In *June*, he corresponded with Jinnah, trying to find some way to alleviate Hindu-Muslim hostility.

In *October*, he returned to the Frontier Province, with Abdul Ghaffar Khan.

In *November*, he commented on the Munich Peace Pact: "The peace Europe gained at Munich is a triumph of violence; it is also its defeat."

1939

On *January 15*, Gandhi held talks with the Aga Khan on the Hindu-Muslim question.

On *January 31*, he decided to go to Rajkot, where he had lived as a boy, to join a satyagraha against the native prince. He commented on the reelection of Subhas Chandra Bose as Congress president, "I must confess that from the very beginning I was decidedly against his re-election."

On *February 4*, he said, "Those who feel uncomfortable in being in Congress must come out, not in a spirit of ill-will [to Bose] but with a deliberate purpose of rendering more effective service."

On *March 3*, he began his fast against the thakore of Rajkot.

On *March 7*, he broke his fast, because of a settlement arranged by the viceroy.

On *April 29*, because of the resistance of Gandhians in Congress, Bose resigned, and Rajendra Prasad, a Gandhi loyalist, became president.

On *August 9 and 10*, acting on his advice, Congress declared its sympathies with the Western democracies and condemned Fascist aggression in Europe.

On *September 3*, Britain and France declared war on Germany.

In *September*, the Working Committee declared that India would cooperate with Britain in the war only if it was treated as an equal and received an unambiguous promise of freedom after the war.

On *November 5*, the viceroy announced the failure of his negotiations with Congress, whose members resigned from the provincial councils.

On December 9, Gandhi appealed to Jinnah to stop holding "Days of Deliverance" (Muslim manifestations), the deliverance being from the rule of Hindus.

1940

In January, he corresponded with Jinnah, about which he said, "It dashes to the ground all hopes of unity."

On January 21, he was invested by the Congress Working Committee with the authority to negotiate with the viceroy again.

Besides the national issues previously mentioned, these selections reflect Gandhi's private concerns—for instance, his understanding and experience of religion and some of his reflections on his education. He maintained, of course, old concerns with his ashram and his family. The very first item is a statement to the press about Harilal's much-publicized (and very brief) conversion to Islam, a gesture performed and reported in mockery of his father. At the end of this period, as the outbreak of war in Europe drew near and its inevitability became obvious, Gandhi was called on to speak about the plight of Hitler's victims; as the leader of satyagraha, he was called on to give advice to the Jews and the Czechs. (His remarks aroused anger and bitter protest both then and in our own time, following the release of the movie Gandhi, and so the reader should study them carefully.) The very last item refers to the sexual scandal that attached itself to him because of his physical intimacy with the women of the ashram, notably his leaning on their shoulders when taking his walks and his allowing them to sleep near him on the porch of his hut. This was not the first time he had been so criticized; the letter to Mirabehn of May 3, 1938, refers to those practices; and at the end of his life the scandal was to become much worse.

79. To My Numerous Muslim Friends

(vol. LXIII, pp. 5–7)

Bangalore,
June 2, 1936

The newspapers report that about a fortnight ago my eldest son Harilal, now nearing fifty years, accepted Islam and that on Friday last 29th May in the midst of a large congregation in the Jumma Musjid at Bombay, he was permitted to announce his acceptance amid great acclamation and that, after his speech was finished, he was besieged by his admirers who vied with one another to shake hands with him. If his acceptance was from the heart and free from any worldly considerations, I should have no quarrel. For I believe Islam to be as true a religion as my own.

But I have the gravest doubt about this acceptance being from the heart or free from selfish considerations. Everyone who knows my son Harilal, knows that he has been for years addicted to the drink evil and has been in the habit of visiting houses of ill-fame. For some years he has been living on the charity of friends who have helped him unstintingly. He is indebted to some Pathans from whom he had borrowed on heavy interest. Up to only recently he was in dread of his life from his Pathan creditors in Bombay. Now he is the hero of the hour in that city. He had a most devoted wife who always forgave his many sins including his unfaithfulness. He has three grown-up children, two daughters and one son, whom he ceased to support long ago.

Not many weeks ago he wrote to the Press complaining against Hindus—not Hinduism—and threatening to go over to Christianity or Islam. The language of the letter showed quite clearly that he would go over to the highest bidder. That letter had the desired effect. Through the good offices of a Hindu councillor he got a job in Nagpur Municipality. And he came out with another letter to the Press recalling the first and declaring emphatic adherence to his ancestral faith.

But, as events have proved, his pecuniary ambition was not satisfied and in order to satisfy that ambition, he has embraced Islam. There are other facts which are known to me and which strengthen my inference.

When I was in Nagpur in April last, he had come to see me and his mother and he told me how he was amused by the attentions that were being paid to him by the missionaries of rival faiths. God can work wonders. He had been known to have changed the stoniest hearts and turned sinners into saints, as it were, in a moment. Nothing will please me better than to find that during the Nagpur meeting and the Friday announcement he had repented of the past and had suddenly become a changed man having shed the drink habit and sexual lust.

But the Press reports give no such evidence. He still delights in sensation and in good living. If he had changed, he would have written to me to gladden my heart. All my children have had the greatest freedom of thought and action. They have been taught to regard all religions with the same respect that they paid to their own. Harilal knew that if he had told me that he had found the key to a right life and peace in Islam, I would have put no obstacle in his path. But no one of us, including his son now twenty-four years old and who is with me, knew anything about the event till we saw the announcement in the Press.

My views on Islam are well known to the Mussalmans who are reported to have enthused over my son's profession. A brotherhood of Islam has telegraphed to me thus:

Expect like your son you truth-seeker to embrace Islam truest religion of world.

I must confess that all this has hurt me. I sense no religious spirit behind this demonstration. I feel that those who are responsible for Harilal's acceptance of Islam did not take the most ordinary precautions they ought to have in a case of this kind.

Harilal's apostasy is no loss to Hinduism and his admission to Islam is a source of weakness to it if, as I apprehend, he remains the same wreck that he was before.

Surely conversion is a matter between man and his Maker who alone knows His creatures' hearts. And conversion without a clean heart is, in my opinion, a denial of God and religion. Conversion without cleanness of heart can only be a matter for sorrow, not joy, to a godly person.

My object in addressing these lines to my numerous Muslim friends is to ask them to examine Harilal in the light of his immediate past and, if they find that his conversion is a soulless matter, to tell him so plainly and disown him and if they discover sincerity in him to see that he is protected against temptations so that his sincerity results in his becoming a godfearing member of society. Let them know that excessive indulgence has softened his brain and undermined his sense of right and wrong, truth and falsehood. I do not mind whether he is known as Abdulla or Harilal if, by adopting one name for the other, he becomes a true devotee of God which both the names mean.

Harijan, 6-6-1936

80. Talk with Jairamdas Doulatram and Devdas Gandhi
(vol. LXIII, pp. 151–52)

[Before July 18, 1936]

I am very happy that you have come here, but, I hope, not to see this dignified hut of mine. I am responsible for little of the planning here, and I have given to it none of my art or my labour. But I wonder if you saw on your way Mirabehn's hut. It was worth while coming all the way to see her hut certainly. That is really and truly HER hut. This is a hut built FOR me, not MY hut. Here is her own hut, planned and built by herself (of course with other people's labour). But it is not merely a hut. It is a poem. I studied it in detail only yesterday, and I tell you I had tears of joy as I saw the villager's mentality about everything in it. You know I often have my quarrels with her, but let me tell you that no one from amongst us can claim to have the real rural-mindedness that she has. Did you study the position of her little bath-room and the inside of it? She has utilized every stone that the blasting of the underground rock in her well made available to her. The seat for the bath is all one stone fixed to the ground. Next to the bathroom in the same little hut is the latrine. No commode or wooden plank or any brickwork. Just two beautiful stones, half buried in the ground, and with two halves of kerosene tins between the stones. Any villager can do this, but never does it. All the water naturally runs to carefully made beds for plants and vegetables. And look at the care with which she has built the little stable for her horse, on the grooming and feeding and keeping of which she lavishes all her love and attention. Her love of animals is a thing to learn from her. Even whilst she is sitting and working in her hut, the stable is so arranged that she can give an occasional look to the horse. And now let us see the inside of the hut—all mud and split bamboo and wattle of palm-branches. You note every little article in the hut and the place given to it. Her *chula* (fire) is all made with her own hands, and though she has learnt it from us no one can beat her in the art. Then see the bamboo mantelpiece (if you will give it that big name) on which she keeps her earthen cooking utensils. Then see the little doorless windows and bamboo bookshelf and note the palms and peacocks over the windows, moulded in relief by herself. Also note her little kitchen and the carding room. The village where she works is about two to three furlongs from the hut. All the women and many of the men in the village know her, and the women confide to her many of their household secrets and look to her for advice and guidance—not always an easy matter, but always unfailingly for solace and comfort. She looks like one of them. Well, if you have not studied her hut carefully I would like you to go there again on your way back.

Harijan, 25-7-1936

81. Of My Recent Illness

(vol. LXIII, pp. 295–97)

I would not tax the reader about my recent malaria fever except for the fact that friends are involved in the decision I have prayerfully made and which I hope God will let me fulfil.

It went against the grain for me, a confirmed believer in nature-cure methods, to go to Wardha and seek admission to the hospital. Left entirely to myself, I would have treated myself in accordance with nature-cure methods as far as possible. But I could not do so without offending the friends who happened to be near me at the time. I knew that Jamnalalji too had a special responsibility, in that I had settled in a village near Wardha, his permanent place of residence. With the choice of the village he has had nothing to do. It was entirely Mirabehn's and it was made because Segaon was predominantly a Harijan village and far enough from Wardha and yet not too far. I was drawn to the village in accordance with a certain declaration I had made when Mirabehn went to Segaon. Jamnalalji to an extent and Sardar Vallabhbhai altogether were against my settling in a village as yet and then in Segaon. But I bore down their opposition when I told them that I was bound by the declaration to which I have referred to settle down in Segaon. No doubt the promise was agreeable to me for my heart was in the village. Having gone to Segaon it was my intention not to stir out of it for full three seasons, i.e., one year. Unfortunately there are obligations undertaken before the decision to settle in Segaon, which I shall have to fulfil and which will disturb the unbroken year's stay. I urge friends, therefore, not to make further inroads upon the period. For me it is my *sadhana*. I set the greatest value upon the village problem. It may not be put off except at the cost of our very existence. India lives in her villages, not in her cities. I am supposed to guide and direct the village industries movement to which at Bombay an autonomous existence was given by the Congress.[1] I am incapable of guiding any movement in which I do not plunge myself actively and directly. Maganwadi, though a village, being a large village, was not good enough for my instruction and inspiration. I needed to be in a real village presenting the problems that face one in the generality of villages. Segaon is one such village.

If then I may not leave Segaon in order not to interrupt my instruction and first-hand experience, I may not also leave it for health reasons. Segaon like most villages has its full share of malaria and other diseases which villagers suffer from. Of its population of 600 there is hardly anyone who has not suffered from malaria or dysentery. Of the record of nearly 200 cases that have come under my observation or Mirabehn's, most are those of malaria and dysentery. The simple remedies at our disposal with dietetic control have served their purpose effectively. The villagers do not go to hospitals, they cannot even go to dispensaries. They usually resort to village quacks or incantations and drag on their weary existence. I claim to have some workable knowledge of common ailments. I have successfully treated myself often enough without the assistance of medical friends though they have been ever ready to help me in my need. If I was not a 'Mahatma,' so-called, no one would have known anything of the recent attack of malaria. I rarely have fever. The last attack I had was nearly 12 years ago and I had treated myself. There is all the greater reason for me now, if I have another attack of malaria or another ailment, not to stir out of Segaon in search of health; and if I must have medical assistance, I must be satisfied with what I can get without fuss and without having to leave Segaon. I am fatalist enough to believe that no one can put off the hour of death when it has struck. Not the greatest medical assistance available has saved kings and emperors from the jaws of death. One like myself struggling to become a humble village servant surely ought to be satisfied with remedies easily accessible to villages. By leaving my village in search of health or the like I deny myself the opportunity of knowing what village life can be when one's health is in peril.

1. In October 1934.

My malaria has quickened my resolve to study the problem of making Segaon malaria-proof. All round me the fields are water-logged. The crops are rotting. The ground is unwalkable unless you are content to wade through knee-deep mud. Fortunately a pukka road was built for my convenience through Jamnalalji's fields which keeps Segaon somewhat accessible to people from Wardha. The road has proved a great convenience for man and beast. If I had listened to friends' advice to postpone settling in Segaon till after the rains, I would have missed the rich experiences I have gained during the heavy rains of the past two months. Everything I have seen hitherto therefore convinces me that, if I am to make any approach to the vil-lage life, I must persevere in my resolve not to desert it in the hour of danger to life or limb. And I ask all the friends to help me in carrying out the resolve and pray with me that God may give me the strength to do so.

Harijan, 19-9-1936

82. Discussion with Protestant Missionaries
(vol. LXIV, pp. 74–75)

Mr. Mathews was curious to know if Gandhiji followed any spiritual practices and what special reading he had found helpful.

G. I am a stranger to yogic practices. The practice I follow is a prac-tice I learnt in my childhood from my nurse. I was afraid of ghosts. She used to say to me: 'There are no ghosts, but if you are afraid, re-peat Ramanama.' What I learnt in my childhood has become a huge thing in my mental firmament. It is a sun that has brightened my darkest hour. A Christian may find the same solace from the repeti-tion of the name of Jesus and a Muslim from the name of Allah. All these things have the same implications and they produce identical results under identical circumstances. Only the repetition must not be a lip expression, but part of your very being. About helpful read-ings we have regular readings of the *Bhagavad Gita* and we have now reached a stage when we finish the *Gita* every week by having read-ings of appointed chapters every morning. Then we have hymns from the various saints of India, and we therein include hymns from the Christian hymn book. As Khan Saheb is with us, we have read-ings from the Koran also. We believe in the equality of all religions. I derive the greatest consolation from my reading of Tulsidas's *Rama-*

yana. I have also derived solace from the New Testament and the Koran. I don't approach them with a critical mind. They are to me as important as the *Bhagavad Gita,* though everything in the former may not appeal to me—everything in the Epistles of Paul for instance, nor everything in Tulsidas. The *Gita* is a pure religious discourse given without any embellishment. It simply describes the progress of the pilgrim soul towards the Supreme Goal. Therefore there is no question of selection.

M. *You are really a Protestant.*

G. I do not know what I am or not; Mr. Hodge will call me a Presbyterian!

M. *Where do you find the seat of authority?*
Pointing to his breast, Gandhiji said:

It lies here. I exercise my judgment about every scripture, including the *Gita.* I cannot let a scriptural text supersede my reason. Whilst I believe that the principal books are inspired, they suffer from a process of double distillation. Firstly, they come through a human prophet, and then through the commentaries of interpreters. Nothing in them comes from God directly. Mat[t]hew may give one version of one text and John may give another. I cannot surrender my reason whilst I subscribe to Divine revelation. And above all, 'the letter killeth, the spirit giveth life.' But you must not misunderstand my position. I believe in Faith also, in things where Reason has no place, e.g., the existence of God. No argument can move me from that faith, and like that little girl who repeated against all reason 'yet we are seven' I would like to repeat, on being baffled in argument by a very superior intellect, 'Yet there is God.'

Harijan, 5-12-1936

83. A Silent Co-worker Gone
(vol. LXVI, pp. 95–97)

[September 1, 1937]
The inmates of the Satyagraha Ashram of Sabarmati are today a scattered family, joined together only by their common vow of silent service. No one, perhaps, with the exception of the late Shri Maganlal Gandhi, personified so nearly this self-effacing ideal as Shri Chhote-

lal Jain whose death, through suicide, has just stunned me. I have not adequate language to describe his insatiable capacity for silent service. He dreaded publicity and loved to live and serve unknown. In fact it may be said of him that his right hand did not know what his left hand was doing. I do not remember his ever visiting his relations or being visited by them. He never even mentioned them to anyone. At the time of writing I do not even know their names or whereabouts.

I have the good luck to have a band of co-workers who are to me as my hands and feet. Without their willing and loyal co-operation I should feel utterly helpless. Prominent among these was Chhotelal. He had a versatile and powerful intelligence which shirked no task however difficult. He was a born linguist. Rajputana being his home, Hindi was his mother tongue, but he knew Gujarati, Marathi, Bengali, Tamil, Sanskrit and English as well. He knew the Urdu script. I have seldom seen anybody with such aptitude for quickly mastering a new language or a new task. He was one of the foundation members of the Sabarmati Ashram. He went through the whole range of Ashram activities with natural ease, and hardly touched anything that he did not adorn. Thus he felt equally at home whether he was engaged in kitchen work, conservancy, spinning or weaving, accounts, or translation work, or correspondence. He had an equal share with the late Maganlal in the writing of *Vanatshastra*.[1]

The riskier a job the more it was welcomed by Chhotelal, and once he took it up, he knew no rest till he had seen it through. He threw himself, with the indefatigable energy which was his characteristic, into any task that he took up, and at the end of it he would still be fresh and ready for the next. The words weariness and fatigue were not in his dictionary. To render service only, never to receive any, was the passion of his life. When the All-India Village Industries Association was started at Wardha, it was Chhotelal who first learnt and then introduced the art of *ghani*[2] in Maganwadi. It was he who introduced the wooden hand-mill for rice-husking. Again, it was he who started bee-culture there. Today I feel disconsolate and crippled by his loss. And I am sure, if we could only know it, the same must be the feeling of the bees whom he had gathered and was looking after with a mother's care. I do not know who else will look after them with the loving care of Chhotelal. For, Chhotelal had literally become apiculture-mad. In the course of his quest he had contracted paratyphoid fever which had a fatal ending. He had been bed-ridden

1. A Gujarati treatise on the science of weaving.
2. Oil-press.

for hardly six or seven days, but the very thought of being a helpless charge upon others evidently ate into him, and on Tuesday night, the 31st of August, leaving everybody asleep, he put an end to his life by throwing himself into the Maganwadi well. The corpse was recovered from the well today, Wednesday, at 4 p.m. and even as I pen these lines at Segaon, at 8 p.m., his body is being cremated at Wardha.

I have not the heart to rebuke Chhotelal for his suicide. He was no coward. He was guilty of no unworthy deed. He could laugh at suffering. I cannot account for this self-immolation except on the supposition that he could no longer brook to be nursed. No doubt that is a sign of subtle pride. But there it was. He was not conscious of it.

His name figured in the Delhi Conspiracy Case of 1915. He was acquitted. He had told me he did not desire acquittal. A casual reading of some of my writings gave a new turn to his life and outlook. He studied my activities in South Africa, and from a violent revolutionary became a votary of ahimsa. He shed his cult of violence as completely and naturally as a snake does it outworn skin, but he could never completely control the proneness to anger and pride that were deeply ingrained in his nature. Did he expiate with his life for these?

By his death (he was 42 [3]) he has left me heavily in his debt. I had entertained high hopes of him. I could not tolerate any imperfection in him and so he had often to bear the brunt of my impatience as, perhaps, only one or two besides him have borne. But he never complained, never even winced. Had I any right to put him through this fire as I used to? I had hoped one day to discharge my debt towards him by offering him as a sacrifice at the altar of Hindu-Muslim unity, untouchability or cow-protection. To my mind these are some of the altars in the great *yajna* of the swaraj of my dream. And Chhotelal was in the front rank of the few who, to my knowledge, had the strength and capacity to claim this privilege.

The country needs an army of silent warriors like him. The achievement of swaraj, which to me is synonymous with *Ramaraj*, is no joke. Let these few glimpses of Chhotelal's life serve as an inspiration in our striving for India's freedom.

Harijan, 11-9-1937

3. *Harijanbandhu* has "45."

84. Statement to the Press

(vol. LXVII, pp. 36–38)

April 22, 1938

I observe that the forthcoming interview between Shri Jinnah and myself is not only attracting very wide attention, but is also inducing high hopes in some. Then there are friends who gravely warn me against this visit and against building any hope on the interview. It is better, therefore, for me to take the public into my confidence and tell them why and how I am waiting upon Shri Jinnah on April 28.

He has himself published my first letter to him, showing my attitude on the question of communal unity, which is as dear to me as life itself. In that letter I clearly stated that all before me was darkness and that I was praying for light. If anything, the darkness has deepened and the prayer become more intense. Add to this the fact that for causes some of which I know and some of which I do not, for the first time in my public and private life I seem to have lost self-confidence. I seem to have detected a flaw in me which is unworthy of a votary of truth and ahimsa. I am going through a process of self-introspection, the results of which I cannot foresee. I find myself for the first time during the past 50 years in a Slough of Despond. I do not consider myself fit for negotiations or any such thing for the moment.

There is no need for any speculation as to the cause of my despondency. It is purely internal. It comes from within. It must be now clear that, if I regarded the forthcoming interview as between two politicians, I should not entertain it in my present depression. But I approach it in no political spirit. I approach it in a prayerful and religious spirit, using the adjective in its broadest sense.

My Hinduism is not sectarian. It includes all that I know to be best in Islam, Christianity, Buddhism and Zoroastrianism. I approach politics as everything else in a religious spirit. Truth is my religion and ahimsa is the only way of its realization. I have rejected once and for all the doctrine of the sword. The secret stabbings of innocent persons and the speeches I read in the papers are hardly the thing leading to peace or an honourable settlement.

Again, I am not approaching the forthcoming interview in any representative capacity. I have purposely divested myself of any such. If there are to be any formal negotiations, they will be between the President of the Congress and the President of the Muslim League. I go as a lifelong worker in the cause of Hindu-Muslim unity. It has been my passion from early youth. I count some of the noblest of Muslims as my friends. I have a devout daughter of Islam as more than a daughter to me. She lives for that unity and would cheerfully die for it. I had the son of the late Muazzin of the Juma Masjid of Bombay as a staunch inmate of the Ashram. I have not met a nobler man. His morning *azan*[1] in the Ashram rings in my ears as I write these lines during midnight. It is for such reasons that I wait on Shri Jinnah.

I may not leave a single stone unturned to achieve Hindu-Muslim unity. God fulfils himself in strange ways. He may, in a manner least known to us, both fulfil himself through the interview and open a way to an honourable understanding between the two communities. It is in that hope that I am looking forward to the forthcoming talk. We are friends, not strangers. It does not matter to me that we see things from different angles of vision. I ask the public not to attach any exaggerated importance to the interview. But I ask all lovers of communal peace to pray that the God of truth and love may give us both the right spirit and the right word and use us for the good of the dumb millions of India.

Harijan, 30-4-1938

85. Letter to Mirabehn

(vol. LXVII, pp. 60–61)

May 3, 1938

I like your letter for its transparent love. It tells me nothing new, but it comes at a moment when I am most receptive. The problem however is not so simple as you have put it. If complete *brahmacharya* under the conditions I am trying is like an attempt to climb the craters in the moon, what is the value of the species that requires the nine fortifications?[1] You are quite right in describing my experiment as new. So is my experiment in ahimsa. The two hang together. Remember that my experiment has natural limitations. I may neither tempt God nor the Devil. I have not the time to prolong the argument.

In your next letter you must tell me in concrete terms what defi-

---

1. Call to prayer.

—

1. The reference is to the nine rules of behaviour known as "the nine-fold hedge or wall" for the protection of *brahmacharya*.

nite changes I should make so as to fit in with your idea. Should I deny myself the service rendered by Sushila?[2] Should I refuse to have *malish*[3] by Lilavati or Amtul Salaam for instance? Or do you want to say that I should never lean on girls' shoulders? Needless to say you won't pain me at all by telling me frankly whatever you think I should do to get out of the terrible despondency. Just now I am most in need of support from those who surround me with service and affection, undeserved as it seems to me, for the time being. In guiding me remember that what I am doing I have done all my life you may say. And my *brahmacharya* has become firmer and more enlightened. Of course I have been far away from perfection. But I felt I was progressing. That degrading, dirty, torturing experience of 14th April shook me to bits and made me feel as if I was hurled by God from an imaginary paradise where I had no right to be in my uncleanliness.[4]

Well, I shall feel pride in my being parent to so many children, if any of them will give a lifting hand and pull me out of the well of despair. My faith in myself and my experiment will revive and will burn all the brighter.

Love.

BAPU

From the manuscript of Mahadev Desai's Diary.

86. Higher Education
(vol. LXVII, pp. 158–63)

The Rt. Hon. Shri Srinivasa Sastri has criticized, as he had a perfect right to do, the views I timidly and very briefly expressed some time ago on higher education. I entertain a very high regard for him as man, patriot and scholar. It is therefore always painful to me when I find myself disagreeing with him. And yet duty compels me to re-express my views on higher education more fully than before, so that the reader may make out for himself the difference between his views and mine.

I admit my limitations. I have no university education worth the name. My high school career was never above the average. I was

2. Sushila was Gandhi's doctor.
3. Massage.
4. This was his experience of involuntary sexual excitement.

thankful if I could pass my examinations. Distinction in the school was beyond my aspiration. Nevertheless I do hold very strong views on education in general, including what is called higher education. And I owe it to the country that my views should be clearly known and taken for what they may be worth. I must shed the timidity that has led almost to self-suppression. I must not fear ridicule, and even loss of popularity or prestige. If I hide my belief, I shall never correct errors of judgment. I am always eager to discover them and more than eager to correct them.

Let me now state my conclusions held for a number of years and enforced wherever I had opportunity of enforcing them:

(1) I am not opposed to education even of the highest type attainable in the world.

(2) The State must pay for it wherever it has definite use for it.

(3) I am opposed to all higher education being paid for from the general revenue.

(4) It is my firm conviction that the vast amount of the so-called education in arts, given in our colleges, is sheer waste and has resulted in unemployment among the educated classes. What is more, it has destroyed the health, both mental and physical, of the boys and girls who have the misfortune to go through the grind in our colleges.

(5) The medium of a foreign language through which higher education has been imparted in India has caused incalculable intellectual and moral injury to the nation. We are too near our own times to judge the enormity of the damage done. And we who have received such education have both to be victims and judges—an almost impossible feat.

I must now give my reason for the conclusions set forth above. This I can best do, perhaps, by giving a chapter from my own experience.

Up to the age of 12 all the knowledge I gained was through Gujarati, my mother tongue. I knew then something of arithmetic, history and geography. Then I entered a high school. For the first three years the mother tongue was still the medium. But the schoolmaster's business was to drive English into the pupil's head. Therefore more than half of our time was given to learning English and mastering its arbitrary spelling and pronunciation. It was a painful discovery to have to learn a language that was not pronounced as it was written. It was a strange experience to have to learn the spelling by heart. But that is by the way, and irrelevant to my argument. However, for the first three years, it was comparatively plain sailing.

The pillory began with the fourth year. Everything had to be learnt through English—geometry, algebra, chemistry, astronomy, history, geography. The tyranny of English was so great that even Sanskrit or Persian had to be learnt through English, not through the mother tongue. If any boy spoke in the class in Gujarati which he understood, he was punished. It did not matter to the teacher if a boy spoke bad English which he could neither pronounce correctly nor understand fully. Why should the teacher worry? His own English was by no means without blemish. It could not be otherwise. English was as much a foreign language to him as to his pupils. The result was chaos. We the boys had to learn many things by heart, though we could not understand them fully and often not at all. My head used to reel as the teacher was struggling to make his exposition on geometry understood by us. I could make neither head nor tail of geometry till we reached the 13th theorem of the first book of Euclid. And let me confess to the reader that in spite of all my love for the mother tongue I do not to this day know the Gujarati equivalents of the technical terms of geometry, algebra and the like. I know now that what I took four years to learn of arithmetic, geometry, algebra, chemistry and astronomy I should have learnt easily in one year if I had not to learn them through English but Gujarati. My grasp of the subjects would have been easier and clearer. My Gujarati vocabulary would have been richer. I would have made use of such knowledge in my own home. This English medium created an impassable barrier between me and the members of my family, who had not gone through English schools. My father knew nothing of what I was doing. I could not, even if I had wished it, interest my father in what I was learning. For though he had ample intelligence, he knew not a word of English. I was fast becoming a stranger in my own home. I certainly became a superior person. Even my dress began to undergo imperceptible changes. What happened to me was not an uncommon experience. It was common to the majority.

The first three years in the high school made little addition to my stock of general knowledge. They were a preparation for fitting the boys for teaching them everything through English. High schools were schools for cultural conquest by the English. The knowledge gained by the three hundred boys of my high school became a circumscribed possession. It was not for transmission to the masses.

A word about literature. We had to learn several books of English prose and English poetry. No doubt all this was nice. But that knowledge has been of no use to me in serving or bringing me in touch with the masses. I am unable to say that if I had not learnt what I did of English prose and poetry, I should have missed a rare treasure. If I had, instead, passed those precious seven years in mastering Gujarati

and had learnt mathematics, sciences, and Sanskrit and other subjects through Gujarati, I could easily have shared the knowledge so
gained with my neighbours. I would have enriched Gujarati, and
who can say that I would not have, with my habit of application and
my inordinate love for the country and the mother tongue, made a
richer and greater contribution to the service of the masses?

I must not be understood to decry English or its noble literature.
The columns of *Harijan* are sufficient evidence of my love of English. But the nobility of its literature cannot avail the Indian nation
any more than the temperate climate or the scenery of England can
avail her. India has to flourish in her own climate and scenery and
her own literature, even though all the three may be inferior to the
English climate, scenery and literature. We and our children must
build on our own heritage. If we borrow another, we impoverish our
own. We can never grow on foreign victuals. I want the nation to
have the treasures contained in that language, and for that matter the
other languages of the world, through its own vernaculars. I do not
need to learn Bengali in order to know the beauties of Rabindranath's
matchless productions. I get them through good translations. Gujarati boys and girls do not need to learn Russian to appreciate Tolstoy's
short stories. They learn them through good translations. It is the
boast of Englishmen that the best of the world's literary output is in
the hands of that nation in simple English inside of a week of its publication. Why need I learn English to get at the best of what Shake-
speare and Milton thought and wrote?

It would be good economy to set apart a class of students whose
business would be to learn the best of what is to be learnt in the different languages of the world and give the translation in the vernaculars. Our masters chose the wrong way for us, and habit has
made the wrong appear as right.

I find daily proof of the increasing and continuing wrong being
done to the millions by our false de-Indianizing education. Those
graduates who are my valued associates themselves flounder when
they have to give expression to their innermost thoughts. They are
strangers in their own homes. Their vocabulary in the mother tongue
is so limited that they cannot always finish their speech without
having recourse to English words and even sentences. Nor can they
exist without English books. They often write to one another in English. I cite the case of my companions to show how deep the evil
has gone. For we have made a conscious effort to mend ourselves.

It has been argued that the wastage that occurs in our colleges
need not worry us if, out of the collegians, one Jagadish Bose can be
produced by them. I should freely subscribe to the argument if the

wastage was unavoidable. I hope I have shown that it was and is even now avoidable. Moreover, the creation of a Bose does not help the argument. For Bose was not a product of the present education. He rose in spite of the terrible handicaps under which he had to labour. And his knowledge became almost intransmissible to the masses. We seem to have come to think that no one can hope to be like a Bose unless he knows English. I cannot conceive a grosser superstition than this. No Japanese feels so helpless as we seem to do.

Nothing but a heroic remedy can deal with the deep-seated evil which I have endeavoured to describe. The Congress Ministers can, if they will, mitigate it if they cannot remove it.

Universities must be made self-supporting. The State should simply educate those whose services it would need. For all other branches of learning it should encourage private effort. The medium of instruction should be altered at once and at any cost, the provincial, languages being given their rightful place. I would prefer temporary chaos in higher education to the criminal waste that is daily accumulating.

In order to enhance the status and the market value of the provincial languages, I would have the language of the law courts to be the language of the province where the court is situated. The proceedings of the Provincial Legislatures must be in the language, or even the languages of the province where a province has more than one language within its borders. I suggest to the legislators that they could, by enough application, inside of a month, understand the languages of their provinces. There is nothing to prevent a Tamilian from easily learning the simple grammar and a few hundred words of Telugu, Malayalam and Kanarese, all allied to Tamil. At the centre Hindustani must rule supreme.

In my opinion this is not a question to be decided by academicians. They cannot decide through what language the boys and girls of a place are to be educated. That question is already decided for them in every free country. Nor can they decide the subjects to be taught. That depends upon the wants of the country to which they belong. Theirs is the privilege of enforcing the nation's will in the best manner possible. When this country becomes really free the question of medium will be settled only one way. The academicians will frame the syllabus and prepare text-books accordingly. And the products of the education of a free India will answer the requirements of the country as today they answer those of the foreign ruler. So long as we the educated classes play with this question, I very much fear we shall not produce the free and healthy India of our dream. We have to grow by strenuous effort out of our bondage, whether it is educational, economical, social or political. The effort itself is three-fourths of the battle.

Thus I claim that I am not an enemy of higher education. But I am an enemy of higher education as it is given in this country. Under my scheme there will be more and better libraries, more and better laboratories, more and better research institutes. Under it we should have an army of chemists, engineers and other experts who will be real servants of the nation and answer the varied and growing requirements of a people who are becoming increasingly conscious of their rights and wants. And all these experts will speak not a foreign language but the language of the people. The knowledge gained by them will be the common property of the people. There will be truly original work instead of mere imitation. And the cost will be evenly and justly distributed.

Harijan, 9-7-1938

87. If I Were a Czech
(vol. LXVII, pp. 404–6)

If I have called the arrangement with Herr Hitler "peace without honour," it was not to cast any reflection on British or French statesmen. I have no doubt that Mr. Chamberlain could not think of anything better. He knew his nation's limitations. He wanted to avoid war, if it could be avoided at all. Short of going to war, he pulled his full weight in favour of the Czechs. That it could not save honour was no fault of his. It would be so every time there is a struggle with Herr Hitler or Signor Mussolini.

It cannot be otherwise. Democracy dreads to spill blood. The philosophy for which the two dictators stand calls it cowardice to shrink from carnage. They exhaust the resources of poetic art in order to glorify organized murder. There is no humbug about their word or deed. They are ever ready for war. There is nobody in Germany or Italy to cross their path. Their word is law.

It is different with Mr. Chamberlain or M. Daladier.[1] They have their Parliaments and Chambers to please. They have parties to confer with. They cannot maintain themselves on a perpetual war footing if their language is to have a democratic accent about it.

Science of war leads one to dictatorship pure and simple. Science of non-violence can alone lead one to pure democracy. England,

1. Edouard Daladier, then prime minister of France.

France and America have to make their choice. That is the challenge of the two dictators.

Russia is out of the picture just now. Russia has a dictator who dreams of peace and thinks he will wade to it through a sea of blood. No one can say what Russian dictatorship will mean to the world.

It was necessary to give this introduction to what I want to say to the Czechs and through them to all those nationalities which are called 'small' or 'weak.' I want to speak to the Czechs because their plight moved me to the point of physical and mental distress and I felt that it would be cowardice on my part not to share with them the thoughts that were welling up within me. It is clear that the small nations must either come or be ready to come under the protection of the dictators or be a constant menace to the peace of Europe. In spite of all the good-will in the world England and France cannot save them. Their intervention can only mean bloodshed and destruction such as has never been seen before. If I were a Czech, therefore, I would free these two nations from the obligation to defend my country. And yet I must live. I would not be a vassal to any nation or body. I must have absolute independence or perish. To seek to win in a clash of arms would be pure bravado. Not so, if in defying the might of one who would deprive me of my independence I refuse to obey his will and perish unarmed in the attempt. In so doing, though I lose the body, I save my soul, i.e., my honour.

This inglorious peace should be my opportunity. I must live down the humiliation and gain real independence.

But, says a comforter, 'Hitler knows no pity. Your spiritual effort will avail nothing before him.'

My answer is, 'You may be right. History has no record of a nation having adopted non-violent resistance. If Hitler is unaffected by my suffering, it does not matter. For I shall have lost nothing worth [preserving]. My honour is the only thing worth preserving. That is independent of Hitler's pity. But as a believer in non-violence, I may not limit its possibilities. Hitherto he and his likes have built upon their invariable experience that men yield to force. Unarmed men, women and children offering non-violent resistance without any bitterness in them will be a novel experience for them. Who can dare say that it is not in their nature to respond to the higher and finer forces? They have the same soul that I have.'

But says another comforter, 'What you say is all right for you. But how do you expect your people to respond to the novel call? They are trained to fight. In personal bravery they are second to none in the world. For you now to ask them to throw away their arms and be trained for non-violent resistance, seems to me to be a vain attempt.'

'You may be right. But I have a call I must answer. I must deliver my message to my people. This humiliation has sunk too deep in me to remain without an outlet. I, at least, must act up to the light that has dawned on me.'

This is how I should, I believe, act if I was a Czech. When I first launched out on satyagraha, I had no companion. We were thirteen thousand men, women and children against a whole nation capable of crushing the existence out of us. I did not know who would listen to me. It all came as in a flash. All the 13,000 did not fight. Many fell back. But the honour of the nation was saved. New history was written by the South African Satyagraha.

A more apposite instance, perhaps, is that of Khan Saheb Abdul Ghaffar Khan, the servant of God as he calls himself, the pride of Afghan as the Pathans delight to call him. He is sitting in front of me as I pen these lines. He has made several thousands of his people throw down their arms. He thinks he has imbibed the lesson of non-violence. He is not sure of his people. Elsewhere I reproduce the pledge that his soldiers of peace make. I have come to the Frontier Province, or rather he has brought me, to see with my own eyes what his men here are doing. I can say in advance and at once that these men know very little of non-violence. All the treasure they have on earth is their faith in their leader. I do not cite these soldiers of peace as at all a finished illustration. I cite them as an honest attempt being made by a soldier to convert fellow soldiers to the ways of peace. I can testify that it is an honest attempt, and whether in the end it suceeds or fails, it will have its lessons for satyagrahis of the future. My purpose will be fulfilled if I suceed in reaching these men's hearts and making them see that if their non-violence does not make them feel much braver than the possession of arms and the ability to use them they must give up their non-violence, which is another name for cowardice, and resume their arms which there is nothing but their own will to prevent them from taking back.

I present Dr. Benes[2] with a weapon not of the weak but of the brave. There is no bravery greater than a resolute refusal to bend the knee to an earthly power, no matter how great, and that without bitterness of spirit and in the fulness of faith that the spirit alone lives, nothing else does.

Peshawar, *October 6, 1938*

Harijan, 15-10-1938

2. Eduard Benes, President of Czechoslovakia.

88. The Jews
(vol. LXVIII, pp. 137–41)

Several letters have been received by me asking me to declare my views about the Arab-Jew question in Palestine and the persecution of the Jews in Germany. It is not without hesitation that I venture to offer my views on this very difficult question.

My sympathies are all with the Jews. I have known them intimately in South Africa. Some of them became life-long companions. Through these friends I came to learn much of their age-long persecution. They have been the untouchables of Christianity. The parallel between their treatment by Christians and the treatment of untouchables by Hindus is very close. Religious sanction has been invoked in both cases for the justification of the inhuman treatment meted out to them. Apart from the friendships, therefore, there is the more common universal reason for my sympathy for the Jews.

But my sympathy does not blind me to the requirements of justice. The cry for the national home for the Jews does not make much appeal to me. The sanction for it is sought in the Bible and the tenacity with which the Jews have hankered after return to Palestine. Why should they not, like other peoples of the earth, make that country their home where they are born and where they earn their livelihood?

Palestine belongs to the Arabs in the same sense that England belongs to the English or France to the French. It is wrong and inhuman to impose the Jews on the Arabs. What is going on in Palestine today cannot be justified by any moral code of conduct. The mandates have no sanction but that of the last war. Surely it would be a crime against humanity to reduce the proud Arabs so that Palestine can be restored to the Jews partly or wholly as their national home.

The nobler course would be to insist on a just treatment of the Jews wherever they are born and bred. The Jews born in France are French in precisely the same sense that Christians born in France are French. If the Jews have no home but Palestine, will they relish the idea of being forced to leave the other parts of the world in which they are settled? Or do they want a double home where they can remain at will? This cry for the national home affords a colourable justification for the German expulsion of the Jews.

But the German persecution of the Jews seems to have no parallel in history. The tyrants of old never went so mad as Hitler seems to have gone. And he is doing it with religious zeal. For he is propound-

ing a new religion of exclusive and militant nationalism in the name
of which any inhumanity becomes an act of humanity to be re-
warded here and hereafter. The crime of an obviously mad but in-
trepid youth is being visited upon his whole race with unbelievable
ferocity. If there ever could be a justifiable war in the name of and for
humanity, a war against Germany, to prevent the wanton persecution
of a whole race, would be completely justified. But I do not believe in
any war. A discussion of the pros and cons of such a war is therefore
outside my horizon or province.

But if there can be no war against Germany, even for such a crime
as is being committed against the Jews, surely there can be no alliance with Germany. How can there be alliance between a nation
which claims to stand for justice and democracy and one which is
the declared enemy of both? Or is England drifting towards armed
dictatorship and all it means?

Germany is showing to the world how efficiently violence can be
worked when it is not hampered by any hypocrisy or weakness
masquerading as humanitarianism. It is also showing how hideous,
terrible and terrifying it looks in its nakedness.

Can the Jews resist this organized and shameless persecution? Is
there a way to preserve their self-respect, and not to feel helpless, neglected and forlorn? I submit there is. No person who has faith in a
living God need feel helpless or forlorn. Jehovah of the Jews is a God
more personal than the God of the Christians, the Mussalmans or
the Hindus, though, as a matter of fact in essence, He is common to
all and one without a second and beyond description. But as the Jews
attribute personality to God and believe that He rules every action of
theirs, they ought not to feel helpless. If I were a Jew and were born
in Germany and earned my livelihood there, I would claim Germany
as my home even as the tallest gentile German may, and challenge
him to shoot me or cast me in the dungeon; I would refuse to be ex-
pelled or to submit to discriminating treatment. And for doing this, I
should not wait for the fellow Jews to join me in civil resistance but
would have confidence that in the end the rest are bound to follow
my example. If one Jew or all the Jews were to accept the prescription here offered, he or they cannot be worse off than now. And suffering voluntarily undergone will bring them an inner strength and
joy which no number of resolutions of sympathy passed in the world
outside Germany can. Indeed, even if Britain, France and America
were to declare hostilities against Germany, they can bring no inner
joy, no inner strength. The calculated violence of Hitler may even result in a general massacre of the Jews by way of his first answer to

the declaration of such hostilities. But if the Jewish mind could be prepared for voluntary suffering, even the massacre I have imagined could be turned into a day of thanksgiving and joy that Jehovah had wrought deliverance of the race even at the hands of the tyrant. For to the godfearing, death has no terror. It is a joyful sleep to be followed by a waking that would be all the more refreshing for the long sleep.

It is hardly necessary for me to point out that it is easier for the Jews than for the Czechs to follow my prescription. And they have in the Indian satyagraha campaign in South Africa an exact parallel. There the Indians occupied precisely the same place that the Jews occupy in Germany. The persecution had also a religious tinge. President Kruger used to say that the white Christians were the chosen of God and Indians were inferior beings created to serve the whites. A fundamental clause in the Transvaal constitution was that there should be no equality between the whites and coloured races including Asiatics. There too the Indians were consigned to ghettos described as locations. The other disabilities were almost of the same type as those of the Jews in Germany. The Indians, a mere handful, resorted to satyagraha without any backing from the world outside or the Indian Government. Indeed the British officials tried to dissuade the satyagrahis from their contemplated step. World opinion and the Indian Government came to their aid after eight years of fighting. And that too was by way of diplomatic pressure not of a threat of war.

But the Jews of Germany can offer satyagraha under infinitely better auspices than the Indians of South Africa. The Jews are a compact, homogeneous community in Germany. They are far more gifted than the Indians of South Africa. And they have organized world opinion behind them. I am convinced that if someone with courage and vision can arise among them to lead them in non-violent action, the winter of their despair can in the twinkling of an eye be turned into the summer of hope. And what has today become a degrading man-hunt can be turned into a calm and determined stand offered by unarmed men and women possessing the strength of suffering given to them by Jehovah. It will be then a truly religious resistance offered against the godless fury of dehumanized man. The German Jews will score a lasting victory over the German gentiles in the sense that they will have converted the latter to an appreciation of human dignity. They will have rendered service to fellow-Germans and proved their title to be the real Germans as against those who are today dragging, however unknowingly, the German name into the mire.

And now a word to the Jews in Palestine. I have no doubt that they are going about it the wrong way. The Palestine of the Biblical conception is not a geographical tract. It is in their hearts. But if they must look to the Palestine of geography as their national home, it is wrong to enter it under the shadow of the British gun. A religious act cannot be performed with the aid of the bayonet or the bomb. They can settle in Palestine only by the goodwill of the Arabs. They should seek to convert the Arab heart. The same God rules the Arab heart who rules the Jewish heart. They can offer satyagraha in front of the Arabs and offer themselves to be shot or thrown into the Dead Sea without raising a little finger against them. They will find the world opinion in their favour in their religious aspiration. There are hundreds of ways of reasoning with the Arabs, if they will only discard the help of the British bayonet. As it is, they are co-sharers with the British in despoiling a people who have done no wrong to them.

I am not defending the Arab excesses. I wish they had chosen the way of non-violence in resisting what they rightly regarded as an unwarrantable encroachment upon their country. But according to the accepted canons of right and wrong, nothing can be said against the Arab resistance in the face of overwhelming odds.

Let the Jews who claim to be the chosen race prove their title by choosing the way of non-violence for vindicating their position on earth. Every country is their home including Palestine not by aggression but by loving service. A Jewish friend has sent me a book called *The Jewish Contribution to Civilization* by Cecil Roth. It gives a record of what the Jews have done to enrich the world's literature, art, music, drama, science, medicine, agriculture, etc. Given the will, the Jew can refuse to be treated as the outcaste of the West, to be despised or patronized. He can command the attention and respect of the world by being man, the chosen creation of God, instead of being man who is fast sinking to the brute and forsaken by God. They can add to their many contributions the surpassing contribution of non-violent action.

Segaon, *November 20, 1938*

Harijan, 26-11-1938

89. Discussion with Charles Fabri [1]

(vol. LXX, pp. 26–30)

Abbottabad,
[On or before July 26, 1939]

GANDHIJI: It is a difficult thing to explain fully what I do when I pray. But I must try to answer your question. The Divine Mind is unchangeable, but that Divinity is in everyone and everything—animate and inanimate. The meaning of prayer is that I want to evoke that Divinity within me. Now I may have that intellectual conviction, but not a living touch. And so when I pray for swaraj or independence for India I pray or wish for adequate power to gain that swaraj or to make the largest contribution I can towards winning it, and I maintain that I can get that power in answer to prayer.

FABRI: *Then you are not justified in calling it prayer. To pray means to beg or demand.*

[G:] Yes, indeed. You may say I beg it of myself, of my Higher Self, the Real Self with which I have not yet achieved complete identification. You may therefore describe it as a continual longing to lose oneself in the Divinity which comprises all.

[F:] *And you use an old form to evoke this?*

[G:] I do. The habit of a lifetime persists, and I would allow it to be said that I pray to an outside Power. I am part of that Infinite, and yet such an infinitesimal part that I feel outside it. Though I give you the intellectual explanation, I feel, without identification with the Divinity, so small that I am nothing. Immediately I begin to say I do this thing and that thing, I begin to feel my unworthiness and nothingness, and feel that someone else, some Higher Power, has to help me.

[F:] *Tolstoy says the same thing. Prayer really is complete meditation and melting into the Higher Self, though one occasionally does lapse in imploration like that of a child to his father.*

1. This appeared under the title "A Dialogue with a Buddhist" by Mahadev Desai, who explains: ". . . an archaeologist . . . Dr. Fabri . . . has been in India for many years. He was a pupil of Prof. Sylvain Levi and came out as assistant to the famous archaeologist, Sir Aurel Stein. . . . He is a Hungarian and had in the past corresponded with Gandhiji and even sympathetically fasted with him. He had come to Abbottabad specially to see Gandhiji. . . . He was particularly exercised about the form and content of prayer and would very much like to know what kind of prayer Gandhiji said. Could the Divine Mind be changed by prayer? Could one find it out by prayer?"

[G:] Pardon me, I would not call it a lapse. It is more in the fitness of things to say that I pray to God who exists somewhere up in the clouds, and the more distant He is, the greater is my longing for Him and [I] find myself in His presence in thought. And thought as you know has a greater velocity than light. Therefore the distance between me and Him, though so incalculably great, is obliterated. He is so far and yet so near.

[F:] *It becomes a matter of belief, but some people like me are cursed with an acute critical faculty. For me there is nothing higher than what Buddha taught, and no great master. For Buddha alone among the teachers of the world said: 'Don't believe implicitly what I say. Don't accept any dogma or any book as infallible.' There is for me no infallible book in the world, inasmuch as all were made by men, however inspired they may have been. I cannot hence believe in a personal idea of God, a Maharaja sitting on the Great White Throne listening to our prayers. I am glad that your prayer is on [a] different level.*

[G:] Let me remind you that you are again only *partially* true when you say my prayer is on a different level. I told you that the intellectual conviction that I gave you is not eternally present with me. What is present is the intensity of faith whereby I lose myself in an Invisible Power. And so it is far truer to say that God has done a thing for me than that I did it. So many things have happened in my life for which I had intense longing, but which I could never have achieved myself. And I have always said to my co-workers it was in answer to my prayer. I did not say to them it was in answer to my intellectual effort to lose myself in the Divinity in me! The easiest and the correct thing for me was to say, 'God has seen me through my difficulty.'

[F:] *But that you deserved by your karma. God is Justice and not Mercy. You are a good man and good things happen to you.*

[G:] No fear. I am not good enough for things to happen like that. If I went about with that philosophical conception of karma, I should often come a cropper. My karma would not come to my help. Although I believe in the inexorable law of karma I am striving to do so many things; every moment of my life is a strenuous endeavour which is an attempt to build up more karma, to undo the past and add to the present. It is therefore wrong to say that because my past is good, good is happening at present. The past would be soon exhausted, and I have to build up the future with prayer. I tell you karma alone is powerless. 'Ignite this match,' I say to myself, and yet I cannot if there is no co-operation from without. Before I strike the match my hand is paralysed or I have only one match and the wind blows it off. Is it an accident or God or Higher Power? Well, I prefer to use the language of my ancestors or of children. I am no better than a child. We may try to talk learnedly and of books, but when it comes to brass tacks—when we are face to face with a calamity— we behave like children and begin to cry and pray and our intellectual belief gives no satisfaction!

[F:] *I know, very highly developed men to whom belief in God gives incredible comfort and help in the building of character. But there are some great spirits that can do without it. That is what Buddhism has taught me.*

[G:] But Buddhism is one long prayer.

[F:] *Buddha asked everyone to find salvation from himself. He never prayed, he meditated.*

[G:] Call it by whatever name you like, it is the same thing. Look at his statues.

[F:] *But they are not true to life. They are 400 years later than his death.*

[G:] Well, give me your own history of Buddha as you may have discovered it. I will prove that he was a praying Buddha. The intellectual conception does not satisfy me. I have not given you a perfect and full definition as you cannot describe your own thought. The very effort to describe is a limitation. It defies analysis and you have nothing but scepticism as the residue.

[F:] *What about the people who cannot pray?*

[G:] 'Be humble,' I would say to them, 'and do not limit even the real Buddha by your own conception of Buddha.' He could not have ruled the lives of millions of men that he did and does today if he was not humble enough to pray. There is something infinitely higher than intellect that rules us and even the sceptics. Their scepticism and philosophy does not help them in critical periods of their lives. They need something better, something outside them that can sustain them. And so if someone puts a conundrum before me, I say to him, 'You are not going to know the meaning of God or prayer unless you reduce yourself to a cipher. You must be humble enough to see that in spite of your greatness and gigantic intellect you are but a speck in the universe. A merely intellectual conception of the things of life is not enough. It is the spiritual conception which eludes the intellect, and which alone can give one satisfaction. Even monied men have critical periods in their lives; though they are surrounded by everything that money can buy and affection can give, they find [themselves] at certain moments in their lives utterly distracted. It is in these moments that we have a glimpse of God, a vision of Him who is guiding every one of our steps in life. It is prayer.'

[F:] You mean what we might call a true religious experience which is stronger than intellectual conception. Twice in life I had that experience, but I have since lost it. But I now find great comfort in one or two sayings of Buddha: 'Selfishness is the cause of sorrow.' 'Remember, monks, everything is fleeting.' To think of these takes almost the place of belief.

[G:] That is prayer.

[F:] What would you say to the right of man to dispose of his life? Life as life I hold of very little importance.

[G:] I think that man has a perfect right to dispose of his life under certain circumstances. A co-worker,[2] suffering from leprosy, knowing that his disease was incurable and that his life was as much an agony for those who had to serve him as it was for him, recently decided to end his life by abstaining from food and water. I blessed the idea. I said to him: 'If you really think you can stand the trial you may do so.' I said this to him for I knew how different it is to die by inches from, say, suddenly killing oneself by drowning or poisoning. And my warning was fully justified, for someone tempted him with the hope that there was one who could cure leprosy, and I now hear that he has resumed eating and put himself under his treatment!

[F:] The criticism seems to me to be that if one's mind is completely obscured by pain, the best thing for him would be to seek nirvana. A man may not be ill but he may be tired of the struggle.

[G:] No, no. My mind rejects this suicide. The criterion is not that one is tired of life, but that one feels that one has become a burden on others and therefore wants to leave the world. One does not want to fly from pain but from having to become an utter burden on others. Otherwise one suffers greater pain in a violent effort to end one's agony. But supposing I have a cancer, and it is only a question of time for me to pass away, I would even ask my doctor to give me a sleeping draught and thereby have the sleep that knows no waking. . . .[3]

No[,] according to you I should have no business to stay if I feel I have finished my task. And I do think I have finished mine!

[F:] No. I am convinced that you can serve humanity for many years. Millions are praying for your life. And though I can neither pray nor desire anything—

[G:] Yes, the English language is so elastic that you can find another word to say the same thing.

[F:] Yes, I can unselfishly opine that you have many years before you.

2. Parachure Shastri.
3. Here, Mahadev Desai explains: "Dr. Fabri got up to go with the parting wish that there may be many more years of helpful activity left for Gandhiji."

[G:] Well, that's it. You have found the word! Here too let me tell you there is the purely intellectual conception of a man being unable to live. If he has not the desire to live, the body will perish for the mere absence of the desire to live.

Harijan, 19-8-1939

90. Discussion with Members of the Oxford Group [1]
(vol. LXX, pp. 195–97)

Segaon, Wardha,
September 23/24, 1939

How I wish I had the same enthusiasm that fires you. Of course I have the experience of listening,[2] not merely of trying to listen. The more I listen, the more I discover that I am still far away from God. While I can lay down rules, the observance of which is essential for proper listening, the reality still escapes me. When we say we are listening to God and getting answers, though we say it truthfully, there is every possibility there of self-deception. I do not know that I am myself altogether free from self-deception. People sometimes ask me if I may not be mistaken, and I say to them, 'Yes, very likely, what I say may be just a picture of my elongated self before you.'

And then see how one may claim to be God-guided in taking a particular course of action, and another may make the same claim in taking an opposite course of action. I will give you a good illustration. Rajaji, whom you know, at any rate whose name you have heard, is I think unsurpassed in godliness or God-mindedness. Now

1. This is extracted from "A Word to the Oxford Groupers." Mahadev Desai explains: ". . . six friends came to Wardha on the 23rd of last month. These included a barrister and his wife, an American journalist, a European who was a railway official, and a gifted lady, daughter of a one-time army officer. . . ."
2. The word "listening" had special meaning in the language of the Oxford Group. Mahadev Desai says: "Their mission may be described in common parlance as one of thinking aloud and, in their language, of 'spiritual sharing.' 'There is good somewhere in all,' said one of the members, 'and there are different ways of finding that out. For us it is by sharing. . . .' Another member said: 'You have always been listening to God. We feel that the solution of those problems for which you have worked would be reached if all the millions of India would start listening to God. We feel we have a place in this plan and have therefore come to you in joy.' Some of the members described their experiences of changes having come over the lives of men and women by this 'listening in.' . . . 'Whereas people of old used to use the word 'prayer,' 'listening in' is the modern word. . . . There was a discussion and Gandhiji spoke out his mind to them."

when I took the 21 days' purificatory fast in the Yeravda Jail in 1933 and proclaimed that it was in answer to a call from God, Rajagopalachari came all the way from Madras to dissuade me. He felt sure that I was deluding myself and that I should probably die and, if I did not, I should certainly be demented. Well, you see that I am still alive and of a sound mind. And yet perhaps Rajaji still thinks I was deluded and it was by an accident that I was saved, and I continue to think that I fasted in answer to the still small voice within.

I say this in order to warn you how unwise it may be to believe that you are always listening to God. I am not at all against the endeavour, but I warn you against thinking that this is a kind of 'open sesame' which has just to be shown to the millions. No one will contradict me when I say I have tried my very best to make India listen to the way of God. I have had some success but I am still far away from the goal. When I listen to the testimonies you have given I become cautious and even suspicious. In South Africa a preacher came who after his sermon got people to sign their names under a pledge, which was published in a book, binding them not to drink. Well, I have been witness to numerous of these promises being broken. It was no fault of these people. They signed the pledge under the temporary influence of the preacher's moving eloquence.

This I know that all that glitters is not gold, and also that if a man has really heard the voice of God, there is no sliding back, just as there is no forgetting it by one who had learnt to swim. The listening in must make people's lives daily richer and richer.

Let me not appear to damp your enthusiasm; but if it is to be built on solid rock, it is better that listening in is also based on solid rock.

This listening in presupposes the fitness to listen, and the fitness is acquired after constant and patient striving and waiting on God. Shankaracharya has likened the process to the attempt to empty the sea by means of a drainer small as the point of a blade of grass. This process thus necessarily is endless being carried through birth after birth.

And yet the effect has to be as natural as breathing or the winking of the eyes, which processes happen without our knowing them. The effort coincides with the process of living. I commend to you this process of eternal striving which alone can take us face to face with God.[3]

3. According to Mahadev Desai, the members of the Oxford group returned the next day and "produced another word begging the same rigorous definition and spiritual striving as 'listening in,' viz., 'repentance.'"

What is India as a nation to do at this juncture? What would you want her to do? How is she to repent? India may say she has committed many sins for which she is suffering and would pray to be given the strength to wipe them out. Or is there anything else at the back of your minds?[4]

Harijan, 7-10-1939

91. My Life

(vol. LXX, pp. 312–15)

The following from its Allahabad correspondent appears in *The Bombay Chronicle:*

Startling revelations have come to light regarding what has been going round the House of Commons about Gandhiji. It is reported that Mr. Edward Thompson, the British historian who visited Allahabad recently, threw some light on the curious mentality prevailing in England. Mr. Thompson, who met some political leaders here, is reported to have told them three things going round the House of Commons regarding Gandhiji:

1. Gandhiji was for unconditional co-operation with the British Government.

2. Gandhiji could still influence the Congress.

3. There were various stories about Gandhiji's sensual life, it being the impression that Gandhiji had ceased to be a saint.

Impressions about Gandhiji's 'sensual life,' it appeared to Mr. Thompson, were based on some Marathi papers. He spoke about them, I understand, to Sir Tej Bahadur Sapru, who repudiated them. He spoke about them to Pandit Jawaharlal Nehru and Mr. P. N. Sapru also, who strongly repudiated them.

It appears Mr. Thompson, before leaving England, has seen several members of the House of Commons. Mr. Thompson, before leaving Allahabad, sent a letter to Mr. Greenwood, M.P., on the suggestion of Pandit Nehru pointing out that the stories regarding Gandhiji were absolutely baseless.

Mr. Thompson was good enough to visit Segaon. He confirmed the report as substantially correct.

The 'unconditional co-operation' is dealt with in another note.

The country will presently know the influence I have over the Congress.

The third charge needs clearing. Two days ago I received a letter

4. Mahadev Desai adds: "There was no satisfactory reply. 'We should begin listening to God as a whole,' was their reply. . . ."

signed by four or five Gujaratis sending me a newspaper whose one mission seems to be to paint me as black as it is possible for any person to be painted. According to its headline it is a paper devoted to 'the organization of Hindus.' The charges against me are mostly taken from my confessions and distorted from their setting. Among many other charges, the charge of sensuality is most marked. My *brahmacharya* is said to be a cloak to hide my sensuality. Poor Dr. Sushila Nayyar has been dragged before the public gaze for the crime of giving me massage and medicated baths, the two things for which she is the best qualified among those who surround me. The curious may be informed that there is no privacy about these operations which take over $1\frac{1}{2}$ hours and during which I often go off to sleep but during which I also transact business with Mahadev, Pyarelal or other co-workers.

The charges, to my knowledge, began with my active campaign against untouchability. This was when it was included in the Congress programme and I began to address crowds on the subject and insisted on having Harijans at meetings and in the Ashram. It was then that some sanatanists, who used to help me and befriend me, broke with me and began a campaign of vilification. Later, a very high-placed Englishman joined the chorus. He picked out my freedom with women and showed up my 'saintliness' as sinfulness. In this chorus there were also one or two well-known Indians. During the Round Table Conference, American journals indulged in cruel caricatures of me. Mirabai who used to look after me was the target of their attack. As far as I could understand Mr. Thompson, who knows the gentlemen who have been behind these charges, my letters to Premabehn Kantak, who is a member of the Sabarmati Ashram, have also been used to prove my depravity. She is a graduate and worker of proved merit. She used to ask questions relating to *brahmacharya* and other topics. I sent her full replies. She thought they might be of general use and she published them with my permission. I hold them to be absolutely innocent and pure.

Hitherto I have ignored these charges. But Mr. Thompson's talks about them and the importunity of the Gujarati correspondents, who say the indictment sent by them is but a sample of what is being said about me, impel me to repudiate them. I have no secrets of my own in this life. I have owned my weaknesses. If I were sensually inclined, I would have the courage to make the confession. It was when I developed destestation of sensual connection even with my own wife and had sufficiently tested myself that I took the vow of *brahmacharya* in 1906, and that for the sake of better dedication to the service of the country. From that day began my open life. I do not remember having ever slept or remained with my own wife or other women with closed doors except for the occasions referred to in my writings in *Young India* and *Navajivan*. Those were black nights with me. But as I have said repeatedly God has saved me in spite of myself. I claim no credit for any virtue that I may possess. He is for me the Giver of all good and has saved me for His service.

From that day when I began *brahmacharya*, our freedom began. My wife became a free woman, free from my authority as her lord and master, and I became free from my slavery to my own appetite which she had to satisfy. No other woman had any attraction for me in the same sense that my wife had. I was too loyal to her as husband and too loyal to the vow I had taken before my mother to be slave to any other woman. But the manner in which my *brahmacharya* came to me irresistibly drew me to woman as the mother of man. She became too sacred for sexual love. And so every woman at once became sister or daughter to me. I had enough women about me at Phœnix. Several of them were my own relations whom I had enticed to South Africa. Others were co-workers' wives or relatives. Among these were the Wests and other Englishmen. The Wests included West, his sister, his wife, and his mother-in-law who had become the Granny of the little settlement.

As has been my wont, I could not keep the new good thing to myself. So I presented *brahmacharya* for the acceptance of all the settlers. All approved of it. And some took it up and remained true to the ideal. My *brahmacharya* knew nothing of the orthodox laws governing its observance. I framed my own rules as occasion necessitated. But I have never believed that all contact with women was to be shunned for the due observance of *brahmacharya*. That restraint which demands abstention from all contact, no matter how innocent, with the opposite sex is a forced growth, having little or no vital value. Therefore natural contacts for service were never restrained. And I found myself enjoying the confidence of many sisters, European and Indian, in South Africa. And when I invited the Indian sisters in South Africa to join the civil resistance movement, I found myself one of them. I discovered that I was specially fitted to serve womankind. To cut the (for me enthralling) story short, my return to India found me in no time one with India's women. The easy access I had to their hearts was an agreeable revelation to me. Muslim sisters never kept *purdah* before me here even as they did not in South Africa. I sleep in the Ashram surrounded by women for they feel safe with me in every respect. It should be remembered that there is no privacy in the Segaon Ashram.

If I were sexually attracted towards women, I have courage enough, even at this time of life, to become a polygamist. I do not believe in free love—secret or open. Free, open love I have looked upon as dog's love. Secret love is besides cowardly.

Sanatanist Hindus may abhor my non-violence. I know many of them think that Hindus will become cowards if they remain under my influence. I know of no man having become a coward under my influence. They may decry my non-violence as much as they like. But they ill serve themselves of Hinduism by indulging in palpable lies.

Segaon, *October 30, 1939*

Harijan, 4-11-1939

CHRONOLOGY VI
1940-1944

This four-year period included India's unhappy and bewildering experience of the war, and Gandhi's self-exhausting attempt to find a policy concerning it to recommend to Congress. The problem was insoluble because of the entanglement of various imperatives. England was leading a war against Fascism, with Soviet Russia as an ally, and for international Socialists such as Nehru, she deserved support. England was holding onto India as an imperial possession, and the war was Congress's chance to wrest the power out of her hands. But, at least once Japan entered the war, India was in danger and needed British arms to protect her. Moreover, both supporting and opposing the British involved Gandhi in employing violence, for under the conditions of war, nonviolent methods looked pale and ineffectual. Jinnah and the Muslim League were able to offer themselves to the British as loyal Indians, cooperating in the war effort in exchange for promises of freedom afterward; sometimes they said they would share power with the Hindus, sometimes they would settle for nothing less in the way of freedom than an independent Muslim state. And finally, the British, especially after Churchill came to power, took a tough line with Gandhi by imprisoning him and isolating him from his followers, which proved ineffectual.

He had tried a campaign of individual satyagraha in which a number of leading Gandhians stepped forward in turn and courted arrest by breaking wartime regulations restraining free speech. They then each accepted imprisonment without protest. It was a pure and dignified form of satyagraha but lacked the excitement of, for instance, the Salt March. Then he tried an opposite sort of campaign—mass civil disobedience with the slogan, directed at the British, "Quit India." Gandhi was arrested as soon as he launched this movement. He disapproved of the violence employed in it, but it seems likely that even if he had been free, he would not have been able to impose nonviolence on everyone.

In jail he felt himself unable to act even in his relations with the British government, with whom alone he was allowed to correspond. More than before he felt himself denied a necessary scope— necessary if he was to be himself—and some of his letters betray an anxiety or plaintiveness we do not see in him at other times.

1940

On February 6, Gandhi said the viceroy assumed that the British would determine India's destiny, whereas Congress insisted that Indians should.

On March 1, the Working Committee declared that it would begin civil disobedience. Also in March, the League, meeting in Lahore, resolved that a separate state for Muslims should be created in areas where they were in a majority.

On March 31, Jinnah asked that the Hindus and the Sikhs consider his proposal for an India divided among the three groups.

During June 17 to 20, the Working Committee divested Gandhi of his responsibility to act for them, leaving Congress free to make its own decisions. Nonviolence no longer compelled their imaginations.

From August 18 to 23, the Committee met again and pledged itself to act under Gandhi's command. He expounded a program of constructive work.

In September, he began to concentrate on the issue of free speech in wartime.

In October, he decided to launch a campaign of individual satyagraha, in which one leader after another would break the laws limiting freedom of speech and would be sent to jail.

On October 21, the first such leader, Vinoba Bhave, delivered an antiwar speech and was arrested four days later.

On October 31, Nehru followed Bhave's example, and others later did the same.

1941

On March 23, "Pakistan Day" was observed by Muslims.

On April 11, Jinnah forwarded to the viceroy the Muslim League resolution on Pakistan.

On July 26, Gandhi declared, "This bloody war indicates that the *world will ultimately be destroyed by machinery, and it is only handicrafts that will sustain or save the world."*

On October 31, he refused to lead a campaign of civil disobedience, on the grounds that it might lead to civil war.

On December 7, Japan entered the war, which made the invasion of India a possibility.

On December 30, he asked to be relieved of leadership again, because of differences of opinion over nonviolence. He wrote to the president, *"It is my certain belief that only nonviolence can save India and the world from self-extinction."*

1942

On January 15, Gandhi again agreed to lead Congress, on his own terms. He also announced, *"Jawaharlal will be my successor."*

On January 18, he restarted the Harijan weeklies after a silence of eighteen months.

On March 22, he asked the government to promise that they would not practice a "scorched earth" policy in India, like that followed in Russia and China.

On March 27, he met Sir Stafford Cripps, who had come out to India with the British government's newest proposals for limited self-rule. Gandhi rejected them.

At this time, Rajaji (the familiar name for C. Rajagopalachari), who had long been one of Gandhi's most devoted followers, recommended acceptance of the idea of Pakistan and cooperation with England in resisting any attack by Japan. Gandhi opposed both proposals.

On July 14, the Working Committee passed a resolution that Gandhi had drafted, calling for the British to "Quit India" and abdicate from power immediately.

On August 8, this resolution was passed by the All India Congress Committee.

On August 9, Gandhi was arrested, along with hundreds of other Congress leaders. He was imprisoned in the Aga Khan palace and was kept out of touch with his followers and the rest of the country.

On August 15, his secretary, Mahadev Desai, died.

1943

He exchanged letters with the viceroy, trying to justify his behavior and to exonerate himself of the charge that he stirred up violence. But some of his followers were engaging, against his wishes, in sabotage. The viceroy replied belatedly and severely.

On May 28, Jinnah described one of Gandhi's letters to him as "a

*move to embroil the Muslim League with the British Government
solely for the purpose of helping his release."*

*By June 30, the number of Indians imprisoned for "Quit India"
activities was 36,000.*

1944

On February 22, Kasturba Gandhi died in the Aga Khan palace.

*During these years, Gandhi began to lose trusted comrades
through death. In the chronicle of his movement in South Africa,
unexpected deaths are frequently recorded—gifted young men, in
whom he had reposed great hopes, died before they could become
co-leaders—but for nearly twenty years in India, death had been on
Gandhi's side, removing rivals rather than comrades. But in 1942
one of his closest millionaire supporters, Jamnalal Bajaj, who had
claimed Gandhi as his adoptive father, died; a little later, a few
days after they had entered jail together, his principal secretary,
Mahadev Desai, died; and in 1944, while still in jail, Kasturba
Gandhi died.*

*We find here addresses to the British and to the Japanese peoples,
and perhaps most characteristic of this period, broodings over the
difficulty of reaching agreement—with the British, with the Muslims, or with his allies in Congress. Gandhi's problems were in this
period larger than he could solve, though his failed efforts were
larger than other people's successes.*

92. How to Combat Hitlerism

(vol. LXXII, pp. 187–89)

Whatever Hitler may ultimately prove to be, we know what Hitlerism has come to mean. It means naked, ruthless force reduced to an
exact science and worked with scientific precision. In its effect it becomes almost irresistible.

In the early days of satyagraha when it was still known as passive
resistance, *The Star* of Johannesburg, stirred by the sight of a handful
of Indians, wholly unarmed and incapable of organized violence even
if they wished it, pitting themselves against an overwhelmingly
armed Government, had a cartoon in which the latter was depicted
as a steam-roller representing irresistible force, and passive resis-

tance was depicted as an elephant unmoved and comfortably planting himself in his seat. This was marked immovable force. The cartoonist had a true insight into the duel between the irresistible and the immovable forces. It was then a stalemate. The sequel we know. What was depicted and appeared to be irresistible was successfully resisted by the immovable force of satyagraha—call it suffering without retaliation.

What became true then can be equally true now. Hitlerism will never be defeated by counter-Hitlerism. It can only breed superior Hitlerism raised to nth degree. What is going on before our eyes is a demonstration of the futility of violence as also of Hitlerism.

Let me explain what I mean by failure of Hitlerism. It has robbed the small nations of their liberty. It has compelled France to sue for peace.[1] Probably by the time this is in print Britain will have decided upon her course. The fall of France is enough for my argument. I think French statesmen have shown rare courage in bowing to the inevitable and refusing to be party to senseless mutual slaughter. There can be no sense in France coming out victorious if the stake is in truth lost. The cause of liberty becomes a mockery if the price to be paid is wholesale destruction of those who are to enjoy liberty. It then becomes an inglorious satiation of ambition. The bravery of the French soldier is world-known. But let the world know also the greater bravery of the French statesmen in suing for peace. I have assumed that the French statesmen have taken the step in a perfectly honourable manner as behoves true soldiers. Let me hope that Herr Hitler will impose no humiliating terms but show that, though he can fight without mercy, he can at least conclude peace not without mercy.

But to resume the thread of the argument. What will Hitler do with his victory? Can he digest so much power? Personally he will go as empty-handed as his not very remote predecessor Alexander. For the Germans he will have left not the pleasure of owning a mighty empire but the burden of sustaining its crushing weight. For they will not be able to hold all the conquered nations in perpetual subjection. And I doubt if the Germans of future generations will entertain unadulterated pride in the deeds for which Hitlerism will be deemed responsible. They will honour Herr Hitler as a genius, as a brave man, a matchless organizer and much more. But I should hope that the Germans of the future will have learnt the art of discrimination

1. The French request for armistice was sent to Hitler on June 16. Hitler's terms were delivered to the French on June 20. On June 22 the German terms were accepted, and three days later on June 25 the armistice became effective.

even about their heroes. Anyway I think it will be allowed that all the blood that has been spilled by Hitler had added not a millionth part of an inch to the world's moral stature.

As against this imagine the state of Europe today if the Czechs, the Poles, the Norwegians, the French and the English had all said to Hitler: 'You need not make your scientific preparation for destruction. We will meet your violence with non-violence. You will therefore be able to destroy our non-violent army without tanks, battleships and airships.' It may be retorted that the only difference would be that Hitler would have got without fighting what he has gained after a bloody fight. Exactly. The history of Europe would then have been written differently. Possession might (but only might) have been then taken under non-violent resistance, as it has been taken now after perpetration of untold barbarities. Under non-violence only those would have been killed who had trained themselves to be killed, if need be, but without killing anyone and without bearing malice towards anybody. I dare say that in that case Europe would have added several inches to its moral stature. And in the end I expect it is the moral worth that will count. All else is dross.

I have written these lines for the European Powers. But they are meant for ourselves. If my argument has gone home, is it not time for us to declare our changeless faith in non-violence of the strong and say we do not seek to defend our liberty with the force of arms but we will defend it with the force of non-violence?

Sevagram, *June 18, 1940*

Harijan, 22-6-1940

93. 'A Cry in the Wilderness'

(vol LXXII, pp. 248–50)

ऊर्ध्वबाहु विरौम्येष न च कश्चिच्छृणोति मे ।
धर्मादर्थश्च कामश्च स धर्मः किं न सेव्यते ॥ [1]

Bapuji Aney [on his way back from Simla] paid a flying visit to me at Delhi on Saturday. Whether we work together or seem to be work-

1. Two lines of verse are quoted, which are translated thus:

"With hands upraised I cry:
(But none listens to me)
Dharma yields both *artha* and *kama*;
Why is that dharma not observed?"

ing in opposite directions, his love for me endures, and so he never misses an opportunity to look in wherever I may be. He expresses himself freely before me, and often shares with me a verse or two from his inexhaustible store. During his Delhi visit he sympathized with me for my having had to sever my connection with the Congress, but he really congratulated me.

They should, I think, leave you in peace, and let you go your way. I read your appeal to every Briton. It will fall on deaf ears. But that does not matter to you. You cannot help telling them what you feel to be their *dharma* (duty). But it is not strange that they will not listen to you—seeing that the Congress itself did not listen to you at the critical moment. When even sage Vyasa failed to make himself heard, how should others fare better? He had to conclude his great epic—*Mahabharata*—with a verse which reveals the cry of his soul.

With this he cited the verse I have quoted at the head of this article. He thereby strengthened my faith, and also showed how difficult was the way I had chosen.

And yet it has never seemed to me so difficult as it is imagined to be. Though the Sardar's way and mine seem to diverge today, it does not mean that our hearts also diverge. It was in my power to stop him from seceding from me. But it did not seem to be proper to do so. And it would have been morally wrong to strive with Rajaji in what he firmly regarded as his clear duty. Instead, therefore, of dissuading Rajaji I encouraged him to follow his course. It was my clear duty to do so. If I have the power to carry my experiment of ahimsa to success in an apparently new field, if my faith endures, and if I am right in thinking that the masses are fundamentally non-violent, Rajaji and the Sardar will again be with me as before.

What are these apparently new fields for the operation of non-violence? Those who have followed the Working Committee's resolutions and writings in *Harijan* are now familiar with these. Non-violence in its operation against constituted authority is one field. We have exercised this up to now with a fair amount of success, and I have always described it as the non-violence of the weak. This non-violence may be said to have come to stay with Congressmen.

The other field is the exercise of ahimsa in internal disturbances—Hindu-Muslim riots and the like. We have not been able to show visible success in the exercise of ahimsa in this field. What then should the Congressmen do when internal chaos is so imminent? Will they return blow for blow, or will they cheerfully bend their heads to receive violent blows? The answer to this is not so easy as we might think. Instead of going into the intricacies, I should say that Congressmen should try to save the situation by laying down their lives, not by taking any. He who meets death without striking a blow fulfils his duty cent per cent. The result is in God's hands.

But it is clear that this non-violence is not the non-violence of the weak. It does not give one the joy of jail-going. One can have that joy and also cover thereby the ill-will one harbours in his breast against the Government. One can also non-co-operate with the Government. But where swords, knives, lathis and stones are freely used, what is a man to do single-handed? Is it possible for one to receive these deadly blows with ill-will in one's heart? It is clear that it is impossible to do so, unless one is saturated with charity. It is only he who feels one with his opponent that can receive his blows as though they were so many flowers. Even one such man, if God favours him, can do the work of a thousand. It requires soul force—moral courage—of the highest type.

The man or woman who can display this non-violence of the brave can easily stand against external invasion. This is the third field for the exercise of non-violence. The Congress Working Committee were of opinion that, while it might be possible for us to exercise ahimsa in internal disturbances, India has not the strength to exercise ahimsa against the invasion of a foreign foe. This their want of faith has distressed me. I do not believe that the unarmed millions of India cannot exercise ahimsa with success in this wide field. It is for Congressmen to reassure the Sardar, whose faith in ahimsa of the strong has for the moment been shaken, that ahimsa is the only weapon that can suit India in the fields mentioned. Let no one ask, "But what about the martial races in India?" For me that is all the more reason why Congressmen should train themselves to defend their country with a non-violent army. This is an entirely new experiment. But who, save the Congress, is to try it—the Congress which has tried it successfully in one field? It is my unshakable faith that, if we have a sufficient number of non-violent soldiers, we are sure to succeed even in this new field, apart from the saving of the needless waste of crores of rupees.

I am therefore hoping that every Gujarati Congressite—man and woman—will declare their adherence to ahimsa and reassure the Sardar that they will never resort to violence. Even if there is sure hope of success in the exercise of violence, they will not prefer it to the exercise of non-violence. We are sure to learn by our mistakes. "We fall to rise, are baffled to fight better, sleep to wake."

On the Train to Wardha, *July 7, 1940*

Harijan, 13-7-1940

94. Why Suspension?

(vol. LXXIII, pp. 124–26)

Wardha,
October 24, 1940

On the 18th instant the Editor of *Harijan* received the following notice from the District Magistrate's Office, Poona:

I am directed by Government to advise you that no account of incidents leading up to satyagraha by Vinoba Bhave and no report of his speeches or any subsequent developments should be published without previous reference to the Chief Press Adviser, Delhi.

I would like to bring to your notice that this is in your own interest to avoid prosecution under Rule 38 of the Defence of India Rules.

Thereupon I entered into correspondence with H. E. the Viceroy. Correspondence is still going on. But it is necessary for me to take a decision today for, if I did not, there m[a]y be waste of public money. In view of the reply hitherto received, I have no course left open but to suspend publication of *Harijan, Harijanbandhu* and *Harijan Sevak*. I cannot function freely if I have to send to the Press Adviser at New Delhi every line I write about satyagraha. It is true that the notice is only advisory, and that therefore I am not bound to act up to it. But the consequence of disregard of advice is also stated in the notice. I have no desire to risk a prosecution against the Editors. The three weeklies have been conducted in the interest of truth and therefore of all parties concerned. But I cannot serve that interest if the editing has to be done under threat of prosecution. Liberty of the Press is a dear privilege, apart from the advisability or otherwise of civil disobedience. The Government have shown their intention clearly by the prosecution of Shri Vinoba Bhave. I have no complaint to make against the prosecution. It was an inevitable result of the Defence of India Rules. But the liberty of the Press stands on a different footing. I am unable to reconcile myself to the notice which although in the nature of advice, is in reality an order whose infringement will carry its own consequence.

I am sorry to have to disappoint the numerous readers of the three weeklies. Next week I shall be able to let the public know whether it is to be merely a suspension or an indefinite stopping of the three weeklies. I shall still hope that it will be merely a suspension and that my fear will prove to be groundless. But should it prove otherwise, I may inform the public that satyagraha is independent of Press advertisement. If it is real, it carries with it its own momentum; and

I believe the present satyagraha to be very real. It will go on. I will not be provoked into any hasty action. I am still not ready with the next move. But as I have said in my previous statement, every act of civil disobedience is complete in itself. This Press notice shows how effective it has been. Every act of repression adds strength to the reality. Satyagraha thrives on repression till at last the repressor is tired of it and the object of satyagraha is gained. Whether, therefore, I take the next step or not and when I take it, is a matter of no consequence to the public. Let those who sympathize with it follow implicitly the instructions I have issued. I believe, and my belief has been tested repeatedly, that thought deliberately thought and controlled is a power greater than speech or writing and any day greater than steam which is husbanded and controlled. We see the latter every day carrying incredible weights even across steep precipices. Thought-power overcomes much greater obstacles and easily carries greater weights. But let me give a practical hint to the non-believer in the power of thought husbanded and controlled. Let everyone become his own walking newspaper and carry the good news from mouth to mouth. This does not mean what boys used to do in the past, viz., trumpeting about of bits of news. The idea here is of my telling my neighbour what I have authentically heard. This no Government can overtake or suppress. It is the cheapest newspaper yet devised and it defies the wit of Government, however clever it may be. Let these walking newspapers be sure of the news they give. They should not indulge in any idle gossip. They should make sure of the source of information, and they will find that the public gets all the information that they need without opening their morning newspaper which, they should know, will contain garbled, one-sided information and therefore not worth the trouble of reading. For it may be that even the public statements such as I am now issuing may also be stopped. It is the condition of life under an autocratic Government, whether foreign or indigenous.

Harijan, 10-11-1940

95. The Ashram Prayer
(vol. LXXV, pp. 280–82)

The Ashram prayer has become very popular. Its development has been spontaneous. The *Ashram Bhajanavali* (Hymn Book) has gone into several editions and is increasingly in demand. The birth and growth of this prayer has not been artificial. There is a history attached to almost every *shloka* and every selected *bhajan*. The *Bhajanavali* contains among others *bhajans* from Muslim Sufis and Fakirs, from Guru Nanak, and from the Christian Hymnary. Every religion seems to have found a natural setting in the prayer book.

Chinese, Burmese, Jews, Ceylonese, Muslims, Parsis, Europeans and Americans have all lived in the Ashram from time to time. In the same way two Japanese sadhus came to me in Maganwadi in 1935. One of them was with me till the other day when war broke out with Japan. He was an ideal inmate of our home in Sevagram. He took part in every activity with zest. I never heard of his quarrelling with anyone. He was a silent worker. He learnt as much Hindi as he could. He was a strict observer of his vows. Every morning and evening he could be seen going round with his drum and heard chanting his *mantra*. The evening worship always commenced with his *mantra* नं म्ये हो रेंगे क्ये, which means "I bow to the Buddha, the giver of true religion." I shall never forget the quickness, the orderliness, and utter detachment with which he prepared himself the day the police came without notice to take him away from the Ashram. He took leave of me after reciting his favourite *mantra* and left his drum with me. "You are leaving us, but your *mantra* will remain an integral part of our Ashram prayer," were the words that came spontaneously to my lips. Since then, in spite of his absence, our morning and evening worship has commenced with the *mantra*. For me it is a constant reminder of Sadhu Keshav's purity and single-eyed devotion. Indeed its efficacy lies in that sacred memory.

While Sadhu Keshav was still with us, Bibi Raihana Tyabji also came to stay at Sevagram for a few days. I knew her to be a devout Muslim but was not aware, before the death of her illustrious father, of how well-versed she was in Koran Sharif. When that jewel of Gujarat, Tyabji Saheb, expired no sound of weeping broke the awful silence in his room. The latter echoed with Bibi Raihana's sonorous recitation of verses from the Koran. Such as Abbas Tyabji Saheb cannot die. He is ever alive in the example of national service which he has left behind.[1] Bibi Raihana is an accomplished singer with an ample repertory of *bhajans* of all kinds. She used to sing daily as well as recite beautiful verses from the Koran. I asked her to teach some verses to any of the inmates who could learn them, and she

---

1. The Hindi here has: "On her arrival I said to Raihana jestingly, 'You convert the Ashram inmates to Islam. I shall convert you to Hinduism.'"

gladly did so. Like so many who come here she had become one of us. Raihana went away when her visit was over, but she has left a fragrant reminder of herself. The well-known 'al Fateha' has been included in the Ashram worship. The following is a translation of it.

> 1. I take refuge in Allah from Satan the accursed.
> 2. Say: He is God, the one and only
> God, the Eternal, Absolute,
> He begetteth not nor is He begotten,
> And there is none like unto Him.
> 3. Praise be to God,
> The Cherisher and Sustainer of the worlds,
> Most Gracious, most Merciful,
> Master of the Day of Judgment,
> Thee do we worship
> And Thine aid we seek.
> Show us the straight way,
> The way of those on whom
> Thou hast bestowed Thy Grace,
> Those whose (portion) is not wrath
> And who go not astray.

I am writing this note in reply to an ardent Hindu friend who has thus gently reproached me: "You have now given the *Kalma* a place in the Ashram. What further remains to be done to kill your Hinduism?"

I am confident that my Hinduism and that of the other Ashram Hindus has grown thereby. There should be in us an equal reverence for all religions. Badshah Khan, whenever he comes, joins in the worship here with delight. He loves the tune to which the *Ramayana* is sung, and he listens intently to the *Gita*. His faith in Islam has not lessened thereby. Then why may I not listen to the Koran with equal reverence and adoration in my heart?

Vinoba and Pyarelal studied Arabic and learnt the Koran in jail. Their Hinduism has been enriched by this study. I believe that Hindu-Muslim unity will come only through such spontaneous mingling of hearts and no other. Rama is not known by only a thousand names. His names are innumerable, and He is the same whether we call Him Allah, Khuda, Rahim, Razaak, the Bread-giver, or any name that comes from the heart of a true devotee.

Sevagram, *February 2, 1942*

Harijan, 15-2-1942

96. Fiery Ordeal

(vol. LXXV, p. 323)

Twenty-two years ago a young man of thirty came to me and said, "I want to ask something of you."

"Ask, and it shall be given, if it is at all within my power to give," I replied with some surprise.

"Regard me as your son Devdas," the young man said.

"Agreed," I replied. "But what have you asked of me? You are the giver, I am the gainer."

The young man was no other than Jamnalal Bajaj. People know something of what this sacrament meant. But few know the extent of the part played by the self-adopted son. Never before, I can say, was a mortal blessed with a 'son' like him. Of course I have many sons and daughters in the sense that they do some of my work. But Jamnalalji surrendered himself and his without reservation. There is hardly any activity of mine in which I did not receive his full-hearted co-operation and in which it did not prove to be of the greatest value. He was gifted with a quick intelligence. He was a merchant prince. He placed at my disposal his ample possessions. He was constantly on the vigil and looked after my work, my comforts, my health and my finances. He would also bring up the workers to me. Where am I to get another son like him now? The day he died he and Janakidevi were to come to me. We had to decide a number of things. But God willed it otherwise and he died almost at the very hour he should have been with me. The death of such a son is a stunning blow to the father. Never before have I felt so forlorn except when Maganlal was snatched from me fourteen years ago.[1] But I had no doubt then, as I have none now, that a calamity of that kind is a blessing in disguise. God wants to try me through and through. I live in the faith that He will give me the strength too to pass through the ordeal.

Sevagram, *February 16, 1942*

[From Hindi]
Harijan Sevak, 22-2-1942

1. In April 1928; *vide* "My Best Comrade Gone."

97. To Every Briton

(vol. LXXVI, pp. 98–100)

When I had just begun my public career in South Africa I wrote "An Open Letter to Every Briton in South Africa."[1] It had its effect. I feel that I should repeat the example at this critical juncture in the history of the world. This time my appeal must be to every Briton in the world. He may be nobody in the counsels of his nation. But in the empire of non-violence every true thought counts, every true voice has its full value. *Vox populi vox dei* is not a copy-book maxim. It is an expression of the solid experience of mankind. But it has one qualification. Its truth is confined to the field of non-violence. Violence can for the moment completely frustrate a people's voice. But since I work on the field of non-violence only, every true thought expressed or unexpressed counts for me.

I ask every Briton to support me in my appeal to the British at this very hour to retire from every Asiatic and African possession and at least from India. That step is essential for the safety of the world and for the destruction of Nazism and Facism. In this I include Japan's 'ism' also. It is a good copy of the two. Acceptance of my appeal will confound all the military plans of all the Axis Powers and even of the military advisers of Great Britain.

If my appeal goes home, I am sure the cost of British interests in India and Africa would be nothing compared to the present ever-growing cost of the war to Britain. And when one puts morals in the scales, there is nothing but gain to Britain, India and the world.

Though I ask for their withdrawal from Asia and Africa, let me confine myself for the moment to India. British statesmen talk glibly of India's participation in the war. Now India was never even formally consulted on the declaration of war. Why should it be? India does not belong to Indians. It belongs to the British. It has been even called a British possession. The British practically do with it as they like. They make me—an all-war resister—pay a war tax in a variety of ways. Thus I pay two pice as war tax on every letter I post, one pice on every postcard, and two annas on every wire I send. This is the lightest side of the dismal picture. But it shows British ingenuity. If I was a student of economics, I could produce startling figures as to what India has been made to pay towards the war apart from what are

1. The title in fact was "Open Letter."

miscalled voluntary contributions. No contribution made to a conqueror can be truly described as voluntary. What a conqueror the Briton makes! He is well saddled in his seat. I do not exaggerate when I say that a whisper of his wish is promptly answered in India. Britain may, therefore, be said to be at perpetual war with India which she holds by right of conquest and through an army of occupation. How does India profit by this enforced participation in Britain's war? The bravery of Indian soldiers profits India nothing.

Before the Japanese menace overtakes India, India's homesteads are being occupied by British troops—Indian and non-Indian. The dwellers are summarily ejected and expected to shift for themselves. They are paid a paltry vacating expense which carries them nowhere. Their occupation is gone. They have to build their cottages and search for their livelihood. These people do not vacate out of a spirit of patriotism. When this incident was referred to me a few days ago, I wrote in these columns that the dispossessed people should be asked to bear their lot with resignation. But my co-workers protested and invited me to go to the evacuees and console them myself or send someone to perform the impossible task. They were right. These poor people should never have been treated as they were. They should have been lodged suitably at the same time that they were asked to vacate.

People in East Bengal may almost be regarded as amphibious. They live partly on land and partly on the waters of the rivers. They have light canoes which enable them to go from place to place. For fear of the Japanese using the canoes the people have been called upon to surrender them. For a Bengali to part with his canoe is almost like parting with his life. So those who take away his canoe he regards as his enemy.

Great Britain has to win the war. Need she do so at India's expense? Should she do so?

But I have something more to add to this sad chapter. The falsity that envelopes Indian life is suffocating. Almost every Indian you meet is discontented. But he will not own it publicly. The Government employees, high and low, are no exception. I am not giving hearsay evidence. Many British officials know this. But they have evolved the art of taking work from such elements. This all-pervading distrust and falsity make life worthless unless one resists it with one's whole soul.

You may refuse to believe all I say. Of course I shall be contradicted. I shall survive the contradictions.

I have stated what I believe to be the truth, the whole truth and nothing but the truth.

My people may or may not approve of this loud thinking. I have consulted nobody. This appeal is being written during my silence day. I am just now concerned with Britain's action. When slavery was abolished in America many slaves protested, some even wept. But protests and tears notwithstanding, slavery was abolished in law. But the abolition was the result of a bloody war between the South and the North; and so though the Negro's lot is considerably better than before, he still remains the outcaste of high society. I am asking for something much higher. I ask for a bloodless end of an unnatural domination and for a new era, even though there may be protests and wailings from some of us.

Bombay, *May 11, 1942*

Harijan, 17-5-1942

98. A Challenge

(vol. LXXVI, pp. 230–32)

I have before me three letters rebuking me for not going to Sind to face the Hurs personally. Two are friendly. The third comes from a critic who has no faith in non-violence. His letter demands an answer. Its main part runs as follows:

I am deeply interested in your writings and in the effect that they make upon the minds of the ignorant masses and your blind followers. I would therefore feel obliged if you enlighten me on the following points, especially because points nos. 3 & 4 raise novel and fundamental issues about non-violence.

You have been training a number of satyagrahis in your Ashram and they must have had the advantage of your supervision and instruction. You have been proclaiming that violence could be effectively met by non-violent means. Japan is now attacking India in the East and Hurs are creating trouble in the West. Is this not then the long-awaited opportunity when you can practise what you have so long preached?

Instead of doing that, you are contenting yourself by writing articles in the *Harijan*. Imagine Hitler or Stalin, without sending their armies to the front line, writing such articles in *Pravda* or such other paper. Instead of asking the Sind M.L.A.s to resign and go to Hurs, why should you not send a 'company' of your trained satyagrahis and try the luck of your doctrine?

Is it not the duty and business of a satyagrahi to go and meet the danger where it exists and threatens the country? Or is it your case that your satyagrahis will meet it only when it reaches the Ashram and not before? If so, is not your doctrine a doctrine of inaction?

I have no doubt that if I could have gone to Sind, I might have been able to do something. I have done such things before, not without success. But I am too old for such missions. What little energy I have, I am storing up for what promises to be the last fight of my life.

I have not conceived my mission to be that of a knight-errant wandering everywhere to deliver people from difficult situations. My humble occupation has been to show people how they can solve their own difficulties. So far as Sind is concerned, I maintain that my advice was perfect. It was clearly Congressmen's duty to proceed to the infested areas and spend themselves in the effort to convert the Hurs to the way of peace. Indeed they could have used arms if they had no faith in non-violence. They should have resigned from the Congress to free themselves from the obligation to observe non-violence. If we are to be fit for independence, we have to learn the art of self-defence either non-violently or violently. Every citizen should consider himself liable to render help to his neighbour in distress.

If I had adopted the role my critic has suggested, I would have helped people to become parasites. Therefore it is well that I have not trained myself to defend others. I shall be satisfied if at my death it could be said of me that I had devoted the best part of my life to showing the way to become self-reliant and cultivate the capacity to defend oneself under every conceivable circumstance.

My correspondent has committed the grave error of thinking that my mission is to deliver people from calamities. That is an arrogation only claimed by dictators. But no dictator has ever succeeded in proving the claim.

Indeed if I could say, as the correspondent thinks I could, that if the menaces of the kind described by him face the Ashram, it will give a good account of itself, I should be quite content and feel that my mission was wholly successful. But I can lay no such claim. The Ashram at Sevagram is only so called. The visitors gave it the name and it has passed current. The Ashram is a medley of people come together for different purposes. There are hardly half a dozen permanent residents having a common ideal. How these few will discharge themselves when the test comes remains to be seen.

The fact is that non-violence does not work in the same way as violence. It works in the opposite way. An armed man naturally relies upon his arms. A man who is intentionally unarmed relies upon the unseen force called God by poets, but called the unknown by scientists. But that which is unknown is not necessarily non-existent. God is the Force among all forces known and unknown. Non-violence without reliance upon that Force is poor stuff to be thrown in the dust.

I hope now my critic realizes the error underlying his question and that he sees also that the doctrine that has guided my life is not one of inaction but of the highest action. His question should really have been put thus:

How is it that, in spite of your work in India for over 22 years, there are not sufficient satyagrahis who can cope with external and internal menaces? My answer then would be that twenty-two years are nothing in the training of a nation for the development of non-violent strength. That is not to say that a large number of persons will not show that strength on due occasion. That occasion seems to have come now. This war puts the civilian on his mettle no less than the military man, non-violent no less than the violent.

Sevagram, *June 18, 1942*

Harijan, 28-6-1942

99. To Every Japanese [1]

(vol. LXXVI, pp. 309-12)

I must confess at the outset that though I have no ill-will against you, I intensely dislike your attack upon China. From your lofty height you have descended to imperial ambition. You will fail to realize that ambition and may become the authors of the dismemberment of Asia, thus unwittingly preventing World Federation and brotherhood without which there can be no hope for humanity.

Ever since I was a lad of eighteen studying in London, over fifty years ago, I learnt, through the writings of the late Sir Edwin Arnold, to prize the many excellent qualities of your nation. I was thrilled when in South Africa I learnt of your brilliant victory over Russian arms. After my return to India from South Africa in 1915, I came in close touch with Japanese monks who lived as members of our Ash-

1. This was published in three Japanese newspapers—*Nichi Nichi, Yomiuri*, and *Miyako*.

ram from time to time. One of them became a valuable member of the Ashram in Sevagram, and his application to duty, his dignified bearing, his unfailing devotion to daily worship, affability, unruffledness under varying circumstances and his natural smile, which was positive evidence of his inner peace, had endeared him to all of us. And now that owing to your delcaration of war against Great Britain he has been taken away from us, we miss him as a dear co-worker. He has left behind him as a memory his daily prayer and his little drum, to the accompaniment of which we open our morning and evening prayers.

In the background of these pleasant recollections I grieve deeply as I contemplate what appears to me to be your unprovoked attack against China and, if reports are to be believed, your merciless devastation of that great and ancient land.

It was a worthy ambition of yours to take equal rank with the great powers of the world. Your aggression against China and your alliance with the Axis powers was surely an unwarranted excess of the ambition.

I should have thought that you would be proud of the fact that that great and ancient people, whose old classical literature you have adopted as your own, are your neighbours. Your understanding of one another's history, tradition, literature should bind you as friends rather than make you the enemies you are today.

If I was a free man, and if you allowed me to come to your country, frail though I am, I would not mind risking my health, maybe my life, to come to your country to plead with you to desist from the wrong you are doing to China and the world and therefore to yourself.

But I enjoy no such freedom. And we are in the unique position of having to resist an imperialism that we detest no less than yours and Nazism. Our resistance to it does not mean harm to the British people. We seek to convert them. Ours is an unarmed revolt against British rule. An important party in the country is engaged in a deadly but friendly quarrel with the foreign rulers.

But in this they need no aid from foreign powers. You have been gravely misinformed, as I know you are, that we have chosen this particular moment to embarrass the Allies when your attack against India is imminent. If we wanted to turn Britain's difficulty into our opportunity we should have done it as soon as the war broke out nearly three years ago.

Our movement demanding the withdrawal of the British power from India should in no way be misunderstood. In fact if we are to believe your reported anxiety for the independence of India, a recognition of that independence by Britain should leave you no excuse for any attack on India. Moreover the reported profession sorts ill with your ruthless aggression against China.

I would ask you to make no mistake about the fact that you will be sadly disillusioned if you believe that you will receive a willing welcome from India. The end and aim of the movement for British withdrawal is to prepare India, by making her free for resisting all militarist and imperialist ambition, whether it is called British Imperialism, German Nazism, or your pattern. If we do not, we shall have been ignoble spectators of the militarization of the world in spite of our belief that in non-violence we have the only solvent of the militarist spirit and ambition. Personally I fear that without declaring the independence of India the Allied powers will not be able to beat the Axis combination which has raised violence to the dignity of a religion. The Allies cannot beat you and your partners unless they beat you in your ruthless and skilled warfare. If they copy it their declaration that they will save the world for democracy and individual freedom must come to naught. I feel that they can only gain strength to avoid copying your ruthlessness by declaring and recognizing *now* the freedom of India, and turning sullen India's forced co-operation into freed India's voluntary co-operation.

To Britain and the Allies we have appealed in the name of justice, in proof of their professions, and in their own self-interest. To you I appeal in the name of humanity. It is a marvel to me that you do not see that ruthless warfare is nobody's monopoly. If not the Allies some other power will certainly improve upon your method and beat you with your own weapon. Even if you win you will leave no legacy to your people of which they would feel proud. They cannot take pride in a recital of cruel deeds however skilfully achieved.

Even if you win it will not prove that you were in the right; it will only prove that your power of destruction was greater. This applies obviously to the Allies too, unless they perform *now* the just and righteous act of freeing India as an earnest and promise of similarly freeing all other subject peoples in Asia and Africa.

Our appeal to Britain is coupled with the offer of free India's willingness to let the Allies retain their troops in India. The offer is made in order to prove that we do not in any way mean to harm the Allied cause, and in order to prevent you from being misled into feeling that you have but to step into the country that Britain has vacated. Needless to repeat that if you cherish any such idea and will carry it out, we will not fail in resisting you with all the might that our country can muster. I address this appeal to you in the hope that our movement may even influence you and your partners in the right direction and deflect you and them from the course which is bound to end in your moral ruin and the reduction of human beings to robots.

The hope of your response to my appeal is much fainter than that of response from Britain. I know that the British are not devoid of a sense of justice and they know me. I do not know you enough to be able to judge. All I have read tells me that you listen to no appeal but to the sword. How I wish that you are cruelly misrepresented and that I shall touch the right chord in your heart! Anyway I have an undying faith in the responsiveness of human nature. On the strength of that faith I have conceived the impending movement in India, and it is that faith which has prompted this appeal to you.

I am,
Your friend and well-wisher,
M. K. GANDHI

Sevagram, *July 18, 1942*

Harijan, 26-7-1942

100. **Talk with Vinoba Bhave and Others**
(vol. LXXVI, pp. 333–35)

July 26, 1942

I have sent for you here so that I can lay before you what is going on in my mind, and if you find in me impatience or any other fault you may let me know.

I have tried, as I am trying, my best to give up the idea of fasting which has occupied my mind these days. But I find that it has taken firm hold of my mind. So far I have undertaken a number of fasts and I do not think any of them was unsuccessful. Some of these were resorted to for personal or domestic reasons. Their result was also good. The fast undertaken for Hindu-Muslim unity, too, had a good effect though it did not last long. The fast unto death undertaken against the proposed separation of the Harijans had instantaneous effect. People did not come and sit down with me but went into action. Even the president of the Hindu Mahasabha came to me and conceded my point. I liked all that. The twenty-one days' self-purification fast, occasioned by the impurity which had crept into the movement, was intended to be the first of a series of such fasts which was to go on for a year. But co-workers did not like the idea and I had to postpone it. But now I find that I cannot postpone it further. At the moment violence is on the rampage and darkness has descended upon the world. The poison has spread to India also. The Government wants to pit our own people against us and watch the spectacle. How can I tolerate that? I therefore feel that without sacrifice this raging fire cannot be quenched.

There are two kinds of fasts: one which is undertaken of one's own volition and the other which is undertaken in obedience to a general. What happens in a violent war? The soldiers put their faith in the general and plunge into the fire. Why cannot this be done in a non-violent war? This time I have also made a slight change in my concept of non-violence. In 1920 and 1930 I had laid down that observance of ahimsa in thought, word and deed was indispensable. Now I feel that it is not right to expect four hundred million people to accept this view and to wait till they do. Now I only tell them to abstain from violence in word and deed. When I send any satyagrahi to break a law, I merely say: "Leave your lathi here and go and do this work without using abusive language." The success of the work which this will ensure will drive out thoughts of violence from his heart also. Supposing a non-violent struggle has been started at my behest and later on there is an outbreak of violence, I will put up with that too, because eventually it is God who is inspiring me and things will shape as He wills. If He wants to destroy the world through violence using me as His instrument, how can I prevent it? He is so subtle that it is beyond man to know Him. Though electricity is a subtler power, we can certainly find out something about it. But God is still subtler and all-pervading. All that we can say about Him is that it is a Power at whose bidding everything goes on. But it is impossible to find out what that Power is. We can only put our faith in Him and it is that faith which is moving me.

When I hear of the destruction of the Germans, the British and the Japanese, the value of their sacrifices greatly increases in my eyes. How brave must have been the man who sank H. M. S., *Prince of Wales!* He threw himself against the engine and sank the enemy ship. What courage!

We have not shown any courage as yet. After going to jail we have fought for small things. A few like you have studied there. But that has no place in my present programme. If Pyarelal says that he would like to finish the Koran or if you say that you would like to complete the writing of an unfinished book, it will not do. This time we have to finish the entire work in three or four days. Breaking all the laws of the Government includes fasting also. If they put us in jail we will give up food and water and immolate ourselves.

Now the question arises—with whom should the beginning be made? For that I have selected myself because the work won't make any progress without my sacrifice. I want your co-operation. There is no cause for anyone to get alarmed or feel unhappy. It is only a matter of doing one's duty. After all the body has to perish one day. It is therefore better to let it perish in a noble cause.

KISHORELAL: *If the general himself should die at the beginning, what would happen to the army! Therefore in my opinion you should choose someone and begin with him. You should first make use of his sacrifice and offer yourself only afterwards, when you think the time has arrived.*

GANDHIJI: Who can that be? Suppose Jankibehn says 'My body is not worth much, let me go' or Shastriji says 'I will go!'

KISHORELAL: *No, no, I meant those who count.*

GANDHIJI: That is what I say. Suppose Shastriji is worth a pice, Jankibehn worth a rupee and I worth a guinea. If we have to pay a guinea for the thing, then I must sacrifice myself. Moreover who will decide that the time to sacrifice myself has come?

KISHORELAL: *You yourself will decide.*

GANDHIJI: If that is so I decide it right now that first of all I should sacrifice myself. What do you think?

VINOBA BHAVE: *I think you are right. But let me repeat what I have understood you to say. To my mind you mean that a fast may be undertaken from one's own choice or in obedience to a general in whom one has faith.*

GANDHIJI: That is right. Let me add that to check the violence that is raging there is no other alternative. This therefore has become necessary. I am prepared to find more time for a fuller discussion if it is considered necessary.

[From Hindi]
Bapuki Chhayamen, pp. 335–38

101. Letter to Lord Linlithgow

(vol. LXXVII, pp. 49–51)

Personal   Detention Camp, [1]
                                               New Year's Eve, 1942

Dear Lord Linlithgow,

This is a very personal letter. Contrary to the biblical injunction, I have allowed many suns to set on a quarrel I have harboured against you, but I must not allow the old year to expire without disburdening myself of what is rankling in my breast against you. I had thought we were friends and should still love to think so. However what has happened since the 9th of August last makes me wonder whether you still regard me as a friend. I have perhaps not come in such close touch with any other occupant of your gadi as with you.

Your arrest of me, the communique you issued thereafter, your reply[2] to Rajaji and the reasons given therefor[e], Mr. Amery's attack[3] on me and much else I can catalogue go to show that at some stage or other you must have suspected my *bona fides*. Mention of other Congressmen in the same connection is by the way. I seem to be the

1. The Aga Khan Palace, Poona, where Gandhi was detained without any charge being framed against him, after his arrest in Bombay on August 9, 1942.

2. The reference, presumably, is to the viceroy's refusal to forward C. Rajagopalachari's telegram to Gandhi, dissuading him from any intended fast, or to permit him to meet Gandhi. A request from Rajagopalachari for an interview with the viceroy had also been negatived. The viceroy's correspondence as published in *The Transfer of Power*, Vol. II, pp. 683–84 and 840, discloses that he was "not prepared to allow communication with Gandhi or the Working Committee. Once that starts, there would be no end to it." Also "a talk with Mr. Rajagopalachari . . . would certainly be taken to mean that we are willing to discuss, and would be regarded as a sign of approaching compromise, possibly even of weakness, by the many substantial interests in this country which are not in agreement with the point of view represented by him."

3. According to *The Indian Annual Register*, 1942, Vol. II, pp. 350–51, on September 11, 1942, L. S. Amery, secretary of state for India, replying to a debate in the House of Commons had, *inter alia*, said: ". . . soon after Sir Stafford Cripps left India, it became clear that under Mr. Gandhi's inspiration, the Congress was steadily swinging towards a policy of direct defiance aimed at paralysing the existing Government of India. . . . He was reported by his secretary, Mr. Desai, in June as saying: 'My attitude has undergone a change. I cannot afford to wait. I must even at obvious risks ask the people to resist slavery.' Mr. Gandhi declared that for national independence they might have to face bombs, bullets and shells. Does this look like a purely non-violent movement? Mr. Gandhi added, as to the method of resistance: 'No doubt the non-violent way is the best but where that does not come naturally . . . violent way is both necessary and honourable, and inaction here is rank cowardice and unmanly.' . . . The Government of India showed remarkable patience. . . . It took no action as long as there was a possibility of the All-India Congress Committee not endorsing the sinister designs of the Working Committee influenced by Mr. Gandhi."

fons et origo of all the evil imputed to the Congress. If I have not ceased to be your friend, why did you not, before taking drastic action, send for me, tell me of your suspicions and make yourself sure of your facts? I am quite capable of seeing myself as others see me, but in this case I have failed hopelessly. I find that all the statements made about me in Government quarters in this connection contain palpable departures from truth. I have so much fallen from grace that I could not establish contact with a dying friend; I mean Prof. Bhansali[4] who is fasting in regard to the Chimur affair; and I am expected to condemn the so-called violence of some people reputed to be Congressmen, although I have no data for such condemnation save the heavily censored reports of newspapers. I must own that I thoroughly distrust these reports. I could write much more but I must not lengthen my tale of woe. I am sure that what I have said is enough to enable you to fill in details.

You know I returned to India from South Africa at the end of 1914 with a mission which came to me in 1906, namely, to spread truth and non-violence among mankind in the place of violence and falsehood in all walks of life. The law of satyagraha knows no defeat. Prison is one of the many ways of spreading the message, but it has its limits. You have placed me in a palace where every reasonable creature comfort is ensured. I have freely partaken of the latter purely as a matter of duty, never as a pleasure, in the hope that some day those that have the power will realize that they have wronged innocent men. I had given myself six months. The period is drawing to a close, so is my patience. The law of satyagraha, as I know it, prescribes a remedy in such moments of trial. In a sentence it is: "Crucify the flesh by fasting." That same law forbids its use except as a last resort. I do not want to use it if I can avoid it. This is the way to avoid it: convince me of my error or errors, and I shall make ample amends. You can send for me or send someone who knows your mind and can carry conviction. There are many other ways, if you have the will. May I expect an early reply? May the New Year bring peace to us all.

I am,
Your sincere friend,
M. K. GANDHI

Gandhiji's Correspondence with the Government, pp. 18–19; also *Correspondence with Mr. Gandhi*, p. 5

4. Jaikrishna P. Bhansali, an inmate of Sevagram Ashram, was on an indefinite fast from November 26 in protest against the government's refusal to institute a public inquiry into Chimur atrocities of October 17.

102. Letter to Lord Wavell

(vol. LXXVII, pp. 244–49)

March 9, 1944

Dear Friend,

I must thank you for your prompt reply to my letter of 17th February. At the outset, I send you and Lady Wavell my thanks for your kind condolences on the death of my wife. Though for her sake I have welcomed her death as bringing freedom from living agony, I feel the loss more than I had thought I should. We were a couple outside the ordinary. It was in 1906 that after mutual consent and after unconscious trials we definitely adopted self-restraint as a rule of life. To my great joy this knit us together as never before. We ceased to be two different entities. Without my wishing it, she chose to lose herself in me. The result was she became truly my *better* half. She was a woman always of very strong will which, in our early days, I used to mistake for obstinacy. But that strong will enabled her to become quite unwittingly my teacher in the art and practice of non-violent non-co-operation. The practice began with my own family. When I introduced it in 1906, in the political field, it came to be known by the more comprehensive and specially coined name of satyagraha. When the course of Indian imprisonment commenced in South Africa, Shri Kasturba was among the civil resisters. She went through greater physical trials than I. Although she had gone through several imprisonments, she did not take kindly to the present incarceration during which all creature comforts were at her disposal. My arrest simultaneously with that of many others, and her own immediately following, gave her a great shock and embittered her. She was wholly unprepared for my arrest. I had assured her that the Government trusted my non-violence, and would not arrest me unless I courted arrest myself. Indeed the nervous shock was so great that after her arrest she developed violent diarrhoea and, but for the attention that Dr. Sushila Nayyar, who was arrested at the same time as the deceased, was able to give her, she might have died before joining me in this detention camp. My presence soothed her, and the diarrhoea stopped without any further medicament. Not so the bitterness. It led to fretfulness ending in painfully slow dissolution of the body.

2. In the light of the foregoing, you will perhaps understand the pain I felt when I read in the papers the statement made on behalf of the Government, which I hold was an unfortunate departure from

truth regarding her who was precious to me beyond measure. I ask you please to send for and read the complaint in the matter which I have forwarded to the Additional Secretary to the Government of India (Home Department). Truth is said to be the first and the heaviest casualty in war. How I wish in this war it could be otherwise in the case of the Allied powers!

3. I now come to your address which you delivered before the Legislature and of which you kindly sent me copy. When the newspapers containing the address were received, I was by the bedside of the deceased. Shri Mirabai read to me the Associated Press report. But my mind was elsewhere. Therefore the receipt of your speech in a handy form was most welcome. I have now read it with all the attention it deserves. Having gone through it, I feel drawn to offer a few remarks, all the more so, as you have observed that the views expressed by you "need not be regarded as final." May this letter lead to a re-shaping of some of them![1]

13. You are flying all over India. You have not hesitated to go among the skeletons[2] of Bengal. May I suggest an interruption in your scheduled flights and a descent upon Ahmednagar and the Aga Khan's Palace in order to probe the hearts of your captives? We are all friends of the British, however much we may criticize the British Government and system in India. If you can but trust, you will find us to be the greatest helpers in the fight against Nazism, Fascism, Japanism and the like.

14. Now I revert to your letter of the 25th February. Shri Mirabai and I have received replies to our representations. The remaining inmates have received their notices. The reply received by me I regard as a mockery; the one received by Shri Mirabai is an insult. According to the report of the Home Member's answer to a question in the Central Assembly, the replies received by us seem to be no replies. He is reported to have said that the stage "for the review of the cases had not yet arrived. Government at present were only receiving representations from prisoners." If the representations in reply to the Government notices are to be considered merely by the executive that imprisoned them without trial, it will amount to a farce and an eye-wash, meant perhaps for foreign consumption, but not as an indication of a desire to do justice. My views are known to the Government. I may be considered an impossible man—though altogether wrongly I would protest. But what about Shri Mirabai? As you know,

1. Several sections of this letter are omitted here.
2. The reference is to the Bengal famine.

she is the daughter of an Admiral[3] and former Commander-in-Chief of these waters. But she left the life of ease and chose instead to throw in her lot with me. Her parents, recognizing her urge to come to me, gave her their full blessings. She spends her time in the service of the masses. She went to Orissa at my request to understand the plight of the people of that benighted land. That Government was hourly expecting Japanese invasion. Papers were to be removed or burnt, and withdrawal of the civil authority from the coast was being contemplated. Shri Mirabai made Chaudwar (Cuttack) airfield her headquarters, and the local military commander was glad of the help she could give him. Later she went to New Delhi and saw General Sir Alan Hartley[4] and General Molesworth,[5] who both appreciated her work and greeted her as one of their own class and caste. It, therefore, baffles me to understand her incarceration.[6]

Gandhiji's Correspondence with the Government, pp. 18–19

3. Sir Edmond Slade.
4. Commander-in-Chief, India.
5. Lt.-Gen. George Noble Molesworth, deputy chief of General Staff, India, 1941–42; secretary, Military Department, India Office, 1943–44.
6. The concluding sections of the letter are omitted.

CHRONOLOGY VII
1944-1948

At the beginning of this last period of his life, Gandhi was preoccupied by an enthusiasm for nature cure, which dated back to his first years in South Africa and which had never left him but which had been crowded out of his life in the intervening years by other matters. We might attribute this revival of interest to the illnesses he had contracted in jail and to a disgust with a political situation in which he was ineffective. But it would be a grave mistake to underestimate this enthusiasm, which is of a piece with much of his cultural politics and which had given him his first great triumphs over his inner weaknesses. Gandhi was a self-created man, in the sense that he had first known himself as a weakling and had made himself into a man of iron and a leader of men, and the means he had employed was nature cure.

However, he was soon drawn back into political activity, because in August 1945, the war ended and a Labor government was returned to power in England, which hurried on the dissolution of the Empire and the freeing of India. Because of Jinnah's general intransigence and his particular antipathy for Gandhi, there proved to be no way to constitute a united free India, even in the form of a loose federation. Gandhi was obliged to sit by as his country was dismembered, which promised a future of even greater cultural hatred because in many cities and provinces the patchwork of Hindu and Muslim districts could not be separated out. The Hindu state was bound to include millions of Muslims, and vice versa, minorities belonging to the new state's national enemy.

This dismemberment also set up two modern nations that immediately began to create armies, and armament factories, and military academies, and ministries of war, and defence taxes, and so on. Gandhi was appalled, though not surprised, as his letter to Nehru of October 5, 1945, shows. He could find a sphere of action only on the periphery of politics (the constitution-writing and the bargaining between British, Congress, and Muslims) in healing particular outbreaks of violence.

1944

On May 6, he was released from prison, suffering from hookworm.

On August 31, the ashram was picketed to prevent Gandhi from going to Bombay to have talks with Jinnah. One of the picketers was Nathuram Godse, the leader of the group who later assassinated Gandhi.

On September 9, he began talks with Jinnah, which broke down on September 27.

1945

In May, in an interview, he said, "War criminals are not confined to the Axis powers alone. Roosevelt and Churchill are no less war criminals than Hitler and Mussolini."

On June 14, the viceroy said he had new proposals to put before Indian leaders.

On June 15, Gandhi said the Congress Working Committee alone could respond to those proposals. Nehru, Patel, and other leaders were then released from prison.

On June 25, the Indian leaders met Lord Wavell, the viceroy, in Simla. (Gandhi was not at the meeting, but he was in Simla.)

On July 11, the failure of the meeting was announced; the Muslim League refused to accept the viceroy's proposal.

On August 15, the war came to an end.

In November, the British put on trial officers of the Indian National Army, which had been led by Subhas Chandra Bose. The Congress took charge of the legal defense of the I.N.A.

1946

On February 19, the Royal Indian Navy mutinied. The British government announced that three Cabinet ministers would go to India to draw up a constitution.

On March 24, they arrived. Both Congress and the Muslim League accepted the Cabinet mission's plan of a three-tiered constitutional structure based on groups of undivided provinces.

In March, Gandhi had talks with Indian Army men.

In April, he said the British should leave the settlement of India's future to the Hindus and Muslims, even at the risk of violence.

In May, there were communal disturbances in many cities.

On June 16, the viceroy and the Cabinet mission abandoned further negotiations.

On August 16, a Muslim League "Direct Action Day" in Calcutta led to mass murders that continued for several days. These then spread to other parts of Bengal, including the Noakhali delta.

On September 2, the first National Interim Government assumed office, under the leadership of Nehru.

On October 10, a reign of terror began in Noakhali, which lasted through the month. The Muslims, who were in a majority there, were the aggressors.

On November 4, he heard the news of similar atrocities in Bihar, where the aggressors were Hindus.

On November 6, he arrived in Noakhali.

On November 16, he began the practice of staying with a Muslim in each Noakhali village he reached.

On November 20, he dispersed his party, sending each member to a separate village as a hostage to peace there.

1947

On January 4, he began a walking tour of Noakhali, spending one night in each village he reached.

On January 22, the Constituent Assembly in New Delhi passed the plans for the new constitution.

On February 20, the prime minister of England announced that power would be transferred into Indian hands no later than June 1948.

On March 2, he said he was going to Bihar, where he arrived on March 5.

On March 21, he said fifty people had confessed their guilt for the violence in Bihar and were willing to take the consequences.

On April 1, he met Lord Mountbatten and proposed an all-Muslim administration.

On April 15, he returned to Bihar. In May, he again met Mountbatten and Jinnah.

On June 3, Congress accepted the British plan for the partition of India. Gandhi criticized the plan but did not openly oppose it.

On July 18, the Partition Council was set up, with the aim of transferring power immediately.

On August 9, he arrived in Calcutta on his way to Noakhali, but he was asked to stay because of fears of violence.

August 15 was Independence Day. Gandhi refused to celebrate it, but he was able to save Calcutta from the communal riots that threatened it and that engulfed other Indian cities.

On September 1, he began a fast against the violence in the city. He broke the fast on September 4, after leaders of the various parties had signed an agreement to end the violence.

On September 7, he left Calcutta for New Delhi.

1948

On January 13, he began a fast to persuade the government to end violence in Delhi and to return to Pakistan its share of the treasury left behind by the British.

On January 18, the agreement was signed and the fast was broken.

On January 20, a bomb was exploded at Gandhi's prayer meeting as part of an assassination attempt, but no one was hurt.

On January 30, the assassination plan succeeded.

We see Gandhi's major concerns mirrored in the selections from this last period. For instance, in the previously mentioned letter to Nehru, Gandhi plainly foresees how far free India, under the leadership of his principal disciple, will diverge from the Gandhian path. We can also detect the general undertone of tragic grief, even, at times, of lassitude, though he suppresses both as much as he can. Gandhi knew himself as a defeated man in this period. But we also hear the more familiar undertone of renewed energy and experimentation in the remarks on nature cure and—however embarrassed and untriumphant this time—in the letters to Munnalal Shah at the ashram and to Nirmal Kumar Bose, who acted as his secretary in Noakhali. These letters refer to Gandhi's defiance of sexual conventions and to the criticism that aroused. And in the final selection we see reflected his extraordinary triumph over sectarian hysteria and mass violence in Calcutta a few months before he was assassinated, perhaps his greatest single feat of politics-and-religion.

103. Letter to Narandas Gandhi
(vol. LXXVII, p. 277)

Juhu,
May 20, 1944

Chi. Narandas,

I went carefully through your Annual Report. I have not yet started writing anything. I have written only three letters to invalids. But *Daridranarayana* is the greatest invalid in the world. You are one of His matchless devotees dedicated exclusively to His service. You celebrate the *Rentia Baras*[1] on the occasion of my birthday and every year you make your plan of service more rigorous. This year the test will be the hardest so far. May you succeed in it. This time, while in jail, I read about Marx and whatever literature I could get about the great experiment in Russia. What a great difference between that experiment and our spinning-wheel? There also, as in India, the whole nation is invited to join in the *yajna*. But the experiments there and here are as different from each other as East from West or North from South.

What a difference between our spinning-wheel and their machines driven by steam or electricity? But all the same I prefer the snail-like speed of the spinning-wheel. The spinning-wheel is a symbol of ahimsa, and ultimately it is ahimsa that will triumph. If, however, we who claim to be its votaries are weak, we shall dishonour ourselves and discredit ahimsa. Your activity is excellent indeed. But you should now introduce some new changes in it. There is a science of the spinning-wheel, as there is one of machines. We have still not fully evolved the "technique" of the spinning-wheel. It requires deep study.

Just as knowledge without faith is useless, even so faith without knowledge is blind.

Blessings from
BAPU

From the Gujarati.

1. Sacrificial spinning initiated by the addressee in honour of Gandhi's birthday; this was also called *Rentia Yajna* meaning nonstop spinning beginning on *Bhadarva Vad* 12, Gandhi's date of birth according to Vikram era, usually falling in the second half of September, to October 2.

104. Tribute to Mahadev Desai

(vol. LXXVIII, pp. 18–20)

Wardhaganj,
August 10, 1944

August 15 is the second anniversary of Mahadev Desai's death. Two or three correspondents have administered a gentle rebuke. The following is my paraphrase of the first of their remarks:

You have become President of the Kasturba Memorial Fund Trust. Mahadev renounced everything for your sake and even laid down his life for you. He died at a much younger age than Kasturba and yet how much he achieved in that relatively short space of time! Kasturba was verily a *sati*, but while India has produced many *satis*, all will admit that it has produced only one Mahadev. If he had not chosen to throw in his lot with you, he might have been living today. His talents would have enabled him to achieve front rank distinction as a savant and man of letters. He might have even been rich, brought up his family in all material comfort and provided his son with the highest education. Instead, he chose to merge himself in you. You regarded him as your son. May I ask what you have done for him?

These sentiments seem to me to be natural. The contrast between the two is too striking to be missed. The one was ready to drop off like a fully ripe fruit. The other had yet to ripen and mature. [L]ife still lay before Mahadev as ordinary standards go. He had aimed at living up to a hundred years. The amount of material that he had piled up in his voluminous note-books called for years of patient labour to work up and he had hoped to do all that. In his trunk was found a memo of my talks taken down on the day previous to his final end. Probably, none besides myself can today make them out, and even I don't know to what use he would have put them. He was a living example of "the wise, who live and work as if they were born to immortality and everlasting youth." But, if all our dreams could be realized, life would become a phantasmagoria, and there would be utter chaos on earth. God in His mercy, therefore, has ordained that His will alone should prevail on earth.

Mahadev, though an idealist and a dreamer, never allowed his feet to be taken off the firm earth. He, therefore, adorned everything that he attempted. To Mahadev's admirers, I can only offer this consolation, that he lost nothing by his association with me. His dreams rose above scholarship or learning. Riches had no attraction for him. God had blessed him with high intellect and versatile tastes but what his soul thirsted for was the devotional spirit. Even before he came to me, he had assiduously sought and cultivated the company of devotees and men of God after his heart. One may say that it was in furtherance of this quest that he came to me and, not obtaining full satisfaction even with me, (shall I say) he turned his back upon me in the fullness of youth, leaving behind him his weeping relations and friends, and set forth to seek realization of his quest in the bosom of his Maker. The only fitting service that I can render his memory is to complete the work which he has left behind him unfinished, and to make myself worthy of his devotion—obviously a more difficult task than merely raising a fund for his memorial. It can be fulfilled only through Divine grace. Mahadev's external goal was the attainment of swaraj; the inner, to fully realize in his own person his ideal of devotion, and if possible to share the same with others.[1]

The raising of a material memorial to the deceased's memory is outside my scope. That is a task for his friends and admirers to take up. Does a father initiate a memorial for his son? I was not responsible for the Kasturba Memorial. In my previous statement I have explained its origin. I have become the President of the Committee only in order to ensure the use of the fund in accordance with its object. If friends and admirers of Mahadev similarly set up a committee to raise a memorial fund and invite me to become its president and give guidance for its proper use, I shall gladly accept it.[2]

A word to litterateurs. They know or should know that he put the charkha above literature. He took delight in spinning for hours. It was a daily duty. He would encroach upon his sleeping hours to finish his daily minimum of spinning. Why this insistence? Not, I assure them, to please me. He threw in his lot with me after much deliberation. I never knew him do a thing without conviction. He thought with me that the material salvation of India's teeming but famishing millions was bound up with the charkha. He discovered too that this daily labour with the hand enriched whatever literary work he did. It gave it a reality which it otherwise lacked. The raising of funds is good and necessary. But a sincere imitation of Mahadev's constructive work is better. The monetary contribution to a memorial fund ought not to be a substitute for the more solid appreciation.

The Hindu, 12-8-1944

1. The Gujarati here adds: "Mahadev did love showing off his erudition. Let no one have any illusion about it. However, he cast it off after coming to me."
2. The Gujarati here adds: "It has been my profession for fifty years." The paragraph which follows is not found in the Gujarati original.

105. Speech at A.I.S.A. Meeting—I
(vol. LXXVIII, pp. 62–65)

Sevagram,
September 1, 1944

More than two years have passed since we last met. I have come to know a little, that is to say, not the whole of what happened outside [the jail] during these two years. It seemed as though one age had succeeded another, bringing in the process trouble for the whole of India. How could the Charkha Sangh have escaped it?

Today, we have once again come together under these circumstances but whatever little work we might yet be able to do would not be enough for us. A large amount of the Charkha Sangh property has either been destroyed or is in Government custody. Besides, many of our colleagues could not be among us today. Here, I am not talking of Congressmen but of those who were especially helpful in the Sangh work and are its trustees. But I have realized that even with these few we can carry on the Sangh work. We are sure of their ability to do it.

I have thought a great deal over the subject of khadi during my detention. I shall briefly state the conclusions I have arrived at.

The most important discovery I made was that the foundation of the A.I.S.A. was so weak that the Association could be easily wiped out of existence. It had not taken root in the life of the people. The Government could destroy it by imprisoning its leaders. Though some of its activities continued, I saw clearly that the Government could exterminate it at its pleasure. That is to say, my belief that the movement for the revival of the spinning-wheel was indestructible, whatever the circumstances, had been dashed to the ground. The work had not been organized on an imperishable basis.

I am not a man to accept defeat easily but it was in the jail that I discovered that we live at government's mercy and it hurts me. If it were in my power I would choose to live at no one's mercy except God's. True, it is Divine dispensation that no man may live without the goodwill of his fellow-beings but I am not talking of such help. My activities are founded on my own thinking. The Charkha Sangh was also founded on the same principles. In South Africa, I discovered that if India was to survive and progress non-violently, it could only be through the charkha—the charkha alone can be a symbol of non-violence. We may draw strength from other symbols as well but such strength may not lead to the world's well-being.

I realized in jail that there was something wrong in our method of khadi work, which must needs be amended. I had asked India to carry on spinning. I knew how this spinning work was to be carried on. But I did not lay the necessary stress on the requisite outlook and the spirit which was to underlie it. I looked at it from its immediate practical aspect. All my co-workers also laid stress on this practical side. So I suffered it, and also lent my helping hand to it. We have gone far in that direction. But today I cannot continue to ask people to spin in that manner.

I contemplated how to work in the future. I even thought of disbanding the Sangh on my own and distributing its property and funds among the people. I saw that our work would be incomplete, so long as we did not carry the message of the charkha to every home. That, I thought, accounted for our being far from our ideal. There are seven lakh villages in India. Thousands of them do not even know what the charkha is. This is our fault and it is because of this fault that we have failed to put khadi work on a sound basis. You must ponder over it.

All the thought and study I have been giving to this subject lately make me feel that the work would have to be decentralized if it is to spread far and wide and take permanent root. The above line of thought led to the idea of decentralization and I thought it would be very good indeed if its worth could be proved. I realize that the difficulties in my way are many but then hardly anyone has devoted as much thought and effort to the charkha as I have. This is a rather tall claim and it also smacks of pride, but not to mention it on the right occasion would be false modesty. In the jail too I had no other thought but the charkha.

The strength behind all my activities including civil disobedience is derived wholly from the charkha to which I have devoted most of my energy and funds. Most of the ten million rupees of the Tilak Swaraj Fund was also used up for the spinning activity. This brought about a spate of charges against me but I regard them as so many bouquets. For whatever I did, I did after due deliberation and with full knowledge of its consequences. I did not deceive anyone. Nothing was spent on the charkha without convincing the public about it. That is how this institution came into being.

After much reflection and study I have arrived at the definite conclusion that, however intense, my *sadhana*[1] of the charkha has remained imperfect and I must admit that my study too has not been

1. Spiritual discipline.

as thorough as it ought to have been. Today, my words have a greater force because I can see these things more clearly.

Besides the Charkha Sangh members, as well as sympathizers and those who share my feelings, today's gathering includes some representatives of the public also. Had we only directed the strength the country displayed during the movement along the right channels, we could have shown how much public support we had. But we failed to do so. The fault is not yours but mine and when I say all this, it is not so much to blame you, as to whip up your intelligence and my own.

We plied the charkha but mechanically, not intelligently. Had you yourselves appreciated the full significance of the charkha, you would have given it the same importance as I do. It also has political significance. It has however no place in the dishonest game of politics. More than any other thing it is the charkha that stands for clean, noble politics. If there is [no] truth in this statement, how can we claim swaraj through the charkha? It certainly does not mean that as soon as the yarn snaps swaraj comes to nought.

It is often alleged that workers of the A.I.S.A. and the A.I.V.I.A., if not Gandhiites in general, are unintelligent and lifeless. People repose trust in them. But they (the Gandhiites) are not able to tell the people what exactly are the problems facing the country and how our programme is calculated to resolve these problems and take us to our goal. On the other hand, Marxian literature is fast increasing in the country and Gandhiites are not able to resist the impact of these external forces.

We say that we are devoted to non-violence. If so, we must reveal in our lives the force of non-violence. Unless we can reveal its force in our own lives, we will not be true Gandhiites. In fact, there is no such thing as Gandhism. If anything, it is non-violence that deserves to be called an ideology. Every member of the Charkha Sangh should be a living witness of non-violence. If he is devotee of non-violence or Gandhism, he must be a live wire. Today Gandhism is a word of reproach. It no more connotes something virtuous or praiseworthy. Let us admit we have failed to make non-violence a part of our being. Otherwise we would find the charkha established in every village. I confess that I have failed. Had I been an adept in this art, I would have produced a concrete pattern of reconstructed village life in Sevagram at any rate. But today even if I put the charkha in the hands of the people of Sevagram they do not accept it. We teach them how to use it, tempt them by providing them with work, pay them more wages and serve them in various ways, yet all to little purpose. But my faith in the charkha is unshakable even when I have failed as President of the Sangh.

[From Hindi]
Charkha Sanghka, Navasamskaran

106. Speech at A.I.S.A. Meeting—III
(vol. LXXVIII, pp. 75–77)

Sevagram,
September 3, 1944

Today, I will try to explain my thoughts to you more clearly and present them to you in a different frame from what I have said during the last two days. Our work had a very humble beginning. When I started khadi I had with me, apart from Maganlalbhai[1] and others who had elected to live and die with me, Vithaldasbhai[2] and a few sisters. Vithaldas was, at that time, fighting for the labourers, but [at my call] he gave up his shop and joined me in this unremunerative work. We had then not the faintest idea as to what the future had in store for us. We have travelled a long way since then and today about two crores of people have come under the influence of the charkha. So far, we have maintained that the charkha has the power to bring us freedom. With its help we have been able to provide the village people with a large amount of money. But can we still hold, as we have always maintained, that swaraj is impossible without the charkha? So long as we do not substantiate this claim the charkha is really no more than a measure of relief, to which we turn because we can do nothing else about it. It would not then be the means of our salvation.

Secondly, we have failed to carry our message to the crores of our people. They have neither any knowledge of what the charkha can do for them nor even the necessary curiosity for it.

The Congress did accept the charkha. But did it do so willingly? No, it tolerates the charkha simply for my sake. The Socialists ridicule it outright. They have spoken and written much against it. We have no clear or convincing reply to offer to them. How I wish I could convince them that the charkha is the key to swaraj! I have not been able to justify the claim all these years.

1. Maganlal Gandhi.
2. Vithaldas Jerajani.

Now for my third point: non-violence is not something of the other world. If it is, I have no use for it. I am of the earth and if non-violence is something really worth while I want to realize it here on this earth while I am still alive. The non-violence I want is one which the masses can follow in practice. And how else can it be realized except in a society which has compassion and other similar virtues as its characteristics?

If you go to the house of one who has use for violence you will find his drawing-room decorated with tigers' skins, deers' horns, swords, guns and such like. I have been to the Viceregal Lodge, I also saw Mussolini. In the houses of both I found arms hanging on the walls. I was given a salute with arms, a symbol of violence.

Just as arms symbolize violence the charkha symbolizes non-violence, in the sense that we can most directly realize non-violence through it. But it cannot symbolize non-violence so long as we do not work in accordance with its spirit. The sword in Mussolini's hall seemed to say 'Touch me and I will cut you.' It gave a vivid picture of violence. It seemed to ask you to touch it and realize its power. So also we must illustrate the power of the charkha so that a mere look at it may speak to us about non-violence. But we are bankrupt today. What is our answer to the Socialists? They complain that we have been harping on the charkha for years and yet we have achieved nothing.

The charkha was there during Muslim rule also. Dacca was famous for its muslin. The charkha then was a symbol of poverty and not of non-violence. The kings took forced labour from women and depressed classes. The same was later repeated by the East India Company. Kautilya[3] mentions in his *Arthashastra* the existence of such forced labour. For ages the charkha was thus a symbol of violence and the use of force and compulsion. The spinner got but a handful of grain or two small coins, while ladies of the court went about luxuriously clad in the finest of muslins, the product of exploited labour.

As against this, I have presented the charkha to you as a symbol of non-violence. If I did not make it clear to you so far, it was my mistake. You know I am among the maimed and can move but slowly. Yet I do believe that the work done so far has not been a waste.

I shall now pass to my fourth point. We have not yet proved that there can be no swaraj without the charkha. It cannot be proved so

3. Chanakya, the celebrated writer on statecraft.

long as you do not explain it to Congressmen. The charkha and the Congress should become synonyms.

The task of proving the superiority of non-violence is a difficult one. We have to fathom its depths if we are to realize its truth. I have always supported all that I have said so far. The world is going to put me to the test. It may declare me a fool for my tall talk about the charkha. The task of making the charkha, which for centuries had been a symbol of poverty, helplessness, injustice and forced labour, the symbol now of mighty non-violent strength, of the new social order and of the new economy, has fallen on our shoulders. We have to change history. And I want to do it through you.

I hope you follow what I am saying. But if in spite of it you do not believe that the charkha has the power to achieve swaraj, I will ask you to leave me. Here you are at the cross-roads. If you continue with me without faith you will be deceiving me and doing a great wrong to the country. I beg of you not to deceive me in the evening of my life.

It is I who am responsible for defects in our working so far. The fault is mine because I have remained the head even when I was conscious of its defects. But let bygones be bygones. Do we honestly believe today that the charkha is the emblem of non-violence? How many of us are there who believe so from the depths of our heart?

Now we have the tricolour flag. What is it but a piece of khadi of specific length and breadth? You can well have another piece in its place. But behind that khadi cloth lie encased your feelings. It is a symbol of swaraj, a symbol of national emancipation. We cannot forget it. We will not remove it. We are prepared to die for it. So also the charkha should be an emblem of non-violence.

What does the charkha, as an emblem of non-violence, signify in the economic sphere? Call it self-sufficiency or what you like. In the name of national reconstruction and self-sufficiency millions are being bled white in Western countries, as also in other countries for their sake. Ours is not a self-sufficiency of that pattern. The charkha is the way to get rid of exploitation and domination. I am not so much concerned with words as with the thing itself. Still, words have a miraculous power. They embody the feelings, which then acquire a definite shape with the aid of language.

We are familiar with the controversy in our religion as to whether God has a form or no. The believers in form prefer to worship God through an emblem. So if non-violence is to be pursued as an ideal, the charkha must be acknowledged as its true form and emblem, and kept ever before view. Whenever I think of non-violence the picture of the charkha comes before me.[4]

[From Hindi]
Charkha Sanghka, Navasamskaran

107. Statement to the Press
(vol. LXXVIII, pp. 371–72)

Sevagram,
December 1, 1944

That 'man proposes and God disposes' constantly proves true in my case, as I expect it does in every case whether we realize it or not. I was contemplating a food fast for reasons I hold to be entirely spiritual. But for the time being, it is being replaced by a day-to-day-work fast. I had hoped that I had recovered sufficiently to be able to go through the routine work without interruption. But nature's warning has been sounding in my ears during the last ten days. I was feeling fatigued. Even after the noonday siesta, the brain seemed tired. There was a complete disinclination to speak or write. But I continued hoping that I would be all right without having to discontinue mental activity.

But nature would have her way. Rajaji who saw me after a month detected a marked change in my face, and he said, 'You must stop all this ceaseless mental activity if you want to avoid a disaster.' I seized the suggestion. He even went so far as to say that I should not mind disappointing invited workers of the Charkha Sangh, although I was looking forward eagerly to meeting them and discussing with them my plan for a new orientation of khadi work. But I would not listen. So I am going through these meetings in the best manner I can in the hope that no crisis will overtake me during the remaining two days of these meetings.

From the 4th to the 31st of this month, I have decided rigidly to discontinue all public activities, all interviews for public or private purposes and all correspondence of any nature whatsoever. I shall read no newspapers during the period. This abstention will be subject to exception for unforeseen circumstances of a grave nature.

I shall not deny myself the pleasure of reading non-political litera-

4. Incomplete.

ture in which I am interested. This also I shall read without in any way unduly taxing the brain. I have asked friends who were expecting to see me during the month to indulgently postpone their visits for the time being.

Let readers not be alarmed at what is only a precautionary measure. Dr. Sushila Nayyar assures me that there is nothing physically wrong with me except that my old friends, the hookworms and the amoebae, have not left me. I am able to take daily walks without the slightest strain and they will be continued. I had hoped to make one or two public statements in connection with a lot of misrepresentations of my views and doings about the communal question and some other public questions. I must forbear for the time being. But I must repeat the warning I have given before, that nothing that is not authoritatively stated by me should be accepted by the public. There are things which I have seen in the Press which I can only say I am incapable of having countenanced directly or indirectly.

There are some vital questions addressed to me by correspondents. They will forgive me for my inability to deal with them for the moment. If, after a month, they still feel the necessity, they will please repeat their letters and if all goes well, I shall gladly reply. Starvation of millions, black markets, and what I cannot but describe as gambling, will continue to worry me as they do now. I can but entreat my numerous co-workers to do what they can to ease the situation, which can be done, I am perfectly sure, if those concerned will make up their minds that the claims of the famishing millions are the first charge on their care and attention.

The Hindu, 3-12-1944

108. Foreword to "Amaran Ba"

(vol. LXXIX, pp. 132–33)

Narahari Parikh is one of those who joined the Satyagraha Ashram when it was first founded at Kochrab. Whatever, therefore, Chi. Vanamala has learnt, she has learnt at the Ashram. She is untouched by any Government school and the education imparted there. It can therefore be said that she knows how to work hard. She has however gone out to collect material for Kasturba's biography. In this she has also secured contributions from others. Up to the time of writing I

have not been able to look at these. It was Chi. Vanamala's wish that
I should go through what she has written. Poor girl, she would write
about Kasturba but how could she forget me, with whom she romped
around and played as a child? I see she has painstakingly collected
her facts and ordered them neatly. Her language is homely and simple.
I see no artificiality in it. Whether Chi. Vanamala has been successful in this her first effort is solely for the readers to judge.

Chi. Sushilabehn, sister of Chi. Pyarelal, has written about Ba's experiences in jail. Chi. Vanamala thought of taking something from
this. But on reading Sushilabehn's account she found that Sushilabehn's writing had a natural flow which she could not disturb. The
original is in Hindi and its Gujarati translation is reproduced in this
collection. Sushilabehn after all holds a doctor's degree. She has
besides an interest in vocal and instrumental music, painting and
literature. She takes interest in public affairs too. The late Mahadev
noticed these qualities of her and took a keen interest in them. But
he has departed from us. His life is ended. Readers should keep this
in mind when they read Sushilabehn's article.

So much for the authors.

But they both assert that if I myself do not say something about Ba
the work will remain incomplete. Since I am writing this foreword to
the book perhaps it will be appropriate if I say something about Ba.
I certainly intend to write more fully about Ba when I have the time.
Here I shall only answer the question, if I can, why Ba was able to
attract people to her. Ba's chief virtue was her voluntary identification
of herself with me. I did not draw her forth. The quality blossomed in
Ba on its own when the time came. I never knew that Ba had this
thing hidden in her. My earlier experience showed her a very stub-
born person. If I tried to compel her in any way she would do exactly
what she herself wanted. This led to bitterness between us—short or
prolonged. But as my public life gradually developed, Ba blossomed
more and more and freely merged herself in me, that is, in my work.
In time no distinction remained between me and my work—which
was service. Ba too became one with that work. This quality perhaps
most naturally arises from the Indian soil. At least that seems to me
the chief reason for Ba's sentiments.

The reason why this virtue reached its pinnacle in Ba is to be
found in our brahmacharya. It came more naturally to Ba than to
me. In the beginning Ba was not even aware of it. The idea came to
me and Ba took it up and made it her own. In the result the relationship between us was as one between true friends. Since 1906—in
fact since 1901—all the time Ba was with me, she had nothing out-

side of my work. She could have lived apart. There would have been no difficulty in her living apart from me. But being a friend she yet considered it her duty as a woman and a wife to merge herself in my work. Ba gave the paramount place to the service of my person and till death never ceased from the task of attending on me.

M. K. GANDHI

Sevagram, *February 18, 1945*

[From Gujarati]
Amaran Ba

109. Letter to Munnalal G. Shah

(vol. LXXIX, pp. 212–13)

March 6, 1945

Chi. Mu.,

Why need you feel embarrassed? This problem cannot be solved in that way. Ask me any question you wish without the slightest hesitation. My statement has undergone some revision and may undergo more. I don't wish to exclude anybody. I have mentioned four. Perhaps they will say, "We were not objects of your experiment; we slept with you as with a mother." I would not contradict them. It is enough here to mention that such a thing has happened. I don't consider Abha, Kanchan and Vina as part of the experiment. If we distinguish between sleeping together and the experiment, the difference between the two in my view is a big one. Abha slept with me for hardly three nights. Kanchan slept one night only. Vina's sleeping with me might be called an accident. All that can be said is that she slept close to me. If Abha had continued, her case would have been an altogether different one. Kanchan's case was rather tragic. I didn't understand her at all. What Abha or Kanchan told me was this; that she had no intention whatever of observing *brahmacharya*, but wished to enjoy the pleasure of sex. She, therefore, stayed only reluctantly and undressed only for fear of hurting me. If I remember rightly, she was not with me even for an hour. I then stopped both the women sleeping with me, for I realized that Kanu and you were upset. I myself advised them that they should tell you both and also Bhansali. You will thus see that these three names cannot be included in the experiment. Lilavati, Amtussalaam, Rajkumari and Prabhavati are not here. I have deliberately included Pra. in the experiment. Maybe I should not. She often used to sleep with me to keep me warm even before I was conscious that I was making an experiment. I used to draw her to me when she lay on the floor, shivering, for my sake. This is an old, old story. I think I have now told you everything. If you have any more questions, you may ask me. Kanchan's labouring under a misunderstanding pained me, but I was helpless.

I formed no judgment regarding Sushila and you. I did not get sufficient material, for doing that either. If she herself wishes and you too wish it, I would spare some time and hear you both. I will examine witnesses and try to weigh the evidence. But let me repeat that if you two feel as brother and sister to each other, you should not ask even your father to examine you and pronounce judgment. But do as you wish.

I understand about a separate kitchen. I shall try. Will the purchase of provisions for the hospital and the Ashram kitchens be under one account or two? I see that a catering service can be run only if it is managed by a third party. I think this is enough for today. About the third party and going to villages, etc., later on. I have not revised this. If you feel that anything needs correction, ask me.

Blessings from
BAPU

From the Gujarati.

110. Note to Munnalal G. Shah
(vol. LXXIX, pp. 215–16)

March 6, 1945

This discussion is somewhat out of place because at present nothing is happening. For this too friends are responsible. I have gone as far as I could to satisfy them. It will not be proper for me to do anything until I have satisfied my co-workers. I am as much against compromise as I am for it. For this very reason my elder brother remained my enemy for 13 years. He asked my forgiveness five or six months before his death. My caste also became my enemy in the same manner. Now it does not show any feeling of animosity. But quite a few sanatanists are still opposed to me. On this account I let myself be deprived of lakhs of rupees. I used to be a friend of the Empire. Today I have become its enemy. What more need I say?

I showed the door to a wife like Ba. Thus, I am what I am. There is therefore no point in talking about the welfare of society. What else may I give up? I cannot give up thinking. As far as possible I have postponed the practice of sleeping together. But it cannot be given up altogether. You can say that ever since I went to England I have been pursuing the idea of *brahmacharya*. It has not harmed anyone. It is true of course that I should do what others too can be permitted to do. If I can restrain myself and sleep beside a woman, others can also do so on the same condition. They can fulfil that condition if they so wish.

The same applies to non-violence. If I completely give up sleeping together, my *brahmacharya* will be put to shame. It is not that I would do anything for the mere pleasure of it. I have not done it for years, and I shall not do it now. It is true that people may indulge in licentiousness by imitating me. Who can stop it? Is there any place where *asatyagraha*[1] has never been practised in the name of satyagraha? In any case, the thing has been postponed because it calls for consideration. But since there is need for a halt let it be so. You can ask any questions. I suggest that you should not ask questions individually. You may all discuss it among yourselves and then ask questions. Let it be understood that right now everything is postponed. Manu has been left alone by the others. Hence there is scope for a mature deliberation. I claim that whatever I have done I have done in the name of God. I go to bed reciting His name. I have got up with His name on my lips. So it is in my dreams, whether alone or with some woman. What God will make me do in days to come He alone knows.

Such restrictions should not be im[p]osed on me. Kishorelalbhai's business should be left to him. Do not drag him into this matter. My advice is that everybody should join hands and stand by him. There is no need to plead his case before me. I am glad that I have answered your question but I am not in a position to listen.

I have said that right now everything stands postponed, leaving aside Manu. But Kishorelal is not satisfied with this. It is your duty to understand him. He is right when he says: "I was not consulted at first. Now I shall not create any confusion." In the present situation whoever has any doubt in his mind should follow him. I would in any case do that. I would not create difficulties for him. You should consider his delicate health when you bother him. If you do this you will be serving him, no doubt, but you will also be serving me. My

1. Opposite of *satyagraha*.

love for him is certainly no less than my love for my brother. What more can I do?

From the Hindi.

111. Foreword to "Varnavyavastha"

(vol. LXXX, pp. 222–24)

I do not have the time to read this book again. I do not even wish to. I have many other things to do.

In my opinion a man daily moves either forward or backward. He never stands still. The whole world is moving. There is no exception to it. I will be making a wrong statement if I say that I am today what I was yesterday and will remain the same in future. In fact I should not even have such a desire.

It is right however that my writings and utterances should not be such as to confuse others. I should not write things which can bear two interpretations. That is to say I should always have an eye to truth and non-violence while writing, speaking or doing anything. I can say that I have been doing that ever since I gave my word to my mother. In fact I became a devotee of truth ever since I reached the age of understanding.

This does not mean that I have had or even today have a full vision of truth and ahimsa. But I do believe that my vision of truth and ahimsa is becoming clearer every day. Therefore it would not be correct to say that my views on Varnashrama are the same as they were in the past. I have said that the varnas and the ashramas are the gifts of Hinduism to the world, and I still adhere to that view. But today neither the varnas nor the ashramas of my conception are in existence anywhere. They should form a part of our religion. But it can be said that these days the ashramas have disappeared altogether and varnas are found in the form of privileges. The claim of being a Brahmin, a Kshatriya, a Vaishya connotes pride. How can there be pride where there is religion? And the Shudras are not taken into consideration at all! Shudras are low and the Ati-Shudras are the lowest of the low. This is not religion but a negation of it.

Where are the four varnas of the *Gita* today? Varna is entirely different from caste. There are numerous castes. I know of no authority for caste in the *Gita* or any other scripture. The *Gita* has prescribed four varnas and they are based on one's aptitudes and karma. I am saying four just to give you an example. There can be more or less varnas than that. But there prevails only one varna today, that is, of Shudras', or, you may call it, Ati-Shudras', or Harijans' or untouchables'. I have no doubt about the truth of what I say. If I can bring round the Hindu society to my view, all our internal quarrels will come to an end. That will also put an end to communal riots between Hindus and Muslims, and the people of India will occupy a place of honour in the world. Just as it is not dharma but *adharma* to believe in the distinctions of high and low, so also colour prejudice is *adharma*. If a scripture is found to sanction distinctions of high and low, or distinctions of colour, it does not deserve the name of scripture. One should approach the scriptures with the assumption that they would not say anything which is contrary to dharma.

Caste distinctions have taken such deep roots that they have infected the Muslims, Christians and others. It is true that there are class distinctions in more or less degree in all the religions, from which one has to conclude that that failing is inherent in every human being. We can cleanse ourselves of that failing only by pure dharma. I have not found sanction for such distinctions between high and low in any scriptures. In the eyes of religion all men are equal. An educated, intelligent and affluent man is not better than an ignorant, stupid and poor man. If he is cultured, that is to say, if he has been purified by dharma, he will utilize his education, intelligence and money in the service of his illiterate, stupid and poor brethren. And he will strive to give them, that is to say, the whole world, what he has got. If that is true of religion, then in our present condition, devoid of religion our dharma lies in becoming Ati-Shudras voluntarily. A man should consider himself not the owner of his property but its trustee or custodian. He will use it for the service of society. He will accept only that much for himself as he has earned with his labour. If that happens, no one will be poor and no one rich. In such a system all religions will naturally be held equal. Therefore all quarrels arising out of religions, caste and economic differences will be ended.

At this stage it is also necessary to ponder over one further point. It is the foremost dharma of a subject nation to free itself of the bondage at the very first opportunity. A subject is compulsorily an Ati-Shudra. It is immaterial whether he has been given titles, or whether he is made a judge or a peon of a judge or whether he is a king or a pauper. The more titles one has the more abject is one's condition under alien rule. Thus by correlating freedom with dharma and making the latter widespread, we shall in the natural course of things arrive at the state described in the previous paragraph.

A man who wants to follow his dharma will not bother about the time when his may be realized. If many people do so, it will not only end our subjection but there will not be any anarchy or confusion in our freedom. This is the swaraj of my dreams. I yearn for that. I want to live for the attainment of it. I am devoting every breath of my life to that effort.

The reader is therefore requested to discard anything in this book which may appear to him incompatible with my views given above.

In order to save me labour, a friend who has digested my views and has done so with great effort, has sent me a brief note of my present views. Shri Kishorelal thought that I could save time if I could affix my signature to it. I was free to make any corrections I liked. But while going through it I found that Shri Kishorelal has, as is his wont, read through the whole book, has pondered over it and then has drafted a note as a testimony of my present views. Even if I cannot sign it, it should be published along with this. There is no incompatibility between his key and mine. Shri Kishorelal's note is based on the study of this book and therefore it would be more helpful to the readers.

May Truth alone triumph.

MOHANDAS KARAMCHAND GANDHI

Mahabaleshwar, *May 31, 1945*

[From Gujarati]
Varnavyavastha, pp. 5–8

112. Two Posers

(vol. LXXX, pp. 299–300)

[On or before June 12, 1945]

Shri Sailendra Nath Chattopadhyaya of the United Press puts the following posers before me: "Why do you wish to live for 125 years, and what is Ram Rajya?"

The questions are so apt and reasonable that, contrary to my wont these days, I want to answer them. Many visitors and correspondents put the same questions. I take this opportunity therefore and once for all, I hope, of answering them to the best of my ability.

The idea of 125 years' life flashed across my mind, while I was speaking on the 8th August, 1942, to the meeting of the A.I.C.C. in Bombay. I might have mentioned the same thing before in private conversation. If I did, I have no recollection.

I am a constant student of the *Ishopanishad* which contains only eighteen *mantras*. The first half of the second *mantra* means: "Only doing works of service on this earth, you should wish to live 120 or 125 years." The word in the original denoting the number is translated by the word 'hundred,' but I had seen just then a commentary which took the number to mean 120 or 125. I purposely used the highest figure at the meeting, as signifying the intense wish to live the longest in order to fulfil my allotted work. In expressing the wish I only followed my old habit of wishing to act according to the best of my belief.

Moreover, as a naturopath, I believe in the feasibility of living the full span of life. I know that, medically speaking, the chances are against me for I have not always followed nature's way. I began to adopt it fairly strictly in South Africa in 1903 or thereabout. Want of *brahmacharya* in early married life must also weigh against the full span.

My conception of nature cure, like everything else, has undergone progressive evolution. And for years I have believed that, if a person is filled with the presence of God and has thus attained the state of dispassion, he can surmount handicaps against long life. I have come to the conclusion, based on observation and scriptural reading, that when a man comes to that complete living faith in the Unseen Power and has become free from passion, the body undergoes internal transformation. This does not come about by mere wish. It needs constant vigilance and practice. In spite of both, unless God's grace descends upon one, human effort comes to naught.

Conquest of passion—passion here does not signify animal appetite; of course, it presupposes full control over such appetite—is more difficult to attain. If it were otherwise, complete non-violence would be easy of achievement. With all my knowledge of, and effort at, non-violence, I have conquered my passion only to the stage of suppression. This involves great strain on both body and mind. Subjugation is the real need. It does not involve absence of feeling. He who identifies himself with every living creature must feel for every kind of woe and yet remain unaffected by it. Action proceeding from such equableness is far-reaching, pervasive and quickest in its effect. Naturally, it is wholly non-violent.

Difficulty of attainment need cause no worry. For, being on the right track leads one nearer to the goal.

Thus, though I wish and even hope to live up to 125 years, what does it matter, if I die tomorrow? There is no sense of regret or frustration in me. And there will be no anguish in me over an early death.

Nor does the wish imply slackness of effort, in view of the prospect of a longer life. The wish, to be capable of being fulfilled, implies readiness to leave this body without a moment's notice. It connotes an easy fulfilment, from day to day, of the daily duty. All strain is an anticipation of death.

Death does not mean an end of all effort. The Eternal Law which we term God will be a mockery, if death were the end of such an effort. 'Hereafter' is a mystery into which we may not peep. We should have enough faith to know that death, after life truly lived, is but a prelude to a better and richer life.

Now for Ram Rajya. It can be religiously translated as Kingdom of God on Earth; politically translated, it is perfect democracy in which, inequalities based on possession and non-possession, colour, race or creed or sex vanish; in it, land and State belong to the people, justice is prompt, perfect and cheap and, therefore, there is freedom of worship, speech and the Press—all this because of the reign of the self-imposed law of moral restraint.

Such a State must be based on truth and non-violence and must consist of prosperous, happy and self-contained villages and village communities. It is a dream that may never be realized. I find happiness in living in that dreamland, ever trying to realize it in the quickest way.

The Hindu, 12-6-1945

113. Letter to Jawaharlal Nehru

(vol. LXXXI, pp. 319–21)

October 5, 1945

Chi. Jawaharlal,

I have long been intending to write to you but can do so only today. I have also been wondering whether I should write in English or Hindustani. In the end I have decided to write in Hindustani.

I take first the sharp difference of opinion that has arisen between us. If such a difference really exists people should also know about it, for the work of swaraj will suffer if they are kept in the dark. I have said that I fully stand by the kind of governance which I have described in *Hind Swaraj*. It is not just a way of speaking. My experience has confirmed the truth of what I wrote in 1909.[1] If I were the only one left who believed in it, I would not be sorry. For I can only testify to the truth as I see it. I have not *Hind Swaraj* in front of me. It is better that I redraw the picture today in my own language. Then it would not matter to me whether or no the picture tallies with that of 1909,[2] nor should it to you. I do not have to establish what I had said before. What is worth knowing is only what I have to say today. I believe that if India, and through India the world, is to achieve real freedom, then sooner or later we shall have to go and live in the villages—in huts, not in palaces. Millions of people can never live in cities and palaces in comfort and peace. Nor can they do so by killing one another, that is, by resorting to violence and untruth. I have not the slightest doubt that, but for the pair, truth and non-violence, mankind will be doomed. We can have the vision of that truth and non-violence only in the simplicity of the villages. That simplicity resides in the spinning-wheel and what is implied by the spinning-wheel. It does not frighten me at all that the world seems to be going in the opposite direction. For the matter of that, when the moth approaches its doom it whirls round faster and faster till it is burnt up. It is possible that India will not be able to escape this moth-like circling. It is my duty to try, till my last breath, to save India and through it the world from such a fate. The sum and substance of what I want to say is that the individual person should have control over the things that are necessary for the sustenance of life. If he cannot have such control the individual cannot survive. Ultimately, the world is made up only of individuals. If there were no drops there would be no ocean. This is only a rough and ready statement. There is nothing new in this.

But even in *Hind Swaraj* I have not said all this. While I appreciate modern thought, I find that an ancient thing, considered in the light of this thought looks so sweet. You will not be able to understand me if you think that I am talking about the villages of today. My ideal village still exists only in my imagination. After all every human

1. The source however has "1908."
2. The source has "1908."

being lives in the world of his own imagination. In this village of my dreams the villager will not be dull—he will be all awareness. He will not live like an animal in filth and darkness. Men and women will live in freedom, prepared to face the whole world. There will be no plague, no cholera and no smallpox. Nobody will be allowed to be idle or to wallow in luxury. Everyone will have to do body labour. Granting all this, I can still envisage a number of things that will have to be organized on a large scale. Perhaps there will even be railways and also post and telegraph offices. I do not know what things there will be or will not be. Nor am I bothered about it. If I can make sure of the essential thing, other things will follow in due course. But if I give up the essential thing, I give up everything.

The other day, at the final day's meeting of the Working Committee, we had taken a decision to the effect that the Working Committee would meet for two or three days to work out this very thing. I shall be happy if it meets. But even if it does not meet, I want that we two should understand each other fully. And this for two reasons. Our bond is not merely political. It is much deeper. I have no measure to fathom that depth. This bond can never be broken. I therefore want that we should understand each other thoroughly in politics as well. The second reason is that neither of us considers himself as worthless. We both live only for India's freedom, and will be happy to die too for that freedom. We do not care for praise from any quarter. Praise or abuse are the same to us. They have no place in the mission of service. Though I aspire to live up to 125 years rendering service, I am nevertheless an old man, while you are comparatively young. That is why I have said that you are my heir. It is only proper that I should at least understand my heir and my heir in turn should understand me. I shall then be at peace.

One thing more. I had written to you about Kasturba Trust and Hindustani. You had said you would write after thinking things over. I find that your name is already figuring in the Hindustani Sabha. Nanavati reminded me that he had approached you and Maulana Saheb and that you had appended your signature. That was in 1942. That was long ago. You know where Hindustani stands today. If you still stand by that signature, I wish to get some work out of you in this regard. It will not involve much running about, but some work will be called for.

The work of Kasturba Memorial Trust is rather complicated. I realize that if what I have said above is going to irk you or is irking you, you will not feel comfortable even in the Kasturba Trust.

The last point concerns the sparks that are flying about in the conflict with Sarat Babu. I have been pained by the episode. I have been unable to trace it to its root. If what you have told me is all there is to it and nothing more remains to be said, then I do not have to inquire further. But if an explanation seems necessary, I very much want to hear it.

If we have to meet to thrash out all these matters, then we should find time for a meeting.

You are working very hard. I trust you are in good health and Indu[3] is well.

Blessings from
BAPU

From the Hindi original: Gandhi-Nehru Papers.

114. **An Englishman's Difficulties**

(vol. LXXXII, pp. 154–55)

Calcutta,
[On or after December 1, 1945]

F.A.U.[1] MEMBER: *However much we may want to be friendly the past tradition clings round your necks and drives you to desperation. It seems to me, that there is hardly any hope of giving to a young Bengali student an idea of the better side of Englishmen unless perhaps he is transferred to England. The atmosphere in India is so poisoned that I wonder if it would not be better for Englishmen not to attempt to come to work in India just now but to wait for better times.*

GANDHIJI: Any friend, who is a real friend, and who comes in a spirit of service, not as a superior, is bound to be welcome. India, when she has come into her own will need all such assistance. The distrust of Englishmen, as you say, is there. It won't disappear even by transporting Indian students to England. You have got to understand it and live it down. It has its roots in history. The late Charlie Andrews and I were bed-fellows. There were scarcely a thought in our mind which we did not share. He even adopted Indian dress though sometimes with grotesque results. But even he could not escape suspi-

3. Indira, Nehru's daughter, the late Mrs. Gandhi, prime minister of India.

1. Friends Ambulance Unit, a wartime organization, begun in 1914, it was reorganized in 1939 to give those with pacifist views an opportunity to serve the suffering and the distressed. It came to India in 1942 after the Midnapore cyclone and again in 1943 during the Bengal famine. Its presence in 1945 was due to widespread famine conditions all over India.

cion. He was even dubbed "a spy." His was a very sensitive spirit. He
suffered unspeakable anguish under these unmerited attacks and I
was hard put to it to dispel the baseless distrust. 'If he is a spy, I am
a spy,' I said to these critics. In the end C. F. A.'s spirit triumphed.

Pearson[2] was C. F. Andrews' disciple and friend. He too came in for
his share of distrust. Then there is Stocks.[3] "If I am to serve India I
must become an Indian," he said to himself and married a Christian
Rajput. He was boycotted by the Rajputs. The Government distrusted him too in the beginning. But he has lived down the distrust
of both the Government and Indians.

If then, even a C. F. Andrews and a Stokes and others had to labour
under distrust, for you to be distrusted may not be wondered at. So
far Indians have known Englishmen only as members of the ruling
race—supercilious when they were not patronizing. The man in the
street makes no distinction between such an Englishman and a good,
humble European, between the Empire-builder Englishman of the
old type that he has known and the new type that is now coming
into being, burning to make reparation for what his forefathers did.
Therefore, if one has not got the fire of sacrifice in him I would say to
him: 'Do not come to India just now.' But if you are cast in a heroic
mould there will be no difficulty. You will in the end be taken at your
worth if you persevere. Anyway those of you who are here have no
reason for going back.

*The same friend was able to elicit from Gandhiji what he considered to
be the weak spots in the Indusco Plan of Chinese co-operatives. Firstly, the
Indusco was a product of abnormal times. Its production was war-time and
war-purposes production stimulated by the Japanese blockade. Secondly, it
was organized by foreign missionary enterprise and their work was tainted
by the proselytization motive.*

G. If you try to merely copy the Chinese co-operatives in India you
will end in miserable failure. Here you have to work among Indian
Christians. The temperament is different, the character is different,
and the circumstances are different. Co-operation which is rooted in
the soil always works. You have therefore to find out for yourself
what type of co-operative is best suited to the Indian temperament
and soil. Even those who have become converts to orthodox Christianity are today veering round.

2. W. W. Pearson, a British missionary worker in Bengal and for some time a teacher
in Santiniketan.
3. Samuel Stokes, a British missionary and an associate of C. F. Andrews. He was a
member of the Congress and courted arrest in 1920; became a Hindu to deliver the
message of Jesus to the Hindus; changed his name to Satyanand; and took up work for
the uplift of the Hill tribes at Kotgarh.

м. *By "veering round" you mean going back!*

G. Yes, I mean going back to real Christianity, to Christ, not Western Christianity. They are beginning to realize that Jesus was an Asiatic. Having seen this they are reading their Bible through Indian eyes. You should study the meaning of Indian Christianity through J. C. Kumarappa's book *Practice and Precepts of Jesus.*

Harijan, 31-3-1946

115. Statement to the Press
(vol. LXXXII, p. 384)

January 9, 1946

Last night (Tuesday) was a terrible night for me. The crowds at every station were unmanageable. The shouts, although well meant, could not please me in my old age, if they ever pleased me before. For I know that swaraj is made of truer and sterner stuff. They serve no useful purpose. In the beginning stages, when people out of fear were afraid to hear their own voice, shouts and slogans had a place, not today when we seem likely to achieve independence, maybe within a few months. I was allowed last night no sleep except for what I could snatch in between stations. I cannot repeat this performance for many days and hope to live to the age of one hundred and twenty-five years. Friends will now appreciate why I have hardened my heart against even a brief tour through East Bengal. I would love to travel throughout Bengal but I know that for the sake of the common cause I must restrain myself and invite friends and co-workers to do likewise. Let them and people at large satisfy themselves with what service I can render without traveling as I used to before. Let the leaders in the various places try to conciliate the populace surrounding them and advise them to restrain from shouts and slogans and from jostling one another.

One vulgar and uncivilized practice must be given up. There is the chain on every train to be used strictly in times of danger or accidents. Any other use of it and the consequent stoppage of the train is not merely a punishable offence but it is a vulgar, thoughtless and even dangerous misuse of an instrument devised for great emergencies. Any such misuse is a social abuse which, if it becomes a custom, must result in a great public nuisance. It is up to every lover of his country to issue a stern warning against such wanton abuse of a humanitarian device intended for public safety.

Amrita Bazar Patrika, 10-1-1946 and 11-1-1946

116. Statement to the Press

(vol. LXXXIII, pp. 182–84)

Poona,
February 26, 1946

I congratulate Shrimati Aruna Asaf Ali on her courageous refutation of my statement on the happenings in Bombay. Except for the fact that she represents not only herself but also a fairly large body of underground workers, I would not have noticed her refutation, if only because she is a daughter of mine not less so because not born to me or because she is a rebel. I had the pleasure of meeting her on several occasions while she was underground. I admired her bravery, resourcefulness and burning love of the country. But my admiration stopped there. I did not like her being underground. I do not appreciate any underground activity. I know that millions cannot go underground. Millions need not. A select few may fancy that they will bring swaraj to the millions by secretly directing their activity. Will this not be spoon-feeding? Only open challenge and open activity is for all to follow. Real swaraj *must* be felt by all—man, woman and child. To labour for that consummation is true revolution. India has become a pattern for all exploited races of the earth, because India's has been an open, unarmed effort which demands sacrifice from all without inflicting injury on the usurper. The millions in India would not have been awakened but for the open, unarmed struggle. Every deviation from the straight path has meant a temporary arrest of the evolutionary revolution.

I do not read the 1942 events as does the brave lady. It was good that the people rose spontaneously. It was bad that some or many resorted to violence. It makes no difference that Shri Kishorelal Mashruwala, Kakasaheb and other workers, in their impatient zeal for the movement, misinterpreted non-violence. That they did so only shows how delicate an instrument non-violence is. My analogy is not meant to cast any reflection on any person. Everyone acted as he or she thought best. Supineness in the face of overwhelming, organized violence would have meant cowardice. I would be weak and wrong, if I failed to give my estimate of the doings of 1942.

Aruna would "rather unite Hindus and Muslims at the barricade than on the constitution front." Even in terms of violence, this is a misleading proposition. [If] the union at the barricade is honest, there must be union also at the constitutional front. Fighters do not always live at the barricade. They are too wise to commit suicide. The barricade life has always to be followed by the constitutional. That front is not taboo for ever.

Emphatically it betrays want of foresight to disbelieve British declarations and precipitate a quarrel in anticipation. Is the official deputation coming to deceive a great nation? It is neither manly nor womanly to think so. What would be lost by waiting? Let the official deputation prove for the last time that British declarations are unreliable. The nation will gain by trusting. The deceiver loses when there is correct response from the deceived.

Let us face facts. The coming mission is claimed to be a friendly mission, entertaining the hope that they will discover a constitutional method of delivery. The problem is knotty, probably the knottiest that has ever confronted statesmen. It is possible that the mission will put forth an insoluble conundrum. So much the worse for them. If they are intent upon finding an honest way out of the difficulties of their own creation, I have no doubt, there is a way. But the nation too has to play the game. If it does, the barricade must be left aside, at least for the time being. I appeal to Aruna and her friends to make wise use of the power their bravery and sacrifice has given them.

It is a matter of great relief that the ratings have listened to Sardar Patel's advice to surrender. They have not surrendered their honour. So far as I can see, in resorting to mutiny they were badly advised. If it was for grievance, fancied or real, they should have waited for the guidance and intervention of political leaders of their choice. If they mutinied for the freedom of India, they were doubly wrong. They could not do so without a call from a prepared revolutionary party. They were thoughtless and ignorant, if they believed that by their might they would deliver India from foreign domination.

Aruna is right when she says that the fighters this time showed grit as never before. But grit becomes foolhardiness when it is untimely and suicidal as this was.

She is entitled to say that the people "*are not* interested in the *ethics* of violence or non-violence," but the people *are* very much interested in knowing *the way* which will bring freedom to the masses—violence or non-violence. The people have, however imperfectly, hitherto gone the way of non-violence. Aruna and her comrades have to ask themselves every time whether the non-violent way has, or has not, raised India from her slumber of ages and created in them a yearning, very vague perhaps, for swaraj. There is, in my opinion, only one answer.

There are other passages in Shrimati Aruna's statement which, as it appears to me, betray confusion of thought. But their treatment can wait.

Needless to say that I have dealt with the message believing it to represent her opinion. If it does not, I apologize to her in advance. My argument, however, is not affected even if it is found that the reporter has not correctly interpreted her. For my argument is, after all, impersonal and directed only to the portions which are calculated to mislead the public, irrespective of their authorship.

Poona, *February 26, 1946*

Harijan, 3-3-1946

117. My Confession and Cure

(vol. LXXXIII, pp. 217–19)

It is plain to me as it has become to some of my friends that I am incorrigible. I can learn only by my mistakes.[1] I do not know why I could not learn through objections or warnings from others. I can learn only when I stumble and fall and feel the pain. As children we all used to learn this way. My condition is just like a child's even in my 76th year. I have just discovered myself making a mistake which I should never have made.

I have known Dr. Dinshaw Mehta for a long time. He has dedicated his life solely to nature cure of his conception. His one ambition is to see a full-fledged nature cure university established in India. A university worth the name must be predominantly for the prevention and cure of the diseases of the poor villagers of India. No such university exists in the world. The institutes in the West are designed more for the rich than for the poor.

I feel that I know the method of nature cure for the villagers of India. Therefore I should at once have known that nature cure for the villagers could not be attempted in Poona city. But a Trust was made. Very sober Jehangirji Patel permitted himself to be a co-trustee with Dr. Mehta and me, and I hastened to Poona to run for the poor Dr. Mehta's erstwhile Clinic which was designed for the rich. I suggested

1. The Gujarati version has: "I can learn only by making mistakes and then acknowledging and correcting them."

some drastic changes; but last Monday[2] the knowledge dawned upon me that I was a fool to think that I could ever hope to make an institute for the poor in town. I realized that if I cared for the ailing poor, I must go to them and not expect them to come to me. This is true of ordinary medicinal treatment. It is much more so of nature cure. How is a villager coming to Poona to understand and carry out my instructions to apply mud-poultices, take sun cure, hip and friction sitz-baths or certain foods cooked conservatively? Will it not be impudence? The villager would go away nodding, but at the same time he would smile and think that the person who advised him to undergo nature cure was a fool. He would expect me to give him a powder or a potion to swallow and be done with it. Nature cure connotes a way of life which has to be learnt; it is not a drug cure as we understand it. The treatment to be efficacious can, therefore, only take place in or near a man's cottage or house. It demands from its physician sympathy and patience and knowledge of human nature. When he has successfully practised in this manner in a village, or villages, when enough men and women have understood the secret of nature cure, a nucleus for a nature cure university is founded. It should not have required eleven days' special stay in the institute to discover this simple truth, and that I did not need a huge building and all its attendant paraphernalia for my purpose. I do not know whether to laugh or weep over my folly. I laughed at it and made haste to undo the blunder. This confession completes the reparation. I have not learnt to give up any work once begun and therefore there is only one alternative left for me. In which village should I start this work?

I should like the reader to draw the moral that he should never take anything for gospel truth even if it comes from a Mahatma unless it appeals to both his head and heart. In the present case my folly is so patent that even if it had continued for some time, very few, if any, would have succumbed to it. The real villagers would not have come for relief to this institute. But if the discovery had come too late, it would have blasted my reputation for I would have lost in my own estimation. Nothing hurts a man more than the loss of self-respect. I do not know that now I deserve the confidence of my fellowmen. If I lost it, I know that I shall have deserved the loss. To complete the story I must tell the reader that not a pice of the money earmarked for the poor ailing villagers has been spent on this abortive enterprise. What shape the present institution will now take and where and how poor man's nature cure will be tried is no part of this confession. The result of the initial mistake must not,

2. March 4, 1946.

however, be an abandonment of the new pursuit that I have taken up in the so-called evening of my life. It must, on the contrary, be a clearer and more vigorous pursuit of the ideal of nature cure for the millions, if such a thing is at all practicable. Possible it certainly is. So far as I am concerned it is enough if this mistake makes me more cautious in realizing my ideals. Time alone can say whether or not poor villagers would welcome nature cure. There is no reason to doubt that it should be welcome.

Poona, *March 6, 1946*

Harijan, 17-3-1946

118. My Sexual Practises

[March 1947]

Chi. Nirmal Babu,[1]

Your letter is full of inaccuracies and unwarranted assumptions. I had asked you to discuss the thing with me. You could not do it. The result is bad. I do not mind what opinion you hold, only it must be well fortified.

You should have ascertained my views from me before accepting second-hand evidence however honest it might be.

I go beyond the orthodox view as we know it. My definition does not admit of laxity. I do not call that *brahmacharya* that means not to touch a woman. What I do today is nothing new for me. So far as I know myself, I hold today the same view I held when about 45 years ago I took the vow. Without the vow in England as a student, I freely mixed with women and yet I called myself a *brahmachari* for the period of my residence there. For me, *brahmacharya* is that thought and practice which puts you in touch with the Infinite and takes you to His presence. In that sense Dayanand Saraswati was not. Most certainly I am not. But I am trying to reach that state and in accordance with my belief, I have made substantial progress in that direction.

I have not become modern at all in the same sense you seem to mean. I am as ancient as can be imagined and hope to remain so to the end of my life. If this displeases you, I cannot help it. Let me appear to you and others as naked as I can.

1. This letter, addressed to Nirmal Kumar Bose, is taken from the latter's book *My Days With Gandhi*, (Calcutta, 1953), pp. 176–78. Bose had protested against Gandhi's practice of lying in bed with women of his party in Noakhali.

You have not done justice to A, B or C. You do not know them fully. Have you any right to judge them before you have taken the trouble of knowing them as fully as possible? That you may not want to or that you have no time, I would appreciate. But that very fact should prevent you from passing judgement on them.

I am amazed at your assumption that my experiment implied any assumption of woman's inferiority. She would be, if I looked upon her with lust with or without her consent. I have believed in woman's perfect equality with man. My wife was 'inferior' when she was the instrument of my lust. She ceased to be that when she lay with me naked as my sister. If she and I were not lustfully agitated in our minds and bodies, the contact raised both of us.

Should there be difference if it is not my wife, as she once was, but some other sister? I do hope you will acquit me of having any lustful designs upon women or girls who have been naked with me. A or B's hysteria had nothing to do with my experiment, I hope. They were before the experiment what they are today, if they have not less of it.

The distinction between Manu and others is meaningless for our discussion. That she is my grand-daughter may exempt me from criticism. But I do not want that advantage.

'Experiment' or *prayog* is an ill-chosen word. I have used it. It differs from the present[2] in the sense that the one could be stopped by me, the other being *dharma* could not be. Now comes the stop.

That I should take the public in my confidence before I do anything new is novel to me. In the present case there is nothing new.

BAPU

119. The Calcutta Fast

On Monday night, September 1st, 1947, Gandhi's press statement said:[1]

I regret to have to report to you that, last night, some young men brought to the compound a bandaged man. He was reported to have been attacked by some Muslims. The Chief Minister had him examined and the report was that he had no marks of stabbing, which he

2. The knotty question, namely, whether Manu should be allowed to use his bed or not, in contrast to his self-examination, which was considered part of his religious or spiritual practice or *dharma*.

1. This is taken from D. G. Tendulkar, *Mahatma* (Ministry of Information, India, 1962), vol. VIII, pp. 102–4.

was said to have received. The seriousness of the injury, however, is not the chief point. What I want to emphasize is that these young men tried to become judges and executioners.

This was about 10 p.m., Calcutta time. The young men began to shout at the top of their voices. My sleep was disturbed, but I tried to lie quiet not knowing what was happening. I heard the window-panes being smashed. I had lying, on either side of me, two very brave girls. They could not sleep, but without my knowledge, for my eyes were closed, they went among the small crowd and tried to pacify them. Thank God, the crowd did not do any harm to them. The old Muslim lady in the house endearingly called Bi Amma and a young Muslim stood near my matting, I suppose, to protect me from harm.

The noise continued to swell. Some had entered the central hall and began to knock open the many doors. I felt that I must get up and face the angry crowd. I stood at the threshold of one of the doors. Friendly faces surrounded me and would not let me move forward. My vow of silence admitted of my breaking it on such occasions, and I broke it and began to appeal to the angry young men to be quiet. I asked the Bengali granddaughter-in-law to translate my few words into Bengali. But all to no purpose. Their ears were closed against reason.

I clasped my hands in the Hindu fashion. Nothing doing. More windowpanes began to crack. The friendly ones in the crowd tried to pacify the crowd. There were police officers. Be it said to their credit that they did not try to exercise authority. They too clasped their hands in appeal. A lathi blow missed me and everybody round me. A brick aimed at me hurt a Muslim friend standing by. The two girls would not leave me and held on to me to the last. Meanwhile, the police superintendent and his officers came in. They did not use force. They appealed to me to retire. Then there was a chance of their stilling the young men. After a time the crowd melted.

What happened outside the compound gate I do not know, except that the police had to use tear-gas to disperse the crowd. Meanwhile, Dr. P. C. Ghosh, Annada Babu and Dr. Nripen walked in and after some discussion left. Happily, Shaheed Suhrawardy Saheb had gone home to prepare for tomorrow's proposed departure for Noakhali. In view of the above ugly incident, which no one could tell where it would lead to, I could not think of leaving Calcutta for Noakhali.

What is the lesson of the incident? It is clear to me that if India is to retain her dearly won independence, all men and women must completely forget the lynch law. What was attempted was an indifferent imitation of it. If the Muslims misbehaved, the complainants could, if they would not go to the ministers, certainly go to me or my friend, Shaheed Saheb. The same thing applies to the Muslim complainants. There is no way of keeping peace in Calcutta or elsewhere, if the elementary rule of the civilized society is not observed. Let them not think of the savagery of the Punjab as outside India. The recognition of the golden rule of never taking the law into one's own hands has no exceptions.

My secretary, Dev Prakash, wires from Patna: 'Public agitated Punjab happenings. Feel statement necessary, impressing duty of public and the press.' Shri Dev Prakash is never unduly agitated. There must be some unguarded word by the press. If that is so, at this time, when we are sitting on a powder magazine, the Fourth Estate has to be extrawise and reticent. Unscrupulousness will act as a lighted match. I hope every editor and reporter will realize his duty to the full.

One thing I must mention. I have an urgent message calling me to the Punjab. I hear all kinds of rumours about recrudescence of trouble in Calcutta. I hope they are exaggerated, if not quite baseless. The citizens of Calcutta have to reassure me that there would be nothing wrong in Calcutta and that peace, once restored, will not be broken.

From the very first day of peace, that is, from August 14th last, I have been saying that the peace might only be a temporary lull. There was no miracle. Will the foreboding prove true and Calcutta again lapse into the law of the jungle? Let us hope not, let us pray to the Almighty that He will touch our hearts and ward off the recurrence of insanity.

Since the foregoing was written, about four o'clock during my silence, I have come to know fairly well the details of what has happened in the various parts of the city. Some of the places, which were safe till yesterday, have suddenly become unsafe. Several deaths have taken place. I saw two bodies of very poor Muslims, I saw also some wretched-looking Muslims being carted away to a place of safety; I quite see that the last night's incidents, so fully described above, pale into insignificance before this flare-up. Nothing that I may do in the way of going about in the open conflagration could possibly arrest it.

I have told the friends, who saw me in the evening, what their duty is. What part am I to play, in order to stop it? The Sikhs and Hindus must not forget what the East Punjab has done during these few days. Now the Muslims in the West Punjab have begun the mad career. It is said that the Sikhs and the Hindus are enraged over the Punjab happenings.

I have adverted above to a very urgent call for me to go to the Punjab. But now that the Calcutta bubble seems to have burst, with what face can I proceed to the Punjab? The weapon which has hitherto proved infallible for me is fasting. To put an appearance before an yelling crowd does not always work. It certainly did not last night. What my word in person cannot do, my fast may. It may touch the hearts of all the warring elements in the Punjab, if it does in Calcutta. I, therefore, begin fasting from 8.15 tonight, to end only if and when sanity returns to Calcutta. I shall as usual, permit myself to add salt and soda bicarb to the water I may wish to drink during the fast.

If the people of Calcutta wish me to proceed to the Punjab and help the people there, they have to enable me to break the fast as early as may be.

GLOSSARY OF TERMS
AND PERSONS MENTIONED

acharya: Teacher.

adharma: Injustice, unrighteousness, vice.

ahimsa: Nonviolence or, positively, the practice of love.

Ali, Maulana Muhammed: The younger of the two Ali brothers, Muslim journalists and politicians, leaders of the Khilafat Movement, and allies of Gandhi for ten years after 1918.

Ali, Maulana Shaukat (1873–1938): Brother to Muhammed Ali.

Ali, Aruna Asaf (b. 1909): A woman who engaged in violent civil disobedience against the British during the second half of World War II.

Ambedkar, B. R., Dr. (1891–1956): born an untouchable, he was educated at the expense of the Maharajah of Baroda, became a lawyer, and made himself a leader in the untouchables' revolt against Hinduism. He was one of Gandhi's bitterest enemies.

amrit: Drink of the gods, supposed to confer immortality.

Anand, Swami (also Swami Anandand; b. 1887): He began life as a Ramakrishna Vedanta *sadhu*, then wrote for Tilak's political newspaper, and after 1918 was editor and press-manager for Gandhi.

Anasuyabehn (Sarabhai): A social worker in Ahmedabad. Gandhi helped her in a strike she led.

Andrews, C. F. (also Dinabandhu and Deenabandhu; 1871–1940): An English missionary, author, educator, and a close friend of Gandhi's.

Aney, Bapuj (1880–1968): He began political life as a follower of Tilak, and after joining Gandhi's movement, often opposed his policies.

anna: One sixteenth of a rupee.

Ansari, M. A., Dr. (1880–1936): A Khilafat leader and Muslim co-worker with Gandhi in Congress.

Arjuna: One of the five Pandava brothers, the heroes of the great Indian epic the *Mahabharata*.

artha: Wealth or prosperity, regarded as one of the four great values of life.

ashram: A quiet place where people with common ideals lead a communal life and follow a common discipline.

atman: The essence or principle of life.

avarna: Not belonging to any of the four castes.

Azad, Maulana Abul Kalam (1888–1958): Politician and scholar of religion, he attacked the British and preached the unity of all religions. He was a prominent congressman and was often in jail between 1920 and 1945.

ba: Mother.

Babu, Nirmal (also Nirmal Kumar Bose; b. 1901): A teacher of anthropology and interpreter for Gandhi in Noakhali during 1946 and 1947. He protested to Gandhi about the latter's sharing his bed with women.

Babu, Brijkishore: *See* Prasad, Brijkishore.

Babur: One of the great Muslim emperors of India.

bahadur: Man of dignity, courage.

bajri: A kind of millet.

Balkrishna (second name, Sharma; 1897–1960): A journalist and writer of Rajasthan.

Bania: Member of the third caste, whose traditional occupation is trade or commerce.

Banker, Shankerlal Ghelabhai (b. 1889): Gandhi's associate for many years as a Congress worker and a labor leader of Gujarat.

bapu: Father.

bardasi: A servant or warder.

Bhagavad Gita: The song of the Lord; part of the sixth section of the *Mahabharata. See* Gita.

bhajans: Hymns.

Bhandarkar, Ramakrishna Gopal (1837–1925): Professor of Sanskrit in Bombay and then Poona. He was also a prominent social reformer when Gandhi began his career.

bhangi: Sweeper or scavenger.

Bhansali, Jaikrishna P.: He was a periodical inmate of Gandhi's ashram and practiced an extreme asceticism.

Bhave, Vinoba (b. 1895): A brilliant intellectual, Vinoba was revolutionary in his youth and believed in violence until he heard Gandhi speak in 1916. He became Gandhi's most trusted collaborator in the field of religion.

Bhishma: The great soldier hero of the *Mahabharata.*

Birla, G. D. (b. 1894): Born rich, he made himself a millionaire but was also a friend and financial supporter of Gandhi.

Bose, Jagadish Chandra (1858–1937): A pioneer in plant physiological research and a doyen of Indian science.

brahmacharya: Celibacy, or a life of self-discipline and continence, dedicated to higher ends.

brahman: All-pervading, self-existent power.

Brahmin: A member of the first caste, whose traditional occupation is priesthood or learning.

Brindaban (also **Vrindaban**): A forest grove near Mathura where Krishna spent his childhood and youth.

chakki: Quern.

chapati: Unleavened bread.

charkha: A spinning wheel.

Choitram (second name, Gidwani), Dr. (1889–1957): A political leader in Sind and co-worker with Gandhi.

Cripps, Sir Stafford (1889–1952): A British Socialist politician; leader of the Cripps Mission of 1942, which tried to rally India behind Britain against Japan.

crore: A hundred *lakhs,* or ten million.

dacoit: A robber.

Dadabhai, Naoroji (1825–1917): A Parsi who became a businessman in London but later was a nationalist social reformer. He criticized England's impoverishment of India.

dal: *Pulse* (beans or lentils) cooked in liquid.

Daridranarayana: God as manifesting Himself in the poorest of men.

darshan: The sight or presence of a holy person or thing.

Das, Chittaranjan (also Deshabandhu and C. R.; 1870–1925): Born in Calcutta, he finished his education in England, returned to India in 1894, and became a barrister and the foremost political leader of Bengal.

Desai, Mahadev (also Mahadevbhai and Mahadev; 1892–1942): Gandhi's principal secretary for twenty-five years and a close friend.

de Valera, Eamonn (1882–1975): A leader of the Irish revolt against English rule and later prime minister and then president of Eire.

Devi, Sarojini (Naidu; 1879–1949): A poet and orator in the Gandhian movement.

dharma: Religion, moral law, or duty.

dhoti: A long piece of cloth wrapped around the lower body.

Doulatram, Jairamdas (b. 1892): A co-worker with Gandhi in Congress.

Draupadi: A heroine and pattern of virtue in the *Mahabharata.*

Dyer, Reginald (1864–1927): A British general responsible for the Amritsar massacre of 1919, when British troops fired on a crowd of civilian Indians. "Dyerism" was a word invented by the Indians to describe such acts of terrorism.

Escombe, Harry: Attorney general of Natal during Gandhi's time there.

gadi: The platform on which rich or superior people sit.

gandharvas: The musicians of Paradise.

Gandhi, Chaganlal (also Chhaganlal): Gandhi's nephew and close co-worker in South Africa and then in India.

Gandhi, Devdas (1900–1957): Gandhi's youngest son, who became a journalist.

Gandhi, Harilal (1888–1948): Gandhi's oldest and unhappiest son.

Gandhi, Kasturba (also Kasturbai and Ba; 1869–1944): Gandhi's wife.

Gandhi, Maganlal (also Maganlal): Gandhi's nephew and collaborator in South Africa and India. Brother to Chaganlal.

Gandhi, Manilal (1892–1956): Gandhi's second son, who lived mostly in South Africa.

Gandhi, Narandas: Manager of Gandhi's ashram in the 1930s.

Gandhi, Navin: Gandhi's grandson.

Gandhi, Ramdas (1897–1969): Gandhi's third son.

Gandhi, Rasik: Son of Harilal Gandhi.

garhasthya: The second of the four stages of life, that of the married householder.

ghee: Clarified butter.

Gita: The religious allegory at the heart of the great Indian epic, the Mahabharata.

Godse, Nathuram (1911–1949): The leader of the group who assassinated Gandhi.

Gokhale, Gopal Krishna (1866–1915): Scholar, patriot, and statesman, associated with Congress from its beginning.

goonda: Hooligan.

Goseva Sangh. A society for the protection of cows.

goshala: Cow shed.

Govind Singh: A great military leader of the Sikhs.

guna: To act; also means "quality" and "strand"; a religious concept, part of a nontheistic system for achieving liberation or salvation.

gur: Jaggery, or molasses.

guru: Teacher or spiritual mentor.

Gurudev: *See* Rabindranath.

gurudev: Great teacher.

Hari: Another name for Vishnu, or simply God.

Harijan: Gandhi's term for the untouchables, meaning "people of God."

Harishchandra: Hero of a fable of dutifulness.

himsa: Violence.

Hindu Mahasabha: Association of Hindus, political party of nationalist Hindus.

Hindu raj: The kingdom or empire of the Hindus.

Hormazd: One manifestation of the divine, in the Zoroastrian religion.

Irwin, Lord (1881–1959): Viceroy of India 1925–31, he negotiated the Gandhi-Irwin Pact in 1930.

Isopanishad: One of the *Upanishads.*

Jamnalalji Seth (also Jamnalal Bajaj and Jamnalalji; 1889–1942): A wealthy merchant who supported Gandhi's work with money and effort.

Janakidevi (also Janakibehn): Wife of Jamnalalji Seth.

Jinnah, M. A. (1875–1948): A Muslim lawyer and politician; at first a co-worker with Gandhi but later an enemy; the founder of Pakistan.

Jowar: A kind of Indian maize.

Kakasaheb Kalelkar (also Kaka Kalelkar; b. 1885): A revolutionary and then a religious ascetic in his youth, from 1915 on he worked with Gandhi on literary and educational projects.

Kali: A female divinity of power.

Kallenbach, Hermann: A German architect, he was a devoted friend and co-worker with Gandhi in South Africa.

Kalma: The Muslim profession of faith in the unity of God.

kama: Love, erotic pleasure, enjoyment, the ordinary pleasure of life.

Kantak, Premabehn: A woman member of Gandhi's ashram.

karma: The moral consequences, in this life or the next, of one's actions.

karmayogi: A man who shows selfless performance of his duties.

Kauravas: The enemies of the Pandavas in the *Mahabharata*.

Kelappan, Sjt. (1888–1971): A teacher and then a lawyer, he joined Gandhi's movement and worked mainly in Kerala.

khadi/khaddar: Handspun and handwoven cloth.

Khan, Saheb Abdul Ghaffar (also Khan Saheb; b. 1890): A leader of the Pathans in the Northwest Territory, he converted his followers to Gandhian nonviolence.

khilafat: The Muslim movement to restore to the caliph (the spiritual leader of Islam) control of the holy places of that religion.

Khurshedbehn Naoroji: A disciple of Gandhi and granddaughter of Dadabhai.

kisan: Peasant.

Kripalani, Acharya (b. 1888): A school and college teacher, he joined Gandhi during the Champaran campaign of 1917 and became one of his most devoted collaborators.

Krishna: Hindu god, manifestation of Vishnu; his life story is told in the *Mahabharata*.

Kshattriya: A member of the second caste, whose traditional occupation is fighting or ruling.

Kurus: An ancient Indian tribe who lived near the Ganges.

lakh: The number 100,000.

Lakshmi: Gandhi's adopted untouchable daughter.

lathi: A wooden pole, often iron-tipped, used as a weapon.

Lilavati: Wife to K. M. Munshi, a lawyer and literary man who joined Gandhi after having resisted him.

Linlithgow, Lord (1887–1952): Viceroy of India, 1936–43.

lokamanya: Chosen of the people; worthy of respect and obedience of the people.

Lokamanya Tilak. *See* Maharaj.

lungi: A loincloth or waist-cloth.

MacDonald, Ramsay (1866–1937): The first Labor Party prime minister of Great Britain.

mahajan: Merchant, banker, or moneylender.

Maharaj, Tilak (also Tilak, B. G.; 1856–1920): A leader of militantly revolutionary youth in the period just before Gandhi's return to India.

Maharashtra: The part of India around Bombay and Poona.

Mahatma: "Great Soul," a title given to saints.

Malaviya, Bharatbushan Pandit (also Madan Mohan Malaviya; 1861–1946).

mantra: A syllable, word, or sentence to be meditated on.

Manu (Gandhi): Gandhi's great-niece, who lived with him in his late years.

Mashruwala, Shri Kishorelal (also Kishorelal): A Gujarati reformer and writer about Gandhi and Gandhism.

Maulana: Man of learning; Muslim.

Mehta, Jivaraj (b. 1887): The doctor who looked after Gandhi in London in 1914.

Mirabehn (also **Mirabai** and **Mira**): Her given name was Madeline. The daughter of Sir Edmond Slade, she came out to India in 1924 and became one of Gandhi's most devoted assistants.

Mirabai (1470–1547): A Hindu poetess and mystic.

moha: Infatuation.

Mountbatten, Lord Louis: (1900–1979): The last viceroy of India, in 1947, and the first governor general of India in 1947–48.

Mussalman: Another word for Muslim.

Nehru, Motilal: Prominent nationalist leader; father of Jawaharlal Nehru; twice president of the Congress.

Nehru, Pandit Jawaharlal (also Panditji; 1889–1964): Gandhi's political lieutenant and heir.

nirvana: Nothingness, or release from the cycle of rebirth.

Panchayata: A five-man village council, to settle disputes.

pandal: Canopy or tent.

Pandavas: The family whose fortunes are followed in the *Mahabharata.*

pandit: Man of learning (Hindu).

Pant, Pandit Govind Vallabh (1887–1961): A Brahmin and prominent congressman.

pariah: Outcast.

Parikh, Narahari (1891–1957): A writer and teacher at Gandhian schools. Joined Gandhi in 1915, with Mahadev Desai.

Parsi: Zoroastrian.

Pasha, Mustafa Kemal (Ataturk; 1881–1938): The founder of modern Turkey.

patel: Village headman.

Patel, Manibehn: A Gandhian disciple and daughter to Vallabhbhai Patel.

Patel, Vallabhbhai (also Vallabhbhai, Shri Vallabhbhai, Sardar, and Sirdar): A Gujarati lawyer who organized political support for Gandhi, especially in Gujarat.

Pherozeshah, Mehta, Sir (1845–1915): A Parsi lawyer of Bombay who helped Gandhi early in his career.

pice: Very small coin.

pinjrapole: Home for old and sick cows.

Prasad, Brajkishore (also Bapu Brajkishore; 1877–1946): A lawyer who helped Gandhi in his Champaran campaign in 1917 and later.

Prasad, Rajendra (1884–1963): Close co-worker with Gandhi; president of free India.

Pratap Singh (1545–1591): A Rajput hero in the wars against the Muslims.

pukka: Genuine.

purdah (also **pardah**): The veil worn by women in some parts of India; also the custom of keeping women in seclusion.

purna swaraj: Complete independence.

Pyarelal, Nayyar (b. 1899): Gandhi's secretary and later his biographer.

Rabindranath (Tagore; also Gurudev; 1861–1941): Nobel Prize–winning poet; also playwright, novelist, educator, actor, singer, etc., who often disagreed with Gandhi but kept on good terms with him.

Radha: The beloved of Krishna.

raja: A king or ruler.

Raja, Rao Bahadur (1883–1943): A leader of the oppressed classes.

Rajagopalachariar, Chakravarti (also Rajagopalachari and Rajaji; 1879–1972): A Brahmin politician of South India, and one of Gandhi's principal lieutenants.

Rajan (T. S. S.; also Dr. Rajan; 1880–1953): A doctor who came under Gandhi's influence in 1914 and led Gandhians in the South.

rajas: The active, stimulating, or fiery principle.

Rajguru (Jayakrishna Mohapatra; 1739–1805): A freedom fighter of Orissa, executed by the British.

Ramaraj (also **Ram Rajya**): The mythical reign of Rama, a golden age for Hindus.

Ramzan: A period of fasting imposed on Muslims by their religion.

Ramanama: A devotion in which Rama's name is repeated.

Ranade, Mahadev Govind (also Justice Ranade; 1842–1901): Social reformer and founder of the Congress.

Ranjit Singh (1872–1933): A Prince and star cricketer, he knew Gandhi in London as a law student.

Ravanarajya: The Kingdom of the Devil on earth.

Ray, Acharya: *See* Ray, Prafulla Chandra.

Ray, Prafulla Chandra (1861–1964): A Bengali scientist and social reformer.

rentia baras: Sacrificial spinning in honor of Gandhi's birthday.

resident: The official representing England in a princely state.

Reynolds, Reginald: An English Quaker who came out to India as a very young man and carried Gandhi's letter to the viceroy in 1930.

rishi: An inspired sage or ascetic of superior sanctity.

Rolland, Romain (1866–1944): A French writer about art and religion, whom Gandhi visited in Switzerland in 1930

roti: A kind of bread.

Rowlatt Acts: Legislation passed by the Government of India in 1919, giving the government emergency powers to arrest and intern suspects.

Royeppen, Joseph: A co-worker of Gandhi's in South Africa.

rupee: An Indian coin.

Rustomji, Sheth: A merchant of Durban, who worked with Gandhi during his years in South Africa.

ryots: Cultivators or peasants.

sadhana: A discipline whereby one attains an important end.

sadhu: A religious ascetic.

saheb: Lord; Westerner; master.

Saheb, Hakim (also Sahib, Hakim; 1863–1927): A Muslim doctor and politician, who joined Gandhi in 1917.

Saheb, Maulana: See Malaviya, Bharatbushan Pandit.

Saheb, Shaheed Suhrawardy (1893–1963): In 1947 chief minister of Bengal; he begged Gandhi to stay in Calcutta for the celebration of independence to avert Hindu-Muslim riots.

Saheb, Thakore: The title of the princely ruler of Rajkot.

sakti: Female power.

sanatanist: Orthodox Hindu.

Sanger, Margaret (1883–1966): Founder of the birth control movement in the United States.

sannyasin: A Hindu of the fourth stage in life, who has renounced the world and lives by mendicancy.

sanskara: Inherited or innate tendency.

Santiniketan: A school founded by Rabindranath Tagore.

Sapru (Tej Bahadur; also Dr. Sapru; 1875–1949): A leading Liberal politician.

Saraswati, Dayanand (1825–1883): founder of Arya Samaj, an organization dedicated to reviving and purifying Hinduism.

Sardar: See Patel, Vallabhbhai.

Sastri, Rt. Hon. Srinivasi (1869–1946): A friendly critic of Gandhi, he spent his life in the public service of various Liberal causes.

Satavlekar (Pandit; 1866–1968): A Sanskrit scholar.

sati: The rite of widow-burning, formerly practiced by certain Hindu groups.

sattva: The principle of peace and reason.

satyagraha: Firmness in truth.

savarna: Caste Hindu.

seer: A measure, as of corn.

Shankaracharya: A philosopher of the eighth century.

Shariat: Muslim Law.

Shastras: Hindu scriptures; legal texts.

Shastri, Parchure: A leper who came to live at the ashram.

sheth: Merchant.

Shiva: The most terrible of the three great Hindu gods.

Shivaji (1627–1680): The founder of the (Hindu) Maratha empire.

shloka: A verse.

shri: Mr.

shrimati: Ms.

Shudra: A member of the fourth caste, whose traditional occupation is work with the hands.

Sind: A province of India.

Singh, Bhagat (1907–1931): A Sikh revolutionary, executed in 1931.

Smuts, Jan Christian (General, 1870–1950): The leader of the Boers in South Africa, with whom Gandhi had to treat between 1906 and 1914.

Spiegel, Dr. Margarete: A schoolteacher from Berlin who came to the ashram in 1934.

Srinivasan, Rao Bahadur (1859–1945): A leader of the Scheduled Castes or "Depressed Classes"—often called untouchables.

Sunderlal, Pandit (b. 1866): A follower of Lalal Lajpat Rai and the Arya Samaj, who was converted to nonviolence by Gandhi in 1916.

Sushila (also Dr. Sushila Nayyar and Sushilabehn): Gandhi's personal doctor in his last years and sister to Pyarelal.

swadeshi: Made in India, or near home; the name given to the political movement to boycott foreign-made goods.

swami/swamin: Master, usually applied to a man of religion.

swaraj: Self-government.

Taiyabji, Badruddin (1844–1906): Born in Bombay, he became a famous lawyer and the first Muslim president of the Congress.

tamas: The principle of darkness, inertia, or helplessness.

tapascharya (also **tapashcharya**): Penance; austerity; single-minded devotion.

Thakkar, Amritlal (1869–1951): An engineer who devoted himself to the cause of the untouchables and worked with Gandhi.

thakore: A princely ruler.

thana: Police station.

Tilak, Bal Gangadhar: *See* Maharaj, Tilak.

tola: A measure of weight.

Tulsidas (1543?–1623): The religious poet of the *Ramayana*, Gandhi's favorite poem.

Tyabji, Bibi Raihana: Member of Gandhi's ashram and daughter to Abbas Tyabji, the nephew of Taiyabji.

Upanishads: Ancient discourses on philosophy; the source of Hindu metaphysics.

"Vaishnava Jana": A hymn about a votary of Vishnu.

Vaishya/Vaisya: Another word for the third caste.

vakil: Lawyer.

vanaprasthya: The third of the four stages of life, when one gives up household duties, and retires from the world to meditate.

"Vande Mataram": Hail the Motherland; a nationalist slogan; title of a hymn that became the unofficial anthem of the Independence movement.

varna system: The four castes.

varnashrama: The four stages of life.

vidyapith: An Indian college.

Virawala, Durbar: The advisor to the Thakore of Rajkot.

Wavell, Field Marshall Sir Archibald (1883–1950): Viceroy of India, 1943–47.

West family: Albert West joined Gandhi's movement in South Africa, and his relatives followed him.

yajna: Religious sacrifice.

Yajnik, Indulal (1892–1972): A congressman who later became hostile to Gandhi.

yama-niyama: The god of death.

yoga: Literally "union"; a method of concentration as a means of self-liberation; the cessation of all conscious mental function.

Yudhishthira: Eldest of the Pandava brothers in the *Mahabharata*.

zamindar (also **zemindar**): Landowner.

INDEX

5/12 (4) 9/1
8/18 (8) 12/16

LaVergne, TN USA
29 September 2010

198957LV00005B/53/A